1001

days out with your

kids

1001

days out with your

kids

The **essential** guide compiled annually,
telling you where the local zoos, theme
parks, museums & fun fairs are in your area

p

This is a Parragon Book
First published in 2003

Parragon
Queen Street House
4 Queen Street
Bath BA1 1HE, UK

ISBN: 1-40540-800-6

A CIP data record for this book is available from the British Library.

Printed in Dubai.

Produced by THE BRIDGEWATER BOOK COMPANY LTD.

DISCLAIMER

The contents of this book are believed correct at the time of printing. The Publisher cannot
be held responsible for any errors or omissions or changes in the information in this guide
or for the consequences of any reliance on the information provided. We have made every
effort to ensure the information is correct but things do change and we strongly advise
readers to telephone before planning a visit. We would be grateful if readers would inform
us of any inaccuracies they may encounter.

ACKNOWLEDGEMENT

The Publishers would like to thank the British Tourist Authority for giving their permission to
use their website www.visitbritain.com and for their assistance in producing this guidebook.

Contents

Introduction

A day out with the children – whether aged 5 or 15 – can be a nerve-wracking experience. But it is surprising how many varied and interesting places there are to visit in the UK which cater in some way for children. These range from beautiful country parks with nature trails specifically for kids, to arts and crafts centres where the whole family are encouraged to get creative. There are the really big attractions, too – such as London Zoo, one of the foremost zoos in the world, with its Children's Zoo; and Alton Towers, with thrills and spills galore for all age groups.

This book covers 1001 such places. It is divided into six regions and each region is divided alphabetically into counties and major cities. The attractions are arranged alphabetically within these locations. You can use the book either by looking through an area to find suitable places to visit; or, if you already know the name of the place you want to visit and where it is, by locating the information quickly within the county.

Each entry gives a brief description of the attraction, vital visitor information and an indication of the facilities on offer. It also gives a rough indication of the amount of time you could spend there. Obviously, this will depend on the age of the children that you are entertaining. A whole day walking in a Scottish park will not be ideal for toddlers. Similarly, teenagers may not want to romp around an adventure playground for too long!

A word about the selection. Though most of the well-known places such as Alton Towers and Legoland are included, we have also listed smaller venues, which may be completely new to you. We have tried to give as varied a selection as possible to provide ideas and inspiration for all manner of exciting day trips.

So, armed with this guide, we wish you a happy day out with the kids.

How To Use This Book

Venue name _____

Region _____

Description _____

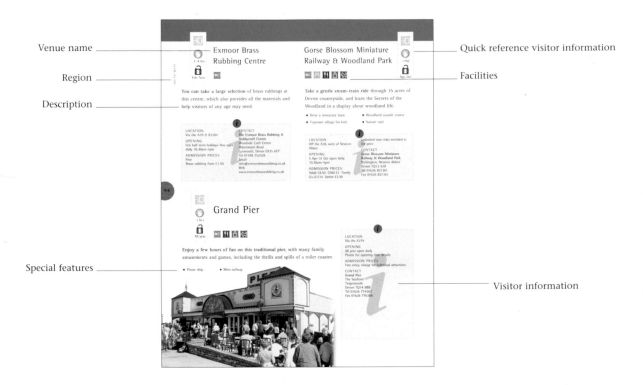

Quick reference visitor information _____

Facilities _____

Special features _____

Visitor information _____

Key to symbols

 All weather – entirely indoor, or outdoor with some indoor facilities such as a visitor centre or indoor café.

 Opening times – in general, the months it is open. There are more details in the Visitor Information.

 Shop – a gift or specialist shop.

 Outdoor – no indoor facilities.

 WC – toilet facilities available

 Restaurant/Café – a restaurant, café or kiosk.

 Duration – a rough indication of the amount of time to spend at the attraction.

 Picnic area – an area, not necessarily a formal picnic area, where you can eat your own food.

 Dogs – dogs allowed, but there may be some restrictions in place, and you may be asked to use a lead.

South-east

The South-east is blessed with an ideal environment for visitors. There are a wealth of historic towns, ports and cities to visit including Oxford, Brighton, Portsmouth, Tunbridge Wells and, of course, London.

Major attractions in this region include London's museums and entertainments such as the London Eye, London Dungeon and Natural History Museum. Sussex has a fabulous multi-award winning animal centre, Drusillas Zoo, which young children will particularly enjoy. Surrey has the superb theme park, Chessington World of Adventures, and in Kent you can, among other things, visit a number of small farm parks, take river trips on an old barge with Caxton River Trips and dip into history at Hever Castle.

In the north of the region, Oxfordshire offers the Cotswold Wildlife Park, and Berkshire and Hampshire have some fantastic country parks offering a wide range of outdoor activities. Bedfordshire has two great wildlife attractions, Whipsnade Zoo, set in 600 acres of beautiful parkland, and Woburn Safari Park. Essex has the award-winning Colchester Zoo which has a programme of daily displays. In Hertfordshire, children of all ages will enjoy Activity World and Animal World, where they can learn and play in a safe environment. And did you know you could dry-ski in Buckinghamshire?

N

Bedfordshire
pp14–17

Buckinghamshire
pp18–22

Oxfordshire
pp54–56

Hertfordshire
pp32–36

Essex
pp22–26

Berkshire
pp17–18

London
pp48–54

Surrey
pp56–61

Kent
pp39–48

Hampshire
pp26–32

Sussex
pp61–69

Isle of Wight
pp36–38

Below is a list of places to visit in the South-east, organised by county and type.

Bedfordshire

MUSEUMS & EXHIBITIONS
John Dony Field Centre 15

ANIMAL ATTRACTIONS
Bedford Butterfly Park 14
HULA Animal Rescue 14
Whipsnade Wild Animal Park 16
Woburn Safari Park 16
Woodside Farm & Wildfowl Park 16

BOAT AND TRAIN TRIPS
Leighton Buzzard Railway 15

PARKS, GARDENS & NATURE TRAILS
Priory Country Park 15

THEME PARKS &
ADVENTURE PLAYGROUNDS
The Playground 15

Berkshire

MUSEUMS & EXHIBITIONS
Household Cavalry Museum 18

SPORT & LEISURE
Premier Karting 18

PARKS, GARDENS & NATURE TRAILS
Beale Park 17
California Country Park 17
Dinton Pastures Country Park 17
The Living Rainforest 18

THEME PARKS &
ADVENTURE PLAYGROUNDS
Legoland Windsor 18

Buckinghamshire

MUSEUMS & EXHIBITIONS
Milton Keynes Museum 20
Roald Dahl Gallery 21
Wycombe Museum 21

SPORT & LEISURE
Wycombe Summit 22

ANIMAL ATTRACTIONS
Bucks Goat Centre 19
Oak Farm Rare Breeds Park 21
Thames Valley Falconry & Conservation
    Centre 21

BOAT & TRAIN TRIPS
Buckinghamshire Railway Centre 19

PARKS, GARDENS & NATURE TRAILS
Denham Country Park 20
Emberton Country Park 20

MISCELLANEOUS
Bekonscot Model Village 19

Essex

HISTORIC BUILDINGS
Hedingham Castle 23

MUSEUMS & EXHIBITIONS
Royal Gunpowder Mills 25

SPORT & LEISURE
Quasar at Rollerworld 25

ANIMAL ATTRACTIONS
Barleylands Farm 22
Colchester Zoo 22
Mole Hall Wildlife Park 24
Old MacDonalds Educational Farm Park 24

PARKS, GARDENS & NATURE TRAILS
Hanningfield Reservoir Visitor Centre 23
High Woods Country Park 23
Lee Valley Park & Information Centre 23
The Original Great Maze 25
Weald Country Park 26

THEME PARKS &
ADVENTURE PLAYGROUNDS
Tumblewood 26

Hampshire

HISTORIC BUILDINGS
Calshot Castle 27

MUSEUMS & EXHIBITIONS
The Bear Museum 26
Beaulieu 26
Hampshire Technology Centre Intech 27
Museum of Army Flying &
    Explorers' World 29

Hertfordshire

Isle of Wight

Kent

London

Oxfordshire

Surrey

Sussex

2 hrs+

Feb–Oct

Bedford Butterfly Park

Set in a landscape of wildflower hay meadows, this fascinating conservation park features a tropical glasshouse where visitors walk through a wonderful scene of waterfalls, ponds and lush foliage, with spectacular butterflies flying around.

★ Adventure playground
★ Nature trails
★ Pygmy goats

LOCATION
From Bedford town centre follow signs for Cambridge. As you leave Bedford turn left for Renhold & Wilden & follow the signs for Wilden

OPENING
18 Feb–31 Oct open daily 10am–5pm

ADMISSION PRICES
Adult £4 Child (3–16 years) £2
Family £11 Concession £3

CONTACT
Bedford Butterfly Park
Renhold Road, Wilden, Bedford
Bedfordshire MK44 2PX
Tel 01234 772770
Fax 01234 772773
Email enquiries@bedford-butterflies.co.uk
Web www.bedford-butterflies.co.uk

14

2 hrs+

Mar–Nov

HULA Animal Rescue:
South Midlands Animal Sanctuary

HULA Animal Rescue is the headquarters of the charity founded in 1972 and its South Midlands Animal Sanctuary. It houses rescued, unwanted and abandoned animals. Ponies, donkeys, cattle, sheep, goats and pigs are residents, and dogs, cats, rabbits, small rodents and caged birds await adoption into new homes. Visitors can look around the animal houses and veterinary unit and learn about the care of animals.

LOCATION
From the village square in Aspley Guise turn into Church Road, then into Salford Road & the entrance to Glebe Farm is on right

OPENING
31 Mar–2 Nov open Sat & Sun 1pm–3pm;
Please phone to confirm Bank holiday opening times

ADMISSION PRICES
Please phone for details

CONTACT
Glebe Farm
Salford Road
Aspley Guise
Milton Keynes
Bedfordshire MK17 8HZ
Tel 01908 584000
Fax 01525 280220
Email hularescue@yahoo.co.uk
Web www.hularescue.org

John Dony Field Centre

1–2 hrs

All year

The Field Centre is located close to a number of important sites of natural historical interest in north-east Luton. There are displays featuring local and natural history, conservation and archaeology.

★ Children's play area ★ Self-guided walks available

LOCATION
In the Bushmead Estate, near the A6, in north Luton. It is signposted from the roundabout at Barnfield College on the A6

OPENING
All year open Mon–Fri 9.30am–4.45pm & Sun 9.30am–12.45pm

ADMISSION PRICES
Free

CONTACT
John Dony Field Centre
Hancock Drive, Bushmead
Luton, Bedfordshire LU2 7SF
Tel 01582 486983
Tel russells@luton.gov.uk
Web www.luton.gov.uk

Leighton Buzzard Railway

65 min

Mar–Oct

When you travel on the Leighton Buzzard Railway, you take a journey into the world of the English light railway – you will experience sharp curves, steep gradients and level crossings.

★ Children's play area ★ Re-created sand train

LOCATION
Off the A4146 on the edge of Leighton Buzzard, close to the junction with the A505, Dunstable–Aylesbury road

OPENING
Open 10 Mar–27 Oct
Please phone for details

ADMISSION PRICES
Adult £5 Child (2–15 years) £2
Concession £4

CONTACT
Leighton Buzzard Railway
Billington Road, Leighton
Buzzard, Bedfordshire LU7 4TN
Tel 01525 373888
Website www.buzzrail.co.uk

15

The Playground

2–4 hrs

All year

An action-packed children's indoor playground with trampolines and a super play village.

★ Conquer the Desert Island ★ Spooky Den Maze
★ Bouncy boxing ★ Dare Devil Drop Slide
★ Trampolines ★ Laser Raider

LOCATION
On the Blackburn Road, off Houghton Regis High Street

OPENING
All year open daily 9.30am–7pm; Closed 25, 26 Dec & 1 Jan

ADMISSION PRICES
Over-5s £4.25 Under-5s £3.95
Under-18 months £2.50

CONTACT
The Playground
Blackburn Road, Houghton
Regis, Bedfordshire
Tel 01582 660111
Web
www.playground.freeserve.co.uk

Priory Country Park

½ day

All year

This country park has over 300 acres of open space, including two lakes and a stunning riverside environment. Fishing is available and watersports can be arranged. The park also has bird-watching hides and a visitor centre.

LOCATION
In Barkers Lane, east of Bedford town centre. Directions indicate Cambridge

OPENING
Visitor centre open all year daily, except Sat
Please phone for details

ADMISSION PRICES
Free

CONTACT
Priory Country Park
Barkers Lane
Bedford
Bedfordshire MK41 9SH
Tel 01234 211182

All day

All year

Whipsnade Wild Animal Park

You can't fail to have fun at **Whipsnade**. With over 2,500 wild animals, it is one of the largest wildlife conservation centres in Europe.

★ Free-flying bird display
★ Penguin feeding
★ Safari tour bus
★ Herds of Asian animals
★ Adventure playground
★ Children's farm

LOCATION
Junction 21 off the M25 & junctions 9 & 12 off the M1. Follow the brown elephant signs

OPENING
All year open daily; 27 Oct–Spring open 10am–4pm; 6 Oct–26 Oct open 10am–5pm; Closed 25 Dec

ADMISSION PRICES
Adult £11.50 Child (3–15 years) £8.50
Under-3s Free Concession £9
Car park £2

CONTACT
Whipsnade Wild Animal Park
Dunstable
Bedfordshire LU6 2LF
Tel 01582 872171
Web www.whipsnade.co.uk

16

All day

All year

Woburn Safari Park

Visitor Attraction of the Year 2000
English Tourism Council

This famous safari drive-through also has an extensive leisure park. There are animal contact areas, a children's playground (indoor and outdoor), boats and a railway train.

LOCATION
Five minutes off junction 13 off the M1. Follow the signposts

OPENING
Mid Mar–31 Oct open daily 10am–5pm; Nov–Feb open weekends 11am–3pm

ADMISSION PRICES
Please phone for details

CONTACT
Woburn Safari Park
Woburn
Bedfordshire MK17 9QN
Tel 01525 290407
Email info@woburnsafari.co.uk
Web www.woburnsafari.co.uk

All day

All year

Woodside Farm & Wildfowl Park

Woodside Farm is home to all manner of creatures, including rabbits and goats, which children are encouraged to make contact with. There are also flamingos, llamas, wallabies, goats, racoons, monkeys and giant tortoises.

LOCATION
From junction 9 or 10 off the M1, follow the tourist signs for the Wildfowl Park

OPENING
All year open daily; In summer 8am–6pm; In winter 8am–5pm; Closed 25, 26 Dec & 1 Jan

ADMISSION PRICES
Adult £3.50 Child (1–16 years) £2.50 Concession £2.50

CONTACT
Woodside Farm & Wildfowl Park, Woodside Road, Slip End Luton, Bedfordshire LU1 4DG
Tel 01582 841044
Web www.woodsidefarm.co.uk

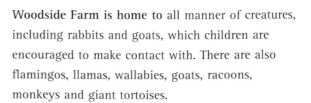

4 hrs

Mar–Dec

Beale Park

Beale Park is dedicated to the conservation of rare birds. There is something for everyone, ranging from gentle walks to madcap adventure play areas.

★ Pets Corner

★ Meerkat & wallaby enclosures

★ Splash pool for children

★ Children's miniature golf

LOCATION	ADMISSION PRICES
On the A329. Follow the brown tourist signs from junction 12 off the M4	Adult £5.50 Child £4 Under-3s Free Many concessions & group rates
OPENING	CONTACT
1 Mar–23 Dec open daily; In summer 10am–6pm (last admission 5pm); In winter 10am–5pm (last admission 4pm or dusk)	**Beale Park** Lower Basildon, Reading Berkshire RG8 9NH Tel 0118 9845172

California Country Park

½ day

All year

This park offers fishing and walks around a scenic lake. It contains an area of heathland and an ancient bog, which is a Site of Special Scientific Interest. A countryside events programme runs all year.

★ Events programme

★ Paddling pool

LOCATION	ADMISSION PRICES
Join Nine Mile Ride from the A321, B3016 or A3095	Free car park £1
	CONTACT
OPENING	**California Country Park** Nine Mile Ride Finchampstead Wokingham RG40 4HT Tel 0118 9342016
Car park open all year Opening times vary Please phone for details Closed 25 Dec	

17

Dinton Pastures Country Park

All day

All year

LOCATION
Off the A329, Reading–Wokingham road. 15 minutes walk from Winnersh station

OPENING
All year open daily; In summer open at 8am (closing times vary); In winter open at 8am (main car park closes at 6pm); Closed 25 Dec

ADMISSION PRICES
Free
Car parking £1

CONTACT
Dinton Pastures Country Park
Davis Street
Hurst
Berkshire RG10 0TH
Tel 0118 9342016
Email countryside@wokingham.gov.uk
Web www.wokingham.gov.uk

Dinton Pastures Country Park is a mosaic of rivers, meadows, lakes and wooded areas for visitors to explore. Countryside events are organised throughout the year, including butterfly and bird walks, pond dips for children and activity days.

★ Family countryside event programme

★ Fishing

★ Watersports

★ Mobility scooter hire

1-2 hrs

All year

Household Cavalry Museum

The collection contains uniforms, weapons, horse furniture and curios of the Life Guards, Horse Grenadier Guards, Royal Horse Guards, 1st Royal Dragoons and the Blues and Royals. Over 300 years of history of the sovereign's mounted bodyguards.

LOCATION
Windsor, via the B3022

OPENING
All year open Mon–Fri 10am–12.30pm, 2pm–4.30pm; Closed Easter (29 Mar–1 Apr), 25, 26 Dec, 1 Jan, Bank holidays

ADMISSION PRICES
Free

CONTACT
Household Cavalry Museum
Combermere Barracks
Windsor SL4 3DN
Tel 01753 755203
Web
www.householdcavalry.co.uk

All day

Mar–Nov

Legoland Windsor

A whole day of fun with more than 40 rides, live shows and attractions, based around six main activity areas and surrounded by extensive gardens and parkland.

★ Pan for gold   ★ Brave the Pirate Falls

LOCATION
2 miles from Windsor town centre on the B3022 Bracknell–Windsor road

OPENING
16 Mar–3 Nov open daily 10am–5pm; 20 Jul–4 Sep open daily 10am–7pm

ADMISSION PRICES
Adult From £18.95 Child From £15.95 Concession From £12.95

CONTACT
Legoland Windsor
Winkfield Road
Windsor SL4 4AY
Tel 0870 5040404
Web www.legoland.co.uk

18

2 hrs

All year

The Living Rainforest

Experience the sights, sounds and smells of a rain-forest under glass at this unique conservation area. There is something for everyone here including special children's activities and art workshops.

★ Events for all ages   ★ Adopt an animal

LOCATION
In the village of Hampstead Norreys, a 10-minute drive from junction 13 on the M4/A34 intersection. Well signposted

OPENING
All year daily from 10am–5.15pm (last admission 4.30pm)
Closed 25, 26 Dec

ADMISSION PRICES
Adult £4.75 Child £2.75–£1.50
Under-3s Free Family £13.50

CONTACT
The Living Rainforest
Hampstead Norreys
Berkshire RG18 0TN
Tel 01635 202444
Web www.livingrainforest.org

Varies

All year

Premier Karting

This indoor karting centre caters for both children and adults. Children must be aged 8–15 years and be over 4ft 6in tall.

★ Cadet parties   ★ Cadet training days

LOCATION
From junction 10 off the M4 take the A329 Reading road & follow signs to Woodley, along the Bader Way. Cross 2 round-abouts & take left exit at 3rd. Venue is found 400 yards on left

OPENING
All year open daily 9am until late

ADMISSION PRICES
Cadet parties £20 each

CONTACT
Premier Karting
Hawkhurst Stadium, Headley Road East, Woodley, Reading Berkshire RG5 4SZ
Tel 0118 9448446
Email
enquiries@premier-karting.com

Bekonscot Model Village

2 hrs

Feb–Nov

LOCATION
Take junction 2 off the M40 & junction 16 off the M4. Signposted to the Model Village on the A355 & M40

OPENING
15 Feb–2 Nov open daily 10am–5pm

ADMISSION PRICES
Adult £4.80 Child £3 Family (2+2) £13.50
Concession £4

CONTACT
Bekonscot Model Village
Warwick Road, Beaconsfield
Buckinghamshire HP9 2PL
Tel 01494 672919
Fax 01494 675284
Email info@bekonscot.co.uk
Web www.bekonscot.com

Bekonscot is a miniature wonderland depicting rural England in the 1930s, with six little villages and their populations going about their daily lives. A large model railway winds its way through the mini-landscape amongst moving models and a cricket match on the green.

★ Sit-on-railway available weekends & school holidays

★ Children's play area

19

2–3 hrs

Apr–Oct

Buckinghamshire Railway Centre

A working steam centre where you can ride behind full-sized steam engines and on the extensive miniature railway. The museum houses a large collection of locomotives, carriages and wagons.

★ Thomas the Tank Engine Days   ★ Santa's Magic Steamings

LOCATION
Off the A41 at Waddesdon & the A413 at Whitchurch. Follow the brown tourist signs

OPENING
Apr–Oct open Sun & Bank holidays 10.30am–5.30pm; Jun–Aug open Sun, Wed & Bank holidays

ADMISSION PRICES
Adult £5 Child £4 Senior £4

CONTACT
Buckinghamshire Railway Centre, Quainton Road Station Quainton, Aylesbury Buckinghamshire HP22 4BY
Tel 01296 655450
Web www.bucksrailcentre.org.uk

Bucks Goat Centre

½ day

All year

A centre with examples of all the British breeds of goat as well as donkeys, pets, reptiles, pigs and poultry. There is also a play barn with facilities for talks and seminars.

★ Guided tours   ★ Trampoline for older children

LOCATION
½ mile south of Stoke Mandeville on the A4010

OPENING
All year open daily 10am–5pm

ADMISSION PRICES
Adult £3 Child (2–16 years) £2
Concession £2

CONTACT
Bucks Goat Centre
Layby Farm, Old Risborough Road, Stoke Mandeville
Aylesbury
Buckinghamshire HP22 5XJ
Tel 01296 612983
Email bucksgoat@ccn.go-free.co.uk
Web www.bucksgoatcentre.co.uk

Denham Country Park

 All day

 All year

This park has the Grand Union Canal to its east and the Colne, Misbourne and Frays rivers, as well as woodland and meadows, to the west.

★ Children's coot trail
★ Play sculpture
★ Maze
★ Visitor centre

LOCATION
Signposted from the A40/M40 at Denham

OPENING
All year open daily
Times displayed at entrance

ADMISSION PRICES
Free

CONTACT
Denham Country Park
Colne Valley Visitor Centre
Denham Court Drive, Denham
Uxbridge
Buckinghamshire UB9 5PG
Tel 01895 833375
Web www.buckscc.gov.uk/countryside/countryparks

Emberton Country Park

 All day

 All year

A country park with 200 acres of beautiful parkland, five lakes and various children's activities centred around the River Ouse.

★ Orienteering courses
★ Junior fishing
★ Nature trail
★ Climbing crag

LOCATION
On the A509, 10 miles north of junction 14 off the M1, close to Milton Keynes

OPENING
All year daily 24 hrs

ADMISSION PRICES
Free
Car park £3

CONTACT
Emberton Country Park
Emberton, Nr Olney
Buckinghamshire MK46 5DB
Tel 01234 711575
Email embertonpark@milton-keynes.gov.uk
Web www.mkweb.co.uk/embertonpark

20

Milton Keynes Museum

 2 hrs

All year

Housed in a beautiful Victorian farmstead, this large museum has something for all the family. Attractions range from room settings covering all aspects of Victorian and Edwardian domestic life to live demonstrations of cooking and printing from a bygone age.

★ Jessie the Shire horse
★ Special events throughout the year
★ Collection of working telephones
★ Hall of transport

LOCATION
Off McConnell Drive in Wolverton, just off the A5 & A422

OPENING
In summer open Wed–Sun 12.30pm–4.30pm;
In winter open Sat & Sun 12.30pm–4.40pm

ADMISSION PRICES
Adult £3.50 Family (2+4) £8
Concession £2.50

CONTACT
Milton Keynes Museum
McConnell Drive, Wolverton
Milton Keynes MK12 5EL
Tel 01908 316222
Email enquiries@mkmuseum.org.uk
Web www.mkmuseum.org.uk

Oak Farm Rare Breeds Park

2 hrs · **Feb–Oct**

This is a small, traditional working farm, with friendly farmyard animals and pets. The animals all have names and many are rare breeds.

★ Play area
★ Nature trail
★ Exhibition area
★ Hand feeding

LOCATION
Just off the A41, signposted to Broughton. Follow the brown tourist signs

OPENING
Mid Feb–end Oct open daily 10am–5.30pm (weather permitting)

ADMISSION PRICES
Adult £3 Child (1–16 years) £2
Concession £2.50

CONTACT
Oak Farm Rare Breeds Park
Broughton, Aylesbury
Buckinghamshire HP22 5AW
Tel 01296 415709
Web
www.pebblesculpt.co.uk/oakfarm

Roald Dahl Gallery

2–3 hrs · **All year**

You really can awaken your senses at this award-winning museum, with its innovative touchable displays and exciting programme of events. Come along and let your imagination run wild!

LOCATION
In the old part of Aylesbury, near the town centre

OPENING
All year open Mon–Sat 10am–5pm & Sun 2pm–5pm; In term time gallery opens at 3pm

ADMISSION PRICES
Dahl Gallery: Adult £3.50
Child £2.75
Main Museum: Free

CONTACT
Bucks County Museum & Roald Dahl Gallery
Church Street, Aylesbury
Buckinghamshire HP20 2QP
Tel 01296 331441
Email museum@buckscc.gov.uk
Web
www.buckscc.gov.uk/museum

21

Thames Valley Falconry & Conservation Centre

2 hrs · **Mar–Nov**

A fascinating centre which has falconry displays, exhibits, static displays and a collection of over 60 raptors from around the world.

★ Falconry courses
★ Birthday parties

LOCATION
From the M4 follow the A404 to Marlow then the A4094 to Bourne End. Turn into Wyeale Garden Centre

OPENING
23 Mar–3 Nov open Tue–Sun, Bank holidays & school holidays 10.30am–5pm

ADMISSION PRICES
Please phone for details

CONTACT
Thames Valley Falconry & Conservation Centre
Pump Lane South
Little Marlow
Buckinghamshire SL7 3RB
Tel 01628 891085
Web
www.thamesvalleyfalconry.com

Wycombe Museum

2 hrs · **All year**

Explore the history of the Wycombe district in the lively modern displays in this museum. There are hands-on activities for children and special events throughout the year.

LOCATION
Take junction 4 off the M40 & follow the A404 through the town centre & up Amersham Hill. Then follow the brown tourist signs

OPENING
All year open daily 10am–5pm; Sun 2pm–5pm; Closed Bank holidays

ADMISSION PRICES
Free

CONTACT
Wycombe Museum
Castle Hill House, Priory Avenue
High Wycombe
Buckinghamshire HP13 6PX
Tel 01494 421895
Web
www.wycombe.gov.uk/museum

Wycombe Summit

2 hrs

All year

The longest ski slope in England and a world-class ski and snowboard centre for all ages and abilities, Wycombe Summit has seven nursery slope areas.

★ Holiday activities   ★ Orienteering

LOCATION
Between junction 3 & 4 of the M40, just ½ hour from London

OPENING
All year open daily; In summer open Mon-Fri 10am-10pm, Sat & Sun 10am-6pm; In winter open 10am-10pm; Closed 25 Dec Please phone to confirm opening dates & times

ADMISSION PRICES
Adult from £10.50 Junior From £9.50

CONTACT
Wycombe Summit
Abbey Barn Lane
High Wycombe
Buckinghamshire HP10 9QQ
Tel 01494 474711/439099
Web www.wycombesummit.com

Barleylands Farm

2-3 hrs

Mar-Oct

A unique farm attraction with a farm museum exhibiting over 2000 farm tools and machines. There is also an animal centre with bunny barn, chick hatchery and duck pond. Children can meet and feed the friendly pigs, cows, goats and sheep.

LOCATION
Follow the brown tourist signs from the A127/A12

OPENING
1 Mar-31 Oct open daily from 10am-5pm

ADMISSION PRICES
Please phone for details

CONTACT
Barleylands Farm
Barleylands Road, Billericay
Essex CM11 2UD
Tel 01268 290229/532253
Email museum@barleylands-farm.co.uk

22

Colchester Zoo

All day

All year

UK Zoo of the Year
The Good Britain Guide

A modern and exciting attraction with a programme of daily displays and a new African Zone for giraffes, elephants, rhinos, cheetahs, warthogs and hyenas. Children and adults can test their knowledge at one of the interactive discovery areas.

★ Disabled access; some steep hills
★ Children's Jungle Safari
★ Familiar Friends Petting Areas
★ Panning for Gold
★ Kalahari Capers soft play area
★ Tanganyika Rope Bridge

LOCATION
South of Colchester. Take the A1124 from the A12 & follow the elephant signs

OPENING
All year open daily from 9.30am;
Closed 25 Dec

ADMISSION PRICES
Adult £9.50 Child (3-14) £6.25
Under-3s Free Senior £6.25
Please confirm prices before visiting

CONTACT
Colchester Zoo
Maldon Road, Stanway
Colchester
Essex CO3 5SL
Tel 01206 331292
Email enquiries@colchester-zoo.co.uk
Web www.colchester-zoo.co.uk

Hanningfield Reservoir Visitor Centre

All day

All year

The visitor centre is the gateway to the 100-acre nature reserve on the shores of Hanningfield Reservoir, on a Site of Special Scientific Interest for its breeding wildfowl.

LOCATION
Turn off the B1007 onto Downham Road & turn left onto Hawkswood Road. The centre is just beyond the causeway, opposite Crowsheath

OPENING
All year open Tue–Sun & Bank holidays 9am–5pm

ADMISSION PRICES
Free; Donations requested

CONTACT
Hanningfield Reservoir Visitor Centre
Hawkswood Road, Downham
Billericay, Essex CM11 1WT
Tel 01268 711001
Web www.essexwt.org.uk

Hedingham Castle

1 hr+

Apr–Oct

Built in 1140 by the Earls of Oxford, this is one of the best-preserved Norman keeps in England. The castle is set in beautiful parkland and holds special events such as jousts throughout the summer.

★ Siege re-enactments   ★ Medieval players

LOCATION
Just off the A1017 between Colchester & Cambridge

OPENING
Apr–Oct open daily 10am–5pm

ADMISSION PRICES
Adult £4 Child £3 Family £14
Concession £3.50

CONTACT
Hedingham Castle
Nr Halstead
Essex CO9 3DJ
Tel 01787 460261
Email hedinghamcastle@aspects.net
Web www.hedinghamcastle.co.uk

High Woods Country Park

All day

All year

LOCATION
Accessible from Mile End Road & Ipswich Road, travelling north from Colchester

OPENING
All year open at any reasonable time
Visitor Centre: 6 Jan–31 Mar open Sat & Sun 10am–4pm; 1 Apr–30 Sep open Mon–Sat 10am–4.30pm, Sun & Bank holidays open 11am–5.30pm; 6 Oct–29 Dec open Sat & Sun 10am–4pm; Closed 22 Dec

ADMISSION PRICES
Free

CONTACT
High Woods Country Park
Visitors Centre, Turner Road
Colchester
Essex CO4 5JR
Tel 01206 853588
Email countryside.team@colchester.gov.uk
Web www.visitweb.com/hwcp

This country park boasts areas of woodland, grassland, farmland and wetland. Numerous footpaths provide an opportunity to see a wide range of wildlife and a visitor centre houses displays on the natural history and history of the area.

★ Guided tours for individuals

★ Fishing

★ Horse-riding trail

Lee Valley Park & Information Centre

The Lee Valley Park, including the River Lee Country Park, offers opportunities for bird-watching, angling and walking. There is an information centre which has details of many different activities.

LOCATION
Signposted from junction 26 off the M25. On the junction of the B194 & A121

OPENING
Park: Open at any reasonable time
Information centre: 1 Jan–28 Mar open daily 10am–4pm; 29 Mar–31 Oct 9.30am–5pm; 1 Nov–31 Dec 10am–4pm

ADMISSION PRICES
Free

CONTACT
Lee Valley Park & Information Centre
Abbey Gardens, Waltham Abbey
Essex EN9 1XQ
Tel 01992 702200
Email info@leevalleypark.org.uk
Web www.leevalleypark.com

Mole Hall Wildlife Park

The park is in gardens adjoining a fully moated manor and has otters, chimps, guanaco, lemurs, wallabies, deer, owls and a butterfly pavilion.

★ Waterfowl   ★ Pets corner
★ Maize maze   ★ Play areas

LOCATION
Off the B1383

OPENING
All year open daily
10.30am–6pm; Closed 25 Dec

ADMISSION PRICES
Adult £5 Child (3–15 years)
£3.50 Family £15 Concession £4

CONTACT
Mole Hall Wildlife Park
Widdington, Saffron Walden
Essex CB11 3SS
Tel 01799 540400
Email enquiries@molehall.co.uk
Web www.molehall.co.uk

Old MacDonald's Educational Farm Park

This educational farm park was created to offer a greater understanding of British farm livestock, wildlife and countryside. There are 17 acres of pasture and woodland, with hard paths to ensure dry feet and access for wheelchairs, and many opportunities to get close to the birds and animals.

★ Guided tours for individuals
★ Interpretation displays on paddocks & pens
★ Playground
★ Essex-style barn

LOCATION
Off the M25 at junction 28 onto the A1023. Left at 1st lights into Wigley Bush Lane, left at the junction with Weald Road, 2 miles on Weald Road. Farm is on the left

OPENING
In winter open 10am–dusk; In summer open 10am–6pm; Closed 25, 26 Dec

ADMISSION PRICES
Adult £3.25 Child (2–15 years) £2
Concession £2.75

CONTACT
Old Macdonald's Educational Farm Park
Weald Road
South Weald
Brentwood
Essex CM14 5AY
Tel 01277 375177
Fax 01277 375393
Email info@oldmacdonaldsfarm.org.uk
Web www.oldmacdonaldsfarm.org.uk

The Original Great Maze

½ day

Jul–Sep

LOCATION
On the A120 between Great Dunmow
& Braintree

OPENING
6 Jul–8 Sep open daily 10am–5pm

ADMISSION PRICES
Adult £4 Under-14s £2.50
Concession £2.50

CONTACT
The Original Great Maze
Blake House Craft Centre
Braintree, Essex CM7 8SH
Tel 01376 553146
Email david@rochesterfm.freeserve.co.uk
Web www.maze.info

A massive, ever-changing maze grown every year from over half a million individual maize and sunflower seeds. It has more than five miles of pathways laid out in over ten acres of Essex farmland.

★ Viewing platform
★ Lost Souls map available

25

Quasar at Rollerworld

Varies

All year

In this laser game each player is armed with a laser gun and shoots the opposition to win points. The game marshal instructs you on how to play, using unlimited lives and headquarter units.

LOCATION
From the A12, take the turn off
to Harwich & Colchester.
Continue straight over the
roundabouts & follow the
brown tourist signs

OPENING
Please phone for details

ADMISSION PRICES
Please phone for details

CONTACT
Quasar at Rollerworld
Eastgates, Colchester
Essex CO1 2TJ
Tel 01206 868868
Fax 01206 870400
Web www.rollerworld.co.uk

Royal Gunpowder Mills

3 hrs+

Mar–Oct

Royal Gunpowder Mills mixes fascinating history, exciting science and beautiful surroundings to produce a magical trip for both old and young.

LOCATION
From the M25, take junction 26
& follow the A121 to Waltham
Abbey. Cross over Highbridge
Street into Beaulieu Drive

OPENING
16 Mar–27 Oct open daily
10am–6pm (last admission 5pm)

ADMISSION PRICES
Adult £5.90 Child £3.25
Family £17 Concession £5.25

CONTACT
Royal Gunpowder Mills
Beaulieu Drive
Waltham Abbey
Essex EN9 1BN
Tel 01992 707370
Fax 01992 710341
Email
info@royalgunpowdermills.com
Web
www.royalgunpowdermills.com

Tumblewood

2 hrs

All year

WC

An **indoor adventure playground** with a baby area with a ball pool and soft shape, a toddler area with a rope climb and ball pool and a large area for the over-5s with slides, rope swings, squeeze rollers, log climbs, ball pool and a spooky dark area.

LOCATION	CONTACT
Take the A131 to Halstead	**Tumblewood**
OPENING	Whitehouse Business Park
All year open daily 10am–6pm;	Whiteash Green, Halstead
Closed 25, 26 Dec	Essex CO9 1PB
	Tel 01787 474760
ADMISSION PRICES	Fax 01787 474808
Under-5s £2.95 Over-5s £3.45	Email tumblewood@aol.com
	Web www.tumblewood.co.uk

Weald Country Park

½ day

All year

This **country park has two lakes**, a deer paddock and country walks and trails. There is a ranger service offering guided walks and events.

★ Visitor centre   ★ Play schemes during holidays

LOCATION	ADMISSION PRICES
Signposted from the M25,	Free
junction 28	
	CONTACT
OPENING	**Weald Country Park**
Park: Open daily 8am–dusk	Weald Road, South Weald
Visitor centre: 2 Apr–31 Oct	Brentwood
open Tue–Sun; Bank holidays	Essex CM14 5QS
open 10am–4pm; 2 Nov–29 Dec	Tel 01277 216297
open Sat & Sun 10am–4pm	Fax 01277 202157

26

The Bear Museum

1 hr

All year

WC

This **museum houses a world-renowned collection** of antique teddy bears displayed in an interesting Edwardian toy shop setting.

LOCATION	ADMISSION PRICES
On the old A3 London–	Free
Portsmouth road. Located in	
Petersfield town centre	CONTACT
	The Bear Museum
OPENING	38 Dragon Street, Petersfield
All year open Tue–Sat	Hampshire GU31 4JJ
10am–4.30pm; Closed 25, 26	Tel 01730 265108
Dec & Bank holidays	Web www.bearmuseum.co.uk

Beaulieu

½ day

All year

The **home of the National Motor Museum**, Beaulieu has over 250 vehicles on display. Visitors can also tour Lord Montagu's home and have fun on the many rides and drives.

LOCATION	ADMISSION PRICES
Between Southampton &	Adult £11.95 Child £6.95 Family
Bournemouth. Reached by road	(2+3) £33.95 Concession £9.95
via the M27, A3	
	CONTACT
OPENING	**National Motor Museum**
Apr–Sep open daily 10am–6pm;	John Montagu Building
Oct–Mar open daily 10am–5pm;	Beaulieu, Brockenhurst
Closed 25 Dec	Hampshire SO45 5DT
	Tel 01590 612345
	Email info@beaulieu.co.uk

Calshot Castle

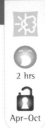

2 hrs

Apr–Oct

WC

Calshot Castle formed part of the chain of coastal forts built by Henry VIII in 1539. Its strategic importance, alongside the deep-water channel between Southampton and Portsmouth, led to it being manned throughout the centuries. In the twentieth century it was best known as a flying boat and marine craft RAF base, and is forever associated with the Schneider Trophy air races. In World War II, Calshot played a key support role, especially in connection with air and sea rescue.

i

LOCATION
From M27 junction 2 take the A326 to Fawley & Calshot

OPENING
1 Apr–31 Oct open daily 10am–4pm

ADMISSION PRICES
Adult £2 Child (5–16 years) £1 Family £5
Concession £1.50

CONTACT
Calshot Castle
Calshot Spit
Calshot
Southampton
Hampshire SO45 1BR
Tel 023 80892023
Email calshot.ac@hants.gov.uk
Web www.hants.gov.uk/calshot

Hampshire Technology Centre Intech

2 hrs+

All year

WC

This centre houses an interactive technology exhibition set up to bring to life the worlds of science, technology, engineering and mathematics. There is something for every age group.

i

LOCATION
On the A3090 Romsey road, 1 mile from the city centre. Turn into Kings Road, then take the 2nd right into Monarch Way

OPENING
All year open daily 10am–4pm; Closed 24 Dec–4 Jan

ADMISSION PRICES
Adult £5 Child £4 Family £13
Concession £3

CONTACT
Hampshire Technology Centre Intech
Telegraph Way, off Alresford Road, Winchester
Hampshire SO21 51H
Tel 01962 863791
Fax 01962 868524
Email htct@intech.uk.com
Web www.intech.uk.com

The Hawk Conservancy & Country Park

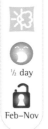

½ day

Feb–Nov

WC

A bird of prey park and hawk conservation centre set in 22 acres of woodland gardens. It has over 250 birds of prey, including hawks, eagles, vultures and owls.

i

LOCATION
4 miles west of Andover, just off the A303

OPENING
9 Feb–3 Nov open daily 10.30am–5.30pm

ADMISSION PRICES
Adult £5.75 Child (3–15 years) £3.25 Family £16.50
Concession £5.25

CONTACT
The Hawk Conservancy & Country Park
Andover
Hampshire SP11 8DY
Tel 01264 772252
Fax 01264 773772
Email
info@hawk.conservancy.org
Web www.hawk-conservancy.org

All day

Feb–Dec

Longdown Activity Farm

A **modern commercial farm** with cows and calves, goats, sheep and different kinds of pigs, including the unusual Kune Kunes. Children particularly enjoy the den, where they can stroke and feed the rabbits, chicks, ducklings, piglets and lambs.

★ Free guided tours for school groups
★ National Dairy Council Museum Collection on show
★ Replica shopfronts & milk delivery vehicle exhibits
★ Bottle feeding & hand feeding

LOCATION
Take the A35 from Lyndhurst–Southampton

OPENING
9 Feb–22 Dec open daily 10am–5pm

ADMISSION PRICES
Adult £4.50 Child (3–14 years) £3.50
Family £10.75–£15 Concession £3.75

CONTACT
Longdown Activity Farm
Deerleap Lane, Longdown
Ashurst, Southampton
Hampshire SO40 4UH
Tel 023 80293326
Fax 023 80293376
Email annette@longdown.uk.com
Web www.longdownfarm.co.uk

4 hrs

All year

Marwell Zoological Park

A **100-acre park** with over 200 species of animals in large paddocks and thoughtfully designed enclosures. Come face-to-face with a Siberian tiger, hear the jungle call of the gibbons and see the stunning colours of tropical frogs and plants.

★ Adventure playground
★ Free car park
★ Holiday specials including camel rides & face painting
★ Encounter Village
★ Tropical World
★ Penguin World
★ Bat House
★ Desert Carnivores
★ World of Lemurs

LOCATION
On the B2177 Winchester–Bishops Waltham road. Signposted from M27 & M3 motorways

OPENING
In summer open daily 10am–6pm; In winter open daily 10am–4pm; Closed 25 Dec

ADMISSION PRICES
Adult £9–£10 Child (3–14 years) £6.50–£7
Family £29.50 Concession £8.50

CONTACT
Marwell Zoological Park
Colden Common, Winchester
Hampshire SO21 1JH
Tel 01962 777407
Fax 01962 777511
Email marwell@marwell.org.uk
Web www.marwell.org.uk

Museum of Army Flying & Explorers' World

1–2 hrs

All year

LOCATION
On the A343, 6 miles south west of Andover, towards Salisbury. Adjacent to the active airfield of the Army Air Corps

OPENING
All year open daily 10am–4.30pm (last admission 4pm); Closed 17–26 Dec

ADMISSION PRICES
Adult £4.80   Under-5s £3.20
Family £13   Concession £3.80

CONTACT
Museum of Army Flying & Explorers' World
Middle Wallop, Stockbridge
Hampshire SO20 8DY
Tel 01980 674421
Fax 01264 781694
Email enquiries@flying-museum.org.uk
Web www.flying.museum.org.uk

The museum traces the development of army flying, from balloons and kites through both World Wars up to the present day. Aircraft include a Sopwith Pup, a Miles Magister and a collection of World War II gliders.

★ Guided tours for individuals
★ Interactive science & education centre

2hrs+

Mar–Sep

The New Forest Owl Sanctuary

The sanctuary includes an incubation room, hospital unit and 100 aviaries of various sizes. There are approximately 300 birds on display and talks and flying displays throughout the day. Otters and red squirrels provide an added attraction.

LOCATION
On the A31

OPENING
4 Mar–30 Sep open daily 10am–5pm

ADMISSION PRICES
Adult £5.50   Child £4   Family £21
Concession £5

CONTACT
The New Forest Owl Sanctuary
Crow Lane
Crow, Ringwood
Hampshire BH24 1EA
Tel 01425 476487
Fax 01425 461222
Email infosowls@aol.com
Web www.owlsanctuary.co.uk

Paultons Park

All day

All year

A family leisure park with over 40 attractions for all ages, including big rides, little rides, play areas, museums and entertainments.

LOCATION
Off the M27 at junction 2

OPENING
9 Mar–3 Nov open daily 10am–6.30pm (last admission 4.30pm); Earlier closing in spring, autumn & winter
Please phone for details

ADMISSION PRICES
Adult £11   Under-14s £10
Concession £10

CONTACT
Paultons Park
Ower, Romsey
Hampshire SO51 6AL
Tel 023 80814442
Fax 023 80813025

2 hrs+

All year

The Royal Armouries – Fort Nelson

This wonderfully restored Victorian fort on 19 acres on Portsdown Hill overlooks Portsmouth Harbour. With underground magazines, tunnels and grass ramparts, there is a lot to explore. Fort Nelson is the home of the Royal Armouries collection of artillery, with over 350 pieces spanning Roman arms to the Iraqi Supergun. A live firing takes place daily and a team of professional actors recreates history by bringing to life characters from the past.

★ Guided tours for individuals

LOCATION
M27 junction 11 to A27 towards Portchester from the Delme Arms round-about. Left at the 2nd set of traffic lights & along Down End Road

OPENING
1 Apr–31 Oct open daily 10am–5pm;
1 Nov–31 Mar open daily 10.30am–4pm
(last admission 1 hour before closing);
Closed 25, 26 Dec

ADMISSION PRICES
Free

CONTACT
The Royal Armouries – Fort Nelson
Down End Road
Fareham
Hampshire PO17 6AN
Tel 01329 233734
Fax 01329 822092
Email sean.mannie@armouries.org.uk
Web www.armouries.org.uk

30

All day

All year

Royal Victoria Country Park

At the **Royal Victoria Country Park** there are over 240 acres of parkland, woodland and foreshore to be explored. The park is in the grounds of an old military hospital which now houses a fascinating exhibition depicting its history, a tower with superb views and a shop.

★ Miniature railway
★ Play areas
★ Activity sheets
★ Play area & sensory garden for the less able
★ Programme of events
★ Orienteering

LOCATION
Take junction 8 off the M27 & follow the tourist signs

OPENING
Park: All year open daily
Exhibition, tower & shop: 24 Mar–Sep open daily 12pm–4.30pm

ADMISSION PRICES
Adult 80p Child (5–16 years) 40p
Concession 40p

CONTACT
Royal Victoria Country Park
Netley Abbey
Southampton
Hampshire SO31 5GA
Tel 023 80455157
Fax 023 80452451
Web www.hants.gov.uk

Southampton Maritime Museum

2 hrs
All year

The museum is a medieval stone warehouse containing exhibitions on the port of Southampton and the Titanic. There are ship models and 'All Hands on Deck', an interactive exhibition.

LOCATION
On waterfront (Town Quay) opposite the old Royal Pier

OPENING
All year open daily except 25, 26 Dec
Please phone for details

ADMISSION PRICES
Free

CONTACT
Southampton Maritime Museum
Wool House, Town Quay
Southampton SO14 2AR
Tel 023 80223941
Web
www.southampton.gov.uk/leisure/heritage

Space Ace

2 hrs
All year

An indoor adventure play area with giant slides, ball pools, rope nets, bouncy castles and much more.

LOCATION
Off the M3 at junction 13

OPENING
All year open daily 10am–4pm

ADMISSION PRICES
Mon–Fri: £2.50; Sat & Sun & school holidays: £3.50

CONTACT
Space Ace
5 Renown Close, School Lane
Chandlers Ford, Eastleigh
Hampshire SO53 4HZ
Tel 023 80255777
Fax 023 80263399

Staunton Country Park

All day
All year

LOCATION
On the B2149 between Havant & Horndean. Follow the brown tourist signs

OPENING
In summer open daily 10am–5pm; In winter open daily 10am–4pm; Closed 25, 26 Dec

ADMISSION PRICES
Adult £3.80 Child £3 Senior £3.40

CONTACT
Staunton Country Park
Middle Park Way
Havant PO9 5HB
Tel 023 92453405
Fax 023 92498156
Web
www.hants.gov.uk/leisure/coparks/staunton

Set in 1,000 acres of parkland with huge glasshouses, walled gardens and follies, this park also has the only remaining ornamental farm in England, with horses, pigs, sheep, llamas, peacocks and waterfowl.

★ Partial disabled access

★ Maze & puzzle garden

★ 1-hr walks on Sun. Prebook at the visitor centre

★ Black Cat Trail

★ Special events throughout the year

All day

All year

Wellington Country Park

LOCATION
Between Reading & Basingstoke

OPENING
15 Feb–3 Nov open daily 10am–5.30pm; 4
Nov–14 Feb open Sat & Sun 10am–4.30pm

ADMISSION PRICES
Adult £4.50 Child (3–13 years) £2.25
Family £12.50 Concession £3.50

CONTACT
Wellington Country Park
Riseley, Reading
Hampshire RG7 1SP
Tel 0118 9266444
Fax 0118 9366445
Email info@wellington-country-park.co.uk
Web www.wellington-country-park.co.uk

Experience peace and tranquillity at Wellington Country Park with woodland walks, a variety of wildlife and a deer park in this wooded parkland. A 35-acre lake offers perch, roach, tench and bream fishing and can be explored by boat or pedalo.

★ Adventure playground

★ Crazy golf

★ Nature trails

★ Miniature railway

★ Children's animal farm

32

2 hrs

All year

Activity World & Animal World

Activity World is an indoor adventure playground with a separate area for toddlers and a baby play pool. Next door to Activity World, Animal World gives children the chance to see close-up a whole range of animals from rabbits and sheep to snakes and spiders.

LOCATION
5 mins from junction 5 (M1) &
10 mins from junction 19 (M25)

OPENING
Activity World: All year daily
9.30am–6.30pm; Animal World:
9.30am–6pm (or dusk, if earlier);
Closed 25, 26 Dec & 1 Jan

ADMISSION PRICES
Adult £1 Child £5 Under-5s Free

CONTACT
Activity World & Animal World
Lincolnsfield Centre, Bushey Hall
Drive, Bushey, Watford
Hertfordshire WD23 2ES
Tel 01923 233841
Web www.lincolnsfields.co.uk

Adventure Island Playbarn

2 hrs

All year

Adventure Island is a children's play centre incorporating a toddler area for the under-5s, a soft play zone, slides, an aerial runway and ball ponds, as well as many other play modules.

LOCATION
500 yards along Parsonage Lane,
off the A1184, just north of
Sawbridgeworth

OPENING
All year open daily 10am–6pm;
Closed 24, 25 Dec &1 Jan

ADMISSION PRICES
Over-5s £3.20 Under-5s £2.50
Under-1s £1

CONTACT
Adventure Island Playbarn
Parsonage Lane, Sawbridgeworth
Hertfordshire CM21 0NG
Tel 01279 600907

Aldenham Country Park

All day

All year

LOCATION
From the M1/A41/A409 Borehamwood is just off the A5183, north of Elstree

OPENING
1 Jan–28 Feb open daily 9am–4pm; 1 Mar–30 Apr 9am–5pm; 1 May–31 Aug 9am–6pm; 1 Sep–31 Oct 9am–5pm; 1 Nov–31 Dec 9am–4pm; Closed 25 Dec

ADMISSION PRICES
Free

CONTACT
Aldenham Country Park
Park Office, Dagger Lane
Elstree, Borehamwood
Hertfordshire WD6 3AT
Tel 020 89539602
Fax 020 89051803
Web www.hertsdirect.org/aldenham

This is the site of Winnie the Pooh's 100-acre wood. With a 65-acre reservoir, circular footpath and 175 acres of woods and meadowland, Aldenham offers a range of activities and interests for the whole family, from nature trails to Winnie the Pooh features.

★ Adventure playground

★ Rare breeds, cattle, sheep & other animals

★ Angling

★ Craft fairs

★ Horse-riding

British Museum of Miniatures

1 hr

All year

The Museum of Miniatures is a doll's house and miniatures museum. Its displays include the largest doll's house in the world.

LOCATION
Take the A603 from Cambridge & the A1198 to Royston

OPENING
All year open Mon–Sat 10am–5pm & Sun 12pm–4pm; Closed 25, 26 Dec & 1 Jan Please phone for Bank holiday opening times

ADMISSION PRICES
Adult £2.50 Child £1.50

CONTACT
British Museum of Miniatures
Maple Street, Wendy, Royston
Hertfordshire SG8 0AB
Tel 01223 207025
Email info@maplestreet.co.uk
Web www.maplestreet.co.uk

Fairlands Valley Park

All day

All year

This 120-acre park has a sailing centre offering watersports, dinghy sailing, windsurfing and powerboat courses.

★ Craft for hire   ★ Children's play area

★ Paddling pools open May–Sep   ★ Fishing bay

LOCATION
Situated on Six Hills Way, 1 mile east of Stevenage near the town centre

OPENING
Open at any reasonable time; Closed 25 Dec & 1 Jan

ADMISSION PRICES
Free

CONTACT
Fairlands Valley Park
Six Hills Way, Stevenage
Hertfordshire SG2 0BL
Tel 01438 353241
Web www.stevenage-leisure.co.uk/fairlands

1 hr
All year

Hertford Museum

A **local history museum** in an old town house with a recreated Jacobean knot garden. There are changing temporary exhibitions to cater for all ages, with related activities for children.

★ Special events in school holidays, bookable in advance
★ Disabled access to ground floor

LOCATION
In the centre of Hertford, a short walk away from the multi-storey car park & within walking distance of the train station

OPENING
All year open Tue–Sat 10am–5pm

ADMISSION PRICES
Free

CONTACT
Hertford Museum
18 Bull Plain
Hertford
Hertfordshire SG14 1DT
Tel 01992 582686
Fax 01992 534797
Email info@hertfordmuseum.org
Web www.hertfordmuseum.org

34

All day
All year

Mill Green Museum & Mill

A visit to this **fully restored eighteenth-century** working watermill that is still producing flour is interesting and educational. The adjacent miller's house is now the local history museum for the district.

★ Events throughout the year

LOCATION
In the hamlet of Mill Green between Hatfield & Welwyn Garden City, at the junction of the A414 & A1000

OPENING
All year open daily; Tue–Fri open 10am–5pm; Sat, Sun & Bank holidays open 2pm–5pm

ADMISSION PRICES
Free
Donations welcome

CONTACT
Mill Green Museum & Mill
Mill Green, Hatfield
Hertfordshire AL9 5PD
Tel 01707 271362
Fax 01707 272511
Email museum@welhatgov.uk

Verulamium Museum

4 hrs

All year

HERTFORDSHIRE

i

LOCATION
Off the A4147, 1 mile from the centre of
St Albans

OPENING
All year open Mon–Sat 10am–5.30pm, Sun
2pm–5.30pm; Closed 25, 26 Dec

ADMISSION PRICES
Adult £3.20 Under-16s £1.85
Family £8.05 Concession £1.85

CONTACT
Verulamium Museum
St Michaels, St Albans
Hertfordshire AL3 4SW
Tel 01727 781810
Fax 01727 859919
Email a.coles@stalbans.gov.uk
Web www.stalbansmuseums.org.uk

Verulamium Museum is the museum of everyday life in Roman Britain.
The award-winning displays include re-created Roman interiors,
accessible collections of glass, pottery, jewellery and coins and
magnificent mosaics, wall paintings and reconstructions of Roman rooms.

★ Hands-on discovery areas

★ Excavation videos

★ Roman invasion every 2nd
weekend of the month

35

Waterhall Farm &
Craft Centre

½ day

All year

i

LOCATION
Off the B651 Whitwell-Hitchin road, in the
village of Whitwell

OPENING
All year open Sat & Sun & open daily during school holidays; In summer open
10am–5pm; In winter open 10am–4pm;
Closed 25, 26 Dec

ADMISSION PRICES
Adult £2.75 Child (2–16 years) £1.75
Family £10 Concession £1.75

CONTACT
Waterhall Farm & Craft Centre
Whitwell, Hitchin
Hertfordshire SG4 8BN
Tel 01438 871256
Fax 01438 871526

An open farm featuring rare
breeds and offering a hands-on
experience for visitors. There is
also a play area featuring a straw
bale battlefield, sand-pit, slide and
an old tractor.

3 hrs+
Apr–Oct

Willows Farm Village

Children enjoy this farm village where they can get to know the farm animals in a countryside setting.

- ★ Parking on site
- ★ Daft Duck Trails
- ★ Guinea Pig Village
- ★ Children's Theatre
- ★ Bouncy Haystack
- ★ Tractor Treck

LOCATION
300 metres from junction 22 of the M25

OPENING
5 Apr–end of Oct open daily 10am–5.30pm

ADMISSION PRICES
Please phone for details

CONTACT
Willows Farm Village
Coursers Road, London Colney
St Albans
Hertfordshire AL2 1BB
Tel 01727 822444
Fax 01727 822365
Email info@willowsfarmvillage.com
Web www.willowsfarmvillage.com

36

All day
Mar–Oct

Blackgang Chine Fantasy Park

This park, originally Victorian gardens, has been developed into a family-friendly theme park. The fun themed areas include Frontierland, Smugglerland, Fantasyland and Nurseryland.

- ★ Water gardens
- ★ Maze
- ★ High speed family water coaster

LOCATION
On the A3005 Chale–Ventnor road

OPENING
26 Mar–27 Oct open daily 10am–5pm; Jul & Aug open daily 10am–10pm (floodlit until 10pm)

ADMISSION PRICES
Adult £6.50 Child (3–13 years) £5.50
Family £21.50 Concession £5.50

CONTACT
Blackgang Chine Fantasy Park
Chale, Ventnor
Isle of Wight PO38 2HN
Tel 01983 730330
Fax 01983 731267
Email vectisventuresltd@btinternet.com
Web www.blackgangchine.com

Flamingo Park Wilflife Encounter

All day

Mar–Oct

LOCATION
Off the B3330 between Ryde & Seaview. Well signposted from Ryde

OPENING
29 Mar–31 Oct open daily 10am–5pm (last admission 4pm)

ADMISSION PRICES
Adult £6.25 Child £4.50 Family (2+2) £20
Senior £35.25

CONTACT
Flamingo Park Wildlife Encounter
Springvale
Seaview
Isle of Wight PO34 5AP
Tel 01983 612153
Email flamingo.park@virgin.net

Set in acres of landscaped gardens overlooking the Solent, this wildlife park has pelicans, flamingos, parrots, beavers and fish, and a Discovery Zone where guests can learn about animal conservation.

★ Special events
★ The Great Easter Treasure Trail
★ Wildlife feeding
★ Keeper talks

37

Fort Victoria Marine Aquarium

2 hrs
Mar–Oct

See poisonous weever fish, graceful ray, beautiful anemones and amazing cuttlefish that change colour before your eyes. Extraordinary tropical fish and much more can be seen at this aquarium.

LOCATION
West from Yarmouth on the A3054, ½ mile past the bridge

OPENING
29 Mar–31 Oct open daily 10am–6pm

ADMISSION PRICES
Adult £1.90 Child (5–16 years) 95p Family £5 Concession £1.50

CONTACT
Fort Victoria Marine Aquarium
Fort Victoria Country Park
off Westhill Lane
Yarmouth PO41 0RR
Tel 01983 760283
Email pblake@globalnet.co.uk
Web www.isleofwightaquarium.co.uk

Fort Victoria Model Railway

1–2 hrs
Mar–Oct

This is the largest and most technically advanced model railway in Britain. It is entirely computer controlled and has over 380 model buildings, 750 model people and 180 vehicles.

LOCATION
Take the Alum Bay/Freshwater road out of Yarmouth. Take the 1st turning right at the brown tourist sign, then follow Westhill Lane to the end

OPENING
29 Mar–7 Apr & 27 May–30 Sep open daily 10am–5pm; Oct open Sat & Sun & half-term 10am–5pm

ADMISSION PRICES
Adult £3.50 Child (1–16 years) £2.50 Family £10
Concession £2.50

CONTACT
Fort Victoria Model Railway
Westhill Lane
Yarmouth
Isle of Wight PO41 0RR
Tel 01983 761553

Isle of Wight Steam Railway

2-4 hrs

Mar-Dec

A five-mile steam railway that uses Victorian and Edwardian locomotives and carriages.

★ Children's playground   ★ Woodland walks

LOCATION
3 miles south-west of Ryde by road

OPENING
29 Mar-2 Apr & 25 May-30 Sep open daily 10am-4.30pm; Please phone for details of Mar, Oct & Dec opening dates & times

ADMISSION PRICES
Adult £7.50-£10.50   Child (4-15 years) £4-£7   Concession £6.50-£9.50   Family £19-£29

CONTACT
Isle of Wight Steam Railway
Railway Station, Havenstreet
Ryde PO33 4DS
Tel 01983 882204
Email havenstreet@iwsteamrail-way.co.uk
Web www.iwsteamrailway.co.uk

Isle of Wight Zoo

½ day

Apr-Oct

Situated on Sandown's beautiful seafront, this zoo is renowned for its collection of magnificent tigers and big cats. There are also rare lemurs and at the Nightmares of Nature exhibit, you can have your photo taken with a harmless snake.

LOCATION
On the B3395

OPENING
Apr-Oct open daily 10am-5pm
Please phone to confirm

ADMISSION PRICES
Adult £5.95 Child (5-16 years) £4.95 Family £18.50
Concession £4.95

CONTACT
Isle of Wight Zoo
Granite Fort, Yaverland Seafront
Sandown PO36 8QB
Tel 01983 403883
Fax 01983 401684
Email jack.corney@iow-zoo.freeserve.co.uk
Web www.isleofwightzoo.com

38

All day

All year

The Needles Park

Overlooking the Needles at the western tip of the island, the park has attractions and rides for all the family. The chairlift to the beach enables visitors to enjoy the most famous view on the island and the unique coloured sand cliffs.

LOCATION
Reached via the B3322

OPENING
29 Mar-early Nov fully open daily 10am-5pm; Nov-Mar open partially for catering, retail, Alum Bay Glass, Isle of Wight Sweet Manufactory; Closed 20 Dec-6 Jan

ADMISSION PRICES
Free

CONTACT
The Needles Park
Alum Bay, Totland Bay
Isle of Wight PO39 0JD
Tel 01983 752401
Email info@theneedles.co.uk
Web www.theneedles.co.uk

Shanklin Chine

1 hr

Mar-Nov

A natural scenic gorge with a 45-foot waterfall and stream leading to a beach with a fascinating history, Shanklin Chine was once a site for shipwrecks and smuggling. It was later used as a training ground for Commandos during World War II.

LOCATION
Enter via the old village, off the A3055 or through the Western end of Shanklin Esplanade, off Chine Hill

OPENING
31 Mar-22 May & 29 Sep-2 Nov open daily 10am-5pm; 22 May-28 Sep open daily 10am-10pm

ADMISSION PRICES
Adult £3.50 Child £2

CONTACT
Shanklin Chine
12 Ponona Road, Shanklin
Isle of Wight PO37 6PF
Tel 01983 866432
Web www.shanklinchine.co.uk

Bredgar & Wormshill Light Railway

2–5 hrs

May–Sep

LOCATION
4½ miles north of Junction 8 off the M20 (Leeds Castle exit). 1 mile south of Bredgar

OPENING
May–Sep open first Sun in the month
11am–5pm

ADMISSION PRICES
Adult £5 Child (over 2 years) £2.50

CONTACT
Bredgar & Wormshill Light Railway
The Warren, Bredgar
Sittingbourne
Kent ME9 8AT
Tel 01622 884254
Fax 01622 884668
Web www.bwlr.co.uk

The steam train service runs along the line between Warren Wood and Stony Shaw, through attractive Kent countryside. There are also eight other restored steam locomotives, vintage cars, a locomotive shed and a model railway to enjoy.

★ Santa Specials (booking essential)
★ Woodland walks

All day

All year

Bridledown Children's Farm

A large, agricultural barn containing a variety of farm animals including rabbits and guinea pigs, ferrets and goats, and birds of prey.

★ Rabbit City
★ Pony rides
★ Play area
★ Woodland walks

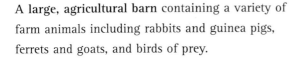

LOCATION
From Dover or Folkestone follow the A20 then turn onto the B2011. Signposted

OPENING
All year open daily 10am–5pm; Closed 25, 26 Dec

ADMISSION PRICES
Adult £2 Child £1

CONTACT
Bridledown Children's Farm & Wildlife Centre
West Hougham, Dover
Kent CT15 7AG
Tel 01304 201382
Fax 01304 204757

The Canterbury Tales

45 min

All year

Join Chaucer's colourful pilgrims on their journey from the Tabard Inn in London to St Thomas a Becket's shrine in Canterbury, in this stunning recreation of medieval England.

LOCATION
Accessible by road via the A2/M2. Follow the signs for Canterbury city centre

OPENING
Jul–Aug open daily 9.30am–5pm; Jan–Jun & Sep open daily 10am–4.30pm; Closed 25 Dec

ADMISSION PRICES
Adult £6.50 Child £5
Family (2+2) £20

CONTACT
The Canterbury Tales
St Margaret's Street
Canterbury CT1 2TG
Tel 01227 479227
Web www.canterburytales.org.uk

Capstone Farm Country Park

All day
All year

Capstone Farm Country Park is set in 280 acres of former farmland on the North Downs and has a variety of habitats to explore, from ancient woodlands and orchards to wildflower meadows and much more.

★ Visitor centre
★ Children's play areas
★ Events programme

LOCATION
Accessible from the M2 & A2

OPENING
Main gates open daily; Jan–Feb 8.30am–5.30pm; Mar–Apr 8.30am–dusk; May–Aug 8.30am–8.30pm; Sep–Dec 8.30am–dusk
Visitor Centre open daily; Jan–Mar open 10am–4pm; Apr–Sep open 10am–5pm; Oct–Dec open 10am–4pm; Closed 25 Dec
Please phone for details

ADMISSION PRICES
Free

CONTACT
Capstone Farm Country Park
Capstone Road
Gillingham ME7 3JG
Tel 01634 812196
Fax 01634 811438
Email capstonefarmcp@medway.gov.uk

40

Caxton River Trips

1 hr
Easter–Sep

Take a return trip from Tonbridge Castle on the barge Caxton. Pass under the town bridge, through a lock and out into open countryside where you may see kingfisher and mink.

★ Guided tours compulsory   ★ Commentary

LOCATION
Leave the M25 at junction 5 & follow the A21 south to Tonbridge

OPENING
Easter–30 Sep open Sat, Sun, Bank holidays & school holidays
Please phone for details

ADMISSION PRICES
Adult £3.50 Child (1–16 years) £2 Concession 50p

CONTACT
Caxton River Trips
Tonbridge Waterways
Riverside Studio, Tonbridge
Kent TN9 1UU
Tel 01732 360630

Crabble Corn Mill

1 hr
Easter–Sep

A restored watermill dating from 1812 and in full working order with devices not seen elsewhere. Demonstrations of flour milling take place and there is a programme of craft and art exhibitions.

LOCATION
M2/A2 from London–Canterbury then the A256 to River. From Folkestone follow the B2060

OPENING
Easter–30 Sep open Sat, Sun, Bank holidays & school holidays
Please phone for details

ADMISSION PRICES
Adult £3.50 Child (1–16 years) £2 Concession 50p

CONTACT
Crabble Corn Mill
Lower Road
River Dover
Kent CT17 0UY
Tel 01304 823292
Web
www.invmed.demon.co.uk/mill

A Day at the Wells

1 hr

All year

Take a **genteel journey** through Georgian England and experience the sights, sounds and smells of a summer's day in 1740s Tunbridge Wells.

LOCATION
Accessible by road via the A26, A21 or A267

OPENING
Apr–Oct open daily 10am–5pm;
Nov–Mar open daily 10am–4pm

ADMISSION PRICES
Adult £5.50 Child £4.50 Family
(2+2) £17.50 Concession £4.50

CONTACT
A Day at the Wells
The Corn Exchange
The Pantiles
Royal Tunbridge Wells,
Kent TN22 5QT
Tel 01892 546545
Email
dayatthewells@hotmail.com

Diggerland

½ day

Mar–Nov

A **unique adventure park** based on the world of construction machinery, where children and adults can ride and drive real JCBs and dumpers in safety.

LOCATION
Exit the M2 at junction 2 onto the A228. Follow the signposts to Strood

OPENING
Mar–Nov open weekdays,
Bank holidays & school holidays
10am–5pm

ADMISSION PRICES
Adults £2.50 Child £2.50
Under-2s Free Senior £1.25
Additional charge to drive real
JCBs and dumpers

CONTACT
Diggerland Ltd
Roman Way, Strood,
Kent ME2 2NU
Tel 08700 344437
Email mail@diggerland.com
Web www.diggerland.com

41

Druidstone Park & Art Park

½ day

Apr–Nov

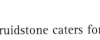

LOCATION
On the A290, from Canterbury or Whitstable

OPENING
1 Apr–30 Nov open daily 10am–5.30pm

ADMISSION PRICES
Adult £3.90 Child (3–16 years) £2.60
Family £11 Concession £3.50

CONTACT
Druidstone Park & Art Park
Honey Hill, Blean
Canterbury
Kent CT2 9JR
Tel 01227 765168
Fax 01227 768860
Web www.druidstone.net

Set in attractive gardens & woodland, Druidstone caters for the imagination of all ages. Go on a discovery trail through the enchanted woodland, explore the Art Park sculpture in many forms and enjoy hands-on experiences in the farmyard.

★ Play areas for all ages

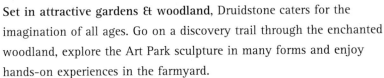

Farming World

There are over 100 traditional breeds of farm animals to meet and have close contact with in this safe environment. In the Hawking Centre visitors can see many indigenous species of birds of prey in spectacular displays.

★ Adventure playground
★ Beehive
★ Tractor & trailer rides
★ Indoor craft activities for children

LOCATION
Off the A299, ¼ mile east of the M2 at junction 7

OPENING
1 Mar–1 Nov open daily 9.30am–5.30pm

ADMISSION PRICES
Adult £4   Child (3–15 years) £3
Concession £3.50

CONTACT
Farming World
Nash Court, Boughton
Faversham, Kent ME13 9SW
Tel 01227 751144
Fax 01795 520813
Email farmingworld@lineone.net
Web www.farming-world.com

42

Fleur de Lis Heritage Centre

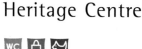

A lively local museum, reflecting Faversham's long and colourful history, from prehistoric times to the present day, and including many exciting features.

★ Historical shops   ★ Edwardian barber's museum

LOCATION
In the town centre, 3 minutes drive from the M2 & 3 minutes walk from the main station

OPENING
All year open Mon–Sat 10am–4pm & Sun 10am–1pm; Closed Sun in Jan & Feb & 24 Dec–1 Jan

ADMISSION PRICES
Adult £2 Under-16s £1
Concession £1

CONTACT
Fleur de Lis Heritage Centre
10–13 Preston Street, Faversham Kent ME13 8NS
Tel 01795 534542
Web www.faversham.org

Hever Castle & Gardens

This thirteenth-century castle, the childhood home of Anne Boleyn, is set in spectacular gardens.

★ Partial disabled access   ★ Adventure playground
★ Yew maze   ★ Miniature house exhibition
★ Water maze (Apr-Oct)   ★ Special events

LOCATION
Take junctions 5 or 6 off the M25. Located 3 miles south-east of Edenbridge off the B2026

OPENING
1 Mar–30 Nov open daily from 11am–4pm

ADMISSION PRICES
Phone for details

CONTACT
Hever Castle, Edenbridge
Kent TN8 7N6
Tel 01732 865244
Email mail@hevercastle.co.uk
Web www.hevercastle.co.uk

The Historic Royal Dockyard Chatham

2–3 hrs

Feb–Nov

Visitors can enjoy 400 years of exciting naval history and architecture set in an 80-acre site. Visitors can see HMS Cavalier, Britain's last World War II destroyer, the submarine Ocelot and the Victorian sloop Gannett, currently under restoration.

★ Wooden Walls exhibit with an
animatronic adventure
★ Riverfront museum

43

Howletts Wild Animal Park

3–4 hrs

All year

Howletts Wild Animal park is set in mature parkland and contains John Aspinall's collection of animals, including one of the largest collections of tigers in the world and the largest breeding colony of gorillas in captivity. Other animals include deer, leopards and elephants.

★ Cave of gems
★ Barbecues in summer
★ Nightlife exhibition
★ Creature close-ups
★ Winter Wonderland
★ Tropical World
★ Adventure playground

1 hr

All year

Kent & East Sussex Railway

Quality Assured Visitor Attraction
English Tourism Council

Take a nostalgic trip behind a full-size steam engine on Britain's first light railway. Journey through 10½ miles of unspoilt countryside between Tenterden and the Sussex village of Bodiam and experience the sights and sounds of steam engines.

★ Video theatre
★ Children's play area
★ Museum
★ Carriage for disabled passengers

LOCATION
Follow the A28 from Ashford or Hastings

OPENING
Opening times vary & are affected by the seasons
Please phone for details

ADMISSION PRICES
Adult £8 Child (3–15 years) £4 Family £22
Concession £7.50

CONTACT
Kent & East Sussex Railway
Tenterden Town Station
Tenterden
Kent TN30 6HE
Tel 01580 765155
Fax 01580 765654
Email enquiries@kesr.org.uk
Web www.kesr.org.uk

44

2–3 hrs

All year

Leeds Castle & Gardens

Set on two islands in the centre of a lake, Leeds Castle has been home to six of the medieval queens of England and a royal palace of King Henry VIII. There are 500 acres of parkland and gardens to explore.

★ Guided tours for individuals
★ Duckery & aviary
★ Maze
★ Grotto
★ Greenhouses & vineyard

LOCATION
7 miles east of Maidstone, off the M20 at junction 8, midway between London & the Channel Ports. The main entrance is on the B2163. Signposted

OPENING
Please phone for details

ADMISSION PRICES
Adult £9.50 Child (4–15 years) £6
Family £27 Concession £8

CONTACT
Leeds Castle
Maidstone
Kent ME17 1PL
Tel 01622 765400
Fax 01622 735616
Email enquiries@leeds-castle.co.uk
Web www.leeds-castle.com

2–4 hrs

All year

Museum of Canterbury

This museum offers exciting interactive displays of archaeology and history, set in the Poor Priest's Hospital. Find out about famous people and precious objects from Canterbury's 2,000-year history.

LOCATION
Follow the M2/A2 from London;
Take the A28 from Ashford.
Located in the city centre

OPENING
All year open Mon–Sat
10.30am–5pm & Sun (Jun–Oct)
1.30pm–5pm (last admission
4pm)

ADMISSION PRICES
Adult £1.90 Child £1.20
Family £5 Concession £1.20

CONTACT
Museum of Canterbury
Stour Street, Canterbury
Kent CT1 2NZ
Tel 01227 452747
Web www.canterbury-
museum.co.uk

Museum of Kent Life

½ day

Feb–Oct

The Museum of Kent is an open-air museum that shows what life was like in Kent during the last 100 years. Children will enjoy the interactive exhibits, animals and boat trips.

LOCATION
Just off junction 6 of the M20.
Follow the signs to Aylesford

OPENING
Feb–Oct open daily
10am–5.50pm

ADMISSION PRICES
Adult £5.50 Child £3.50 Family
£16 Concession £4

CONTACT
Museum of Kent Life
Lock Lane, Sandling
Maidstone
Kent ME14 3AU
Tel 01622 763936
Email
enquiries@museum-kentlife.co.uk
Web www.museum-kentlife.co.uk

45

2–4 hrs

Mar–Oct

M. W. Amusement Park

An amusement park with various rides including dodgems, log flume, ghost train, balloon rides and indoor amusement arcades.

LOCATION
The A259 from Folkestone/Rye

OPENING
Mar–end Oct open daily
10am–late

ADMISSION PRICES
1 ride: 70p 4 rides: £2.50
9 rides: £5 20 rides: £10

CONTACT
M. W. Amusement Park
20 High Street
Dymchurch
Romney Marsh
Kent TN29 0NG
Tel 01303 873120

Planet Lazer

Varies

All year

Planet Lazer contains Europe's largest laser centre and has 20 machine video games. Visitors can also take part in a futuristic fantasy world role-play.

LOCATION
Off the M2/A2 from London or
Dover or the A28 from Ashford

OPENING
All year open daily except
24–27, 31 Dec & 1, 2 Jan
Please phone for details

ADMISSION PRICES
Adult £6 Child £6
Concession £4.50

CONTACT
Planet Lazer
City Gate Centre, 41 St George's
Place, Canterbury, Kent CT1 1UT
Tel 01227 787377
Web www.planetlazer.co.uk

2 hrs

All year

Port Lympne Wild Animal Park

LOCATION
Leave the M20/A20 at junction 11 & follow the signs to Lympne

OPENING
All year open daily; Closed 25 Dec

ADMISSION PRICES
Adult £11.95 Child £8.95 Senior £8.95

CONTACT
Port Lympne Wild Animal Park
Port Lympne
Lympne, Hythe
Kent CT21 4PD
Tel 01303 264647
Fax 01303 264944
Email info@howletts.net
Web www.howletts.net

A **300-acre wild animal park** situated on a panoramic sloping woodland estate where spacious paddocks contain herds of rare horses, deer, antelopes, rhinos, elephants and many other animals including tigers, lions, leopards and gorillas.

★ Free safari trailer journeys through animal paddocks

★ Historic house & formal garden

46

1–2 hrs

Apr–Sep

Ramsgate Model Village

This **model village** offers a charming reproduction of England's picturesque countryside in miniature.

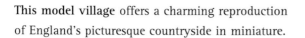

LOCATION
Take the A2 from London to Canterbury, then follow the A28/A253 to Ramsgate

OPENING
Apr–Sep open daily from 10am
Please phone for details

ADMISSION PRICES
Adult £3 Under-14s £1.50
Family £8 Concession £2

CONTACT
Ramsgate Model Village
West Cliff, Ramsgate
Kent CT11 9NY
Tel 01843 850043
Web www.model-village.com

Roman Museum

1 hr

All year

This **underground museum** houses excavated objects, reconstructions and the preserved remains of a Roman town house. Reconstructions include a Roman market place with a shoemaker, fabric seller and fruit and vegetable stall.

LOCATION
Take the M2/A2 from London or the A28 from Ashford

OPENING
All year open daily except Good Fri & Christmas period
Please phone for details

ADMISSION PRICES
Adult £2.50 Child £1.60
Family £6.50 Concession £1.60

CONTACT
Roman Museum, Butchery Lane
Canterbury, Kent CT1 2JR
Tel 01227 785575
Web
www.canterbury-museum.co.uk

2 hr+

All year

Romney, Hythe &
Dymchurch Railway

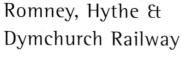

This 13½-mile tourist railway was opened in 1927 by millionaire Jack Howey. It runs steam and diesel engines with comfortable carriages, and has a toy and model railway museum.

LOCATION
3 miles from junction 11 off the M20

OPENING
Easter–30 Sep open daily from 9.35am–6.35pm; Oct–Mar open weekends 9.35am–6.35pm

ADMISSION PRICES
Please phone for details

CONTACT
Romney, Hythe & Dymchurch Railway, New Romney Station New Romney, Kent TN28 8PL
Tel 01797 36235
Web www.rhdr.demon.co.uk

Snappy's Adventure
Play Centre

½ day

All year

Snappy's is a large indoor adventure play centre with an extensive range of approved play equipment all set within an exciting dinosaur theme. There is a dedicated area for under-4s, together with a Game Zone for parents and older children.

LOCATION
From Whitstable take the A290 up Borstal Hill & turn left onto the A2990. At the next round-about turn right then right again

OPENING
All year open daily 10am–6.30pm; Closed 25 Dec–1 Jan

ADMISSION PRICES
Please phone for details

CONTACT
Snappy's Adventure Play Centre, 45b Joseph Wilson Estate, Millstrood Road Whitstable, Kent CT5 3PS
Tel 01227 282100
Fax 01227 282101

47

LOCATION
Take junction 10 off the M20 & follow the A2070 to Hamstreet. Follow the B2067 towards Woodchurch

OPENING
Apr–Sep open daily 10.30am–5.30pm; Oct–Mar open Tue–Sun 10.30am–4.30pm

ADMISSION PRICES
Adult £4 Child (3–15 years) £2.50
Playbarn £2 Senior £3.50

CONTACT
South of England Rare Breeds Centre
Woodchurch, Ashford
Kent TN26 3RJ
Tel 01233 861493
Fax 01233 861457
Email visit@rarebreeds.org.uk
Web www.rarebreeds.org.uk

South of England
Rare Breeds Centre

2–4 hrs

All year

This is a fun family day out in a traditional farmyard where children can meet and pet young animals and play in the playground, sandpit and paddling pool. Parents can relax in beautiful rural surroundings.

★ Indoor soft play area
★ Outdoor playground
★ Trailer rides (seasonal)
★ Easter Bunny Hunt
★ Piggy Picnics
★ Animal Action Day

All day

All year

Wildwood

See **wolves**, **beaver**, **deer**, badger, fox, red squirrel, ravens, otter and many other examples of rare British wildlife in this unique woodland discovery park. There are also special historic events.

LOCATION
On the A291, midway between Herne Bay & Canterbury

OPENING
All year open daily 10am–5pm or dusk, if earlier; Closed 24, 25, 31 Dec & 1 Jan

ADMISSION PRICES
Adult £5.25 Child £3.75
Concession £3.85

CONTACT
Wildwood
Herne Common, Herne Bay
Kent CT6 7LQ
Tel 01227 712111
Web www.wildwood-centre.co.uk

1 hr

All year

Bank of England Museum

This **museum is housed** within the Bank of England and traces the history of the bank. Visitors can view gold bars dating from ancient times, the modern market bar, coins, a unique collection of banknotes and much more.

LOCATION
Bank & Liverpool Street underground stations

OPENING
All year open daily 10am–5pm; Also open on the day of the Lord Mayor's Show; Closed Sat, Sun & Bank holidays

ADMISSION PRICES
Free

CONTACT
Bank of England Museum
Threadneedle Street
London EC2R 8AH
Tel 020 76015545
Web www.bankofengland.co.uk

48

½ day

All year

Battersea Park Children's Zoo

The **children's zoo** is situated in pleasant surroundings with a paddock area, farmyard animals, flamingos, otters, monkeys, a tactile area, deer enclosure and a reptile and amphibian house. Otters are fed daily at 11am and 4pm.

LOCATION
In Battersea Park, near the Peace Pagoda on North Carriage Drive

OPENING
23 Mar–1 Oct open daily 10am–5pm; 30 Sep–22 Mar open Sat & Sun 11am–3pm (last admission 2.30pm); Closed 22, 23, 28, 29 Dec

ADMISSION PRICES
Adult £2   Child (2–16 years) £1
Concession £1

CONTACT
Battersea Park Children's Zoo
Battersea Park
London SW11 4NJ
Tel 020 88717540
Fax 020 73500477

½ hr

All year

British Airways London Eye

The **London Eye** is the tallest observation wheel in the world. It takes guests on a gradual 30-minute flight high above London and offers fantastic views of the capital's celebrated landmarks.

★ Children's playground   ★ Views of up to 25 miles

LOCATION
On the South Bank, 5 minutes walk from Waterloo & Westminster underground

OPENING
All year open daily, except Jan; In summer open 9.30am–10pm; In winter open 9.30am–8pm (weekdays); 9.30am–10pm (weekends)

ADMISSION PRICES
£10.50

CONTACT
British Airways London Eye
Riverside Building, County Hall
Westminster Bridge Road
London SE12 7PB
Tel 0870 5000600 (bookings)
Tel 0870 9908883 (customer services)

BBC Television Centre Tours

1½ hrs
All year

On this tour you will see behind the scenes of the BBC TV Centre. You may visit areas such as the News Centre, dressing-rooms and studios. No two tours are ever the same. All tours must be pre-booked and visitors must be 10 years and over.

LOCATION
White City underground station

OPENING
Please phone for details

ADMISSION PRICES
Adult £7.95 Child £5.95
Family £21.95
Concession £6.95

CONTACT
BBC Television Centre Tours
BBC Television Centre
Wood Lane
London W12 7RJ
Tel 0870 6030304
Web www.bbc.co.uk/tours

HM Tower of London

1 day
All year

A visit to the Tower of London's 11 towers encompasses 1,000 years of history – some of it bloody. Far more than just a trip to see the Crown Jewels, there are talks, tours, holiday events and family trails, all included in the basic ticket price.

LOCATION
Tower Hill underground station

OPENING
All year; In summer Mon–Sat open 9am–5pm; Sun 10am–5pm; In winter Mon & Sun open 10am–4pm; Tue–Sat 9am–4pm

ADMISSION PRICES
Adult £11.30 Child £7.50
Concession £8.50

CONTACT
The Tower of London
Tower Hill, London EC3N
Tel 0870 7567070 for tickets
Tel 0870 7566060 for info
Web www.hrp.org.uk

49

Imperial War Museum

Quality Assured Visitor Attraction
English Tourism Council

2 hrs
All year

Come and relive life during World War I and II. Walk through the trenches and share the dramatic Blitz experience, complete with the sounds and smells of London during an air raid. Find out about spies in the Secret War Exhibition.

LOCATION
Lambeth North, Southwark, Elephant and Castle & Waterloo underground stations

OPENING
All year open daily 10am–6pm; Closed 24–26 Dec

ADMISSION PRICES
Free

CONTACT
Imperial War Museum
Lambeth Road
London SE1 6HZ
Tel 020 74165320
Fax 020 74165374
Email mail@iwm.org.uk
Web www.iwm.org.uk

Livesey Museum for Children

1–2 hrs
Feb–Nov

The Livesey Museum runs a changing programme of lively, unusual, interactive exhibitions for children up to the age of 12.

LOCATION
Elephant & Castle underground station, then the 53 or 172 bus

OPENING
Tue–Sat open 10am–5pm; Closed Dec & Jan

ADMISSION PRICES
Free

CONTACT
Livesey Museum for Children
682 Old Kent Road
London SE15 1JF
Tel 020 76395604
Fax 020 72775384
Email livesey.museum@south-wark.gov.uk
Web www.liveseymuseum.org.uk

London Aquarium

½ day

All year

Dive down deep beneath the Thames and submerge yourself in one of Europe's largest displays of aquatic life. Come face-to-face with two-yard long sharks and watch fearless divers hand-feeding gigantic conger eels.

LOCATION
On the South Bank via Waterloo station

OPENING
All year open daily 10am–6pm (last admission 5pm); Closed 25 Dec
Opening times are subject to change

ADMISSION PRICES
Adult £8.75 Child £5.25
Family £15 Concession £6.50

CONTACT
London Aquarium
County Hall, Riverside Building
London SE1 7PB
Tel 020 79678000
Web www.londonaquarium.co.uk

London Butterfly House

1–2 hrs

All year

See hundreds of butterflies flying free in a tropical greenhouse garden. Watch the butterflies feeding, courting and laying their eggs. The insect gallery has giant spiders, locusts, lizards, scorpions and stick insects and there is a walk-through aviary.

LOCATION
Tube to Gunnersbury then bus 237 or 267 to Brent Lea Gate

OPENING
Jan–27 Mar & 25 Oct–Dec open daily 10am–3.30pm; 28 Mar–24 Oct open daily 10am–5pm; 1 Jan open 10am–3pm; Closed 25, 26 Dec

ADMISSION PRICES
Adult £3.80 Child £2.80
Family £10 Concession £2.80

CONTACT
London Butterfly House
Syon Park, Brentford
London TW8 8JF
Tel 020 85607272
Web www.butterflies.org.uk

2 hrs

All year

The London Dungeon

Best Unusual Venue of 1999/2000
Meetings and Incentive Travel

The London Dungeon is an interactive historic horror attraction which dispenses fear and fun in equal doses. Visitors can encounter The Great Fire of London, Jack The Ripper and the Judgement Day boatride, which includes a trip down the River Thames.

LOCATION
Nearest station London Bridge Station. 400 yards from Monument/Bank Station

OPENING
All year open daily; Nov–Mar 10.30am–5pm; Apr–Oct 10am–5.50pm; Closed 25 Dec

ADMISSION PRICES
Adult £10.95 Child £6.95 Senior £6.95
Student £9.50

CONTACT
The London Dungeon
28/34 Tooley Street
London SE1 2SZ
Tel 020 74037221
Email londondungeon@merlin-entertainment.com
Web www.thedungeons.com

★ Not recommended for those of a nervous disposition
★ Children under 15 must be accompanied by an adult

London Planetarium

1 hr+
All year

A **virtual reality trip through space!** Before the star show, wander through the interactive Space Zones, see Stephen Hawkings, Einstein and Armstrong and learn about Black Holes and the search for Extra Terrestrial intelligence.

LOCATION	CONTACT
Baker Street underground station	**London Planetarium**
	Marylebone Road
OPENING	London NW1 5LR
Shows Mon–Fri 12.30pm–5pm,	Tel 0870 4003000
Sat & Sun 10.30am–5pm	Web www.london-planetarium.com
ADMISSION PRICES	Ticket hotline 0870 4003000
Adult £7.50 Child £5.35	
Concession £6.10	

London Zoo

All day
All year

Set in the leafy surroundings of Regent's Park, London Zoo opened in 1828 and was the world's first scientific zoo. Today it houses over 650 species of animals and hosts a daily programme of events.

LOCATION	ADMISSION PRICES
In Regents Park. Nearest under-ground is Camden Town, nearest British Rail station is Euston	Adult £11 Child (3–15) £8 Under-3s Free Family (2+2) £34 Concession £9.50
OPENING	**CONTACT**
All year daily; In summer open 10am–5.30pm; In winter open 10am–4pm; Closed 25 Dec	**London Zoo** Outer Circle, Regents Park London NW1 4RY Tel 020 77223333

51

Natural History Museum

4 hrs+
All year

The Natural History Museum has hundreds of exciting, interactive exhibits. Highlights include 'Dinosaurs', 'Creepy-Crawlies', 'Human Biology' the must-see exhibition about ourselves and 'Mammals', with its unforgettable huge blue whale.

LOCATION	ADMISSION PRICES
On the Cromwell Road, the A4 into London from the M4	Free; Charges for specific exhibitions
OPENING	**CONTACT**
All year open Mon–Sat, Bank holidays 10am–5.50pm, Sun 11am–5.50pm (last admission 5.30pm); Closed 24, 25, 26 Dec	**Natural History Museum** Cromwell Road London SW7 5BD Tel 020 79425000 Web www.nhm.ac.uk

Polka Theatre

Varies
All year

Polka is the only theatre building in Britain producing and presenting work just for children. Shows range from classic and contemporary book adaptations to new work for the stage.

★ Playground   ★ Exhibits of costumes & props

LOCATION	ADMISSION PRICES
Turn left down the Broadway & the theatre is on the left	Please phone for details
OPENING	**CONTACT**
Performances all year Tue–Sat; Closed Sun & Mon, Easter & 4-25 Sep; Please phone for per-formance times	**Polka Children's Theatre** 240 The Broadway, Wimbledon London SW19 1SB Tel 020 85434888 Web www.polkatheatre.com

Pollock's Toy Museum

2 hrs
All year

At this museum you will find toys of all kinds, including dolls, dolls' houses, a Victorian nursery, toy theatres, teddy bears, tin toys and folk toys from around the world. Live Toy Theatre performances are held during school holidays.

LOCATION
Tottenham Court Road to Goodge Street

OPENING
All year open Mon–Sat 10am–5pm (last admission 4.30pm); Closed Easter, 25, 26 Dec & 1 Jan

ADMISSION PRICES
Adult £3 Child £1.50
Concession £3

CONTACT
Pollock's Toy Museum
1 Scala Street, London W1T 2HL
Tel 020 76363452
Web
www.pollocksmuseum.co.uk

Ragged School Museum

2 hrs+
All year

This museum is dedicated to the East End. On the old site of Barnardo's ragged school, the museum has a reconstructed Victorian classroom, along with exhibits on housing, education and work in the East End from the 1880s to 1900.

LOCATION
In London's East End. Nearest underground station is Mile End

OPENING
All year open Wed & Thu 10am–5pm; First Sun of each month open 2pm–5pm

ADMISSION PRICES
Free

CONTACT
Ragged School Museum
46–50 Copperfield Road
London E3 4RR
Tel 020 89806405
Fax 020 89833481
Email enquiries@raggedschool-museum.org.uk
Web www.raggedschool.muse-um.org.uk

Royal Air Force Museum

4 hrs
All year

The exciting interactive displays,
film shows and over 80 aircraft on
display make this aviation museum
a fun day out for all the family.

★ Fun 'n' Flight interactive section
★ Touch & Try jet provost

LOCATION
Easy access from the M25. Signposted from the M1, A41, A5 & A406; Nearest underground is Colindale (Northern Line); Nearest overground station is via Thameslink Rail, Mill Hill Broadway

OPENING
All year open daily 10am–6pm; Closed 25, 26th Dec & 1 Jan

ADMISSION PRICES
Free
Under-16s must be accompanied by an adult

CONTACT
The Royal Air Force Museum
Grahame Park Way
London NW9 5LL
Tel 020 83584849
Fax 020 83584981
Web www.rafmuseum.com

Science Museum

All day

All year

Come and see over 40 galleries and 2,000 hands-on imaginative exhibits at this amazing museum. You can step into the future in the Wellcome Wing, change your sex, age 30 years in 30 seconds and create your own identity profile – all in a day!

LOCATION
South Kensington underground station

OPENING
All year open daily 10am–6pm; Closed 24–26 Dec

ADMISSION PRICES
Free
Charges for some attractions

CONTACT
Science Museum
Exhibition Road
London SW7 2DD
Tel 0870 8704868
Fax 020 79424421
Email
sciencemuseum@nmsi.ac.uk
Web www.sciencemuseum.org.uk

Sherlock Holmes Museum

2 hrs+

All year

The museum consists of Holmes' apartment on the first floor, and the entire second and third floors and attic which contain the new exhibition area, featuring several life-size wax figures from the more exciting and best known Sherlock Holmes adventures.

LOCATION
Baker Street underground station

OPENING
All year open daily
9.30am–6.30pm; Closed 25 Dec

ADMISSION PRICES
Adult £6 Child £4
Concession £6

CONTACT
Sherlock Holmes Museum
221B Baker Street
London NW1 6XE
Tel 020 79358866
Fax 020 77381269
Email sherlock@easynet.co.uk
Web www.sherlock-holmes.co.uk

Stepping Stones Farm

½ day

All year

This is an urban working farm with a full range of livestock. Structured demonstrations, such as dairy sessions and sheep shearing, are arranged for groups, according to season.

★ Play area   ★ Farm trail

LOCATION
Stepney Green underground station

OPENING
All year open Tue–Sun
9.30am–6pm; Closed Mon
except Bank holidays; Open
Easter, Christmas period &
New Year

ADMISSION PRICES
Free

CONTACT
Stepping Stones Farm
Stepney Way
Stepney High Street
London E1 3DG
Tel 020 77908204
Web www.stepneynews.com

Tate Britain

3 hrs

All year

Tate Britain is the national gallery of British art from 1500 to the present day – the Tudors to the Turner Prize. Tate holds the greatest collection of British art in the world. It presents the best collection of British art in a dynamic series of displays.

LOCATION
From Vauxhall station cross
Vauxhall Bridge Road, turn right
at end of road & then turn left
onto Millbank

OPENING
All year open daily 10am–5.50pm;
Open Good Fri, May Bank
holiday; Closed 24–26 Dec

ADMISSION PRICES
Free
Charges for some exhibitions

CONTACT
Tate Britain
Millbank, London SW1P 4RG
Tel 020 78878000
Email information@tate.org.uk
Web www.tate.org.uk

1 hr+

All year

Thames Barrier

The £500 million Thames Barrier spans the Thames at Woolwich Reach. There is an exhibition with a video and a working scale model. You can also enjoy riverside walkways, a children's play area and a learning centre with a teaching room.

LOCATION
On the A206. On the south side of the Thames between the south exit of the Blackwall Tunnel & the Woolwich ferry

OPENING
1 Apr–30 Sep open 10.30am–4.30pm; 1 Oct–31 Mar 11.30am–3.30pm; Closed 24–26 Dec

ADMISSION PRICES
Adult £1 Child 50p
Concession 75p

CONTACT
Thames Barrier Information & Learning Centre
1 Unity Way, Woolwich
London SE18 5NJ
Tel 020 83054188

1–2 hrs

All year

Tower Bridge Experience

Inside the Tower Bridge Experience you will learn how the world's most famous bridge works and the history of its construction. Enjoy the panoramic views from the walkways situated high above the Thames and visit the original Victorian engines.

LOCATION
Turn right out of the station onto Tower Bridge Road

OPENING
Apr–Oct open daily 10am–6.30pm; Nov–Mar daily 9.30am–6pm; Open Easter daily 10am––6.30pm; Closed 24, 25 Dec

ADMISSION PRICES
Adult £4.50 Child £3
Family £14 Concession £3

CONTACT
Tower Bridge Experience
Tower Bridge
London SE1 2UP
Tel 020 74033761
Web www.towerbridge.org.uk

54

1–2 hrs

All year

Winston Churchill's Britain at War Experience

This museum portrays Britain's home front during World War II. The special effects and original artefacts re-create everyday life for ordinary British people – rationing, blackouts and evacuation.

LOCATION
London Bridge underground station

OPENING
Oct–Mar open daily 10am–4.30pm; Apr–Sep open daily 10am–5.30pm; Closed 24–26 Dec

ADMISSION PRICES
Adult £5.95 Child £2.95
Family £14 Concession £3.95

CONTACT
Winston Churchill's Britain at War Experience
64–66 Tooley Street
London Bridge, London SE1 2TF
Tel 020 74033171
Web www.britainatwar.co.uk

---

3 hrs

Mar–Nov

Cogges Manor Farm Museum

Find out what life was like for the Victorians of rural Oxfordshire. The farm has beautiful original Cotswold buildings, traditional animal breeds, a walled garden and a manor house and riverside walk.

LOCATION
½ mile south-east of Witney, off the A40

OPENING
Mid Mar–30 Nov open Tue–Fri & Bank holidays 10.30am–5.30pm; Sat & Sun open 12pm–5.50pm

ADMISSION PRICES
Adult £4.20 Child £2.10
Concession £2.65

CONTACT
Cogges Manor Farm Museum
Church Lane, Witney
Oxfordshire OX28 3LA
Tel 01993 772602
Web www.westoxon.gov.uk

Cotswold Wildlife Park

All day
All year

LOCATION
2½ miles south of Burford & midway between Oxford & Cheltenham

OPENING
In summer open daily 10am–5pm (last admission 5pm); In winter 10am–3.30pm or dusk; Closed 25 Dec

ADMISSION PRICES
Adult £7 Child (3–16 years) £4.50
Concession £5

CONTACT
Cotswold Wildlife Park
Bradwell Grove, Burford
Oxford
Oxfordshire OX18 4JW
Tel 01993 823006
Fax 01993 823807
Web www.cotswoldwildlifepark.co.uk

The park is set around a Victorian manor house in 200 acres of gardens and woodland with a wide variety of animals in landscaped surroundings.

- ★ Bat house
- ★ Reptile house
- ★ Insect house
- ★ Adventure playground
- ★ Brass rubbing centre
- ★ Narrow-gauge railway

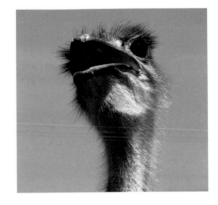

Didcot Railway Centre

Varies
All year

A living museum of the Great Western Railway, based around the original depot, and now housing a collection of steam locomotives, carriages and wagons. On Steamdays the locomotives come to life and visitors can ride in the 1930s trains.

LOCATION
Signposted from the M4 at junction 13 & the A34. Easily reached from the M40

OPENING
Please phone for details; Closed 25, 26 Dec

ADMISSION PRICES
Adult £4–£8.50 Child (3–15 years) £3–£7.50
Concession £3.50–£8

CONTACT
Didcot Railway Centre
Great Western Society, Didcot
Oxfordshire OX11 7NJ
Tel 01235 817200

The Oxford Story

1 hr
All year

Climb aboard this amazing 'dark' ride and travel through 900 years of history complete with sights, sounds and smells. Discover the connection between Alice in Wonderland and the University of Oxford.

LOCATION
Accessible by road via the A44. Follow the city centre signs. A Park & Ride service is available

OPENING
Jul–Aug open daily 9.30am–5pm; Jan–Jun & Sep–Dec open Mon–Sat 10am–4.30pm & Sun 11am–4.30pm; Closed 25 Dec

ADMISSION PRICES
Adult £6.50 Child £5
Family (2+2) £20

CONTACT
The Oxford Story
6 Broad Street
Oxford OX1 3AJ
Tel 01865 728822
Email info@oxfordstory.co.uk
Web www.oxfordstory.co.uk

All day
All year

Oxfordshire Museum

This award-winning redevelopment of Fletcher's House provides a home for the new county museum. The new museum celebrates Oxfordshire and features collections of local history, art, archaeology, landscape and wildlife, as well as a gallery exploring the county's innovative industries – from nuclear power to nanotechnology. Interactive exhibits offer new learning experiences for all ages.

LOCATION
On the A44

OPENING
All year open Tue–Sat 10am–5pm; Sun, Bank holidays 2pm–5pm (last admission 4.30pm)
Please phone for Easter & Christmas opening times

ADMISSION PRICES
Adult £2.50 Child 50p Family £4.50
Concession £1

CONTACT
Fletcher's House
Park Street
Woodstock
Oxford
Oxfordshire OX20 1SN
Tel 01993 811456
Email oxon.museum@oxfordshire.gov.uk
Web www.oxfordshire.gov.uk

1 hr
All year

Wellplace Zoo

A small zoo designed for children, with a museum and garden centre.

LOCATION
On the A4074

OPENING
Jan–Mar open Sat & Sun 10am–4pm; Apr–end Sep open daily 10am–5pm; Oct–end Dec open Sat & Sun 10am–4pm

ADMISSION PRICES
Adult £2 Child 50p

CONTACT
Wellplace Zoo
Ipsden, Wallingford
Oxfordshire OX10 6OZ
Tel 01491 680473
Web www.zooweb.com

Beaver Zoological Gardens

½ day

All year

Visitors to Beaver Zoological Gardens can see reptiles, tropical and cold-water fish, Canadian beavers, aviary birds, rabbits, chipmunks and chickens. There is also a play area and sand-pit.

LOCATION
Located 4 miles north-west of Westerham

OPENING
In summer open 10am–6pm; In winter 10am–5pm; Closed 25 Dec

ADMISSION PRICES
Adult £2.50   Child £1.50

CONTACT
Waylands Farm
Approach Road
Tatsfield
Westerham
Surrey TN16 2JT
Tel 01959 577747
Web www.beaverwaterworld.com

½ day

Feb–Oct

Birdworld

These gardens and parkland have an impressive collection of bird displays, including the parrots in flight aviary, a heron theatre and penguin feeding.

★ Seashore walk   ★ Tropical walk

★ Children's farm   ★ Aquarium

LOCATION
On the A325, 3 miles south of Farnham

OPENING
9 Feb–end Oct open daily; In winter open 9.30am–4.30pm; Closed 25, 26 Dec

ADMISSION PRICES
Please phone for details

CONTACT
Birdworld, Holt Pound, Farnham Surrey GU10 4LD
Tel 01420 22140
Fax 01420 23715
Email bookings@birdworld.co.uk
Web www.birdworld.co.uk

Bocketts Farm Park

All day
All year

This is a working family farm set in beautiful downland countryside with many friendly farm animals who enjoy being fed and touched. There are also play areas for children.

★ Tractor & pony rides   ★ Daily pig races

LOCATION
From Leatherhead follow the B2122 to the junction with the A246. From Dorking follow the A24, then the A246. Turn left at the junction with the B2122

OPENING
All year open daily 10am–6pm; Closed 25, 26 Dec & 1 Jan

ADMISSION PRICES
Adult £3.95   Child £3.75 or £2.95 Concession £3.75

CONTACT
Bocketts Farm Park
Young Street, Fetcham
Leatherhead, Surrey KT22 9DA
Tel 01372 363764
Web www.bockettsfarm.co.uk

½ day

Easter–Oct

British Wildlife Centre

The British Wildlife Centre is home to one of the finest collections of native mammals in the country, with over 25 species set in 30 acres.

LOCATION
Leave the M25 at junction 6, then follow the A22 south to Newchapel

OPENING
Easter–Oct open Sun, Bank holidays & daily during school holidays 10am–5pm

ADMISSION PRICES
Adult £4 Child (3–14) £3

CONTACT
British Wildlife Centre
Newchapel, Lingfield
Surrey RH7 6LF
Tel 01342 834658
Web www.british-wildlife.co.uk

Brooklands Museum

½ day

All year

A family-friendly motorsport and aviation museum with walk-on exhibits, a hands-on discovery centre and regular family activities. There are motorsport events and fly-ins throughout the year.

★ Trails & Timetraveller packs   ★ Holiday activities & events

LOCATION
From junction 10 off the M25, take the A3 north to London & the exit for Weybridge. Follow the tourist signs to Weybridge

OPENING
All year open Tue–Sun 10am–5pm (4pm in winter); Closed during Christmas period

ADMISSION PRICES
Adult £7 Child £5
Family (2+3) £18 Concession £6

CONTACT
Brooklands Museum
Brooklands Road, Weybridge
Surrey KT13 0QN
Tel 01932 857381
Web www.brooklandsmuseum.com

Box Hill

All day

All year

Box Hill is a large area of **woodland** and downland with outstanding views. There are waymarked trails and an information centre.

LOCATION	ADMISSION PRICES
Off the A24, near Dorking	Free
OPENING	CONTACT
Park: All year open daily dawn–dusk	**Box Hill**
Information centre: Open daily 10am–5pm; Closed 25, 26 Dec	The Old Fort, Box Hill Road Tadworth Surrey KT20 7LB Tel 01306 885502 Fax 01306 875030

Burpham Court Farm Park

½ day

All year

A **76-acre conservation centre** for endangered breeds of farm livestock including cattle, sheep, pigs, goats and llamas. There is also a nature trail and many opportunities for hands-on contact with the animals including collecting eggs with the farmer.

LOCATION	ADMISSION PRICES
Off the A320 from Guildford	Adult £3.95 Child (2–16 years) £2.95 Concession £3.25
OPENING	CONTACT
Jan open 10am–6pm (or dusk if earlier); Feb–Oct open 10am–6pm; Nov & Dec open 10am–6pm (or dusk if earlier); Please phone to check winter times; Closed 25, 26 Dec	**Burpham Court Farm Park** Clay Lane, Jacobswell Guildford, Surrey GU4 7NA Tel 01483 576089

58

Cherry Tree Farm (ILPH)

½ day

All year

Cherry Tree Farm offers guided tours of picturesque stables and paddocks where visitors can see rescued horses, ponies and donkeys that are rehabilitated by the ILPH before being re-homed.

LOCATION	ADMISSION PRICES
On the A22 to East Grinstead. Turn right at Newchapel round-about. The farm is on the right	Free
	CONTACT
OPENING	**Cherry Tree Farm (ILPH)** Westpark Road, Newchapel Lingfield, Surrey RH7 6HP Tel 01342 832420 Email info@ilph.org Web www.ilph.org.uk
All year open Wed 2pm–4pm, Sat, Sun & Bank holidays open 11am–4pm; Closed 25 Dec, 1 Jan	

Chessington World of Adventures

All day

Mar–Nov

An exciting range of themed attractions, rides, games and adventures.

★ Tomb Blaster   ★ Toytown
★ Beanoland   ★ Toadie's Crazy Cars
★ Trail of the Kings

LOCATION	ADMISSION PRICES
On the A243, 2 miles from the A3 & M25	Adult £21 Child £17 Family £63 Concession £14
OPENING	CONTACT
22 Mar–3 Nov open daily 10am–5pm or 6pm (times vary); 27 Jul–1 Sep open daily 10am–7pm Please phone 0870 4447777 for details	**Chessington** World of **Adventures**, Leatherhead Road Chessington, Surrey KT9 2NE Tel 01372 729560 Web www.chessington.com

½ day

All year

Godstone Farm

Set in 40 acres of wooded farmland with three ponds and a stream, Godstone Farm is home to a variety of animals including cows, sheep, pigs, horses, ponies, goats, ducks, chickens and rabbits. Children can hold the smaller animals.

LOCATION
Leave the M25 at junction 6, then follow the road to Godstone village. Signposted from the village

OPENING
All year open daily 10am–6pm; Closed 25 Dec

ADMISSION PRICES
Adult £4.10 Child (2–16 years) £4.10

CONTACT
Godstone Farm
Tiburstow Hill Road, Godstone
Surrey RH9 8LX
Tel 01883 742546
Web www.godstonefarm.co.uk

Horton Park Children's Farm

2 hrs+

All year

A friendly children's farm set up for the under-9s. There are lots of different farm animals including cows, sheep, pigs, goats, ponies, a donkey, poultry, rabbits, guinea pigs, gerbils, mice and birds. There is even a friendly snake!

LOCATION
Leave the M25 at junction 9 & follow the A243 north

OPENING
In summer open daily 10am–6pm; In winter open daily 10am–5pm; Closed 25, 26 Dec

ADMISSION PRICES
Adult £3.90 Child £3.90

CONTACT
Horton Park Children's Farm
Horton Lane, Epsom
Surrey KT19 8PT
Tel 01372 743984
Fax 01372 749069
Email childrensfarm@horton-park.co.uk
Web www.hortonpark.co.uk

59

2 hrs

Jul–Sep

Ladyland Farm

A traditional, family-run farm set in beautiful gardens. Run by teachers and farmers, it gives children a hands-on learning experience. Visitors have the opportunity to hold, feed and bed-down calves, goats, sheep, ducklings, piglets and rabbits.

LOCATION
On the A2 from Redhill or Gatwick, or the A217 from Reigate

OPENING
27 Jul–4 Sep open daily 11am–3pm

ADMISSION PRICES
Adult £3 Child (2–16 years) £3

CONTACT
Ladyland Farm
Meath Green Lane, Horley
Surrey RH6 8JA
Tel 01293 784469
Web www.ladylandfarm.demon.co.uk

Painshill Park

½ day

All year

An eighteenth-century landscaped garden with a Gothic temple, ruined abbey, Turkish tent, spectacular waterwheel, 14-acre serpentine lake, Chinese bridge and much more.

LOCATION
Via M25 junction 10 & the A3. Exit at the junction with the A245

OPENING
Apr–Oct open Tue–Sun & Bank holidays 10am–6pm (last admission 4.30pm); Nov–Mar open Tue–Thu, Sat & Sun & Bank holidays 11am–4pm or dusk if earlier (last admission 3pm); Closed 25, 26 Dec

ADMISSION PRICES
Adult £4.80 Child (5–16) £2.40
Under-5s Free Concession £4.20

CONTACT
Painshill Park
Portsmouth Road
Cobham
Surrey KT11 1JE
Tel 01932 864674

2½ hrs

Mar–Nov

River Wey &
Godalming Navigations

Surrey Industrial History Group
Conservation Award
Guildford Borough Council Access Award

Discover the story of Surrey's oldest waterway and the people who lived and worked on it. Climb aboard a wey barge and enjoy the interactive exhibits or take a boat trip.

★ Family trail & trail for younger visitors
★ Programme of family fun days and holiday trails
★ Hands-on discovery room

LOCATION
On Wharf Road, off Woodbridge Road (A322), ½ mile north of Guildford town centre

OPENING
22 Mar –2 Nov open Thu–Mon 11am–5pm

ADMISSION PRICES
Adult £3 Child £1.50 Family £7.50 (National Trust members free)

CONTACT
River Wey & Godalming Navigations
Navigations Office & Dapdune Wharf
Wharf Road
Guildford GU1 4RR
Tel 01483 561389
Email riverwey@smtp.ntrust.org.uk
Web www.nationaltrust.org.uk/riverwey

60

3 hrs+

All year

Rural Life Centre

The Rural Life Centre occupies 10 acres of fields and woodland and houses around 40,000 artefacts. There are realistic settings within the museum showing aspects of traditional village life, and craftsmen are regularly available to demonstrate their skills. There is a reconstructed village playground for young children.

★ Family trails
★ Special events
★ Old Kiln Light Railway rides on Sundays

LOCATION
3 miles south of Farnham, off the A287, midway between Frensham & Tilford

OPENING
Apr–Oct open Wed–Sun & Bank holidays 11am–6pm; Nov–Mar open Wed only 11am–4pm

ADMISSION PRICES
Adult £5 Child (5–15) £3 Family (2+2) £12
Senior £4

CONTACT
Rural Life Centre
Reeds Road, Tilford
Farnham
Surrey GU10 2DL
Tel 01252 795571
Email rural.life@lineone.net
Web www.rural-life.org.uk

All day

Mar–Nov

Thorpe Park

A park with thrilling roller coasters and water rides including the New Rumba Rapids, a white-water ride that twists and turns, tosses and twirls riders through a river, and Colossus, the world's first 10-looping coaster.

LOCATION	ADMISSION PRICES
Leave the M25 at junction 11 or 13 & follow the signs via the A320 to Thorpe Park	Adult £17–£23 Child (4–11 years) £14.50–£17 Family £52–£65
OPENING	CONTACT
22 Mar–3 Nov open daily, except for some mid-week days during the off-peak season Please phone for details	Thorpe Park, Staines Road Chertsey, Surrey KT16 8PN Tel 0870 4444466 Web www.thorpepark.com

2 hrs

Mar–Nov

Amberley Working Museum

A working museum set in the beautiful South Downs, where visitors can experience the sights, smells and sounds of craftsmen at work, take a ride on a narrow-gauge railway and sample the delights of the early motor bus.

LOCATION	ADMISSION PRICES
On the B2139, between Arundel & Storrington, adjacent to Amberley rail station	Adult £6.75 Child (5–16 years) £3.75 Family £19 Concession £6
OPENING	CONTACT
20 Mar–3 Nov open Wed & Sun 10am–6pm & daily during school holidays (last admission 5pm)	Amberley Working Museum Houghton Bridge, Amberley Arundel, West Sussex BN18 9LT Tel 01798 831370 Web www.amberleymuseum.co.uk

61

1–2 hrs

Feb–Nov

Bentley Wildfowl & Motor Museum

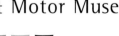

A lovely setting with lakes, ponds, shrubs and trees surrounding Bentley House and its gardens, with a private collection of over 1,000 interesting and beautiful birds.

LOCATION	ADMISSION PRICES
A26, 5 miles north of Lewes. Signposted from the A26 & A22	Adult £5 Child £3.20 Family £14.80 Concession £4
OPENING	CONTACT
Grounds & museum: 2 Feb–10 Mar open Sat & Sun 10.30am–4.30pm; 18 Mar–31 Oct open daily 10.30am–5pm; 1–28 Nov open Sat & Sun 10.30am–4.30pm House: 1 Apr–31 Oct open daily 12pm–5pm	Bentley Wildfowl & Motor Museum Bentley, Halland, Lewes East Sussex BN8 5AF Tel 01825 840573 Email barrysutherland@pavil-ion.co.uk Web www.bentley.org.uk

1½ hrs

All year

Bluebell Railway

The Bluebell Railway operates standard-gauge steam trains through nine miles of scenic Sussex countryside between Sheffield Park, Horsted Keynes and Kingscote.

LOCATION	ADMISSION PRICES
Take the A275 from East Grinstead or Lewes	Adult £8 Child (3–15 years) £4 Family £21.50 Concession £6.40
OPENING	CONTACT
Jan–Apr open Sat & Sun; May–Sep & local school holidays open daily; Oct–Dec open Sat & Sun Please phone for details	Bluebell Railway Sheffield Park Station Sheffield Park, Uckfield East Sussex TN22 3QL Tel 01825 720800 Web www.bluebell-railway.co.uk

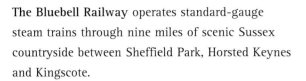

Borde Hill Garden

Visitor Attraction of the Year 1999
South East England Tourist Board

½ day
All year

Brighton Sea Life Centre

2 hrs
All year

A **romantic garden** with areas of outstanding beauty including The Round Dell, home to a number of exotic palms, with its distinctively sub-tropical atmosphere, and The Garden of Allah, a haven of peace and tranquillity.

An **aquarium with** up-to-date marine life habitats. The spectacular underwater tunnel – the longest in England – winds its way through an enormous seabed, alive with sharks, rays and conger eels. Children under 14 must be accompanied.

LOCATION
On the A23, exit junction 10a

OPENING
All year open daily 10am–6pm, or dusk if earlier

ADMISSION PRICES
Adult £5.50 Child (3–16 years) £3
Family £15 Concession £5

CONTACT
Borde Hill Garden
Balcombe Road
Haywards Heath
West Sussex RH16 1XP
Tel 01444 450326
Fax 01444 440427
Email info@bordehill.co.uk
Web www.bordehill.co.uk

LOCATION
Take the M23/A23 from London & the A27 from Portsmouth & Lewes

OPENING
All year open daily from 10am Please phone for details of winter opening times

ADMISSION PRICES
Adult £6.99 Child £4.50
Senior £4.95

CONTACT
Brighton Sea Life Centre
Marine Parade
Brighton BN2 1TB
Tel 01273 604234
Web www.sealife.co.uk

Chichester Harbour Water Tours

1½ hr
All year

A **leisurely 1½-hour sightseeing** trip from West Itchenor around Chichester Harbour – an Area of Outstanding Natural Beauty and noted wildlife reserve. Bird-watching trips are available during winter months.

LOCATION
Follow the A27 & take the A286 towards West Wittering. Signposted from the A27

OPENING
In spring, summer & autumn open daily; In winter open once every 2 weeks; Please phone for details of sailing times

ADMISSION PRICES
Adult £5.50 Child (4–14 years) £2.50

CONTACT
Chichester Harbour Water Tours
9 Cawley Road
Chichester
West Sussex PO19 1UZ
Tel 01243 786418
Web
www.chichesterharbourwatertours.co.uk

2001 Sussex Family Attraction of the Year
The Good Britain Guide

Drusillas Park

5 hrs
All year

WC

LOCATION
Off the A27 between Lewes & Eastbourne

OPENING
In summer open daily 10am–6pm (last admission 5pm); In winter open daily 10am–5pm (last admission 4pm); Closed 24, 25, 26 Dec

ADMISSION PRICES
Adult £9.49 Over-13s £9.95
Please phone for details of other individual/family/group prices

CONTACT
Drusillas Park
Alfriston
East Sussex BN26 3QS
Tel 01323 874100
Fax 01323 874101
Email drusillas@drusilla.demon.co.uk
Web www.drusillas.co.uk

Drusillas Park has over 100 animal species in naturalistic environments including meerkats, otters, monkeys, penguins, bats and lemurs. The excellent children's play areas include ample climbing, jumping, sliding and swinging fun and there are areas set aside for toddlers.

★ Panning for gold
★ Jungle adventure golf
★ Explorer's lagoon
★ Bouncy castle
★ Train rides
★ Monkey Kingdom
★ Sensory trail

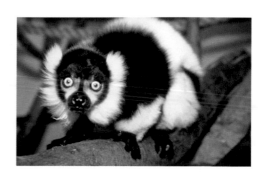

Earnley Butterflies & Gardens

½ day
Mar–Oct

WC

LOCATION
Follow the A286 from Chichester to the Witterings. After 3 miles turn left & follow the Butterflies Garden signs

OPENING
23 Mar–28 Oct open daily 10am–6pm

ADMISSION PRICES
Adult £3.85 Child £2.60 Family £12.50
Concession £3.30

CONTACT
Earnley Butterflies & Gardens
133 Almodington Lane
Earnley
Chichester PO20 7JR
Tel 01243 512637
Email william.priddle@ntlworld.com

At Earnley visitors can see the ornamental butterfly house, covered theme gardens from around the world and an exotic bird garden. There is also a children's play area, a small animal farm, a shipwreck museum and a 15-hole crazy golf course.

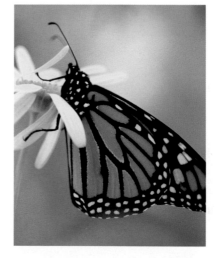

All day

All year

Fishers Farm Park

*Millennium Visitor Attraction
of the Year Winner*

A **mixture of rural farmyard** and dynamic adventure play, Fishers Farm Park has a combine harvester ride and tractor, pony and horse rides.

LOCATION
Near the village of Wisborough Green. Follow the brown tourist signs on the A272 & B2133

OPENING
Dec–Oct open daily 10am–5pm; Nov open Mon–Fri 10am–5pm; Closed 25, 26 Dec

ADMISSION PRICES
High season: Adult £8
Child £7.50 Family £30
Please phone for low & mid-season prices

CONTACT
Fishers Farm Park
Newpound Lane
Wisborough Green
West Sussex RH14 0EG
Tel 01403 700063
Web www.fishersfarmpark.co.uk

1 day

All year

Harbour Park
Family Amusement Park

A **family amusement park** with traditional dodgems, waltzer, video games, soft play areas and adventure golf.

- ★ Indoor swimming centre
- ★ Boating lake
- ★ Pitch & putt
- ★ Miniature railway

LOCATION
Take the A27 from Brighton or Chichester, then follow the A280 or the A284 to Littlehampton

OPENING
Children's play area: Open all year 10am–6pm
Outside attractions: Open 24 Mar–1 Oct 10am–6pm (weather permitting)

ADMISSION PRICES
Free
Charges for individual rides

CONTACT
**Harbour Park Family
Amusement Park**
Sea Front, Littlehampton
West Sussex BN17 5LL
Tel 01903 721200
Email fun@harbourpark.com

64

2 hrs

All year

Hastings Castle
& 1066 Story

Come to the first Norman castle in Britain. At Hastings you can enjoy a spectacular audio-visual show, The 1066 Story, in a medieval siege tent.

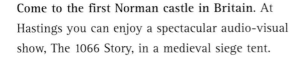

LOCATION
Leave the M25 at junction 5 & follow the A21 to Hastings. Take the A259 from Eastbourne or Rye

OPENING
1 Jan–31 Mar open daily 11am (last admission 3.30pm); 1 Apr–30 Sep open daily 10am (last admission 5pm); 1 Oct–23 Dec open daily 10am (last admission 3.30pm); Closed 24, 25 Dec

ADMISSION PRICES
Adult £3.20 Child £2.10
Senior £2.60

CONTACT
Hastings Castle & 1066 Story
Castle Hill Road, West Hill
Hastings
East Sussex TN34
Tel 01424 781112
Fax 01424 781133
Email bookings@discover hastings.co.uk

2 hrs

All year

'How We Lived Then' Museum
of Shops & Social History

Over 100,000 exhibits of old shops, room-settings and displays depicting 100 years of shopping and social history. Stroll through the Victorian-styled streets, wonder at the chemist's 'cure-all' preparations or visit the ironmonger.

LOCATION
Take the A22 from London or the A27 from Brighton

OPENING
All year open daily 10am–5.30pm; Winter closing time subject to change; Closed 24–26 Dec; Please phone before visiting

ADMISSION PRICES
Adult £3 Child £2 Concession £2

CONTACT
**'How We Lived Then' Museum
of Shops & Social History**
20 Cornfield Terrace, Eastbourne
East Sussex BN21 4NS
Tel 01323 737143
Web www.seetb.org.uk/hwlt

Mohair Centre

2 hrs

All year

A **children's farm** with Angora goats and other farm animals. Come along and watch the lambing and kidding in the spring.

★ Spinning & weaving demonstrations

★ Play area

LOCATION
Located just off the A22. Take the A22 from Eastbourne or East Grinstead; the B2124 from Lewes

OPENING
Please phone for details

ADMISSION PRICES
Please phone for details

CONTACT
Mohair Centre
Brickfield Farm, Laughton Road
Chiddingly, Lewes
East Sussex BN8 6JG
Tel 01825 872457

LOCATION
M23/A23 from London to Brighton then follow the A27 towards Eastbourne. At Lewes follow the A26 to Newhaven. It is signposted from there

OPENING
1–22 Mar open Sat & Sun 10.30am–6pm;
23 Mar–3 Nov open daily 10.30am–6pm

ADMISSION PRICES
Adult £4.75 Child (4–15 years) £3.25
Family £14 Concession £4.25

CONTACT
Newhaven Fort
Fort Road, Newhaven
East Sussex BN9 9DL
Tel 01273 517622
Fax 01273 512059
Email enquiries@newhavenfort.org.uk
Web www.newhavenfort.org.uk

Mount Farm

½ day

Mar–Oct

A **family-run, working organic mixed farm** offering a rare opportunity to experience an authentic farm environment. There are 17 acres of ancient woodland and a nature trail.

LOCATION
Follow the A267 south from Tunbridge Wells to Frant, then turn left onto the B2099. After passing under the railway bridge take the 1st right turn. Farm is on the right

OPENING
4 Mar–31 Oct open Sat & Sun 10am–4.45pm & daily during Sussex school holidays

ADMISSION PRICES
Adult £2 Child £1.50
Season ticket: Adult £8 Child £6

CONTACT
Mount Farm
Faircrouch Lane
Wadhurst
East Sussex TN5 6PT
Tel 01892 783152

65

Newhaven Fort

2 hrs

Mar–Nov

The massive ramparts, tunnels and gun emplacements fire the imagination with exciting glimpses into England's wartime past. Sights, sounds and smells of the period are found in displays and exciting 'real-life' sets and audio-visual presentations. Discover what the soldiers' living conditions were like, walk through a 'blitzed' home and experience an air raid from the safety of an underground shelter. Step into the lives of people on the Home Front.

4–6 hrs
All year

Paradise Park Botanical Gardens

A **blend of exotic plant houses**, dinosaur fossils and Sussex history, with lots of activities and sights to interest children, including a miniature railway and fantasy golf.

★ Voyage of Discovery Exhibition
★ The Dark Ages
★ Halloween Spooktacular
★ Santa's Magical Wonderland
★ Sussex History Trail
★ Children's rides
★ Boating pool
★ Gold panning

LOCATION
Reached via the A27 Brighton/Lewes bypass & the A26

OPENING
All year open daily 9am–6pm; Closed 25, 26 Dec

ADMISSION PRICES
Adult £4.99 Child £3.99 Family £16.99

CONTACT
Paradise Park Botanical Gardens
Avis Road
Newhaven
East Sussex BN9 0DH
Tel 01273 616006 (24-hr info line)
Tel 01273 512123
Email paradisepark.co.uk
Web www.paradisepark.co.uk

66

2–3 hrs

Apr–Oct

Shipwreck Heritage Centre

A **unique collection of historic treasures** recovered from shipwrecks, including the warship Anne (1690) and the Dutch treasure ship Amsterdam (1749).

LOCATION
Take the A259 from Rye or Eastbourne or the A21 from London

OPENING
Apr–Oct open daily 10am–5pm

ADMISSION PRICES
Free
Donations welcomed

CONTACT
Shipwreck Heritage Centre
Rock-a-Nore Road
Hastings
East Sussex TN34 3DW
Tel 01424 437452

A Smuggler's Adventure

2 hrs

All year

A **hands-on opportunity** to learn more about the secrets of smugglers in a series of spooky caverns and passages. Find out what happened when the smugglers got caught and how they were punished!

LOCATION
Junction 5 off the M25 & follow the A21 to Hastings. Take the A259 from Eastbourne or Rye

OPENING
Jan-Easter open daily 11am–4.30pm; Easter–Sep open daily 10am–5.50pm; Oct–Dec open daily 11am–4.30pm; Closed 24–26 Dec

ADMISSION PRICES
Adult £5.50 Child £3.50 Family £15.25 Concession £4.50

CONTACT
A Smuggler's Adventure
West Hill, Hastings
East Sussex TN34 3HY
Tel 01424 422964
Web www.smugglersadventure.co.uk

Stoneywish Country Park

1 day

All year

LOCATION
Take the A23 from Brighton or London, then the B2116. Located ¼ mile east of Ditchling

OPENING
2 Jan–28 Feb open Sat & Sun 10am–5pm (last admission 3pm); 1 Mar–31 Oct open daily 10am–7pm (last admission 5pm); 1 Nov–31 Dec open Sat & Sun 10am–5pm (last admission 3pm); Closed 25, 26 Dec & 1 Jan

ADMISSION PRICES
Adult £3 Child (3–14 years) £2
Concession £2

CONTACT
Stoneywish Country Park
Spatham Lane
Ditchling, Hassocks
East Sussex
Tel 01273 843498

Stoneywish Country Park is set in 52 acres of meadows and ponds. A wildlife walk enables visitors to pass through fields to a play and picnic area. You can then move on to a farm centre and flint buildings which house a tearoom, a museum and gallery.

★ Pets corner

★ Museum

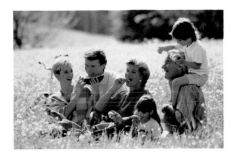

Tilgate Park & Nature Centre

2 hrs

All year

LOCATION
Take the A23 from London or Brighton

OPENING
In summer open daily 10am–6pm; In winter open daily 10am–4pm; Closed 25, 26 Dec & 1 Jan

ADMISSION PRICES
Free
Admission by donation to nature centre & walled garden

CONTACT
Tilgate Park & Nature Centre
Tilgate Park
Crawley
West Sussex RH10 5PQ
Tel 01293 521168
Email tilgate@crawley.gov.uk
Web www.crawley.gov.uk

Come and see a collection of wild and domestic animals, with the emphasis on endangered species and breeds. Visitors can see White Park cattle, Exmoor ponies, pigs, sheep, goats, deer, red squirrels, pheasants, cranes and ibises. There are also themed gardens and Shire horses.

★ Maze

★ Lawns, lakes & woodland

★ Stables & ornamental gardens

★ Golf centre

½ day
May–Sep

Treasure Island

This is a children's adventure playground with life-size models of jungle animals and Treasure Island characters.

★ Paddling pools
★ Indoor play area
★ Sand-pits
★ Climbing apparatus

LOCATION
Take the A27 from Brighton &
the A22 from London. Follow
the signs for seafront east

OPENING
5 May–30 Sep open 10am–6pm

ADMISSION PRICES
Adult £1 Child £3.50

CONTACT
Treasure Island
Royal Parade, Eastbourne
East Sussex BN22 7AA
Tel 01323 411077
Fax 01323 641984
Email treasure.island@east-
bourne.gov.uk

½ day
All year

Tulleys Farm

A farm with pick-your-own soft fruit and vegetables and a seven-acre maize maze to entertain all the family.

★ Special seasonal events
★ Pets corner
★ Play area
★ Farm shop

LOCATION
Take the B2110 from East
Grinstead to Turners Hill.
Signposted from there

OPENING
Tearoom & farm shop open
daily; Maize Maze open Jul–early
Sep daily 10am–6pm (last
admission 5pm)

ADMISSION PRICES
Admission to maze: Adult £4.50
Child (4–14 years) £3.50
Family £12

CONTACT
Tulleys Farm, Turners Hill
Crawley, West Sussex RH10 4PE
Tel 01342 718472
Web www.tulleysfarm.com

---

2 hrs
All year

Underwater World, Hastings

Tidal rock pools, sandy seabeds and seaside touch pools let visitors get close to the marine inhabitants at Underwater World. Visitors can walk through a glass tunnel beneath a 'reef pool' that is home to a multitude of sharks, rays, crabs and starfish.

LOCATION
Follow the signs to Old Town, Hastings.
Underwater World is located next to the
Shipwreck Heritage Centre

OPENING
1 Jan–28 Mar open daily 11am–4.30pm;
Easter–30 Sep open daily 10am–5pm;
1 Oct–31 Dec open daily 11am–4.30pm;
Closed 24–26 Dec

ADMISSION PRICES
Adult £5.50   Child (5–16 years) £3.50
Family £15.25   Concession £4.50

CONTACT
Underwater World, Hastings
Rock-a-Nore Road
Hastings
East Sussex TN34 3DW
Tel 01424 718776
Email sharks@discoverhastings.co.uk
Web www.discoverhastings.co.uk

Washbrooks Farm Centre

2 hrs

All year

LOCATION
On the B2117 from Hurstpierpoint

OPENING
All year open daily 9.30am–5pm; Closed 25–31 Dec

ADMISSION PRICES
Adult £2.75 Child (3–14 years) £2.50 Family £9.50

CONTACT
Washbrooks Farm Centre
Washbrooks Farm
Brighton Road
Hurstpierpoint
Hassocks
West Sussex BN6 9EH
Tel 01273 832201
Email familyfarm@washbrooks.com
Web www.washbrooks.com

A working farm with rare breed pigs, cows, goats, ponies, donkeys, chicken, ducks and sheep – usually with their young. Visitors can see and touch all the animals. There are tractor and trailer and quad bike rides around the farm and an adventure playground too.

★ Sand-pit

★ Swings

★ ½-mile Brookside Walk

69

All day

All year

Weald & Downland Open Air Museum

A **museum consisting of over 45 historic buildings** set in a beautiful South Downs park, and depicting the rural homes and work places of the past.

LOCATION
6 miles north of Chichester on the A286

OPENING
3 Nov–28 Feb open weekends only; 26 Dec–1 Jan open daily; 1 Mar–31 Oct open daily; Open daily during Sussex half-terms

ADMISSION PRICES
Adult £7 Child £4 Family £19 Senior £6.50

CONTACT
Weald & Downland Open Air Museum, Singleton, Chichester Sussex PO18 0EU
Tel 01243 811363
Web www.wealdown.co.uk

Wish Tower Puppet Museum

1 hr

Easter–Oct

Housed in one of a series of Martello towers built against possible Napoleonic invasion, this museum displays puppets from all over the world, ranging from early shadow puppets to modern television puppets. There are good views from the tower.

LOCATION
On the B2103, off the A259

OPENING
Easter–mid Jul open Sat & Sun 11am–5pm; Mid Jul–Aug open daily 11am–5pm; Sep–Oct open Sat & Sun 11am–5pm

ADMISSION PRICES
Adult £1.80 Child (2–16 years) £1.25 Family £5

CONTACT
Wish Tower Puppet Museum
King Edward's Parade
Eastbourne BN21 4BY
Tel 01323 417776
Web www.puppets.co.uk

South-west

This region includes the West Country, Gloucestershire and South Wales. The West Country, in particular, has long been a popular tourist destination and is known for sandy beaches and natural beauty that entice families year after year. Visitors to the region can explore historic towns and cities, such as Glastonbury and Bristol, and the wild beauty of South Wales with its parks and ancient castles.

In Cornwall, you will find the internationally famous Eden Project and many small farm attractions, where children can come into close contact with a variety of animals. Devon offers the wonderful experience of a visit to tranquil Lundy Island, with its wealth of wildlife and car-free paths, and Blackpool Sands, an award-winning beach. You can go llama-trekking in Dorset and visit the famous Cheddar Gorge caves in Somerset, where you can play the Crystal Quest Challenge Game. Gloucestershire has fun and interesting farms to visit and the National Birds of Prey Centre with its collection of magnificent eagles, condors and kestrels. In Wiltshire, you can visit Steam – the Museum of the Great Western Railway, and in South Wales, why not enjoy walking in the beautiful Brecon Beacons National Park and exploring fairy-tale Cardiff Castle.

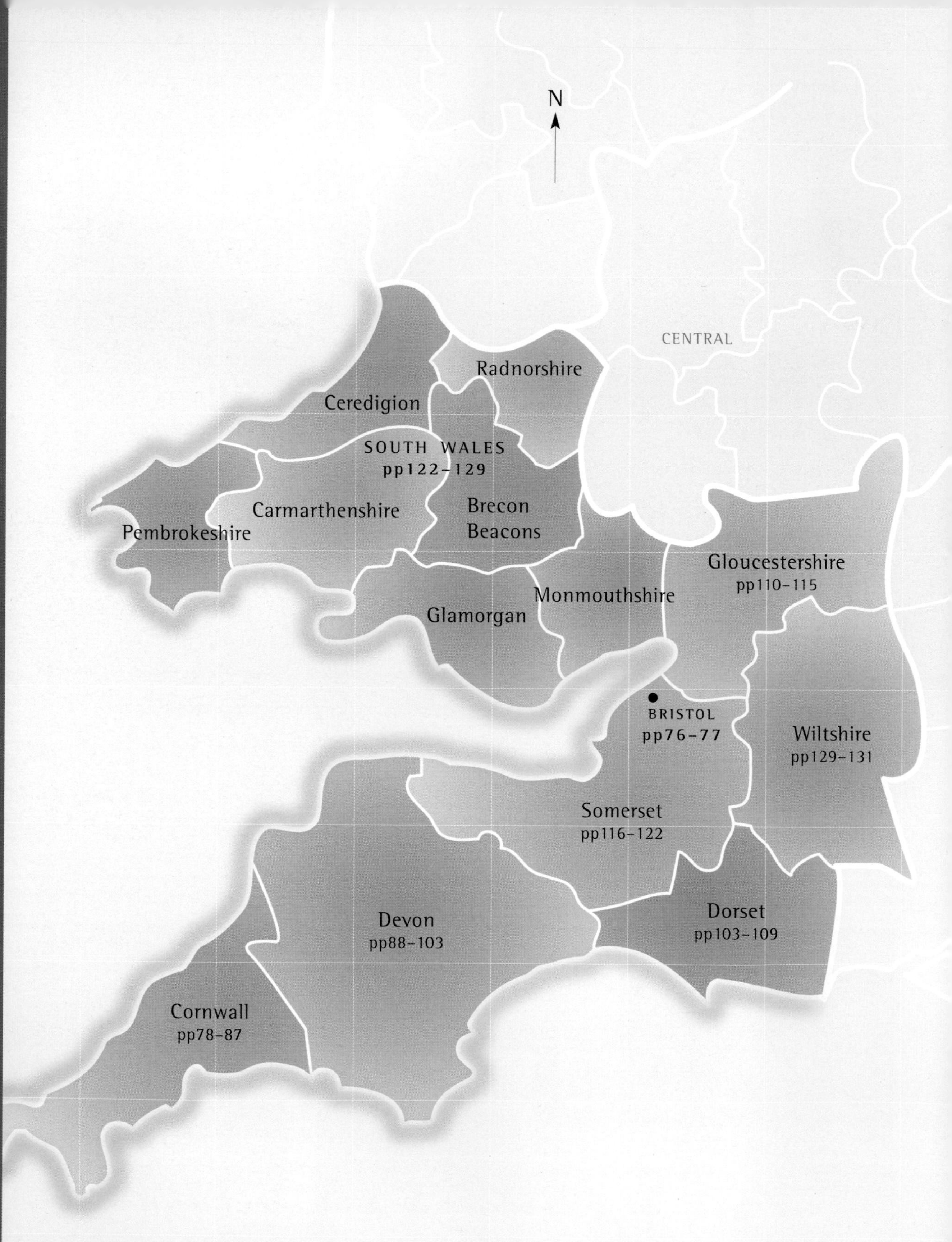

N

CENTRAL

Radnorshire

Ceredigion

SOUTH WALES
pp122–129

Carmarthenshire

Brecon
Beacons

Pembrokeshire

Gloucestershire
pp110–115

Monmouthshire

Glamorgan

● BRISTOL
pp76–77

Wiltshire
pp129–131

Somerset
pp116–122

Devon
pp88–103

Dorset
pp103–109

Cornwall
pp78–87

Below is a list of places to visit in the South-west, organised by county and type.

Bristol

MUSEUMS & EXHIBITIONS
At Bristol 76
Clifton Suspension Bridge Visitor Centre 76

SPORT & LEISURE
Bristol Ice Rink 76

ANIMAL ATTRACTIONS
Horseworld 77

PARKS, GARDENS & NATURE TRAILS
Oldown Country Park 77

Cornwall

HISTORIC BUILDINGS
Lanhydrock 83

MUSEUMS & EXHIBITIONS
The Cheese Farm 79
Goonhilly Satellite Earth Station 81
National Maritime Museum Cornwall 84
The Pilchard Works 85
Royal Cornwall Museum 86

SPORT & LEISURE
Colliford Lake Park 79
Dragon Leisure Centre 80
Killarney Springs Leisure Park 82
Polkyth Leisure Centre 85

ANIMAL ATTRACTIONS
Dairyland Farm World 79
The Monkey Sanctuary 83
National Seal Sanctuary 84
Newquay Zoo 84
Porfell Animal Land 86
Springfields Pony Centre & Fun Park 87
Trethorne Leisure Farm 87

BOAT & TRAIN TRIPS
Bodmin & Wenford Railway 78
Isles of Scilly Steamship Company 81
Lappa Valley Steam Railway 83

PARKS, GARDENS & NATURE TRAILS
Camel Train 78
Charlestown Shipwreck & Heritage Centre 78
Eden Project 80
Land's End Visitor Centre 82
Mount Edgcumbe House & Park 83
Tehidy Country Park 87

THEME PARKS & ADVENTURE PLAYGROUNDS
Brocklands Adventure Park 78
Flambards Theme Park 80
Holywell Bay Fun Park 81
Kids Kingdom Ltd 82
Spirit of the West Theme Park 86

MISCELLANEOUS
Poldark Mine 85

Devon

HISTORIC BUILDINGS
Arlington Court 88
Crownhill Fort 92
Knightshayes Court 96
Watermouth Castle 103

MUSEUMS & EXHIBITIONS
Barnstaple Heritage Centre 89
Bygones 91
Eggesford Country Centre 93
The Great Exmouth '00' Model Railway 95
The Green House Visitor Centre 95
Norman Lockyer Observatory & James Lockyer
   Planetarium 97
Overbecks Museum & Garden 98
Tiverton Museum of Mid Devon Life 102
Torrington 1646 102
Totnes Costume Museum 102
Totnes Museum 102
Tuckers Maltings 103

SPORT & LEISURE
Ashcombe Adventure Centre 88
Riverdart Adventures 99
The Riviera International Centre 100
Woodlands Leisure Park 103

ANIMAL ATTRACTIONS
The Big Sheep 90
Buckfast Butterfly Farm & Dartmoor
   Otter Sanctuary 91
Dartmoor Wildlife Park 92
The Donkey Sanctuary 93
Hedgehog Hospital Farm 95
North Devon Farm Park 97
Paignton Zoo 98
Pennywell Farm Centre 99
Sorley Tunnel Adventure Farm 101

Gloucestershire

74

Dorset

South Wales

Wiltshire

Somerset

At Bristol

½ day
All year

At **Explore, an interactive science centre**, you can play virtual volleyball, test your memory and run in a giant hamster wheel. Wildwalk takes you on a journey through the story of life on earth using botanical houses, live animals and multimedia displays. The IMAX Theatre is the biggest cinema screen in the region.

LOCATION
1 mile from the M32, M4, M5

OPENING
All year open daily 10am–6pm;
Closed 25 Dec

ADMISSION PRICES
For 1 attraction: Adult £6.50 Child (3–15)
£4.50 Family £19 Concession £5.50
Please phone for prices of multiple attractions

CONTACT
At Bristol
Anchor Rod
Harbourside
Bristol BS1 5DB
Tel 08453 451235
Email information@at-bristol.org.uk
Web www.at-bristol.org.uk

Bristol Ice Rink

2 hrs
All year

Bristol Ice Rink offers a variety of family and disco sessions every day. Learn-to-ice-skate courses are available throughout the year.

★ Birthday parties

LOCATION
In Bristol city centre

OPENING
All year open daily from 10.30am

ADMISSION PRICES
From £4.80 per person

CONTACT
Bristol Ice Rink
Frogmore Street
Bristol BS1 5NA
Tel 0117 9292148
Email jnlbristol@nikegroup.co.uk
Web www.jnll.co.uk

Clifton Suspension Bridge Visitor Centre

45 mins
All year

Clifton Suspension Bridge Visitor Centre illustrates the story of Brunel's famous landmark. The centre has a series of displays on the construction of the bridge, an intricate scale model and an interactive bridge.

LOCATION
200 yards from the bridge on the Clifton side, in Bridge House (relocating 2003)

OPENING
Apr-Oct open daily 10am–5pm;
Nov–Mar open Mon–Fri
11am–4pm & Sat, Sun
11am–5pm

ADMISSION PRICES
Adult £1.90 Child £1.30 Family
(2+2) £5 Concession £1.70

CONTACT
Clifton Suspension Bridge Visitor Centre
Tel 0117 9744664
Email visitinfo@clifton-suspension-bridge.org.uk

Horseworld

½ day

All year

LOCATION
Between Bristol & Bath, just off the A37 Wells road at Whitchurch

OPENING
Jan–Sep open daily; Oct–Jan open Tue–Sun; Easter–Sep open 10am–5pm; Oct–Easter open 10am–4pm

ADMISSION PRICES
Adult £4.50 Child (3–15) £3 Family (2+2) £14 Concession £3

CONTACT
Horseworld
Staunton Manor Farm
Staunton Lane
Whitchurch
Bristol BS14 0QJ
Tel 01275 540173
Email info@horseworld.org.uk
Web www.horseworld.org.uk

Horseworld is the visitor centre of an equine welfare charity where guests can meet and touch many of the rescued horses, donkeys and ponies. Children will love the pony rides and the miniature ponies.

★ Indoor & outdoor play areas
★ Interactive museums
★ Nature trail

Oldown Country Park

3 hrs+

Feb–Oct

LOCATION
Near the M4/M5 interchange north of Bristol & junction 16 off the M5. Go north on the A38 towards Thornbury & follow the brown Oldown signs

OPENING
Feb half-term–autumn half-term; School holidays open daily 10am–5pm; Jun–Jul open Tue–Sun 10am–5pm

ADMISSION PRICES
Adult £4.50 Child £4.50 Under-3s Free

CONTACT
Oldown Country Park
Foxholes Lane
Tockington
Bristol BS32 4PG
Tel 01454 413605
Email info@oldown.co.uk
Web www.oldown.co.uk

This park has adventure equipment for all ages, a forest challenge, tractor and trailer rides. Visitors can meet the animals, take country walk and a trip on a miniature steam train.

★ Ball pool
★ Go-karts
★ Ferret-racing
★ Pig-racing
★ Husky-racing
★ Santa Special at Christmas

½ day

Apr–Oct

Bodmin & Wenford Railway

A **trip on this standard-gauge railway** operated mainly by steam engines runs for 6½ miles from Bodmin town to Bodmin Parkway and passes through the beautiful River Fowey valley.

★ Guided tours

LOCATION	CONTACT
On the B3268 in central Bodmin	**Bodmin & Wenford Railway** Bodmin General Station Lostwithiel Road Bodmin Cornwall PL31 1AQ Tel 01208 73666 Web www.bodminand wenfordrailway.co.uk
OPENING Open Apr–Oct & at Christmas & New Year; Please phone for details	
ADMISSION PRICES All line ticket: Adult £8 Child £4.50 Under-3s Free Family (2+4) £23	

78

All day

All year

Brocklands Adventure Park

Quality Assured Visitor Attraction

English Tourism Council

Children as young as 18 months will enjoy the playroom with sand-pit, swings and slides at this activity-packed park. For older kids there is a mini assault course and aqua blaster, pony rides, bumper boats, two-seater super karts and much more.

LOCATION	CONTACT
On the A39 between Bude & Bideford	**Brocklands Adventure Park** West Street Kilkhampton Bude Cornwall EX23 9QW Tel 01288 321920 Fax 01288 321387
OPENING Please phone for details	
ADMISSION PRICES Adult £6.30 Child (2–14) £4.80 Concession £3	

All day

All year

Camel Train

Take a whole day to explore this waymarked path, which runs along 17 miles of the Camel Estuary and Camel Valley from Padstow to Poley's Bridge. The route is suitable for pedestrians and cyclists.

LOCATION	CONTACT
Accessible from Wadebridge town, or the A389 from Bodmin or the main car park in Padstow	**Camel Trail** Planning Directorate Truro Cornwall TR1 3AY Tel 01208 322000
OPENING All year	
ADMISSION PRICES Free	

Charlestown Shipwreck & Heritage Centre

2 hrs

Mar–Oct

Learn about diving, rescues and shipwrecks in this major display of maritime history, the largest shipwreck artefact collection in the British Isles. There is also an exhibition about the Titanic.

LOCATION	CONTACT
Reached via the A390 & A3061	**Charlestown Shipwreck & Heritage Centre** Quay Road, Charlestown St Austell Cornwall PL25 3NJ Tel 01726 69897 Web www.shipwreckcharlestown.com
OPENING 1 Mar–31 Oct open daily 10am–5pm	
ADMISSION PRICES Adult £4.95 Child £1.95	

The Cheese Farm

2 hrs

Mar–Oct

A working farmyard with animals, milking, calf-rearing and cheese-making where children can watch and learn about these activities.

★ Park with nature walk   ★ Museum of memorabilia

LOCATION
From Launceston follow the A30 west, then the B3257; from Callington follow the B3257; from Liskeard follow the B3254

OPENING
25 Mar–31 Oct open Mon–Fri 9.30am–4pm & Sat 9.30am–2pm

ADMISSION PRICES
Adult £3 Child (5–16) £1.50
Concession £2

CONTACT
The Cheese Farm
Lynher Dairies, Netherton Farm
Upton Cross
Liskeard, Cornwall PL14 5BD
Tel 01579 362244

Colliford Lake Park

All day

Easter–Sep

Spend a whole day at this 40-acre park where you can enjoy a range of activities, including driving pedal-karts, undertaking challenging agility trails and target range practice. There is also a nature trail and small-animal centre.

LOCATION
On the A30

OPENING
Please phone for details

ADMISSION PRICES
Please phone for details

CONTACT
Colliford Lake Park
Bodmin Moor
Liskeard
Cornwall PL14 6PZ
Tel 01208 821469

Dairyland Farm World

½ day

Mar–Oct

LOCATION
On the A3058, 4 miles from Newquay

OPENING
25 Mar–27 Oct open 10am–5pm

ADMISSION PRICES
Adult £5.25 Child (3–15) £4.25
Family £15.95 Concession £4.75

CONTACT
Dairyland Farm World
Tresillian Barton
Summercourt
Newquay
Cornwall TR8 5AA
Tel 01872 510246
Email farmworld@yahoo.com
Web www.dairylandfarmworld.com

One of the UK's leading working farm attractions, Dairyland has a wealth of animals that children love to pet – among the menagerie are kittens, kids, lambs, rabbits, donkeys, chipmunks and chinchillas. You can even have a go at milking Clarabelle, the cyber cow.

★ Pony rides
★ Daily events

½ day

All year

Dragon Leisure Centre

You and your family can enjoy a wide range of leisure activities here, including coaching courses and tournaments. Beginners are welcome.

LOCATION
Take the A30 to Bodmin. The centre is 1½ miles from Bodmin town centre

OPENING
All year open daily except for Christmas break
Please phone for details

ADMISSION PRICES
Please phone for details

CONTACT
Dragon Leisure Centre
Lostwithiel Road
Bodmin
Cornwall PL31 1DE
Tel 01208 75715
Fax 01208 78004

Eden Project

½ day

All year

Visit the largest greenhouses in the world with plants from many diverse habitats such as the tropical rainforest, Mediterranean fruit groves and fields of California.

★ Free events throughout the year

LOCATION
Signposted from the A390, A30 & A391. Near to St Austell

OPENING
All year open daily except for 25 & 25 Dec
Please phone for details

ADMISSION PRICES
Adult £8.90 Child £4 Family £23
Senior £7.50

CONTACT
Eden Project
Bodelva, St Austell
Cornwall PL24 2SG
Tel 01726 811911
Web www.edenproject.com

80

All day

Easter–Nov

Flambards Theme Park

Set in glorious gardens, this theme park combines internationally acclaimed exhibitions such as Britain in the Blitz with thrilling playground rides and family shows.

★ Cornwall's Science Centre
★ Undercover children's play areas
★ Go-karts
★ Paddle boats
★ Roller coaster
★ Buggy hire for small children
★ Creepy Crawly Show

LOCATION
On the A3083 Lizard road. Well signposted from the A394 Truro to Helston road & on the A394 Penzance to Helston road

OPENING
Easter–Nov open most days from 10.30am–5pm; In peak season open 10am–5.30pm

ADMISSION PRICES
Super Family Saver tickets available for 4, 5 or 6 persons
Please phone for details

CONTACT
Flambards Theme Park
Tel 01326 564093 (24-hr info)
Email info@flambards.co.uk
Web www.flambards.co.uk

Goonhilly Satellite Earth Station

½ day

Mar–Sep

CORNWALL

Visit Goonhilly, the largest satellite station on Earth, to learn about space and modern communications through the multimedia visitors centre, interactive exhibits and film shows.

★ High-speed touch-screen internet facilities
★ Virtual reality booth
★ Play areas
★ Guided tour

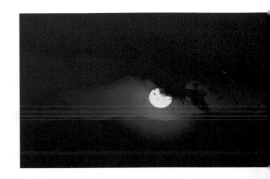

LOCATION
On the Lizard Peninsula, 7 miles from Helston on the B3293 St Keverne Road

OPENING
Please phone for details

ADMISSION PRICES
Please phone for details

CONTACT
Goonhilly Earth Station
The Visitors Centre
Goonhilly Downs
Helston
Cornwall TR12 6LQ
Tel 0800 679593
Email goonhilly.visitorscentre@bt.com
Web www.goonhilly.bt.com

81

All day

Holywell Bay Fun Park

Mar–Oct

Great rides, go-karts, crazy golf and a maze are just a few the attractions at this fun park.

★ Bumper boats
★ Children's fun rides
★ Pitch 'n' putt

★ Beach nearby
★ Junior karts
★ Climbing wall

LOCATION
Follow the A3075 Newquay–Perranporth road, turn right to Cubert. Located on the right-hand side, 1 mile past Cubert

OPENING
28 Mar–31 Oct from 10.30am

ADMISSION PRICES
Free entry; Pay as you play tokens

CONTACT
Holywell Bay Fun Park
Holywell Bay, Newquay
Cornwall TR8 5PW
Tel 01637 830531
Email info@trevornick.co.uk
Web www.holywellbay.co.uk

Isles of Scilly Steamship Company

All day

Mar–Nov

Cruise to the Isles of Scilly on a leisure boat. During the journey you can see an interesting exhibition about the islands and enjoy a commentary by the ship's captain.

LOCATION
On the A30, A394 to Penzance

OPENING
30 Mar–16 Nov open daily
Please phone for details

ADMISSION PRICES
Day trip: Adult £35
Child (2–15) £17.50 Family £72

CONTACT
Isles of Scilly Steamship Company Limited
Steamship House
Quay Street
Penzance, Cornwall TR18 4BZ
Tel 01736 334220
Email sales@isles of scilly-travel.co.uk
Web www.ios-travel.co.uk

2 hrs+

All year

Kids Kingdom Ltd

Tots and toddlers will love this imaginative soft play area with its wealth of fun, exciting, challenging and sometimes scary activities.

★ Demon Drop

★ Monster Hut Maze

★ Gladiator Rings

★ Rollerway Challenge

★ Go-karts

★ Slides

LOCATION
Signposted off the A390 & close to the town centre

OPENING
Easter–30 Sep open daily 10am–6pm;
Closed Mon in winter, except during school holidays

ADMISSION PRICES
Child £3.95

CONTACT
Kids Kingdom Ltd
St Austell
Cornwall PL25 4TZ
Tel 01726 77377
Fax 01726 77177

82

All day

Apr–Oct

Killarney Springs Leisure Park

An adventure park that caters for children of all ages. It has an adventure playground, water coasters, super-karts, an under-6s play area with bouncy castle, a boating lake, toboggan rides and a nature trail.

LOCATION
On the A39, 8 miles north of Bude. No suitable public transport

OPENING
Open daily 7 Apr–31 Oct, winter weekends & holidays
10.30am–6pm

ADMISSION PRICES
Adult £4.95 Child (3–14) £4.95

CONTACT
Killarney Springs
Morwenstow
Bude
Cornwall EX23 9PX
Tel 01288 331475

Land's End Visitor Centre

This heritage centre is set in the breathtaking scenery of Land's Ends, one of the UK's most famous sites. The centre has exhibitions and shows on the theme of Land's End including the Air Sea Rescue theatre experience. There is also a playground.

2 hrs+

All year

LOCATION
At the end of the A30, 12 miles from Penzance

OPENING
In summer open 10am–4pm; In winter open 10am–3pm; Closed 25 & 26 Dec

ADMISSION PRICES
Adult £9.50 Child (4–14) £5
Family £25 Concession £5

CONTACT
The Custom House
Land's End, Sennen, Penzance
Cornwall TR19 7AA
Tel 01736 871501
Web www.landsend-landmark.co.uk

Lanhydrock

2 hrs+

All year

One of the finest houses in Cornwall, built in the late nineteenth century. It is set in wooded parkland and surrounded by a garden with rare shrubs and trees.

★ Woodland walks

★ Children's guide & quizzes

★ Organised activities in school holidays

LOCATION
Signed from the A30, A38
Bodmin–Liskeard road & the
B3269 Bodmin–Lostwithiel road

OPENING
Garden & park: All year open
daily, except 24, 25, 26 Dec
& 1 Jan
House: 23 Mar–3 Nov open

Tue–Sun & Bank holiday Mon

ADMISSION PRICES
Adult £7 Child £3.50
Family £17.50

CONTACT
Lanhydrock, Bodmin
Cornwall PL30 5Ad
Tel 01208 733320

Lappa Valley
Steam Railway

All day

Apr–Oct

Enjoy a two-mile steam train journey, paddle boats, crazy golf, a maze and woodland walks in scenic countryside. Included in the admission price is the entrance to the viewing platform of the largest mine engine house in Cornwall.

LOCATION
Follow the A3075 to Newquay.
Just past Newquay turn east to
St Newlyn East & follow the
tourist signs to the railway

OPENING
Mid Apr–Oct
Please phone for details

ADMISSION PRICES
Please phone for details

CONTACT
Lappa Valley Steam Railway
St Newlyn East, Newquay
Cornwall TR8 5HZ
Tel 01872 510317
Web www.lappa-railway.co.uk

83

The Monkey Sanctuary

½ day

All year

Children can see Amazon woolly monkeys in their own spacious territory. Talks are given throughout the day about the species and its threatened rainforest habitat. The centre encourages environmental awareness.

LOCATION
Signposted on the B3253
Looe–Plymouth road at No
Man's Land. Distance from Looe
4 miles, from Plymouth 18 miles

OPENING
Sun before Easter–end Sep open
Sun–Thu 11am–4.30pm

ADMISSION PRICES
Adult £4 Child £1.50
Concession £3

CONTACT
The Monkey Sanctuary
Looe, Cornwall PL13 1NZ
Tel 01503 262532
Email info@monkeysanctuary.org
Web www.monkeysanctuary.org

Mount Edgcumbe
House & Park

½ day

All year

For 400 years this was the home of the Earls of Edgcumbe. The landscaped park has fallow deer, woodland and coastal walks.

★ Programme of special exhibitions & events

LOCATION
Take the Torpoint ferry from
Plymouth

OPENING
House: 4 Apr–30 Sep open
Wed–Sun 11am–4.30pm
Park: All year open daily

ADMISSION PRICES
Adult £4.50 Child (5–15) £2.25
Family £10 Concession £3.50

CONTACT
Mount Edgcumbe House
& Park
Cremyll, Torpoint
Cornwall PL10 1HZ
Tel 01752 822236

2–4 hrs
All year

National Maritime Museum Cornwall

National Seal Sanctuary

2 hrs
All year

Enjoy the unique interactive displays of over 140 boats and their place in people's lives over the past 150 years, explore a Cornish quayside, study small craft from under the water in the Tidal Zone and visit the special conservation area.

Get to know the seals at this leading marine mammal rescue centre. Watch them at feeding time and listen to the talks. The centre also has other rescued animals such as donkeys, ponies and goats.

★ Barbecues in summer   ★ See the otters in Otter Creek

LOCATION
At the south-eastern end of Falmouth's harbour. Follow the signs to Falmouth, then the brown tourist signs to the museum

OPENING
In summer open 10am–6pm; In winter open 10am–5pm; Closed 25 Dec & in Jan 2004

ADMISSION PRICES
Adult £5.90 Child £3.90
Family £15.50 Concession £3.90

CONTACT
National Maritime Museum Cornwall, Discovery Quay Falmouth TR11 3QY
Tel 01326 313388
Web www.nmmc.co.uk

LOCATION
Follow the A3083 from Helston towards The Lizard. Turn left onto the B3291 & into Gweek

OPENING
All year open daily from 9am; Closed 25 Dec

ADMISSION PRICES
Adult £6.95 Child (4–14) £4.95
Senior £4.95

CONTACT
The National Seal Sanctuary Gweek, Helston Cornwall TR12 6UG
Tel 01326 221361
Web www.sealsanctuary.co.uk

84

½ day

All year

Newquay Zoo

Home to many of the world's endangered species, Newquay Zoo is set in beautiful subtropical gardens. Explore the rainforest and its fascinating wildlife in the Tropical Zone and learn about farmyards from around the world in the Village Farm.

★ Tarzan Trail
★ Dragon Maze
★ Special events

LOCATION
Off the A3075 Edgcumbe Avenue in Trenance Gardens, Newquay

OPENING
Apr–Oct open daily 9.30am–6pm (last admission 5pm); Nov–Mar open daily 10am–5pm (last admission 4pm)

ADMISSION PRICES
Please check website or phone for details

CONTACT
Newquay Zoo Trenance Gardens Newquay Cornwall TR7 2LZ
Tel 01637 873342
Email info@newquayzoo.co.uk
Web www.newquayzoo.co.uk

The Pilchard Works

2 hrs

Easter-Oct

A **working factory museum** that produces salt fish and records the history of Cornwall's fishing heritage over the last 400 years including the trades of salting, pressing and stencilling. Children can use the pulleys and presses and make their own stencil prints.

LOCATION
From Penzance follow the promenade for 1 mile to Newlyn. From the A30 follow the signs on the Penzance bypass

OPENING
Easter-Oct open Mon–Fri 10am–6pm (last admission 5.15pm)

ADMISSION PRICES
Adult £3.25 Child (4–13) £1.95
Family £10   Concession £2.95

CONTACT
The Pilchard Works
Tolcarne, Newlyn, Penzance
Cornwall TR18 5QH
Tel 01736 332112
Web www.pilchardworks.co.uk

Poldark Mine

1 hr

Apr–Dec

A **guided tour of a genuine** eighteenth-century Cornish tin mine, with a museum, gardens, children's play areas and craft demonstrations.

LOCATION
3 miles from Helston on the B3297

OPENING
Apr–1 Oct open daily 10am–6pm (last tour 4pm); Oct–Dec open Sat–Thu 10.30am–4.30pm (last tour 3pm); Closed Christmas, Jan & Feb

ADMISSION PRICES
Underground guided tour:
Adult £5.75 Child (5–15) £3.60
Family £15.50

CONTACT
Poldark's Mine, Wendron
Helston, Cornwall TR13 0ER
Tel 01326 573173
Web www.poldark-mine.com

85

Polkyth Leisure Centre

2 hrs+

All year

LOCATION
Accessible via the A390 & A391. Follow the brown tourist signs

OPENING
2 Jan-30 Dec open daily, except 24-27 Dec & 1 Jan Mon–Fri 9am–10pm; Sat 9am–5pm; Sun 9am–5pm

ADMISSION PRICES
Please phone for details

CONTACT
Polkyth Leisure Centre
Carlyon Road
St Austell
Cornwall PL25 4DB
Tel 01726 223344
Fax 01726 70041

Well-equipped sports hall with badminton courts, squash courts, tennis courts and swimming pools, with a hoist for disabled visitors.

★ Hydrotherapy pool
★ Fitness room

Porfell Animal Land

2 hrs+
Apr–Oct

See and feed the deer, goats, ponies, chickens, ducks and peacocks that live here in a natural environment of woodland paths and open fields. There is also a children's playground.

LOCATION
Take the A38 from Liskeard to Dobwalls. Turn onto A390 & at East Taphouse turn left onto the B3359. First turning on right

OPENING
1 Apr–31 Oct open daily
10am–6pm

ADMISSION PRICES
Adult £4 Child (3–13) £3
Concession £3.50

CONTACT
Porfell Animal Land
Trecangate, Nr Lanreath, Liskeard
Cornwall PL14 4RE
Tel 01503 220211
Web
www.PorfellAnimalLand.co.uk

Royal Cornwall Museum

2 hrs
All year

A fascinating museum for older children interested in history and archaeology. It has displays on the history and natural history of Cornwall, a magnificent collection of minerals and crystals and antiquities from ancient Egypt, Rome and Greece.

LOCATION
Situated off the city centre, 5 minutes walk from the railway station & 10 minutes from the main bus terminal. Long term parking available nearby

OPENING
All year open Mon–Sat
10am–5pm

ADMISSION PRICES
Adult £4 Accompanied child Free

CONTACT
Royal Cornwall Museum
River Street
Truro
Cornwall TR1 2SU
Tel 01872 272205

Spirit of the West Theme Park

All day
May–Sep

A theme park dedicated to the Wild West with Native American artefacts and live street-action shows. Set in 100 acres, it contains two whole themed towns.

★ Panning for gold
★ Fishing at Retallack
★ Westworld auto raceway
★ Shooting gallery
★ Train ride
★ Museums

LOCATION
On the A39 St Columb-Wadebridge road, just off Winnards Perch roundabout on the B3274

OPENING
Theme Park: 1 May–30 Sep open Mon–Fri, Sun
Fishery: Open all year daily

ADMISSION PRICES
Theme Park: Adult £5 Child (4–14) £4
Family £16 Concession £4
Fishery: Adult £6 Child (4–14) £5
Concession £5

CONTACT
The Spirit of the West
Retallack Park
Winnards Perch
Nr St Columb
Cornwall TR9 6DE
Tel 01637 881160

Springfields Pony Centre & Fun Park

This is a large undercover complex with indoor water gardens, free-fall slides, trampolines and much more. Just outside is a park with a lake for boating.

★ Small pets area

★ Pony cart & train rides

LOCATION
From the A30 follow the signs for the airport for 2 miles. Signposted from the St Columb roundabout bypass on the A3

OPENING
Easter–Oct open daily 9.30am–5.50pm; Nov–Mar open daily 10am–4.30pm

ADMISSION PRICES
Adult £4.95 Child (2–16) £3.95
Concession £4.50

CONTACT
Springfields Pony Centre
St Columb Major, St Columb
Cornwall TR9 6HU
Tel 01637 881224
Web www.chycor.co.uk/springfields

Tehidy Country Park

Enjoy an active day at this country park in 345 acres of woodland, lakes and ponds, with nine miles of footpaths to explore.

★ Woodland trails

★ Horse & bike trails

★ Sensory trail for the visually impaired

LOCATION
Access on the B3301 from Portneath to North Cliffs

OPENING
All year

ADMISSION PRICES
Free

CONTACT
Tehidy Country Park
Tehidy
Cambourne
Cornwall TR14 0HA
Tel 01209 714494
Fax 01209 612764

87

Quality Assured Visitor Attraction
English Tourism Council

LOCATION
On the A395, 3 miles west of Launceston, just off the A30

OPENING
All year open daily except Sun & 25, 26 Dec

ADMISSION PRICES
Adult £4.95 Child (3–16) £4.50
Family £18 Concession £4

CONTACT
Trethorne Leisure Farm
Kennards House
Launceston
Cornwall PL15 8QE
Tel 01566 86324
Email trethorneleisure@eclipse.co.uk
Web www.cornwall-online.co.uk/trethorne

Trethorne Leisure Farm

3hrs+

All year

Children can feed the lambs and touch the animals at this farm combined with an indoor leisure park. There are numerous activities including pony rides and a virtual climbing wall.

★ Ball pools

★ Assault course

★ Rollerblading

★ Pony rides

★ Crazy golf

★ Tenpin bowling (you pay extra for this)

2 hrs+

Apr–Oct

Arlington Court

The Victorian home of Miss Rosalie Chichester, Arlington Hall is full of fascinating artefacts that she collected. In the basement, from May to September, visitors can follow the activities of Devon's largest colony of lesser horseshoe bats.

★ Carriage rides around the grounds
★ Parkland & woodland walks
★ Children's sculpture trail & quizzes

LOCATION
On the A39, 8 miles north-east of Barnstaple

OPENING
29 Mar–2 Nov open Wed–Mon 10am–5pm (last admission 4.30pm)

ADMISSION PRICES
Adult £5.60 Child £2.80 Family £13.90

CONTACT
Arlington Court
Arlington
Nr Barnstaple
Devon EX31 4LP
Tel 01271 850296
Web www.nationaltrust.org.uk

88

1 hr+

All year

Ashcombe Adventure Centre

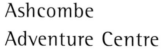

Burn off some energy at this adventure centre, where a wide range of fun and challenging activities is available.

★ Paintball
★ Archery
★ The Hyperslide
★ Clay pigeon shooting
★ Quad biking

LOCATION
Follow the A380 & the B3192 towards Teignmouth

OPENING
All year open Mon–Sat 9am–5pm; Sun 9am–1am

ADMISSION PRICES
Please phone for details

CONTACT
Ashcombe Adventure Centre
Ashcombe, Dawlish
Devon EX7 0QD
Tel 01626 866766
Email info@ashcombeadventure.co.uk
Web www.ashcombeadventure.co.uk

Babbacombe Model Village

2 hrs

All year

There are hundreds of 1:12 scale models set in award-winning gardens at this model village. There are villages, farms and rural areas, beautiful lakes and waterfalls, railways and details of everyday life.

LOCATION
Take the A380 to Torquay, then the B3199 to Babbacombe

OPENING
In winter open 10am–4pm; In summer open 9am–5pm; End of Sep open until 10pm

ADMISSION PRICES
Adult £5.40 Child £3.50

Family £14.95

CONTACT
Babbacombe Model Village
Hampton Avenue, Babbacombe
Torquay TQ1 3LA
Tel 01803 315315
Web www.babbacombemodel village.co.uk

Babbacombe Pottery

1 hr+
Varies

You can watch pots being thrown and can join in at the potter's wheel and make one of your own. If that seems too ambitious, try your hand at painting a ready-made pot.

i

LOCATION
On the A380

OPENING
Please phone for details

ADMISSION PRICES
Please phone for details

CONTACT
Babbacombe Pottery
Babbacombe Road
Torquay
Devon TQ1 3SY
Tel 01803 329222
Fax 01803 314159

Barnstaple Heritage Centre

2 hrs
All year

Over 1,000 years of Barnstaple's history is on show here, with hands-on visual and audio displays and life-size models and reconstructions.

i

LOCATION
In the centre of Barnstaple, on the quayside

OPENING
1 Apr–31 Oct open Mon–Sat 10am–5pm; 1 Nov–31 Mar open Tue–Fri 10am–4.30pm & Sat 10am–3.30pm; Closed Easter Sun & 25, 26 Dec & 1 Jan

ADMISSION PRICES
Adult £2.50 Child (7–16) £1.50
Family £7.50 Concession £2

CONTACT
Barnstaple Heritage Centre
Queen Anne's Walk
The Strand
Barnstaple
Devon EX31 1EU
Tel 01271 373003
Email barnstapletowncouncil
@northdevon.gov.uk

Beer Quarry Caves

1 hr+
Apr–Oct

i

LOCATION
Take the B3174 to Beer; follow the brown tourist signs from there

OPENING
1 Apr–30 Sep open daily 10am–5pm; 1–31 Oct open daily 11am–4pm

ADMISSION PRICES
Adult £4.50 Child (0–16) £3.25
Family £14

CONTACT
Beer Quarry Caves
Quarry Lane
Beer
Seaton
Devon
Tel 01297 680282
Email john@beerquarrycaves.fsnet.co.uk
Web www.beerquarrycaves.fsnet.co.uk

Take an eerie tour of this vast underground quarry with a long and eventful history. There is a fascinating commentary about the people who worked it over the centuries, from the Romans to the Victorians.

2 hrs+

All year

Bicton Park Gardens

Gardeners, young or old, will be interested in this historic garden with its nineteenth-century palmhouse, glasshouses and Italian garden. There are also indoor and outdoor play areas and train rides on offer.

★ Guided tours
★ Train rides
★ Shell house & museum

LOCATION
On the B3178 from Exmouth

OPENING
In summer open daily 10am–6pm; In winter open daily 10am–5pm; Closed 25 Dec

ADMISSION PRICES
Adult £4.75 Child (3–16) £2.75
Family £12.75 Concession £3.75
Annual membership available

CONTACT
Bicton Park Gardens
East Budleigh
Budleigh Salterton
Devon EX9 7BJ
Tel 01395 568465
Email gardens@bictonpark.co.uk
Web www.bictonpark.co.uk

90

All day

All year

The Big Sheep

Quality Assured Visitor Attraction
English Tourism Council

Traditional sheep crafts like sheep-shearing and sheep dog trials are combined with more modern attractions such as The Amazing Ewetopia Adventure Zone playground and sheep-racing to make this a fun and unusual day out for all the family.

★ Guided tours
★ Educational visits welcome
★ Indoor playground
★ Horse whispering shows
★ Sheep racing
★ Shearing & wool craft demonstrations

LOCATION
On the A39 North Devon link road,
2 minutes west of Bideford bridge

OPENING
1 Apr–31 Oct open daily 10am–6pm
Please phone for winter details

ADMISSION PRICES
Adult £5.95 Child £4.95 Family (2+4) £22

CONTACT
The Big Sheep
Abbotsham
Bideford
Devon EX39 5AP
Tel 01237 472366
Email info@thebigsheep.co.uk
Website www.thebigsheep.co.uk

All day

Apr-Oct

Blackpool Sands

Quality Assured Visitor Attraction

English Tourism Council

Blackpool Sands is an award-winning beach set in a beautiful and unspoilt sheltered bay amongst evergreens and pines.

★ Playground & watersports centre

i

LOCATION
On the A379, 3 miles from Dartmouth

OPENING
31 Mar-31 Oct open daily 9am-7pm; Closed 3-25 Dec

ADMISSION PRICES
Free

CONTACT
Blackpool Sands
Blackpool
Dartmouth
Devon TQ6 0RG
Tel 01803 770606
Email
info@blackpoolsands.co.uk
Web www.blackpoolsands.co.uk

Brannan Pottery

1 hr+

May-Oct

Take a guided tour of the factory to see how pots are thrown and, if you are interested, have a go at making one of your own.

i

LOCATION
On the A39 Barnstaple-Bideford road

OPENING
May-Oct open Mon-Sat 9am-5pm

ADMISSION PRICES
Please phone for details

CONTACT
Brannan Pottery
Roundswell Industrial Estate
Barnstaple
Devon EX31 3NJ
Tel 01271 343035
Email brannam@brannam.com

---

2 hrs+

Mar-Oct

Buckfast Butterfly Farm & Dartmoor Otter Sanctuary

Walk among some of the most beautiful butterflies in the world, flying free in a tropical garden with waterfalls, ponds and bridges. At the otter sanctuary visitors can see the playful otters from above and below the water and at feeding time.

i

LOCATION
Follow the brown tourist signs from Dart Bridge junction of the A38

OPENING
Butterflies: 1 Apr-31 Oct open daily 10am-5.30pm
Otters: Mar open 10.30am-3pm; 1 Apr-31 Oct open 10am-5.30pm

ADMISSION PRICES
Adult £4.45 Child £2.95
Senior £3.95

CONTACT
Buckfast Butterfly Farm & Dartmoor Otter Sanctuary
Buckfastleigh, Devon TQ11 0DZ
Tel 01364 642916
Web www.ottersandbutterflies.co.uk

Bygones

2 hrs

All year

Bygones has a life-size Victorian exhibition street with period rooms. Children will enjoy the large Hornby railway layouts, medals and militaria and an illuminated 'fantasyland'.

i

LOCATION
On the A379

OPENING
1 Mar-30 Jun & Sept-31 Oct open daily 10am-6pm; Jul & Aug open Mon-Thur 10am-9.30pm, Fri-Sun 10am-6pm; Nov-end Feb open 10am-5pm; Closed 24, 25 Dec

ADMISSION PRICES
Adult £3.95 Child £3.50
Family £16

CONTACT
Bygones
Fore Street
St Marychurch
Torquay TQ1 4PR
Tel 01803 326108

All day

Mar–Oct

Cascades Tropical Adventure Pool

Spend a whole day at this adventure pool, which is set beside an award-winning sandy beach. There are safe pools and mini-waterfalls for younger children.

★ 230ft flume, geysers & rapids rides

LOCATION
Take junction 27 off the M5 & follow the signs to Barnstaple and Braunton. Turn left at the traffic lights in Braunton centre onto the B3231 & follow the signs to Croyde

OPENING
Mid-Mar–end Oct open 10am–6pm (9pm in peak season) Please phone for details

ADMISSION PRICES
Please phone for details

CONTACT
Ruda Holiday Park
Croyde Bay, Braunton
Devon EX33 1NY
Tel 01271 890671

All day

All year

Crealy Adventure Park

One of the South-west's best days out, Crealy Adventure Park combines magic, adventure, animal rides and slides.

★ Special events throughout the year

LOCATION
Take junction 30 on the M5 onto the A3052. Follow the signs to Crealy

OPENING
In summer open 10am–6pm; In winter 10am–5pm; Closed 24, 25, 26 Dec & 1 Jan

ADMISSION PRICES
Please phone for details

CONTACT
Crealy Adventure Park
Clyst St Mary, Sidmouth Road
Exeter, Devon EX5 1DR
Tel 01395 233200
Email fun@crealy.co.uk
Web www.crealy.co.uk

92

---

2 hrs+

Apr–Nov

Crownhill Fort

The largest of Plymouth's great Victorian forts, visitors can discover the underground tunnels, explore the ramparts, marvel at Victorian architecture and view the guns, including the 'disappearing' Moncrieff.

LOCATION
From Plymouth town centre follow the A386 & the signs to Crownhill, which appear north of the A38

OPENING
Please phone for details
Open daily for pre-booked groups & schools

ADMISSION PRICES
Adult £4.75 Child £2.85 Family (2+2) £14 Senior/Student £4.80

CONTACT
Crownhill Fort
Crownhill Fort Road
Plymouth PL6 5BX
Tel 01752 793754
Web www.crownhillfort.co.uk

All day

All year

Dartmoor Wildlife Park

At this wildlife park, visitors can mingle with the friendly animals in a two-acre walk-in enclosure.

★ Daily flying displays except Fridays
★ Close Encounters of the Animal Kind event every afternoon

LOCATION
3 miles from Plymouth on the A38. Follow the brown tourist signs

OPENING
All year open daily 10am–6pm

ADMISSION PRICES
Adult £6.95 Child (4–14) £4.50 Family £20 Concession £5.50

CONTACT
Dartmoor Wildlife Park
Sparkwell
Plymouth, Devon PL7 5DG
Tel 01752 837209
Email ellisdaw@wildlifepark.freeserve.co.uk
Web www.dartmoorwildife.co.uk

Dart Valley Railway

2 hrs

Jun–Sep

Travel Torbay's spectacular coast and the beautiful river Dart by steam train from Paignton to Kingswear. The trip can be combined with river excursions to picturesque Dartmouth.

★ Thomas the Tank Engine weekends & Santa Specials in December

LOCATION
Follow the brown tourist signs to the centre of Paignton. Situated next to mainline trains

OPENING
Jun–Sep open daily; Apr, May & Oct open on selected dates
Please phone for details

ADMISSION PRICES
Please phone for details

CONTACT
Dart Valley Railway
Queens Park Station
Torbay Road, Paignton
Devon TQ4 6AF
Tel 01803 555872
www.paignton-steamrailway.co.uk

Diggerland

3 hrs

Mar–Nov

Based on the world of construction machinery, this is a unique adventure park where children and adults can experience the thrill of riding and driving real JCBs and dumpers in safety.

LOCATION
Exit the M5 at junction 27, head east on the A38, turn right at the roundabout onto the B2181. 3 miles on the left

OPENING
Mar–Nov weekdays, Bank hols & school hols from 10am–5pm

ADMISSION PRICES
Adult £2.50 Child £2.50

Under-2s Free Senior £1.25
Additional charge to drive real JCBs & dumpers

CONTACT
Diggerland Ltd
Verbeer Manor
Cullompton, Devon EX15 2PE
Tel 08700 344437
Email mail@diggerland.com

The Donkey Sanctuary

2–3 hrs

All year

The donkey sanctuary is a refuge for over 400 rescued donkeys. Set in beautiful surroundings, it has five walks and a donkey trail.

LOCATION
Off the A3052 between Sidford & Branscombe. Well signposted

OPENING
All year open daily 9am–dusk

ADMISSION PRICES
Free

CONTACT
The Donkey Sanctuary
Sidmouth, Devon EX10 0NU
Tel 01395 578222
Email
thedonkeysanctuary@compuserve.com
Web www.thedonkeysanctuary.org.uk

Eggesford Country Centre

All day

All year

A heritage centre depicting local social history, set in the beautiful Taw Valley.

★ Cycle trails   ★ Guided tours
★ Large rural garden centre

LOCATION
Take the A377 from Barnstaple or Exeter

OPENING
Please phone for details

ADMISSION PRICES
Free

CONTACT
Eggesford Country Centre
Eggesford Gardens
Chulmleigh
Devon EX18 7QU
Tel 01769 580250
Fax 01769 581041

2–4 hrs

Feb–Nov

Exmoor Brass Rubbing Centre

You can take a large selection of brass rubbings at this centre, which also provides all the materials and help visitors of any age may need.

LOCATION
Via the A39 & B3284

OPENING
Feb half-term holidays–Nov open daily 10.30am–5pm

ADMISSION PRICES
Free
Brass rubbing from £1.50

CONTACT
The Exmoor Brass Rubbing & Hobbycraft Centre
Woodside Craft Centre
Watersmeet Road
Lynmouth, Devon EX35 6EP
Tel 01598 752529
Email
info@exmoorbrassrubbing.co.uk
Web
www.exmoorbrassrubbing.co.uk

½ day

Apr–Oct

Gorse Blossom Miniature Railway & Woodland Park

Take a gentle steam-train ride through 35 acres of Devon countryside, and learn the Secrets of the Woodland in a display about woodland life.

★ Drive a miniature train
★ Toytown village for kids
★ Woodland assault course
★ Nature trail

LOCATION
Off the A38, west of Newton Abbot

OPENING
5 Apr–31 Oct open daily 10.30am–5pm

ADMISSION PRICES
Adult £4.50 Child £3 Family (2+2) £14 Senior £3.50

Unlimited train rides included in the price

CONTACT
Gorse Blossom Miniature Railway & Woodland Park
Bickington, Newton Abbot
Devon TQ12 6JD
Tel 01626 821361
Fax 01626 821361

1 hr+

All year

Grand Pier

Enjoy a few hours of fun on this traditional pier, with many family amusements and games, including the thrills and spills of a roller coaster.

★ Pirate ship
★ Mini-railway

LOCATION
Via the A379

OPENING
All year open daily
Phone for opening time details

ADMISSION PRICES
Free entry; charge for individual attractions

CONTACT
Grand Pier
The Seafront
Teignmouth
Devon TQ14 8BB
Tel 01626 774367
Fax 01626 776388

The Great Exmouth 'OO' Model Railway

1 hr

Easter–Sep

With over 7,500 feet of track, this is one of the world's largest scenic 'OO'-gauge model railways. It runs through villages and towns, all exquisitely modelled in great detail.

★ Model railway accessories for sale

LOCATION
Via the A376 & A377

OPENING
Please phone for details

ADMISSION PRICES
Adult £2.25 Child (3–13) £1.75
Family £7 Concession £1.75

CONTACT
The Great Exmouth 'OO'
Model Railway
Sea Front
Exmouth
Devon EX8 2AY
Tel 01395 278383
Fax 01395 273307

The Green House Visitor Centre

1 hr+

All year

The Green House is the UK's first leisure-based sustainable waste exhibition. Suitable for all the family, its imaginative interactive exhibits are designed to intrigue and challenge children.

LOCATION
2 miles east of Plymouth, off the A379 Kingsbridge Road. Follow the signs for Chelson Meadow

OPENING
All year open daily except Christmas break
Please phone for details

ADMISSION PRICES
Please phone for details

CONTACT
The Green House Visitor Centre
The Ride
Plymouth PL9 7JA
Tel 01752 482392
Email tghvc@hotmail.com
Web www.tghvc.co.uk

Quality Assured Visitor Centre
English Tourism Council

LOCATION
On the A381, 1½ miles from Newton Abbot town centre

OPENING
In summer open daily; In winter open on specific dates
Please phone for details

ADMISSION PRICES
Adult £4.95 Child (3–14) £3.95
Family (2+2) £16.90

CONTACT
Hedgehog Hospital Farm
Prickly Ball Farm
Denbury Road
East Ogwell
Newton Abbot
Devon TQ12 6BZ
Tel 01626 362319
Email hedgehog@hedgehog.org.uk
Web www.hedgehog.org.uk

Hedgehog Hospital Farm

2 hrs

All year

You can see baby hedgehogs bottle feeding, and amble in a hedgehog-friendly garden at this hospital for sick and injured hedgehogs. In addition there is a variety of outdoor activities on offer at the busy, working farm.

★ Meet the farm animals
★ Donkey & pony rides
★ Nightwatch in Aug (for adults only)

1 hr

All year

House of Marbles & Teign Valley Glass

A **working glass-blowing factory** which also has a museum full of glass artefacts including toys, marbles and games. Visitors can watch glass-blowing when work is in progress.

LOCATION
On the A382 from Newton Abbot to Bovey Tracey & the A38 from Exeter to Bovey Tracey

OPENING
All year open daily except 25, 26 Dec

ADMISSION PRICES
Free

CONTACT
House of Marbles & Teign Valley Glass
The Old Pottery
Pottery Road
Bovey Tracey, Newton Abbot
Devon TQ13 9DS
Tel 01626 835358
Email uk@houseofmarbles.com
Web www.houseofmarbles.com

2 hrs+

Mar-Oct

Knightshayes Court

The **lavish house** was built around 1870 by William Burges. Its much-admired garden features a water-lily pond, topiary, formal terraces and rare shrubs.

★ Woodland walks   ★ Children's quizzes

LOCATION
2 miles north of Tiverton, off the A396 at Bolham

OPENING
23 Mar-3 Nov open daily 11am-5.30pm; Oct open 11am-4.30pm Closed Fri except Good Fri

ADMISSION PRICES
Adult £5.50 Child £2.75
Family £13.70

CONTACT
Knightshayes Court
Bolham, Tiverton
Devon EX16 7RQ
Tel 01884 254665
Web www.nationaltrust.org.uk

All day

All year

Lundy Island

Enjoy a day walking on this beautiful island. Three miles long and only 24 miles out in the Bristol channel, it has a lighthouse and castle and is ideal for bird-watching. It is a great place to take children, not least because there are no roads or cars.

LOCATION
Take the A361 to Ilfracombe & the A386 to Bideford for the MS Oldenburg to Lundy Island

OPENING
Please phone for details

ADMISSION PRICES
£3.50; entrance fee included in MS Oldenburg fare

CONTACT
Lundy Island
Bideford, Devon EX39 2LY
Tel 01271 863636
Email info@lundyisland.co.uk
Web www.lundyisland.co.uk

3 hrs+

All year

The Milky Way Adventure Park

Set in 18 acres of landscaped grounds, this is an all-weather attraction with games and slides for all age groups. The North Devon Bird of Prey Centre is also located here.

★ Clone Zone Alien Encounter   ★ Dodgems

LOCATION
On the A39 Bideford-Bude road, 2 miles from Clovelly

OPENING
Easter-Oct open daily 10.30am-6pm

ADMISSION PRICES
Adult 6.50 Child £5.50 Family (2+2) £23 Concession £5.50

CONTACT
The Milky Way Adventure Park
Downland Farm
Clovelly
Bideford
Devon EX39 5RY
Tel 01237 431255
Email info@themilkyway.co.uk
Web www.the milkyway.co.uk

Norman Lockyer Observatory & James Lockyer Planetarium

½ day

Mar–Sep

WC 🏕 🍴 🛍

LOCATION
Take the A3052 Exeter–Seaton road, turn right after the Blue Ball Inn at Sidford & follow the signs

OPENING
Please phone for details

ADMISSION PRICES
Adult £4 Child £2

CONTACT
Norman Lockyer Observatory & James Lockyer Planetarium
Salcombe Hill Road
Sidmouth
Devon EX10 0NY
Tel 01395 579941
Email g.e.white@exeter.ac.uk
Web www.ex.ac.uk/nlo/

The solar system, space travel, communications and the weather are all explained and explored in fascinating exhibitions, models and hands-on activities at this working observatory and planetarium.

★ Radio room where visitors can talk to people all over the world
★ Satellite station where weather pictures are seen as soon as they are received from satellites
★ Meteorology station with three telescopes for public nighttime use
★ Woodland & coastal walks nearby
★ Exhibition hall with models of the solar system & space ships

97

---

3 hrs

All year

North Devon Farm Park

WC 🏕 🍴 🛍

A **visit to this farm park** gives children a chance to see animals in their natural environment, as well as enjoying a choice of beautiful woodland walks.

★ Indoor Jungle World   ★ Outdoor adventure play
★ Tractor rides

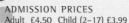

LOCATION
On the A361

OPENING
Easter–31 Oct open Tue–Sun
10am–5pm; Aug open daily
Please phone for winter opening details

ADMISSION PRICES
Adult £4.50 Child (2–17) £3.99
Family £16 Concession £2.99

CONTACT
North Devon Farm Park
Marsh Farm, Landkey
Barnstaple, Devon EX32 0NN
Tel 01271 830255

All day

Easter –Sep

Once Upon a Time Theme Park

WC 🏕 🍴

Take a whole day to visit this children's theme park. It has themed train rides, adventure trails, fairy-tale grottoes and some gentle enjoyable rides for younger children.

LOCATION
On the B3343, 1 mile from Woolacombe

OPENING
Easter–30 Sep open Sun–Fri
Please phone for details

ADMISSION PRICES
Adult £3 Child (2–13) £5.50

CONTACT
Once Upon A Time Theme Park
The Old Station
Woolacombe, Devon EX34 7HH
Tel 01271 870999
Email enquiries@
watermouthcastle.com
Web www.watermouthcastle.com

2 hrs+

All year

Overbecks Museum & Garden

The unusual and eclectic collection of the scientist Otto Overbeck is on display at this Edwardian house. It ranges from model boats and toys to shipbuilding tools and stuffed animals. Children love the secret room and the beautiful sub-tropical garden.

LOCATION
Signposted from Malborough & Salcombe

OPENING
Garden: All year open daily
Museum: 24 Mar–31 & Jul & Sep open Sun–Fri; Aug open daily; Oct open daily except Fri & Sat; Opening times 11am–5.30pm

ADMISSION PRICES
Adult £4.20 Child £2.10
Family £10.50

CONTACT
Overbecks
Sharpitor, Salcombe
Devon TQ8 8LW
Tel 01548 842893
Fax 01548 844038

Paignton Zoo

½ day+

All year

Visitors can cover thousands of miles in just a few hours on foot on a worldwide nature trail at Paignton Zoo. The fascinating journey takes you from scorching deserts to frozen Poles and from African savannah to South American rain forest.

LOCATION
1 mile from Paignton town centre on the A3022 Totnes road. The bus stop is in the zoo grounds

OPENING
In summer open 10am–6pm; In winter open 10am–dusk
Please phone for details

ADMISSION PRICES
Adult £8.25 Child £6
Under-3s Free Senior 75p

CONTACT
Paignton Zoo
Totnes Road
Paignton
Devon TQ4 7EU
Tel 01803 697500

2–3 hrs

Mar–Sep

Pecorama Pleasure Gardens & Exhibition

At a visit to these pleasure gardens visitors can enjoy a gentle stroll around the Peco Millenium Celebration Garden, which has five linked and themed gardens, and a one-mile steam-locomotive journey on the Beer Heights Light Railway.

★ Daily children's entertainment except peak season Sat

★ Children's activity areas

★ Crazy golf

LOCATION
Follow the A3052 westbound from Lyme Regis or eastbound from Exeter & then the B3174 to Beer

OPENING
25 Mar–27 Sep open Mon–Fri 10am–5pm, Sat open 10am–5.30pm
Outdoor facilities closed Nov–Easter

ADMISSION PRICES
Combined tickets, separate tickets & optional extras are available
Please phone for details

CONTACT
Pecorama Pleasure Gardens & Exhibition
Underleys
Beer
Seaton
Devon EX12 3NA
Tel 01297 21542
Web www.peco-uk.com

½ day

Feb–Nov

Pennywell Farm Centre

With a different activity every 30 minutes, children won't get bored at this fun farm. From feeding the animals to egg-collecting, this is also a great educational experience.

★ Pony & donkey rides   ★ Go-karts

LOCATION
Follow the A38 from Exeter or Plymouth–Buckfastleigh

OPENING
9 Feb–3 Nov open daily from 10am–5pm

ADMISSION PRICES
Adult £6.75 Child (3–16) £5.45 Family (2+2) £24

CONTACT
Pennywell Farm Centre Buckfastleigh
Devon TQ11 0LT
Tel 01364 642023
Fax 01364 642122
Email information@pennywellfarmcentre.co.uk

Plymouth Boat Cruises Limited

Varies

Feb–Nov

Plymouth Boat Cruises offers daily cruises around the naval harbour, as well as regular cruises to Calstock on the River Tamar, and sea trips to the River Yealm, east of Plymouth.

LOCATION
Take usual route into Plymouth then Barbican onto Phoenix Wharf

OPENING
1 Feb–30 Nov open daily 10am–3pm; Closed Christmas & New Year

ADMISSION PRICES
Please phone for details

CONTACT
Plymouth Boat Cruises Limited Phoenix Wharf, Barbican
Plymouth PL10 1AW
Tel 01752 822797
Email pbc@pbc.onyxnet.co.uk

½ day

All year

Plymouth Pavilions

A shopping, exhibition, conference and leisure attraction with an ice rink, tropical pool with water rides, restaurants and cafés.

LOCATION
Follow City Centre & Pavilions signs from the A38

OPENING
Please phone for details

ADMISSION PRICES
Please phone for details

CONTACT
Plymouth Pavilions Millbay Road
Plymouth PL1 3LF
Tel 01752 222200
Fax 01752 262226
Web www.plymouthpavilions.com

Riverdart Adventures

All day

Mar–Sep

Have a go at rafting or climbing, or enjoy a long ramble at this activity centre set in a 90-acre country estate with parkland.

★ Campsite   ★ Climbing wall
★ Rafting   ★ Paddle zone

LOCATION
Follow the brown tourist signs on the A38 to Ashburton

OPENING
29 Mar–Sep open daily 10am–5pm

ADMISSION PRICES
Adult £5.75 Child (5–14) £4.85 Family £19.50

CONTACT
Riverdart Adventures Holne Park
Ashburton, Newton Abbot
Devon TQ13 7NP
Tel 01364 652511
Email info@riverdart.co.uk
Web www.riverdart.co.uk

½ day

All year

The Riviera International Centre

WC ∥ 🔒

There is something for children of all ages at this leisure complex. It has a health and fitness centre, a choice of children's play areas, leisure pool, restaurants, cafés and shops.

★ Children's soft play area
★ Children's water spray area
★ Leisure pool, flume & wave machine

LOCATION
Take the M5 from Exeter or the A380 from Newton Abbot

OPENING
All year open 7.30am–9pm;
Closed 25, 26 Dec

ADMISSION PRICES
Please phone for details

CONTACT
The Riviera International Centre
Chestnut Avenue
Torquay
Devon TQ2 5LZ
Tel 01803 299992
Email enquiries@rivieracentre.co.uk
Web www.rivieracentre.co.uk

100

2–3 hrs

Apr–Dec

Seaton Tramway

WC 🪑 ∥ 🔒 🐕

Take a leisurely journey through the glorious Axe Valley in a unique narrow-gauge tramway. In good weather, bird-watchers can enjoy excellent views of wading birds from the open-top tram cars. In poorer weather, enclosed tram cars are used.

★ Disabled access by arrangement
★ Drive-a-Tram lesson available
★ Santa Specials
★ Vintage rallies

LOCATION
Follow the brown tourist signs on the A3052 Exeter–Lyme Regis road

OPENING
12 Apr–2 Nov open daily; 8–30 Nov open Sat–Sun; 7–21 Dec open Sun
Please phone for details

ADMISSION PRICES
1 Day Rover Ticket: Adult £8.25
Child (4–14) £5.50 Senior £7
Please phone or check the website for details

CONTACT
Seaton Tramway
Harbour Road
Seaton
Devon EX12 2NQ
Tel 01297 20375
Web www.tram.co.uk

Sorley Tunnel Adventure Farm

A **working organic dairy farm** with farm animals, riding stables and pony rides, and a children's nature trail which runs through an eerie, reputedly 'haunted', railway tunnel.

★ Indoor play area
★ Pedal-karts
★ Trampolines
★ Slides

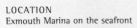

LOCATION
On the B3196, 1 mile north of Kingsbridge

OPENING
Feb half-term & Easter–end of Oct open daily 10am–6pm; Mar, Nov & Dec open Mon–Fri 10am–5pm

ADMISSION PRICES
Adult £2.50 Child £2.50

CONTACT
Sorley Tunnel Adventure Farm
Loddiswell Road
Kingsbridge, Devon TQ7 4BP
Tel 01548 854078
Email info@sorleytunnel.co.uk
Web www.sorleytunnel.com

½ day
All year

South Devon Railway

Enjoy a **traditional steam train journey** through a beautiful stretch of Devon countryside.

★ Free vintage bus service around town in summer
★ Small museum
★ Play area

LOCATION
Between Exeter & Plymouth on the A38 Expressway

OPENING
Apr–Oct open daily

ADMISSION PRICES
Adult £6.80 Child (5–14) £4
Family £19.60 Concession £6.10
Please phone for discount details

CONTACT
South Devon Railway
The Station
Buckfastleigh, Devon TQ11 0DZ
Tel 01364 643338
Email southdevonrailway.org
Web www.southdevonrailway.org

Varies
Apr–Oct

Stuart Line Cruises & Boat Trips

Varies
All year

LOCATION
Exmouth Marina on the seafront

OPENING
All year open daily
Please phone for details

ADMISSION PRICES
Fares depend on trip
Please phone for details

CONTACT
Stuart Line Cruises & Boat Trips
Exmouth Marina
Exmouth Docks
Exmouth
Devon EX8 1DV
Tel 01395 279693
Email info@stuartlinecruises.co.uk
Web www.stuartlinecruises.co.uk

Enjoy a **pleasureboat cruise** along the beautiful River Exe or a sea trip along the East Devon coast – the latter is known for the extraordinary fossils exposed in its rocks and is now an official World Heritage Site.

★ Guided tours for individuals
★ Mackerel and evening deep-sea fishing trips
★ Evening barbecue cruises
★ Day trips to Torquay

Tiverton Museum of Mid Devon Life

Torrington 1646

This is a comprehensive regional museum. The railway gallery contains a Great Western Railway locomotive and there is a Heathcote lace machine gallery. Also on show are agricultural and domestic implements and a collection of Devon farm waggons.

LOCATION
Via the A396, A373 or A361

OPENING
Feb–Dec open Mon–Fri 10.30am–4.30pm, Sat 10am–1pm; Closed 22 Dec–end Jan

ADMISSION PRICES
Please phone for details

CONTACT
Tiverton Museum of Mid Devon Life
Beck's Square, Tiverton
Devon EX16 6PJ
Tel 01884 256295
Email tivertonmus@eclipse.co.uk
Web www.tivertonmuseum.org.uk

At Torrington 1646 visitors travel through time back to the seventeenth century. The multi-media displays, costumed interpreters, and living history displays bring history to life.

LOCATION
In Great Torrington town centre

OPENING
All year
Please phone for details

ADMISSION PRICES
Please phone for details

CONTACT
Torrington 1646
Castle Hill
South Street
Great Torrington
Devon EX38 8AA
Tel 01805 626146
Web www.great-torrington.com

102

Totnes Costume Museum

Totnes Museum

At the Totnes Costume Museum there is a new exhibition of costumes and accessories each season, displayed in one of the historic merchants' houses of Totnes, Bogan House, restored by Mitchell Trust.

LOCATION
On the A385 & A381

OPENING
26 May–end of Sep open Mon–Fri 11am–5pm

ADMISSION PRICES
Please phone for details

CONTACT
Totnes Costume Museum – Devonshire Collection of Period Costume
Bogan House
43 High Street
Totnes
Devon TQ9 5NP
Tel 01803 862857

A sixteenth-century Tudor merchant's house complete with cobbled courtyard and Elizabethan herb garden. There is a Tudor bedroom, and a Victorian nursery, kitchen and grocer's shop, as well as the archaeology and costume rooms.

LOCATION
In the main street in front of East Gate Arch in Totnes

OPENING
3 Apr–27 Oct open Mon–Fri; Closed Easter, 13, 16 Apr

ADMISSION PRICES
Adult £1.50 Child 25p
Concession £1

CONTACT
Totnes Museum
70 Fore Street
Totnes, Devon TQ9 5RU
Tel 01803 863821

Tuckers Maltings

Take a unique guided tour of England's only working malthouse. Visitors can watch working Victorian machinery producing malt from barley. Suitable for all ages to see, touch, smell and taste.

★ Audio effects, video and hands-on discovery centre

LOCATION
Follow the brown tourist signs from Newton Abbot station

OPENING
Easter–31 Oct open Mon–Sat; Jul & Aug open daily

ADMISSION PRICES
Adult £4.35 Child £2.75 Family £12.25 Concession £3.95

CONTACT
Tuckers Maltings
Teign Road
Newton Abbot
Devon TQ12 4AA
Tel 01626 334734
Fax 01626 330153

Watermouth Castle

A castle with a difference, Watermouth has numerous activities and exhibitions of interest to all the family, ranging from cider-making exhibits and mechanical music demonstrations to a gnome village, crazy mirrors, maze and model railway.

LOCATION
On the A399 from Ilfracombe–Combe Martin

OPENING
Please phone for details

ADMISSION PRICES
Adult £7 Child (3–13) £6

CONTACT
Watermouth Castle
Berrynarbor
Ilfracombe
Devon Ex34 9SL
Tel 01271 863879
Web www.watermouthcastle.com

Woodlands Leisure Park

Action rides, games and water slides and an animal zone with rabbits, pigs, deer and llamas.

★ Under-6s Ice Palace play zone
★ Falconry demonstrations
★ Live entertainment
★ Empire of the Sea Dragon indoor play area

LOCATION
5 miles from Dartmouth on the B3122

OPENING
15 Mar–3 Nov open daily 9.30am–6pm; 4 Nov–14 Mar open weekends 9.30am–5pm

ADMISSION PRICES
Adult £6.75 Child £6.75 Family (2+2) £24.95

CONTACT
Woodlands Leisure Park
Dartmouth, Devon TQ9 7DQ
Tel 01803 712598
Email fun@woodlandspark.com
Web www.woodlandspark.com

Abbotsbury Swannery

Visitors can walk among the free-flying mute swans that live here and, during the hatching period (end of May–end June), watch the eggs hatch.

★ Guided tours available
★ Shire horse cart rides
★ Audio-visual show

LOCATION
On the B3157 between Bridport & Weymouth

OPENING
5 Apr–2 Nov open daily 10am–6pm (last admission 5pm)

ADMISSION PRICES
Adult £5.50 Child £3.50 Senior/Disabled £5.20

CONTACT
Abbotsbury Swannery
New Barn Road, Abbotsbury
Weymouth, Dorset ST3 4JG
Tel 01305 871858
Email info@abbotsbury-tourism.co.uk
Web www.abbotsbury-tourism.co.uk

All day

All year

Avon Heath Country Park

Enjoy a day at Dorset's largest country park, walking or cycling in the beautiful heathland and woods.

★ Barbecue hire available

★ Nature trails

★ Activities & events at the visitor centre

LOCATION
On the A31, 2 miles west of Ringwood

OPENING
Park: All year open daily
Visitor centre: All year open daily 11am–4pm

ADMISSION PRICES
Free
Car park charge

CONTACT
Avon Heath Country Park
Visitor Centre, Brocks Pine
St Leonards, Ringwood
Dorset BH24 2DA
Tel 01425 478470

1 hr

All year

Brewers Quay & Timewalk Journey

Visit this redeveloped Victorian brewery in Weymouth's Old Harbour to see an award-winning exhibition that takes the visitor on a voyage with Miss Paws, the brewery cat, through 19 life-size scenes, recreating 600 years of local history.

LOCATION
Follow the brown tourist signs on the A354

OPENING
All year open daily 10am–5pm, extended to 9pm in peak season; Closed 25, 26, 27 Dec & last 2 weeks of Jan

ADMISSION PRICES
Adult £4.25 Child (5–16) £3
Family £12.50 Concession £3.75

CONTACT
Brewers Quay & Timewalk Journey
Hope Square, Weymouth
Dorset DT4 8TR
Tel 01305 777622

104

3 hrs

All year

Corfe Castle

Explore this ruined castle with a long and fascinating history as a fortress, prison and home. The Castle View Visitor Centre has hands-on displays and children are encouraged to touch castle artefacts and try on replica medieval clothing.

★ Children's activities during the summer holidays

★ Special events including history enactments

★ Guided tours

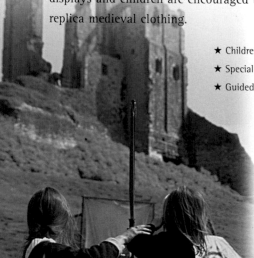

LOCATION
On the A351 Wareham–Swanage road

OPENING
All year except 25, 26 Dec & 2 days in mid Mar
Please phone for details of opening times

ADMISSION PRICES
Adult £4.30 Child (5–16) £2.15
Family £10.50
Free for National Trust members

CONTACT
Corfe Castle
The Square
Wareham
Dorset BH20 5EZ
Tel 01929 481294
Email wcfgen@smtp.ntrust.org.uk
Website www.nationaltrust.org.uk

Dorset Belle Cruises

½ day

Mar–Sep

Take a cruise around the Purbeck coast, visit the Isle of Wight for a day or explore Brownsea Island.

★ Boats available for charter

★ Evening cruises

★ Link-up with Swanage Railway

★ Bikes carried free

LOCATION
From the east take the A338 to Bournemouth. From the west take the A35. Follow the signs to the pier

OPENING
Please phone for details

ADMISSION PRICES
Bournemouth to Swanage: Adult £8
Bournemouth to Poole or Brownsea: Adult £5
Child £1

CONTACT
Dorset Belle Cruises
Croson Limited
Pier Approach
Bournemouth BH2 5AA
Tel 01202 558550
Email karllamb@aol.com
web www.dorsetbelles.co.uk

105

---

1 hr+

All year

Dorset County Museum

Best Social History Museum 1998
Museum of the Year Awards

Explore **Dorset wildlife, geology** and social history in interactive exhibitions and audio-visual displays.

★ Gallery of Dorset's writers
including Thomas Hardy study

★ Art gallery

★ Schools' service

LOCATION
In the town centre

OPENING
1 May–31 Oct open daily
10am–5pm; 1 Jan–30 Apr & 1
Nov–31 Dec open Mon–Sat
10am–5pm; Closed Good Fri &
24, 25, 26 Dec

ADMISSION PRICES
Please phone for details

CONTACT
Dorset County Museum
High West Street, Dorchester
Dorset DT1 1XA
Tel 01305 262735
Web
www.dorsetcountymuseum.co.uk

The Dorset Teddy Bear Museum

1 hr

All year

An unusual museum where the teddy bears are life-sized. See the teddy bear family at work, rest and play. A large selection of teddy bears is available at the period shop.

LOCATION
In the town centre

OPENING
All year open daily 9.30am–5pm;
Closed 25, 26 Dec

ADMISSION PRICES
Adult £2.95 Child (4–16) £1.50
Family £7.95

CONTACT
The Dorset Teddy Bear Museum
Teddy Bear House
Antelope Walk
Dorchester
Dorset DT1 1BE
Tel 01305 263200
Email
info@teddybearhouse.co.uk
Web www.teddybearhouse.co.uk

All day

All year

Durlston Country Park

A **country park** with wildflower meadows, downland, cliffs, sea and a wealth of wildlife. There is also a visitor centre for local information.

★ Theme trails   ★ Ranger-guided walks

LOCATION
Take the A351 to Swanage &
then follow the brown tourist
signs

OPENING
Park open all year daily
Phone visitor centre for details

ADMISSION PRICES
Free; Car park charge

CONTACT
Durlston Country Park
Durlston, Swanage
Dorset BH19 2JL
Tel 01929 424443
Email info@durlston.co.uk
Web www.durlston.co.uk

---

3 hrs

Feb–Dec

Farmer Palmer's Farm Park

A **delightful farm** where children can feed the lambs, ride on a tractor and watch cows being milked.

★ Woodland walk & maize maze (in summer)
★ Large & small climbing frames

★ Undercover straw mountain
★ Bouncy castle
★ Pedal karts

LOCATION
Take the A35 towards Dorchester,
take 2nd turning left at the
roundabout to Organford, then
1st road on the right

OPENING
Open 8 Feb–29 Dec; Closed 25,
26 Dec
Please phone for details

ADMISSION PRICES
Adult £4.25 Child (3–14) £3.25
Family £13.90 Concession £3.75

CONTACT
Falmer Palmer's Farm Park
Organford, Poole
Dorset BH16 6EU
Tel 01202 622022
Email farmerpalmers@bigfoot.com

---

3 hrs+

All year

Kingston Maurward Gardens & Animal Park

Enjoy a **tranquil day at this beautiful park.** There are Edwardian gardens with a croquet lawn, rose garden, herbaceous borders and large displays of tender perennials.

LOCATION
1 mile east of Dorchester off the
A35. Signposted from the
roundabout on the eastern end
of the Dorchester bypass

OPENING
6 Jan–23 Dec open daily
10am–5.30pm or dusk if earlier

ADMISSION PRICES
Adult £4 Child £2.50

CONTACT
**Kingston Maurward Gardens
& Animal Park**
Kingston Maurward, Dorchester
Dorset DT2 8PY
Tel 01305 215003
Web www.kmc.ac.uk

½ day

Feb–Dec

Lulworth Castle

An **interesting historic building** with plenty to entertain children. After viewing the house, you can take a woodland walk and visit a nearby animal farm where children can help to feed the animals.

★ Adventure playground
★ Woodland walk

★ Children's indoor activity room

LOCATION
Follow the brown tourist signs
on the B3070 & B3071

OPENING
16 Feb–23 Dec
Please phone for details

ADMISSION PRICES
Adult £5.50 Child (5–16) £3.50
Family £15

CONTACT
Lulworth Castle
Lulworth Estate
East Lulworth
Wareham
Dorset BH20 5QS
Tel 01929 400352
Email hennie@lulworth.com
Web www.lulworth.com

Model World

2 hrs+

All year

WC

An impressive model world featuring places of local interest and working models, including a railway, zoo and circus, all operated at the touch of a button.

LOCATION	ADMISSION PRICES
On the A353 Preston–Weymouth road	Adult £3.25 Child £2 Senior £5.75 Group rates available
OPENING	**CONTACT**
All year open daily 10am–5pm (later in Jul & Aug); Closed Christmas & New Year	**Model World** Lodmoor Country Park Weymouth, Dorset DT4 7SX Tel 01305 781797

Oceanarium

3 hrs

All year

WC

From the tropical rainforest to the ocean depths take a fascinating voyage of discovery through the planet's greatest natural wonders and experience close encounters with an array of underwater life ranging from elegant seahorses to sinister sharks.

LOCATION	ADMISSION PRICES
On the west beach promenade opposite Bournemouth pier. From the A338 Wessex Way, follow signs to the Oceanarium	Adult £5.85 Child £3.75 Family £18 Concession £4.75
OPENING	**CONTACT**
In summer open daily 10am–8pm; In winter open daily 10am–4pm	**Oceanarium** Pier Approach, West Beach Bournemouth BH2 5AA Tel 01202 311993 Web www.oceanarium.co.uk

107

Poole Aquarium & Serpentarium

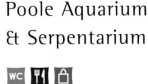

2 hrs

All year

WC

See the sharks and piranhas, marvel at the wonders of the coral reef and have your photo taken as you dare to touch the snakes in the snake pit.

★ Model railway   ★ Partial disabled access

LOCATION	CONTACT
Follow the brown tourist signs to Poole Quay	**Poole Aquarium & Serpentarium** Hennings Wharf, The Quay Poole BH15 1JS Tel 01202 686712
OPENING Sep–Jun open 10am–5.30pm; Jul & Aug 9am–9pm; Closed 25 Dec	
ADMISSION PRICES Adult £4 Child (3–16) £3 Concession £3	Email pooleaquarium@tiscali.co.uk Web www.poolenaturalworld.co.uk

Putlake Adventure Farm

3 hrs

Feb–Dec

WC

Enjoy the relaxed atmosphere at this all-weather farm park. Children can enjoy the indoor and outdoor play areas, make friends with the animals and take pony and trailer rides. At 4pm interested visitors can try their hand at milking.

LOCATION	CONTACT
Take the B3069 to Langton Matravers	**Putlake Adventure Farm** Langton Matravers Swanage Dorset BH19 3EU Tel 01929 422917 Fax 01929 422917
OPENING 9 Feb–23 Dec Please phone for details	
ADMISSION PRICES Adult £3.80 Child (3–14) £2.80 Concession £2.80	

Sherborne Museum

2 hrs

Apr–Oct

This museum is based around Sherborne's Norman castle. It has a Victorian doll's house as well as many other agricultural and household artefacts. The museum also houses geological and archaeological collections and Roman artefacts.

LOCATION
In the centre of town near Sherborne Abbey

OPENING
Apr–31 Oct open Tue–Sat 10.30am–4.30pm; Sun, Bank holidays open 2.30pm–4.30pm

ADMISSION PRICES
Adult £1 Child Free

CONTACT
Sherborne Museum
Abbey Gate House
Sherborne
Dorset DT9 3BP
Tel 01935 812252
Web www.aboutbritain.com

Stapehill Abbey, Crafts & Gardens

2 hr+

All year

Thirty acres of award-winning gardens and woodland surround this nineteenth-century Cistercian Abbey. It has a craft centre, countryside museum and home farm, where a range of domestic animals can be seen at close quarters.

LOCATION
8 miles from Ringwood on the A31

OPENING
1 Apr–30 Sep open daily 10am–5pm; 1 Oct–31 Mar open Wed–Sun 10am–4pm; Closed 22 Dec–4 Feb

ADMISSION PRICES
Adult £4 Child (4–16) 2.50
Concession £4

CONTACT
Stapehill Abbey, Crafts & Gardens, Wimbourne Road West Stapehill, Wimbourne Minster, Dorset BH21 2EB
Tel 01202 861686

Studland Beach & Nature Reserve

All day

All year

These fine sandy beaches stretch for three miles from South Haven Point to the chalk cliffs of Old Harry Rocks. The heathland behind the beach is a National Nature Reserve and is ideal for walking and birdwatching.

LOCATION
From Wareham take the A351 & B3351

OPENING
Shell Bay car park open all year; The Knoll & Middle Beach car park open East–Sep 9am– 8pm; South Beach car park 9am–11pm

ADMISSION PRICES
Free; Car park charge

CONTACT
Studland Beach & Nature Reserve, Countryside Office Middle Beach, Studland Swanage, Dorset BH19 3AX
Tel 01929 450259

Swanage Railway

Varies

All year

Enjoy a nostalgic steam-train journey through magnificent countryside. The train runs through the village of Corfe Castle, offering good views of the historic ruins.

★ Special events throughout the year, including train-driving lessons

LOCATION
On the Dorset coast, between Poole Harbour & Weymouth

OPENING
Apr–Oct open daily; Nov–Mar open most weekends; Closed 25 Dec

ADMISSION PRICES
Return ticket from Swanage to

Norden: Adult £6 Child (5–15) £4 Family £18 Concession £4

CONTACT
Swanage Railway
Station House, Swanage
Dorset BH19 1HB
Tel 01929 425800
Web www.swanagerailway.co.uk

3 hrs
All year

The Tank Museum

The Tank Museum houses the world's finest indoor collection of Armoured Fighting Vehicles. Tanks in Action displays are held throughout the summer.

★ Family activity trail

LOCATION
Off the A352, between
Dorchester & Wareham,
near Wool

OPENING
All year open daily except
Christmas week

ADMISSION PRICES
Please phone for details

CONTACT
The Tank Museum
Tel 01929 405096
Email info@tankmuseum.co.uk
Web www.tankmuseum.co.uk

2 hrs
All year

UK Llamas

Gentle and easy to handle, walking with llamas is a unique experience and fun for all ages.

★ Day treks available
★ Children's birthday parties

LOCATION
On the A3066, north of
Beaminster

OPENING
Please phone for details

ADMISSION PRICES
Pre-booking essential; please
phone for details on prices

CONTACT
UK Llamas
New House Farm
Beaminster
Dorset DT8 3HE
Tel 01308 868674
Email jo@ukllamas.co.uk
Web www.ukllamas.co.uk

109

All day
All year

Upton Country Park

Upton House has pretty formal gardens which lead into woodland, meadow, and a saltmarsh teeming with wildlife on the edge of Poole harbour.

★ Countryside heritage centre   ★ Cycling allowed on
with nature trails   waymarked cycle route

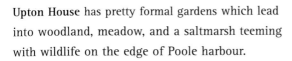

LOCATION
On the south side of the
A35/A3409, 4 miles west of
Poole town centre

OPENING
All year open daily 9am–dusk

ADMISSION PRICES
Free

CONTACT
Upton Country Park
Upton Road
Upton
Poole
Dorset BH17 7BJ
Tel 01202 672625
Fax 01202 678140

2 hrs
Mar–Sep

Wimbourne Model Town & Gardens

Set in award-winning gardens, the models are exact 1:10 scale replicas of the town of Wimbourne Minster as it was in the 1950s. Children will enjoy the play houses in Wendy Street.

LOCATION
Accessible via the A31

OPENING
22 Mar–29 Sep open daily
10.30am–5pm

ADMISSION PRICES
Adult £3 Child (3–15) £2
Concession £2.50

CONTACT
Wimbourne Model Town
& Gardens
16 King Street
Wimbourne Minster
Dorset BH21 1DY
Tel 01202 881924
Email wimbournemodeltown
@ hotmail.com
Web www.wimbourne-
modeltown.com

SOUTH-WEST

1 hr
All year WC

Beatrix Potter's House of the Tailor of Gloucester

The attraction and shop are in the house used by Beatrix Potter for her story The Tailor of Gloucester. Displays and interactive models bring this classic English tale to life.

LOCATION
In College Court, off Westgate Street in the centre of Gloucester (pedestrian area)

OPENING
1 Apr-30 Sep open daily 10am-5pm; 1 Nov-31 Mar 10am-4pm; Closed 21 Apr, 25, 26 Dec & 1 Jan

ADMISSION PRICES
Please phone for details

CONTACT
Beatrix Potter's House of the Tailor of Gloucester
9 College Court
Gloucester
Gloucestershire
GL1 2HJ
Tel 01452 422856
Email enquiries@hop-skip-jump.com

110

1 hr+
Mar-Oct

Berkeley Castle

Berkeley Castle is a stately home full of treasures. There are paintings by English and Dutch masters, tapestries, furniture of a wide variety of styles, silver and porcelain. The castle is surrounded by beautiful terraced Elizabethan gardens where the family can relax and enjoy the scenery.

LOCATION
Situated on the A38 (M5, exit 13 or 14) west of Dursley

OPENING
29 Mar-31 May open Tue-Sun 2pm-5pm; Jun & Sep open Tue-Sat 11am-5pm; Sun 2pm-5pm; Jul & Aug open Mon-Sat 11am-5pm, Sun 2pm-5pm, Oct open Sun 2pm-4.30pm; Bank holidays open 11am-5pm

ADMISSION PRICES
Adult £5.70 Child £3.10 Family £15.50 Concession £4.70

CONTACT
Berkeley Castle
Berkeley
Gloucestershire GL13 9BQ
Tel 01453 810332

Birdland Park Ltd

½ day

All year

Visit the penguins, flamingos, storks, cranes, parrots, ibises, hornbills and many other birds at this centre, set in woodland and gardens.

★ Children's play area

LOCATION
Follow the A436 to Bourton-on-the-Water

OPENING
1 Apr–31 Oct open 10am–6pm;
1 Nov–31 March open 10am–4pm
(last admission 1 hr before closing time); Closed 25 Dec

ADMISSION PRICES
Adult £4.50 Child (4–14) £2.50
Concession £3.50

CONTACT
Birdland Park Ltd
Rissington Road
Bourton-on-the-Water
Cheltenham
Gloucestershire GL54 2BN
Tel 01541 820480
Email sb.birdland@virgin.net

Butts Farm
Rare Farm Animals

3 hrs

Feb–Oct

Children can feed and pet some of the animals and birds at this working farm. There are piglets, ponies, rabbits, roosters, goats and geese.

★ Pets corner   ★ Daily programme of events

LOCATION
On the A419, east of Cirencester

OPENING
11 Feb–31 Oct open Wed–Sun
11am–5pm; open daily during the
school holidays

ADMISSION PRICES
Adult £3.75 Child £2.75
Family £12 Concession £3

CONTACT
Butts Farm Rare Farm Animals
The Butts Farm
South Cerney
Cirencester
Gloucestershire GL7 5QE
Tel 01285 862205
Email buttsfarm@aol.com

2–4 hrs

All year

Cattle Country
Adventure Park

A **farm park specialising in exotic** cattle such as Gloucester Old Spot and American Bison. It also has a large adventure playground with big slides and an outdoor paddling pool.

LOCATION
On the B4066, near Berkeley
town

OPENING
In winter open Sun 10am–5pm;
Please phone for summer details

ADMISSION PRICES
£4.70 (group discounts available)

CONTACT
Cattle Country Adventure Park
Berkeley Heath Farm
Berkeley Heath
Berkeley
Gloucestershire GL13 9EN
Tel 01453 810510
Web www.cattlecountry.co.uk

Cotswold Farm Park

3 hrs

Mar–Sep

The home of rare breed conservation with over 50 herds in a beautiful setting.

★ Farm safari ride   ★ Farm nature trail

★ Pets corner   ★ Indoor tractor school

LOCATION
Follow the B4077 from Stow for
5 miles. Signposted

OPENING
23 Mar–29 Sep open daily
10.30am–5pm

ADMISSION PRICES
Adult £4.75 Child (3–16) £3
Family £14.50 Concession £4.25

CONTACT
Cotswold Farm Park
Guiting Power, Cheltenham
Gloucestershire GL54 5UG
Tel 01451 850307
Email
info@cotswoldfarmpark.co.uk
Web
www.cotswoldfarmpark.co.uk

2 hrs+

All year

Dick Whittington Family Leisure Park

Among the indoor and outdoor facilities at this family leisure park are a toy corner, pets corner, giant sand-pit and the Dick Whittington Exhibition.

★ Scenic walks & spectacular viewing point

LOCATION
On the A4136 Gloucester–Monmouth Road

OPENING
All year open daily 10.30am–6pm; Closed 25 Dec

ADMISSION PRICES
Adult £4 Child £3.50

CONTACT
Dick Whittington Family Leisure Park
Blakemore Park, Little London
Longhope
Gloucestershire GL17 0PH
Tel 01452 831137
Email brian@dickwhittington.net
Web www.dickwhittington.net

---

2 hrs+

All year

Folly Farm Waterfowl

A beautiful aquatic landscape with 100 breeds of ducks and geese and a variety of farm animals including chickens, pigs and donkeys, and Highland cattle, llamas and rheas. Children can hand-feed the ducks.

LOCATION
On the A436, about 2½ miles from Bourton-on-the-Water

OPENING
31 Mar–30 Sep open daily 10am–5pm; 1 Oct–30 Mar open Sat & Sun 10am–5pm

ADMISSION PRICES
Adult £3.50 Child (4-14) £1.50

CONTACT
Folly Farm Waterfowl
Folly Farm
Bourton-on-the-Water
Cheltenham
Gloucestershire GL54 3BY
Tel 01451 820940
Web
www.follyfarmwaterfowl.co.uk

112

3 hrs+

All year

Lechdale Trout Farm

An organic trout farm with trout and fly-fishing, Lechdale is open to disabled anglers, and offers tuition and boats for hire.

LOCATION
On the A361 between Highworth & Carterton

OPENING
1 Apr–31 Oct open daily 7.30am–5.30pm; 1 Nov–31 Mar open daily 8am–5pm; Closed 25, 26 Dec

ADMISSION PRICES
Day tickets: Adult £40 Junior (accompanied) £25
Half-day tickets available

CONTACT
Lechdale Trout Farm
Burford Road, Lechdale
Gloucestershire GL7 3QQ
Tel 01367 253266
Email tim@timtrout.co.uk

---

2 hrs+

All year

Museum in the Park

An innovative outdoor museum set in a park, it has imaginative displays including dinosaurs and a Roman temple.

★ Guided tours

LOCATION
From junction 13 of the M5, take the A419 Ebley bypass towards Stroud

OPENING
1 Apr–30 Sep open Tue–Fri 12pm–5pm, Sat & Sun 11am–5pm; 1 Oct–31 Mar open Tue–Fri 1pm–5pm, Sat–Sun 11am–4pm

ADMISSION PRICES
Adult £2.50 Child (5–18) £1.25
Concession £1.25

CONTACT
Museum in the Park
Stroud District Museum
Stratford Park, Stratford Road
Stroud, Gloucesterhire GL5 4AF
Tel 01453 763394
Web www.stroud.gov.uk

½ day
Feb–Oct

National Birds of Prey Centre

Vultures, eagles, condors, kites, buzzards and kestrels can all be seen here.

★ Children's play area

★ Education room

★ Guided tours for groups

★ Woodland walk

LOCATION
Take junction 3 off the M50 & junction 11 off the M5 & follow the signs

OPENING
1 Feb–31 Oct open daily 10.30am–5.30pm

ADMISSION PRICES
Adult £5.95 Child £3.65

Under-4s Free Family £17
Senior £4.95

CONTACT
National Birds of Prey Centre
Great Boulsdon
Newent
Gloucestershire GL18 1JJ
Tel 0870 9901992

---

2 hrs
All year

National Waterways Museum

Take a Journey Through Britain in this award-winning museum, which tells the 200-year story of inland waterways. There are two different quaysides of historic craft to investigate, a traditional blacksmith's shop and an activities room.

LOCATION
On the A430, off junction 11 off the M5. Follow the brown signs for Historic Docks

OPENING
All year open daily 10am–5pm; Closed 25 Dec

ADMISSION PRICES
Please phone for details

CONTACT
National Waterways Museum
Llanthony Warehouse
Gloucester Docks, Gloucester
Gloucestershire GL1 2EH
Tel 01452 318054
Email info@nwm.demon.co.uk
Web www.nwm.org.uk

Varies
All year

Pedalbikeaway Cycle Centre

A bike hire centre with bikes for all ages and catering for special needs. Information on cycling in the Forest of Dean, Wye Valley, Black Mountains, Brecon Beacons and Herefordshire is available.

★ Guided tours for individuals

LOCATION
Take the B4226 out of Coleford towards Cinderford. Turn left at the crossroads with the B4234 & follow signs for a ¼ mile

OPENING
1 Apr–31 Oct open Tue–Sun 9am–6pm; Jul & Aug open daily 9am–6pm; 1 Nov–31 Mar open

Sat & Sun 9am–6pm

CONTACT
Pedalabikeaway Cycle Centre
Cannop Valley
Coleford
Gloucestershire GL16 7EH
Tel 01594 860065
Email info@pedalbikeaway.com
Web www.pedalbikeaway.com

---

3 hrs+
All year

Prinknash Bird Park

Enjoy a wildlife experience walking in this bird park with fallow deer and pygmy goats, peacocks and cranes. There is a reputedly haunted fish pond teeming with large trout.

LOCATION
Exit the M5 at junction 11a & then take the A46 towards Stroud

OPENING
1 Apr–31 Oct open daily 10am–5pm; 1 Nov–31 Mar open daily 10am–4pm; Closed 29 Mar, 25, 26 Dec

ADMISSION PRICES
Adult £3.70 Child £1.90

CONTACT
Prinknash Bird Park, Prinknash Abbey, Cranham, Gloucester
Gloucestershire GL4 8EX
Tel 01452 812727
Web www.prinknash-bird-and-deerpark.com

2 hrs

Mar–Oct

Puzzle Wood (Open Iron Mines)

Puzzle Wood contains iron workings dating back to Roman times. The paths were laid to form a very unusual maze covering 14 acres. Visitors can walk through them, playing the Indoor Puzzle Wood game, in which they are challenged to spot particular features.

LOCATION
Take the B4228 from Colford to Chepstow. Puzzle Wood is ½ mile from Coleford

OPENING
26 Mar–31 Oct open Tue–Sun & Bank holiday Mon 11am–6pm (last admission 4.30pm); Aug open 11am–9pm (last admission 8pm)

ADMISSION PRICES
Adult £3.25 Child £2.25

CONTACT
Puzzle Wood (Open Iron Mines)
Lower Perrygrove Farm
Coleford
Gloucestershire GL16 8RB
Tel 01594 833187

114

All day

All year

Robinswood Hill Country Park

Enjoy 250 acres of open countryside with way-marked nature trails and a visitor centre.

LOCATION
Take the Gloucester outer ring road, south of the city road

OPENING
All year open daily dawn–dusk

ADMISSION PRICES
Free

CONTACT
Robinswood Hill Country Park
Reservoir Road
Gloucester
Gloucestershire GL4 6SX
Tel 01452 303206
Fax 01452 304779

Sandford Parks Lido

½ day

Apr–Sep

Set in beautiful grounds, the whole family can enjoy swimming in the 50-metre heated outdoor pool.

★ Playground   ★ Children's pool

LOCATION
Off the A40, near the centre of Cheltenham

OPENING
20 Apr–29 Sep open daily 11am–7.30pm
Early morning swims available
Please phone for details

ADMISSION PRICES
Adult £2.60 Child (5–16) £1.60
Family £7.50 Concession £1.60

CONTACT
Sandford Parks Lido
Keynsham Road, Cheltenham
Gloucestershire GL53 7PU
Tel & Fax 01242 524430
Email swim@sandfordlido.freeserve.co.uk

2 hrs

All year

Soldiers of Gloucestershire Museum

The story of Gloucestershire's soldiers and their families in peacetime and war over the last 300 years is told of this award-winning museum.

★ Archive film

★ Computer games

★ Life-size displays & sound effects

LOCATION
Take the A38 & follow the brown signs to Historic Docks

OPENING
All year open daily 10am–5pm; Nov & Mar closed Mon

ADMISSION PRICES
Adult £4 Child (5–16) £2 Family £10.50 Concession £3

CONTACT
Soldiers of Gloucestershire Museum
Custom House
Gloucester Docks
Gloucestershire GL1 2HE
Tel 01452 522682
Web www.glosters.org.uk

½ day
All year

The Wildfowl & Wetlands Trust

Visit a large collection of exotic, rare and endangered ducks, geese and swans in this reserve. The Discovery Centre has hands-on displays.

★ Face-painting & badge-making

★ Special activities during school holidays

LOCATION
Between Bristol & Gloucester. Follow the signs from the M5, junctions 13 or 14

OPENING
All year open daily except 25 Dec

ADMISSION PRICES
Adult £6.30 Child £3.80
Family ticket (2+2) £5

Concession for single parents

CONTACT
WWT Slimbridge
Slimbridge
Gloucestershire GL2 7BT
Tel 01453 890333
Email slimbridge@wwt.org.uk
Web www.wwt.org.uk

Woodchester Park

½ day
All year

LOCATION
1 mile north-west of Nailsworth; 4 miles south-west of Stroud

OPENING
All year open daily 9am–5pm (last admission 1 hr before closing)

ADMISSION PRICES
Free

CONTACT
Woodchester Park
Nympsfield
Stonehouse
Gloucestershire
Tel 01453 750455
Web www.the-mansion.co.uk

Known as 'The Secret Valley', this park was formerly an eighteenth-century park with five lakes, now virtually covered in forestry plantation. It contains the remains of a Victorian mansion. There are waymarked walks and trails through the woods.

All day

All year

Animal Farm Adventure Park

Children can pet and feed many of the friendly animals at this farm. There is a playbarn with big indoor slides, a large play park and several delightful walks.

★ Phone for details of special events

LOCATION
10 mins from junction 22 on the M5. Head for Berrow & follow the signs

OPENING
In summer open daily 10am–5.30pm; In winter open daily 10am–4.30pm

ADMISSION PRICES
Adult £4.70 Child £4.70 Family £18
Senior £4.20

CONTACT
Animal Farm Adventure Park
Red Roan
Berrow
Somerset TA8 2RW
Tel 01278 751628
Email mike at AFAP.FSNET.co.uk
Web www.animal-farm.co.uk

116

2 hrs

All year

Aquarium Weston-super-Mare

Walk through the underwater tunnel to view hundreds of fascinating fish, including sharks and rays, at close quarters, in 20 naturally themed marine habitats.

★ Soft play area   ★ Finzone adventure trail

LOCATION
Take junctions 21 or 22 off the M5 into Weston-Super-Mare. Follow the brown tourist signs

OPENING
Sep–Oct open daily; Jan open weekends only
Please phone for details

ADMISSION PRICES
Adult £4.75 Child (4–14) £3.75
Concession £3.75

CONTACT
Aquarium Weston-super-Mare
Marine Parade
Weston-super-Mare
Somerset BS23 1BE
Tel 01934 641603

Barrington Court

2 hrs+

Mar–Nov

WC

An enchanting garden laid out in a sequence of walled rooms, with a working kitchen garden. The Tudor manor house is now an antique furniture showroom.

★ Children's activities   ★ Nature trail

LOCATION
On the A378 between Taunton & Langport

OPENING
Mar & Oct–3rd Nov open Thu–Sun 11am–4.50pm; 1 Apr–30 Jun & Sep open Sat–Thu 11am–5.50pm; Jul & Aug open daily 11am–5.30pm

ADMISSION PRICES
Adult £5 Child (5–16) £2.50
Family £12.50

CONTACT
Barrington Court
Barrington Ilminster
Somerset TA19 0NQ
Tel 01460 241938
Web www.nationaltrust.org.uk

Cheddar Caves & Gorge

½ day

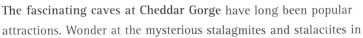

All year

LOCATION
On the B3135 with easy access from the M5 (junction 33)

OPENING
Easter–Sep open daily 10am–5pm;
Oct–Mar open daily 10.30am–4.30pm

ADMISSION PRICES
Caves & Gorge: Adult £8.90 Child £5.90

CONTACT
Cheddar Caves & Gorge
Cheddar
Somerset BS27 3QF
Tel 01934 742343
Email caves@visitcheddar.co.uk
Web www.cheddarcaves.co.uk

The fascinating caves at Cheddar Gorge have long been popular attractions. Wonder at the mysterious stalagmites and stalactites in Gough's Cave and enjoy the Crystal Quest Challenge in the underground fantasy adventure game.

★ Open-top scenic bus tours in summer

★ Heritage centre

★ Guided tours for individuals

★ Cliff-top walk

Dunster Castle

2 hrs+

All year

LOCATION
Dunster, 3 miles south-east of Minehead

OPENING
Castle: 23 Mar–3 Nov open Sun–Wed
Garden & Park: Open all year daily except 25, 26 Dec
Please phone for opening times

ADMISSION PRICES
Castle & Grounds: Adult £6.20 Child (5–15) £3.10 Family £15.50
Grounds & Park: Adult £3 Child £1.50 Family £7.50

CONTACT
Dunster Castle
Dunster
Minehead
Somerset TA24 6SL
Tel 01643 821314
Email dunstercastle@ntrust.org.uk

The fortified home of the Luttrels for 600 years, this castle is set in beautiful parkland and has a terraced garden of rare shrubs.

★ Children's guidebook

★ Activity trails & activity days

Varies

All year

The East Somerset Railway

Take a steam-engine trip through the beautiful Somerset countryside on the line known locally as the Strawberry Line. The station complex has a collection of steam-engines and a model train shop.

★ Special events (please phone for details)

LOCATION
On the A361 between Frome & Shepton Mallet

OPENING
All year open daily
Please phone for details

ADMISSION PRICES
Site only: Adult £2 Child (3–16) £1
Concession £1.50
Site & train ride: Adult £5.75 Child £3.75
Family £16 Concession £4.75

CONTACT
The East Somerset Railway
Cranmore Station
Cranmore
Shepton Mallet
Somerset BA4 4QP
Tel 01749 880417
Web www.soft.net.uk/carver

118

½ day

All year

Ferne Animal Sanctuary

Quality Assured Visitor Attraction
English Tourism Council

Take your time to stroll around the 51 acres of tranquil surroundings for 300 unwanted and retired animals, ranging from horses to chipmunks.

LOCATION
3 miles west of Chard in Somerset, signposted from the A30

OPENING
All year open daily 10am–5pm; Closed 25 Dec & 1 Jan

ADMISSION PRICES
Free; donations welcomed

CONTACT
Ferne Animal Sanctuary
Warnbrook
Chard
Somerset TA20 3DH
Tel 01460 65214
Email info@ferneanimalsanctuary.org
Web www.ferneanimalsanctuary.org

Fleet Air Arm Museum

4 hrs

WC ⊞ ⊪ 🔒

All year

LOCATION
On the B3151, just off the A303 near
Ilchester, 5 miles north of Yeovil

OPENING
Apr–Oct open daily 10am–5.30pm; Nov–Mar
open daily 10am–4.30pm; Closed 24, 25 &
26 Dec

ADMISSION PRICES
Please phone for details

CONTACT
Fleet Air Arm Museum
RNAS Yeovilton
Ilchester
Yeovil
Somerset BA22 8HT
Tel 01935 842614
Email info@fleetairarm.com
Web www.fleetairarm.com

You can see historic aircraft and hundreds of rare documents, medals and uniforms at this fascinating museum. Situated next to an operational military airfield, aircraft flying from the Royal Naval Air Station Yeovilton can be viewed from the airfield viewing galleries.

★ Interactive touch screen displays
★ Tour of an aircraft carrier's nerve centre

Glastonbury Abbey

½ day

WC ⊞ ⊪ 🔒

All year

Quality Assured Visitor Attraction

English Tourism Council

LOCATION
Take junction 23 off the M5, the A39 or
A303 to Ilchester, then the B3151. Or take
the A37/A39 from Bristol or Bath

OPENING
Jun–Aug open 9am–6pm; Dec–Feb open
10am–6pm; Mar, Apr, Sep, Oct & Nov open
daily 9.30am–6pm; Closed 25 Dec

ADMISSION PRICES
Adult £3.50 Child (5–15) £1.50
Family £8 Concession £3

CONTACT
Glastonbury Abbey
Abbey Gatehouse
Magdalene Street
Glastonbury
Somerset BA6 9EL
Tel 01458 832267
Web www.glastonburyabbey.com

Steeped in history and legend, this ancient abbey, though now ruined, is still a Christian sanctuary and an oasis of peace and quiet. Set in parkland with ponds and a wildlife centre, the whole family can relax in its tranquil surroundings. Its award-winning museum has a special children's display.

All day

All year

Hamdon Hill Country Park

Enjoy the large wildflower meadows, a deserted medieval village, native woodlands, Iron Age ramparts and superb views of the Somerset Levels, Exmoor and the Mendip Hills at this beautiful country park.

★ Ranger service &

free guidebooks

LOCATION
West of Yeovil off the A303

OPENING
All year

ADMISSION PRICES
Free

CONTACT
Hamdon Hill Country Park
The Rangers Office
Stoke sub Hamdon
Yeovil
Somerset TA14 6RW
Tel 01935 823616
Email katy.menday@southsomerset.gov.uk
Web www.southsomerset.gov.uk

120

2 hrs

All year

The Helicopter Museum

Somerset County Museum

2–3 hrs

All year

Over 60 helicopters dating from 1931 to the present day are displayed here in authentic hangar surroundings.

★ Open cockpit days (please phone for details)

★ Guided tours for groups of 12 or more

LOCATION
Off junction 21 of the M5 in Weston-super-Mare in Somerset

OPENING
All year open Wed–Sun & Bank holidays, Easter & summer holidays; Apr–Oct open daily 10am–6pm; Nov–Mar open daily 10am–4pm

ADMISSION PRICES
Adult £3.95 Child (5–16) £2.75
Under-5s Free Family (2+2) £11

CONTACT
The Helicopter Museum
The Heliport, Locking Moor Road, Weston-super-Mare Somerset BS24 8PP
Tel 01931 635227

An interesting museum housed in Taunton Castle, it has costumes, silver and a sixteenth-century almshouse on display. Recent additions include the shipwreck coin hoard – the largest hoard of Roman silver coins found in Britain.

LOCATION
Reached via the A38, M5

OPENING
3 Mar–4 Nov open Tue–Sat 10am–5pm; 4 Nov–Easter open Tue–Sat 10am–3pm; Closed 29 Mar, 25, 26 Dec & 1 Jan

ADMISSION PRICES
Adult £2.50 Child £1
Concession £1

CONTACT
Somerset County Museum
Taunton Castle, Castle Green Taunton, Somerset TA1 4AA
Tel 01823 320201
Web www.somerset.gov.uk

Viaduct Fishery

3 hrs+
All year

Set in the beautiful Cary Valley, this fishery offers six coarse lakes spread out over a peaceful 25-acre site. Tuition is available for beginners.

★ Limited disabled access
★ Tackle shop

LOCATION
On the northern outskirts of Somerton

OPENING
All year open dawn–dusk

ADMISSION PRICES
Adult £5 Child £4 Concession £4

CONTACT
Viaduct Fishery
Cary Valley
Somerton
Somerset TA11 6LJ
Tel 01458 274022

Weston-super-Mare Heritage Centre

1 hr
All year

The heritage centre is an exhibition of what is was really like to be rich or poor in a Victorian town, and highlights the main features that can still be visited today. A working model gives children a good idea of all the fun of the Edwardian seaside.

LOCATION
Turn onto the A370 from the M5. Follow the signs to seafront north and turn right at traffic lights at the High Street

OPENING
All year open Mon–Sun 10am–5pm; Closed Bank holidays

ADMISSION PRICES
Please phone for details

CONTACT
Weston-super-Mare Heritage Centre
3–6 Wadham Street
Weston-super-Mare
Somerset BS23 1JY
Tel 01934 412144

West Somerset Railway

Varies
Feb–Sep

This preserved steam railway operates between Minehead and Bishop's Lydeard, near Taunton. It is the longest independent railway in Britain.

★ Visitor centre & model railway
★ Great Western Railway Museum
★ Somerset & Dorset Railway Museum
★ Diesel & Electric Group depot

LOCATION
Reached via the A39, A358

OPENING
Please phone for details

ADMISSION PRICES
Adult £9.80 Child £4.90
Family £26

CONTACT
West Somerset Railway
The Railway Station, Minehead
Somerset TA24 5BG
Tel 01643 704996
Email info@west-somerset-railway.co.uk
Web www.west-somerset-railway.co.uk

West Somerset Rural Life Museum

2 hrs+
May–Oct

Visit the schools of the past in this museum, housed in an old school building, with a thatched roof and riverside garden. Children can dress up in Victorian clothes, write on slates and play with traditional toys.

LOCATION
On the A39 from Minehead

OPENING
Easter & 6 May–25 Oct
Please phone for details

ADMISSION PRICES
Adult £1.50 Child (5–14) 50p
Senior £1.20

CONTACT
West Somerset Rural Life Museum
The Old School
Allerford
Minehead
Somerset TA24 8HN
Tel 01643 862529
Web www.allerfordwebsite.ic24.net

1 hr+

All year

Wookey Hole Caves & Papermill

It is said that the infamous Witch of Wookey lived in these spectacular caves. Guided tours of the caves are amazing. Visitors can also watch demonstrations of traditional paper-making at a 400-year-old papermill and there are numerous activities for children.

★ Magical Mirror Maze

★ Old Penny Arcade

★ Paper-making workshop

★ Paper shop

★ Museum

LOCATION
Accessible by the A39, M4 & M5. Leave the M5 at junction 22 & follow the brown tourist signs on the A371

OPENING
Apr–Oct open 10am–5pm; Nov–Mar open 10.30am–4.50pm; Closed 17–26 Dec

ADMISSION PRICES
Adult £8 Child £5

CONTACT
Wookey Hole Caves & Papermill
Wookey Hole
Wells
Somerset BA5 1BB
Tel 01749 672243
Email witch@wookey.co.uk
Web www.wookey.co.uk

122

½ day

All year

Animalarium

The Animalarium is a collection of small exotic and domestic animals, many of which have come from pet rescue centres. There are many activities for children including pony rides in summer, the chance to touch snakes and the opportunity to watch crocodiles and piranhas being fed.

★ Pony rides

★ Animal feeding

★ Petting barn

★ Ball pool

★ Playground

★ Close to a quiet beach

LOCATION
At Borth, between Aberystwyth & Machynlleth

OPENING
All year open daily; In summer open 10am–6pm; In winter open 11am–4pm

ADMISSION PRICES
Adult £4.20 Child £2.40 Family (2+3) £12
Senior £3.50

CONTACT
Animalarium
Borth
Ceredigion SY25 6RA
Tel 01970 871224

Brecon Beacons National Park

2 hrs+

All year

LOCATION
Midway between Brecon & Swansea on the A4067

OPENING
Please phone for details

ADMISSION PRICES
Free
Pay & display car parking

CONTACT
Brecon Beacons National Park
Tel/Fax 01639 730395
Email
cyncp@breconbeacons.org
Web www.breconbeacons.org/cyncp

Tall trees and rushing rivers make this a delightful country park and a great place to explore, have a picnic or enjoy the peace and quiet.

Caldicot Castle

2 hrs

Mar–Oct

LOCATION
From the M4 take junction 23 & the B4245. From the M48 take junction 2, the A48 & B4245. The castle is signposted from the B4245

OPENING
Mar–Oct open daily 1am–5pm

ADMISSION PRICES
Adult £3 Child (5–17) £1.50
Family (2+3) £8.50

CONTACT
Caldicot Castle
Church Road
Monmouthshire NP26 4HU
Tel 01291 420241
Web www.caldicotcastle.co.uk

A fine medieval castle set in 55 acres of beautiful parkland with plenty on offer for children. The children's activity station includes puzzles and games, tree and leaf identification and the chance to make a castle to take home.

3 hrs

All year

Cardiff Castle

Discover 2,000 years of history in the heart of the city. View the Roman wall, climb the Norman keep and take a guided tour of the fairy-tale apartments, created in the nineteenth century for the 3rd Marquess of Bute.

★ Guided tours

★ Fairy-tale interiors featuring many carved & painted animals throughout

LOCATION
From the M4 or A470 follow the signs to Cardiff City Centre. Use the city centre car parks

OPENING
Mar–Oct open 9.30am–6pm (last admission 5pm); Nov–Feb open 9.30am–5pm (last admission 3.30pm); Closed 25, 26 Dec & 1 Jan

ADMISSION PRICES
Adult £5.50 Child & Senior £3.30
Family £15.50

CONTACT
Cardiff Castle
Castle Street
Cardiff CF10 3RB
Tel 029 20878100
Email cardiffcastle@cardiff.gov.uk
Web www.cardiffcastle.com

124

1 hr

Mar–Oct

Cardigan Heritage Centre

The heritage centre tells the story of Cardigan from Norman times to the present day. A child-friendly centre, it has arts activities for younger children and small quizzes for older children.

★ Special summer interactive exhibitions

★ Guided tours by appointment

LOCATION
On the bank of the river Teifi, next to Cardigan bridge

OPENING
Mid Mar–end Oct open daily from 10am–5pm

ADMISSION PRICES
Adult £2 Child £1 Family £5
Concession £1.50

CONTACT
Cardigan Heritage Centre
Teifi Wharf
Cardigan
Wales
Tel 01239 613416

Carew Castle

½ day

WC Apr–Oct

LOCATION
5 miles east of Pembroke, just off the A477

OPENING
Apr–Oct open daily 10am–5pm

ADMISSION PRICES
Adult £2.80 Family £7.50 Concession £1.90

CONTACT
Carew Castle & Tidal Mill
Carew
Nr Tenby
Pembrokeshire SA70 8SL
Tel 01646 651782
Email enquiries@carewcastle.com
Web www.carewcastle.com

A **magnificent Norman castle** and later an Elizabethan residence with links to the Tudors, it was the setting for the Great Tournament in 1507. It has the only restored tidal mill in Wales with original machinery.

★ Educational programmes for key stages 1 & 2
★ Holiday activities for young people
★ Daily guided tours

Colby Woodland Garden

2 hrs+

Mar–Oct

LOCATION
Off the A477 Tenby–Carmarthen road or off the coast road at Amroth Castle

OPENING
23 Mar–3 Nov open daily 10am–5pm

ADMISSION PRICES
Adult £2.80 Child £1.40 Family £7

CONTACT
Colby Woodland Garden
Amroth
Narberth
Pembrokeshire SA67 8PP
Tel 01834 811885
Fax 01834 831766

This pretty woodland garden has many pleasant meadow and woodland walks through secluded valleys and along open and wooded pathways.

★ Braille guide
★ Children's quiz & safari packs

SOUTH-WEST

3 hrs

Mar–Nov

Dinefwr

An eighteenth-century park with a medieval deer park in which children can marvel at fallow deer and Dinefwr White Park Cattle.

★ Children's quizzes & events

★ Boardwalk through Bog Wood to Mill Pond Dam (suitable for wheelchair users)

LOCATION
On the outskirts of Llandeilo

OPENING
23 Mar–3 Nov open Thu–Mon 11am–5pm

ADMISSION PRICES
House & Park Adult £3.30 Child £1.60
Family 38

CONTACT
Dinefwr
Llandeilo SA19 6RT
Tel 01558 825912
Fax 01558 822036

126

1 hr

Mar–Sep

Dolaucothi Gold Mines

Begun by the Romans, this mine was worked again in the nineteenth and twentieth centuries. Visitors are taken on fascinating guided tours of the Roman and more recent underground workings (the latter are not open to under-5s).

★ Gold panning

★ Waymarked walks

★ Cycle hire

★ Activity room

★ Events

LOCATION
On the A482 between Lampeter & Llanwrda

OPENING
22 Mar–22 Sep open daily 10am–5pm

ADMISSION PRICES
Combines site & underground tour: Adult
£6.50 Child £3.20 Family £16
Reduced rates for National Trust members

CONTACT
Dolaucothi Gold Mines
Pumsaint
Llanwrda SA19 8RR
Tel 01558 650177
Infoline 01558 825146

Felinwynt Rain Forest & Butterfly Centre

1–2 hrs

Easter–Oct

LOCATION
6 miles north of Cardigan. Follow the brown tourist signs

OPENING
Easter–Oct open daily 10.30am–5pm; Nov, Dec & March limited opening from 11.30am–4.30pm

ADMISSION PRICES
Adult £3.75 Child 50p Senior £3.50

CONTACT
Felinwynt Rain Forest & Butterfly Centre
Felinwynt, Cardigan SA43 1RT
Tel 01239 810882
www.butterflycentre.co.uk

This fascinating experience offers a glimpse into the rain forest with tropical butterflies and exotic plants, waterfalls and stream. A personal guide can make the experience unique.

★ Art activities for children
★ Video room

127

Heatherton Country Sports Park

½ day

All year

LOCATION
2 miles outside Tenby on the B4318 Tenby–Pembroke road

OPENING
Jun–Sep open 10am–10pm; Oct–May open 10am–6pm; Closed 25, 26 Dec & 1 Jan

ADMISSION PRICES
Charge for each activity

CONTACT
Heatherton Country Sports Park
St Florence
Tenby
Pembrokeshire SA69 9EE
Tel 01646 651025
Web www.heatherton.co.uk

Heatherton is set in the beautiful West Wales countryside and hosts a range of activities for all the family including golf, karting and paintball. All equipment is provided.

★ Maize Maze & Puzzle Zone (Jun–Sep only)

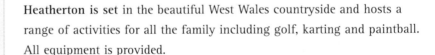

2 hrs

Apr-Oct

King Arthur's Labyrinth

Take an underground boat ride and walk in spectacular caves deep under the mountain, where Welsh tales of King Arthur unfold with magical sound and light effects.

LOCATION
At the Corris Craft Centre. On the A487, 6 miles north of Machynlleth & 10 miles south of Dolgellan, mid-Wales

OPENING
Apr-Oct open daily 10am-5pm

ADMISSION PRICES
Adult £4.85 Child £3.40 Senior £4.30

CONTACT
King Arthur's Labyrinth
Corris
Machynlleth SY20 9RF
Tel 01654 761584
Email
king.arthurs.labyrinth@corris-wales.co.uk

128

5 hrs

Easter–
Oct

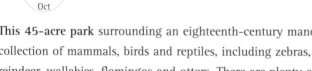

Manor House Wild Animal Park

This 45-acre park surrounding an eighteenth-century manor houses a fine collection of mammals, birds and reptiles, including zebras, camels, reindeer, wallabies, flamingos and otters. There are plenty of activities for children of all ages ranging from feeding penguins to go-karting.

★ Model railway exhibition

★ Natural history museum

★ Snake experience

★ Owl & iguana handling

★ Falconry displays

★ Penguin feeding

_i_

LOCATION
3 miles outside Tenby on the B4318

OPENING
Easter–end of Sep open 10am-6pm

ADMISSION PRICES
Adult £4.50 Child £3.50 Family £14.50
Senior £4 Party rates available for 20 paying people or more

CONTACT
Manor House Wild Animal Park
St Florence
Tenby
Pembrokeshire SA70 8RJ
Tel 01646 651201
Email
mail@manorhousewildanimalparkfreeserve.co.uk
Web www.safaripark.co.uk

Oakwood Coaster Country

All day

Apr–Sep

LOCATION
Follow the M4 until junction 29. Take the A48 to Carmarthen. Oakwood is clearly signposted from Carmarthen

OPENING
12 Apr–28 Sep; Please phone for details

ADMISSION PRICES
Adult £12.95 Child (3-9) £11.95 Family £46.80 Senior & disabled £8.70

CONTACT
Oakwood Coaster Country
Canaston Bridge
Narbeth
Pembrokeshire SA67 8DE
Tel 0870 1226951
Email parkenquiries@oakwood-leisure.com
Web www.oakwood-leisure.com

Enjoy the award-winning rides at Wales' largest theme park. There are thrills and spills for adults and teenagers and many small rides and attractions for young children.

★ Kidzworld for younger children with carousel, mini-ferris wheel, pirate ship, clown coaster & more

★ Megafobia roller coaster & Hydro (water coaster) for older children & adults

129

Rhondda Heritage Park

½ day

All year

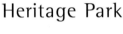

With an ex-miner as a guide, visitors are taken down in 'the cage' to the pit bottom and, after a tour of the mine, take a thrilling ride back to the surface.

★ Energy Zone outdoor adventure playground

★ Children's art sessions

LOCATION
Exit junction 33 off the M4. Signposted on the A470 to the Rhondda Valley

OPENING
Easter–Oct open daily 10am–6pm (last tour at 4.30pm); Rest of year open Tue–Sun 10am–6pm

ADMISSION PRICES
Adult £5.60 Child £4.90 Family (2+2) £16.50 Senior £4.95

CONTACT
Rhondda Heritage Park
Lewis Merthyr Colliery
Coed Cae Road, Trehafod
Tel 01443 682036

Athelstan Museum

1 hr+

All year

Situated within Malmesbury town hall, this museum has local history exhibits such as costumes, an early fire engine, a collection of photographs of the town and an educational hands-on activity for children called The Mini Museum Detective.

LOCATION
5 miles from junction 17 off the M4

OPENING
1 April–30 Sep open Mon-Sat 10am–2pm; 1 Oct–31 Mar open Tue & Thu 10am–2pm & Sat 10am–12pm; Please phone for details

ADMISSION PRICES
Free

CONTACT
Athelstan Museum
Cross Hayes, Malmesbury
Wiltshire SN16 9BZ
Tel 01666 829258
Web www.northwilts.com

2 hrs+

Mar–Oct

Cholderton Rare Breeds Centre

From pig-racing to tractor rides, this farm park for rare farm animals has a wealth of things to see and do. A haven for rabbit lovers, it is home to one of Britain's largest collections of rabbit breeds.

★ Toddler's play area   ★ Pig-racing

★ Adventure playground   ★ Tractor rides (in season)

LOCATION
Reached by the A303 from Andover or the A338 from Salisbury or Marlborough

OPENING
23 Mar–31 Oct open daily 10am–6pm (last admission 4.45pm)

ADMISSION PRICES
Adult £4.25 Child (2–14) £2.75
Family £13 Concession £3.75

CONTACT
Cholderton Rare Breeds Farm Park, Amesbury Road Cholderton, Salisbury Wiltshire SP4 0EW
Tel 01980 629438

Farmer Giles Farmstead

3 hrs

All year

Children will love getting to know the farmyard animals, watching cows being milked and having a go at bottle-feeding lambs at this working dairy farm.

★ Adventure playground   ★ Scenic walk

LOCATION
Off the A303 London–Exeter road at Teffont, 11 miles west of Salisbury

OPENING
1 Jan–20 Mar & 10 Nov–31 Dec open Sat & Sun 10.30am–dusk; 21 Mar–8 Nov open daily 10am–6pm; Closed 25 Dec

ADMISSION PRICES
Adult £3.95 Child (2–16) £2.85
Concession £3.50

CONTACT
Farmer Giles Farmstead Teffont, Salisbury Wiltshire SP3 5QY
Tel 01722 716338
Web www.farmergiles.co.uk

130

All day

Apr–Nov

Longleat

Family Attraction of the Year 2002
Good Britain Guide

From safari to stately home and from miniature trains to mazes and boat rides, there is always something to discover round every corner. Visitors can enjoy close encounters with some the world's most exotic animals.

★ Safari boats

★ World's longest hedge maze

★ Adventure castle & Blue Peter maze

★ King Arthur's Mirror Maze

★ Butterfly garden

★ Pets corner

★ Longleat railway

★ Ugh! Show (5 Jul–7 Sep 2003 only)

LOCATION
Off the A36 between Bath & Salisbury

OPENING
All attractions open 5 Apr–2 Nov; In summer Longleat House & Safari Park open 10am–5.30pm; Other attractions open 11am–5.30pm
Please phone for winter details

ADMISSION PRICES
Adult £15 Child (4–14) £12 Senior £12

CONTACT
Longleat
Warminster
Wiltshire BA12 7NW
Tel 01985 844400
Email enquiries@longleat.co.uk
Web www.longleat.co.uk

Oasis Leisure Centre

2 hrs+

All year

LOCATION
Follow the brown tourist signs on all major roads to Swindon

OPENING
Please phone for details

ADMISSION PRICES
Please phone for details

CONTACT
Oasis Leisure Centre
North Star Avenue
Swindon SN2 1EP
Tel 01793 445401
Fax 01793 465132

This leisure centre has activities for all age groups including an under-5s play area, giant water slides and lagoon pool wave machine.

★ Outdoor multi-play pitches
★ Soft play centre

131

UK Commendation
Museum of the Year Award 2002

STEAM – Museum of the Great Western Railway

3 hrs

All year

LOCATION
Take junction 14 off the M4 & follow the brown tourist signs to 'Outlet Centre'

OPENING
In summer open Mon–Sat 10am–5.30pm & Sun 11am–5.30pm; In winter open Mon–Sat 10am–5pm Mon–Sat & Sun 11am–5pm; Closed 25, 26 Dec & 1 Jan

ADMISSION PRICES
Adult £5.95 Child £3.90 Senior £3.90

CONTACT
STEAM
Kemble Drive
Swindon
Wiltshire SN2 2TA
Tel 01793 466646
Web www.steam-museum.org.uk

STEAM tells the story of workers of the Great Western Railway. Housed in beautiful railway buildings, this award-winning museum has hands-on exhibits and famous locomotives and is a great day out for all the family.

★ Day out with Thomas
the Tank Engine
★ Seasonal events
throughout the year

Central

This area covers a range of counties in the centre of England. It includes Lincolnshire and Derbyshire to the north; East Anglia to the east; Shropshire and Herefordshire to the west; Worcestershire, Warwickshire and Northamptonshire to the south and the conurbation around Birmingham and Coventry known as the West Midlands.

In such a diverse area there are many different family attractions. At the Donington Grand Prix Collection in Derbyshire, you can take a lap around the largest grand prix circuit in the world. In the same county, a totally different experience can be found at Gulliver's Kingdom, a theme park designed for the younger family. In Herefordshire, there are the distinctive historic buildings of Belmont Abbey and Berrington Hall, the latter with a children's play area and quizzes. In Leicestershire, you can visit the National Space Centre and in Lincolnshire, the fabulous Butterfly and Wildlife Park, where you can see wallabies, llamas, snakes and crocodiles to name but a few. Norfolk offers a lovely boat trip on the River Ant and in Suffolk, visit the West Stow Anglo-Saxon Village, which regularly hosts costume events. In Wickstead Park in Northamptonshire you can choose from over 30 attractions including a scary roller coaster. Staffordshire's most famous attraction is Alton Towers Theme Park, with over 200 acres of landscaped gardens, rides and entertainments, while Warwickshire boasts the leading primate zoo in the country, Twycross Zoo.

N

NORTH-EAST

NORTH-WEST

Derbyshire
pp139–143

Lincolnshire
pp149–155

Nottinghamshire
pp170–175

Staffordshire
pp179–182

Rutland
pp176–177

Leicestershire
pp145–149

Norfolk
pp155–167

Shropshire
pp177–178

West Midlands
pp190–192

Cambridgeshire
pp138–139

Worcestershire
pp192–193

Northamptonshire
pp168–169

Suffolk
pp182–187

Warwickshire
pp188–189

Herefordshire
pp144–145

SOUTH-WEST

SOUTH-EAST

Below is a list of places to visit in the central region, organised by county and type.

Cambridgeshire

ANIMAL ATTRACTIONS
Raptor Foundation 139

PARKS, GARDENS & NATURE TRAILS
Brampton Wood 138
Grafham Water 138

Derbyshire

HISTORIC BUILDINGS
Bolsover Castle 140
Hardwick Old Hall 142
Peveril Castle 143
Wingfield Manor 143

MUSEUMS & EXHIBITIONS
Derby Industrial Museum 140

SPORT & LEISURE
Donington Grand Prix Collection 141

ANIMAL ATTRACTIONS
Chestnut Centre Otter Haven & Owl Sanctuary 140
Freshfields 141

Matlock Bath Aquarium & Hologram Gallery 143

THEME PARKS & ADVENTURE PLAYGROUNDS
The American Adventure 139
Gulliver's Kingdom 142

Herefordshire

HISTORIC BUILDINGS
Belmont Abbey 144
Berrington Hall 144
Eastnor Castle 144

ANIMAL ATTRACTIONS
Shortwood Family Farm 145

THEME PARKS & ADVENTURE PLAYGROUNDS
Splendours of the Orient 145

ARTS & CRAFTS
Ledbury Ceramics 144

Leicestershire

HISTORIC BUILDINGS
Ashby de la Zouch Castle 145
Belvoir Castle 146
Kirby Muxloe Castle 147

MUSEUMS & EXHIBITIONS
Charnwood Museum 146
Foxton Canal Museum 147
The Leicester Gas Museum 148
Leicester Royal Infirmary: History Museum 148
The National Space Centre 148
Snibston Discovery Park 148

ANIMAL ATTRACTIONS
Tumbledown Farm 149

Lincolnshire

HISTORIC BUILDINGS
Lincoln Medieval Bishop's Palace 151
Sibsey Trader Windmill 155
Tattershall Castle 155

MUSEUMS & EXHIBITIONS
Lincolnshire Aviation Heritage Centre 151
Museum of Lincolnshire Life 152
North Lincolnshire Museum 154

SPORT & LEISURE
Lakeside Leisure Ltd 151

ANIMAL ATTRACTIONS
Baytree Garden Centre (Owl Centre) 149
The Butterfly & Wildlife Park 150
Hardy's Animal Farm 150
Natureland Seal Sanctuary 153
Northcote Heavy Horses 153
The Seal Sanctuary 154

THEME PARKS & ADVENTURE PLAYGROUNDS
Butlins 149
Fun Farm 150
Magical World of Fantasy Island 152
Panda's Palace 154

ARTS & CRAFTS
Lincolnshire's Lifelong Adventure 152

Norfolk

Northamptonshire

Nottinghamshire

Rutland

Brampton Wood

2 hrs+

Varies

 WC

Brampton Wood supports a wide variety of plants and animals. It is particularly well known for butterflies. The woodland itself consists primarily of ash and field maple with hazel coppice. There are also many other trees and shrubs to enjoy on your walk.

LOCATION
On the north side of the road between Grafham & Brampton, about 1 mile west of the A1, & 2 miles east of Grafham village

OPENING
Please phone for details

ADMISSION PRICES
Free

CONTACT
Brampton Wood
Brampton, Huntingdon
Cambridgeshire
Tel 01480 810844
Email cambswt@cix.co.uk
Web www.wildlifetrust.org.uk/bcnp

138

Grafham Water

3 hrs

All year

WC

This water park has extensive views, sailing, trout fishing, a nature reserve, trails and walks, play areas, and a visitor centre.

★ Cycle hire
★ Bird feeding station
★ Dragonfly pond
★ Wildlife garden
★ Wildlife cabin in Mander car park for information

LOCATION
On the A1 or A14, 2 miles off the A1 (Buckden roundabout). Near the A1–M1 link

OPENING
5 Jan–24 Mar open Sat & Sun 11am–4pm; 25 Mar–1 Nov open Mon–Fri 11am–4pm, Sat & Sun 11am–4pm; Bank holidays open 11am–5pm; 2 Nov–15 Dec Sat & Sun 11am–4pm

ADMISSION PRICES
Oct–Mar: Car park £1
Apr–Sep: Car park £2

CONTACT
Grafham Water
Visitor Centre, Marlow Park
Grafham, Huntingdon
Cambridgeshire PE28 0BH
Tel 01480 812154
Web www.wildlifetrust.org.uk

The Raptor Foundation

3–4 hrs

All year

LOCATION
Off the A14 St Ives exit.
Turn onto the B1040 to Somersham
& follow the brown tourist signs

OPENING
In summer open daily 10.30am–5pm; In
winter open daily 10.30am–4pm; Closed
Christmas & New Year

ADMISSION PRICES
Adult £3 Child £1.75
Under-5s Free Senior £2

CONTACT
The Raptor Foundation
The Heath, St. Ives Road
Woodhurst
Cambridgeshire PE28 3BT
Tel 01487 741140
Email heleowl@aol.com
Web www.raptorfoundation.org.uk

Home to over 30 raptors and more than 25 species, the Raptor Foundation is a unique and exciting place for children and adults alike. Pay a visit to meet and learn about owls, falcons, hawks and buzzards.

★ Adopt a raptor
★ Flying displays
★ Guided tours
★ Quizzes for children

139

The American Adventure

Quality Assured Visitor Attraction
English Tourism Council

All day

Mar–Nov

LOCATION
Take junction 26 off the M1 & follow sign-posts along the A610 to the A608 & then
the A6007

OPENING
23 Mar–3 Nov open daily 10am onwards

ADMISSION PRICES
Adult £13.99 Child £10.99 Family £42.50
Concession £3.50

CONTACT
The American Adventure
Ilkeston
Derbyshire DE7 5SX
Tel 0845 3302929
Email sales@americanadventure.co.uk
Web www.americanadventure.co.uk

Visit The American Adventure and discover the epic story of the USA, from the Western Pioneers to the Pioneers of Space. With over 100 attractions, live shows and rides, The American Adventure is an enjoyable family day out for everyone.

1–1½ hrs

All year

Bolsover Castle

Bolsover is an enchanting early seventeenth-century castle, set on a hill with restored Venus Gardens, a magnificent indoor riding house and outstanding craftmanship on view everywhere. Visit the Discovery Centre, enjoy the interactive scale model of a castle and take the audio tour.

★ Activity sheets available
★ Medieval Knights events
★ King Arthur events
★ Ghost tours
★ Free audio tour

LOCATION
Just off the M1 at junctions 29 or 30, 6 miles from Mansfield. Once in Bolsover the castle is 6 miles east of Chesterfield on the A632

OPENING
1 Apr–30 Sep open daily 10am–6pm; Oct open daily 10am–5pm; 1 Nov–31 Mar open daily Thu–Mon 10am–4pm; Closed 24–26 Dec & 1 Jan

ADMISSION PRICES
Adult £6.20 Child £3 Family £15 Concession £4.60

CONTACT
Bolsover Castle
Castle Street
Bolsover
Derbyshire S44 GPR
Tel 01246 822844
Web www.english-heritage.org.uk

2 hrs+

All year

Chestnut Centre Otter Haven & Owl Sanctuary

Enjoy watching captive-bred otters and owls in their natural surroundings. Set in an extensive nature trail of 1¼ miles, there are 50 acres of grounds. The sanctuary is a member of the Federation of Zoological Gardens of Great Britain.

LOCATION
Off the A625. Follow the brown tourist signs

OPENING
Jan open Sat & Sun 10.30am–dusk; Feb–Dec open daily 10.30am–5.30pm

ADMISSION PRICES
Adult £5.50 Child £3.50 Family £16

CONTACT
Chestnut Centre Otter Haven & Owl Sanctuary, Castleton Road Chapel-en-le-Frith, High Peak Derbyshire SK23 0QS
Tel 01298 814099

Derby Industrial Museum

2 hrs+

All year

Displays at this museum form an introduction to the history of Derby's industries. They include a major collection of Rolls Royce aero engines, a railway engineering gallery, a railway research gallery and a Power for Industry gallery.

LOCATION
Off the A6, near Derby Cathedral

OPENING
All year open Mon 11am–5pm, Tue–Sat 10am–5pm, Sun & Bank holidays 2pm–5pm Please phone for details of Christmas opening

ADMISSION PRICES
Free

CONTACT
Derby Industrial Museum
Silk Mill Lane, off Full Street
Derby DE1 3AR
Tel 01332 255308
Web www.derby.gov.uk/museums

Donington Grand Prix Collection

1½ hrs

All year

LOCATION
2 miles from M1 junction 23a/24 & M42/A42, close to Nottingham, Derby & Leicester

OPENING
All year open daily 10am–5pm (last admission 4pm)
Please phone for details of Christmas opening

ADMISSION PRICES
Adult £7 Child £2.50 Family £14
Senior & Student £5

CONTACT
Donington Grand Prix Collection
Donington Park
Castle Donington
Derby DE74 2RP
Tel 01332 811027
Email enquiries@donington

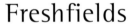

Take a lap around the largest Grand Prix grid in the world, and prepare to be amazed as the exciting history of motorsport unfolds before you. Donington Park has the largest collection of McLaren racing cars on public display, along with numerous other unique racing cars.

- ★ Memorials to Senna & Fangio
- ★ Rare four-wheel-drive racing cars
- ★ BRM display
- ★ Ferraris
- ★ Lotus
- ★ Tyrells
- ★ Maserati
- ★ Alfa Romeo
- ★ Williams F1 cars from 1983–1999
- ★ Children's activity packs available
- ★ Guided tours available for pre-bookings

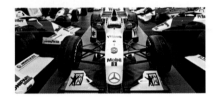

Freshfields

3 hrs+

All year

LOCATION
From the village of Peak Forest, take the road to Wormhill & Smalldale, then take the 5th entrance on the right. Watch out for a small sign & a long drive

OPENING
All year open Mon–Fri 10am–4.30pm, Sat & Sun 10am–5.30pm

ADMISSION PRICES
Free

CONTACT
Michael Elliott Trust
Freshfields
Peak Forest
Buxton
Derbyshire SK17 8EE
Tel 01298 79775

Freshfields is a therapeutic centre for children with special needs. It is home to a herd of rescue donkeys. Enjoy the remarkable experience of spending time in the meadows with over 60 rescue animals.

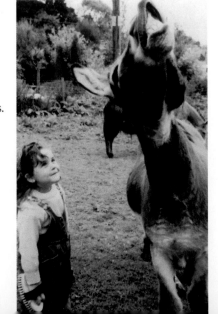

All day

Apr–Sep

Gulliver's Kingdom

The park is designed for the younger family, where the adults can have as much fun as the children. It is set on a wooded hillside and includes over 40 attractions ranging from a log flume, roller coaster and chairlift to the Royal Mine Ride and family shows.

★ Outdoor fantasy eating

LOCATION
Off the A6 between Matlock & Cromford

OPENING
Open Apr–Sep
Please phone for details

ADMISSION PRICES
Adult £6.80 Child £6.80
Children under 3ft tall Free
Senior £5.80
Special rates available for late admissions

CONTACT
Gulliver's Kingdom
Temple Walk
Matlock Bath
Matlock
Derbyshire DE4 3PG
Tel 01629 580540
Web www.gulliversfun.co.uk

1 hr

Apr–Oct

Hardwick Old Hall

This large ruined house was completed in 1591 and was constructed with huge windows and interesting plasterwork. There are spectacular views from the top floor over the country park and New Hall.

★ Free audio tour of the Bess of Hardwick story

LOCATION
9½ miles south-east of Chesterfield, off the A6175 from junction 29 off the M1

OPENING
1 Apr–31 Oct open Mon, Wed, Thu, Sat & Sun 11am–6pm (5pm in Oct)

ADMISSION PRICES
Adult £3 Child £1.50 Family £7.50
Concession £2.30

CONTACT
Hardwick Old Hall
Doe Lea
Near Chesterfield
Derbyshire S44 5QJ
Tel 01246 850431
Web www.english-heritage.org.uk

Matlock Bath Aquarium & Hologram Gallery

3 hrs

All year

LOCATION
Off the A6 in Matlock Bath

OPENING
23 Mar–3 Nov open daily 10am–5.30pm
(times extended during high season);
Nov–Mar open Sat & Sun 10am–5.30pm

ADMISSION PRICES
Adult £1.80 Child £1.80
Concession £1.80

CONTACT
Matlock Bath Aquarium &
Hologram Gallery
110-114 North Parade
Matlock Bath, Matlock
Derbyshire DE4 3NS
Tel 01629 583624

This **fantastic aquarium has various aquaria** containing species of British and tropical freshwater fish. There is a large open pool which is fed by a thermal spring and illuminated at night. It contains common carp, mirror carp and koi carp.

Peveril Castle

1 hr+

All year

There are **breathtaking views of** the Peak District from Peveril Castle, perched high above the pretty village of Castleton. Come and see the famous Great Square Tower of Henry II.

★ Special events organised regularly

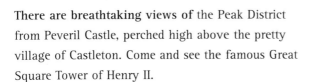

LOCATION
On the south side of Castleton,
15 miles west of Sheffield on
the A6187

OPENING
1 Apr–31 Oct open daily
10am–6pm (5pm in Oct); 1
Nov–31 Mar open Wed–Sun
10am–4pm

ADMISSION PRICES
Adult £2.40 Child £1.20
Concession £1.80

CONTACT
Peveril Castle, Market Place
Castleton, Hope Valley S33 8WQ
Tel 01433 620613
Web www.english-heritage.org.uk

Wingfield Manor

1 hr

Apr–Oct

A **huge ruined mansion**, Wingfield was built in the mid-fifteenth century. It was used as a prison for Mary Queen of Scots, and several TV shows and films have been made at this impressive location.

★ Free audio tour   ★ Orientation guide available

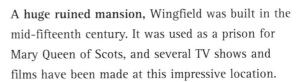

LOCATION
17 miles north of Derby, 11
miles south of Chesterfield on
the B5035 (½ mile south of
South Wingfield)

OPENING
1 Apr–31 Oct open daily
10am–6pm (5pm in Oct)

ADMISSION PRICES
Adult £3.20 Child £1.60
Concession £2.40

CONTACT
Wingfield Manor
Garner Lane, South Wingfield
Derbyshire DE5 7NH
Tel 01773 832060

Belmont Abbey

1 hr

All year

WC

This classic mid-Victorian Pugin church has a sacristy with a treasury (viewed by arrangement only) and beautiful grounds. There are fascinating talks by monks on Benedictine monastic life and its history.

LOCATION
On the A465,
Hereford–Abergavenny road

OPENING
All year open daily 8am–5pm

ADMISSION PRICES
Free

CONTACT
Belmont Abbey
Hereford HR2 9RZ
Tel 01432 277475
Email Procoffice@aol.com
Web www.belmontabbey.org.uk

Berrington Hall

½ day
Mar–Oct

WC

Berrington Hall is an eighteenth-century mansion with a Georgian dairy, a Victorian laundry, a walled garden and a children's play area. Orienteering courses are available.

★ Ugly bug safaris   ★ Quizzes organised

LOCATION
4 miles north of Leominster & 7 miles south of Ludlow, on the west of the A49

OPENING
29 Mar–29 Oct open Sat–Wed (closed Thu & Fri); Mar–Sep open Sat–Wed 12pm–4.30pm; Oct open Sat–Wed 12pm–4pm

ADMISSION PRICES
Adult £4.60 Child £2.30
Family £11.50

CONTACT
Berrington Hall, Leominster
Herefordshire HR6 0DW
Tel 01568 615721
Email susan.brace@national-trust.org.uk

144

Eastnor Castle

2 hrs+
Mar–Oct

Quality Assured Visitor Attraction
English Tourism Council

WC

In the dramatic setting of the Malvern Hills and surrounded by a beautiful deer park, arboretum and lake, this fairy-tale castle has undergone a renaissance in recent years and many of the castle treasures are now displayed for the first time.

LOCATION
2 miles from Ledbury on the A438 Ledbury–Tewkesbury road. 5 miles from the M50 junction 2 via Ledbury

OPENING
3 Mar–6 Oct open Sun & Bank holidays 11am–5pm; Jul & Aug open daily except Sat

ADMISSION PRICES
Adult £5.50 Child £3 Family £14
Concession £4.75

CONTACT
Eastnor Castle
Eastnor
Ledbury HR8 1RL
Tel 01531 633160
Web www.eastnorcastle.com

Ledbury Ceramics

2 hrs
All year

WC

Paint pottery to your own design and personalise it. When you've created your masterpiece, staff glaze and fire the finished article and you collect it later.

★ Birthday parties   ★ Mobile studio

★ Regular workshops   ★ Non-toxic & washable paint

LOCATION
In Ledbury within easy reach of Worcester, Gloucestershire & Herefordshire

OPENING
All year open Mon–Fri 11am–6pm, Sat & Sun 11am–5pm; Closed Christmas & New Year

ADMISSION PRICES
Adult £5   Child £3

CONTACT
Glazydayz Ceramic Café
Homend Trading Estate
Ledbury HR8 1AR
Tel 01531 636018
Email
ledburyceramics@supanet.com

Shortwood Family Farm

2 hrs

Easter–Oct

Shortwood is a modern dairy farm with a trail and pets corner. Guided tours are run between 2pm and 4pm every afternoon. Visitors can collect eggs, feed animals, milk a cow and watch a milking machine.

LOCATION
Signed from the A417 between Burley Gate, Bodenham & from Pencombe village

OPENING
Easter–Oct open daily from 10am

ADMISSION PRICES
Adult £4.50 Child £1.90

CONTACT
Shortwood Family Farm
Shortwood, Pencombe, Bromyard
Herefordshire HR7 4RP
Tel 01885 400205
Web www.janet.legge.btinternet

Splendours of the Orient

3 hrs

All year

This indoor attraction has scenes from many fairy-tales. The wide range of activities include Easter Bunnies, Teddy Bears' Treasure Hunt and Father Christmas in Wonderland.

★ Easter Egg Hunt   ★ Winter Wonderland

LOCATION
Off the A40, midway between Ross-on-Wye & Monmouth

OPENING
In summer open daily 10am–6pm; In winter open Oct–Dec 10am–5pm; Jan–Mar open 10am–4pm; Closed 25 Dec

ADMISSION PRICES
Adult £2 Child £2

CONTACT
Splendours of the Orient
Jubilee Park, Symonds Yat West
Herefordshire HR9 6DA
Tel 01600 890668
Email
info@orientalsplendour.co.uk

Ashby de la Zouch Castle

1 hr

All year

LOCATION
In Ashby de la Zouch, 12 miles south of Derby on the A511

OPENING
1 Apr–31 Oct open daily 10am–6pm (5pm in Oct); 1 Nov–31 Mar open Wed–Sun 10am–4pm; Closed 24–26 Dec & 1 Jan

ADMISSION PRICES
Adult £3.20 Child £1.60 Family £8
Concession £2.40

CONTACT
Ashby de la Zouch Castle
South Street
Ashby de La Zouch
Leicestershire LE65 1BR
Tel 01530 413343
Web www.english-heritage.co.uk

Ashby de la Zouch Castle is a late medieval castle with impressive ruins which are dominated by the Hastings Tower. It offers panoramic views of the surrounding countryside and the chance to explore the secret tunnel used in the Siege of Ashby.

★ Visit the secret tunnel from the kitchen
★ Free audio tour
★ Storytelling weekends
★ Ivanhoe: Heroes & Villains themed weekends
★ The Magic of Merlin weekends

½ day

Apr–Sep

Belvoir Castle

Belvoir Castle is home to the Duke and Duchess of Rutland. This stunning castle has a hilltop position, breathtaking views and glorious gardens. Events are staged every weekend throughout the season.

LOCATION
Off the A52, 7 miles from Grantham & 9 miles from Melton Mowbray

OPENING
Apr–Sep open 11am–5pm
Please phone for details

ADMISSION PRICES
Adult £7.25 Child £4.75 Family £19
Senior £6.75

CONTACT
Belvoir Castle
Grantham
Leicestershire NG32 1PD
Tel 01476 871002
Email nwheeler@belvoircastle.com

3 hrs

All year

Charnwood Museum

Quality Assured Visitor Attraction
English Tourism Council

The museum opened in 1999 and features a wide range of exhibits which reflect local history and industries. Permanent exhibitions have been grouped into four areas: Coming to Charnwood, Natural History, The People and Industries of Charnwood and Digging for Victory.

★ Interactive displays

★ Handle rocks from Charnwood's volcanic past

★ Walk below the giant oak tree

★ Hear stories from the local Land Girls via special listening posts

LOCATION
In the centre of town in Queen's Park. Exit at junction 23 of the M1

OPENING
All year open Mon–Sat 10am–4.30pm, Sun 2pm–5pm; Open Bank holidays & by request for groups at other times

ADMISSION PRICES
Free

CONTACT
Charnwood Museum
Queen's Hall, Granby Street
Loughborough
Leicestershire LE11 3QW
Tel 01509 233784
Email charnwoodmuseum@leics.gov.uk
Web www.leics.gov.uk/museums/charnwood

Foxton Canal Museum

3 hrs
All year

LOCATION
Follow the brown tourist signs from the A6
Market Harborough–Leicester road or the
A4304 at Lubenham, or M1 junction 20
to the Market Harborough road

OPENING
29 Mar–31 Oct open daily 10am–5pm;
1 Nov–Easter & Sat & Sun open
11am–4pm; Closed 24 Dec–2 Jan

ADMISSION PRICES
Adult £2 Child Free Concession £1.50

CONTACT
Foxton Canal Museum
Middle Lock
Gumley Road
Foxton, Market Harborough
Leicestershire LE16 7RA
Tel 0116 2792657
Email mike@foxcm.freeserve.co.uk
Web www.foxcanal.fsnet.co.uk

A canal museum featuring the story of the local canals and the unique boat lift, set in beautiful countryside with 10 locks and all supporting facilities. The museum contains models of the lift, interactive displays, social history and a canal play boat for younger visitors.

Kirby Muxloe Castle

1 hr
Apr–Oct

LOCATION
4 miles west of Leicester, off the B5380 &
close to junction 21a off the M1

OPENING
1 Apr–31 Oct open Sat, Sun & Bank
holidays 12pm–5pm

ADMISSION PRICES
Adult £2.20 Child £1.10 Concession £1.70

CONTACT
Kirby Muxloe Castle
Oakcroft Avenue, Kirby Muxloe
Leicestershire LE9 9MD
Tel 01162 386886
Web www.english-heritage.org.uk

Kirby Muxloe Castle is an 'unfinished castle'. Building work at Kirby Muxloe was started in 1480 by William Hastings. However, work was never finished at this picturesque, brick-built castle because Hastings was executed in 1483 by Richard III. The castle has a moat and tower.

★ Tours

2 hrs

All year

The Leicester Gas Museum

The Leicester Gas Museum traces the development of the gas industry from 1792 to the advent of natural gas. There is also an extensive collection of domestic appliances, from hairdryers to a gas-driven radio and a 1920s all-gas kitchen.

i

LOCATION	ADMISSION PRICES
Off the A426, south of Leicester city centre	Free
OPENING	**CONTACT**
All year open Tue, Wed & Thu 12pm–4.30pm; Closed Bank holidays	**The Leicester Gas Museum** British Gas Services 195 Aylestone Road Leicester LE2 7QH Tel 0116 2503190 Web www.gasmuseum.co.uk

Leicester Royal Infirmary: History Museum

3 hrs

All year

Learn about the history of the Royal Infirmary (opened in 1771) with exhibitions charting the history of medical and surgical instruments.

★ Educational visits welcomed

i

LOCATION	ADMISSION PRICES
Off the A50 on the ring road into the city centre	Free Donations welcomed
OPENING	**CONTACT**
All year open Tue & Wed 12pm–2pm Closed all public holidays	**Leicester Royal Infirmary: History Museum** Knighton Street Leicester Tel 0116 2541414

148

2–3 hrs

All year

The National Space Centre

The National Space Centre is the UK's largest attraction dedicated to the exciting subject of space. Be amazed by the rockets, forecast the weather, visit the Space Theatre and the Newsdesk or travel to a distant planet – all in a few hours!

i

LOCATION	ADMISSION PRICES
1 mile north of Leicester city centre, off the A6. Follow the brown tourist signs off the M1	Adult £7.95 Child £5.95
OPENING	**CONTACT**
Daily in school hols; Closed Mon in term time; Open all year Tue–Sun 9.30am–4.30pm (closes 6pm); Mon 12.30pm–6pm	**National Space Centre** Mansion House 41 Guildhall Lane, Leicester Leicestershire LE1 5FR Tel 0116 2610201 Web www.spacecentre.co.uk

Snibston Discovery Park

All day

All year

Snibston Discovery Park is the award-winning, all-weather tourist attraction where visitors of all ages can explore the wonders of technology with over 30 hands-on experiments, and delve into the world of Leicestershire's industrial heritage.

i

LOCATION	ADMISSION PRICES
Located west of Coalville & 10 mins from junction 22 of the M1 or junction 13 of the A42/M42	Adult £4.75 Child £2.95 Family £13.50 Concession £3.25
OPENING	**CONTACT**
All year open daily 10am–5pm; Closed 25 & 26 Dec	**Snibston Discovery Park** Ashby Road, Coalville, Leicester Leicestershire LE67 3LN Tel 01530 278444 Email snibston@leics.gov.uk

Tumbledown Farm

2–4 hrs

All year

A traditional family-run working farm set in unspoiled countryside where the farmers breed animals, milk goats and grow cereal crops. You can watch people work with the animals and the land and enjoy the craft workshop and weekend events.

LOCATION
1 mile from Melton Mowbray & signposted from the A607 between Melton Mowbray & Grantham

OPENING
All year open daily; In summer open 10am–5pm; In winter open 10am–4pm; Closed 24–26 Dec

ADMISSION PRICES
All £2.95 Under-2s Free
Family £11

CONTACT
Tumbledown Farm
Spinney Road
Melton Mowbray
Leicestershire LE14 4SB
Web www.leics.gov.uk

Baytree Garden Centre (Owl Centre)

2 hrs+

All year

Baytree Garden Centre has 72 owls from around the world, and is set in a beautiful landscaped area. There are tame owls to hold or just to enjoy watching in flying displays.

LOCATION
On the main A151 at Weston between Spalding & Holbeach

OPENING
All year open daily 10am–4pm; Closed 31 Mar, 25, 26 Dec

ADMISSION PRICES
Adult £2.75 Child £2
Senior £2.50

CONTACT
Baytree Garden Centre
Baytree Nursery, High Road
Weston, Spalding
Lincolnshire PE12 6JU
Tel 01406 372840
Web www.spalding.org.uk/owl-museum.html

149

Quality Assured Visitor Attraction
English Tourism Council

LOCATION
3 miles north of Skegness, situated on the A52 Ingoldmells, Chapel St Leonards, Sutton-on-Sea & Mablethorpe Road

OPENING
30 Apr–27 Oct open daily 10am–11pm (last admission 4pm)

ADMISSION PRICES
Please phone for details

CONTACT
Butlins
Roman Bank
Ingoldmells
Skegness
Lincolnshire PE25 1NJ
Tel 01754 762311
Web www.butlins.co.uk

Butlins

All day

Apr–Oct

Children can have great fun at Butlins, from Splash, an indoor sub-tropical waterworld, with its exciting water rides, to Hotshots, a terrific tenpin bowling centre and the amazing Skyline Pavilion with live shows. Younger children can meet Noddy, Big Ears and Mr Plod in toyland.

★ Foodcourts
★ Live shows & street theatre

1 hr

Mar–Oct

CENTRAL

The Butterfly & Wildlife Park

Quality Assured Visitor Attraction
The English Tourist Board

When you visit this park, you will see wallabies, llamas, ponies and lots more. Indoor attractions include tropical butterflies, snakes, crocodiles, an ant room and an insectarium.

★ Wildflower walks
★ Ride-on tractors
★ Toddlers' play area
★ Flying displays
★ Mini golf

LOCATION
Signposted off the A17 at Long Sutton, Lincolnshire

OPENING
Mid-Mar–end Oct open daily from 10am
Please phone for details

ADMISSION PRICES
Adult £5 Child £3.70 Senior £4.70
Family ticket available

CONTACT
The Butterfly & Wildlife Park
Long Sutton, Spalding
Lincolnshire PE12 9LE
Tel 01406 363833
Email butterflypark@hotmail.com
Web www.butterflyandwildlifepark.co.uk

150

---

2 hrs+

All year

Fun Farm

At Fun Farm you can enjoy slides, ball pools, scramble nets, climbing frames and more.

★ Party bookings available

LOCATION
In Dysart Road next to Grantham Bowl, Kempton Way

OPENING
All year open daily 10am–6pm
Closed 25, 26 Dec & 1 Jan

ADMISSION PRICES
Peak: Child £3.99
Off-peak: Child £2.49

CONTACT
Fun Farm
Dysart Road, Grantham
Lincolnshire NG31 7LE
Tel 01476 562228
Email enquiries@funfarm.co.uk
Web www.funfarm.co.uk

Hardy's Animal Farm

3 hrs

All year

See commercial and rare breeds of cattle, sheep and goats. Visit the calf unit where you can see the care and attention necessary to keep animals healthy and contented. The pig breeding unit offers you the chance to see the day-to-day development of pigs.

LOCATION
Take the A52 north from Skegness to Ingoldmells. Go through Ingoldmells & take the 1st right down Anchor Lane

OPENING
All year open daily 10am–6pm
(last admission 5pm)

ADMISSION PRICES
Adult From £3 Child From £2
Senior From £2

CONTACT
Hardy's Animal Farm
Grays Farm, Anchor Lane
Ingoldmells, Skegness
Lincolnshire PE25 1LZ
Tel 01754 872267

Lakeside Leisure Ltd

4 hrs
Mar–Oct

Fun for all the family with boats to hire, quads to try and loads of activities to keep everyone happy.

★ Astro slide
★ Amusement arcade
★ Bouncy castle
★ Roller coaster
★ Crazy golf
★ Fishing

LOCATION
Off the A52 between Chapel-St. Leonard's & Ingoldmills. 6 miles north of Skegness

OPENING
Mid-Mar–31 Oct; In summer open daily 8am–late; In winter open daily dawn–dusk

ADMISSION PRICES
All rides & attractions are priced separately

CONTACT
Lakeside Leisure Ltd
Trunch Lane, Chapel-St. Leonard's, Skegness
Lincolnshire PE25 5TU
Tel 01754 872631

Lincoln Medieval Bishop's Palace

1 hr
All year

Set in the shadow of Lincoln Cathedral, the palace was the centre of the largest diocese in medieval England. Visit the superb new visitor facilities and the delightful contemporary heritage garden.

★ Video and audio tour
★ Vineyard

LOCATION
On the south side of Lincoln Cathedral, in the centre of the city of Lincoln

OPENING
1 Apr–31 Oct open daily 10am–6pm (5pm in Oct); 1 Nov–31 Mar Sat & Sun 10am–4pm; Closed 24–26 Dec & 1 Jan

ADMISSION PRICES
Adult £3.20 Child £1.60
Family £8 Concession £2.40

CONTACT
Lincoln Medieval
Bishop's Palace
Bishop's Palace, Lincoln
Lincolnshire LN2 1PU
Tel 01522 527468

151

LOCATION
Off the A155

OPENING
29 Mar–31 Oct open Mon–Sat 10am–5pm; 1 Nov–28 Mar open 10am–4pm
Closed 25, 26 Dec

ADMISSION PRICES
Adult £4 Child £1.50 Concession £3.50

CONTACT
Lincolnshire Aviation Heritage Centre
The Airfield, East Kirkby
Spilsby
Lincolnshire PE23 4DE
Tel 01790 763207
Fax 01790 763677
Web www.lincsaviation.co.uk

Lincolnshire Aviation Heritage Centre

2 hrs
All year

The Heritage Centre is part of a wartime bomber airfield under restoration, which includes the control tower and displays depicting the history of flying in Lincolnshire. There is also an exhibition by the Royal Air Force Escaping Society.

★ Educational visits
★ Photographic exhibition
★ Blast shelter & military vehicles
★ A complete AVRO Lancaster NX611

Varies

All year

Lincolnshire's Lifelong Adventure

At **this craft studio,** visitors can have a go at ceramics, pottery, archery and fencing. Groups can book a day's activities including pottery, archery and fencing.

★ Fishing lake

★ Adventure playground

★ Group booking can include lunch with day's activities

LOCATION
On the A1031 Grimsby–Mablethorpe road

OPENING
All year open daily dawn–dusk

ADMISSION PRICES
Free; charge for activities

CONTACT
Lincolnshire's Lifelong Adventure
Pigeon Cottage
Conisholme Road
North Somercotes
Louth
Lincolnshire LN11 7PS
Tel 01507 359063
Email LLA.HILL@ukgateway.net

2–3 hrs

All year

Magical World of Fantasy Island

This **indoor theme park** has rides and attractions to suit all ages, as well as live entertainment during the evenings throughout the main season. There are also outdoor rides and Europe's largest looping roller-coaster, The Millennium Coaster.

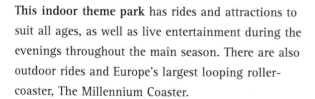

LOCATION
Off the A52, 4 miles north of Skegness

OPENING
All year open daily from 10am; Closing times vary according to season
Please phone for details

ADMISSION PRICES
Free

CONTACT
Magical World of Fantasy Island
Sea Lane, Ingoldmells
Skegness
Lincolnshire PE25 1RH
Tel 01754 872030
Web www.fantasyisland.co.uk

Museum of Lincolnshire Life

Experience the **domestic,** agricultural, industrial and social history of Lincolnshire with agricultural and industrial machinery built in the county. Also on show are Victorian room settings and a World War I tank. Special events are held throughout the year.

LOCATION
Take the A15 & the B1398 & follow signs from the A46

OPENING
1 May–31 Oct open daily 10am–5.30pm; 1 Nov–30 Apr Mon-Sat 10am–5.30pm, Sun 2pm–5.30pm
Closed 24-26, 31 Dec & 1 Jan

ADMISSION PRICES
Adult £2 Child 60p
Family £4.50

CONTACT
Museum of Lincolnshire Life
Burton Road, Lincoln
Lincolnshire LN1 3LY
Tel 01522 528448
Email finchj@lincolnshire.gov.uk

Natureland Seal Sanctuary

1–2 hrs

All year

LINCOLNSHIRE

Skegness Seal Sanctuary is well known for rescuing and rehabilitating orphaned and injured seal pups. The sanctuary has penguins, reptiles and insects and tropical birds. There is also an aquarium and a pets corner, and from April to October you can view the tropical butterflies.

★ Seal hospital
★ Underwater viewing pool
★ Chipmunk Island
★ Floral Palace
★ Feeding times
★ Crocodiles

153

Northcote Heavy Horse Centre

2–5 hrs

Apr–Sep

Northcote Heavy Horse Centre offers genuine close contact with some of the tallest horses in the world. A unique experience where you learn about the horses and their story.

★ Groom the horse of your choice
★ Learn about the history & future of heavy horses
★ Harnessing demonstration

North Lincolnshire Museum

 3 hrs · All year · WC

This is the regional museum for North Lincolnshire. Archaeology, local history, geology and a countryside gallery can all be found here. The art galleries feature a constantly-changing programme of temporary exhibitions.

LOCATION
Take the M180 & M181 to Scunthorpe town centre

OPENING
All year open Tue–Sat 10am–4pm, Sun 2pm–5pm; Bank holidays 10am–4pm; Closed 25, 26 Dec & 1 Jan

ADMISSION PRICES
Free

CONTACT
North Lincolnshire Museum
Oswald Road
Scunthorpe DN15 7BD
Tel 01724 843533
Fax 01724 270474

Panda's Palace

WC · 2 hrs · All year

An indoor adventure centre for children with ball pools, soft play areas, slides and jungle rope walks.

LOCATION
In the centre of Skegness via the A52 or A158

OPENING
Apr–Nov open daily 10.30am–6pm; Nov–Apr open weekends & school holidays

ADMISSION PRICES
Child £3
Please phone for further details

CONTACT
Panda's Palace
Tower Esplanade, Skegness
Lincolnshire PE25 3HJ
Tel 01754 765494

The Seal Sanctuary

   2 hrs · Mar–Oct ·  WC

The Seal Trust is a registered charity with the twin aims of caring for local wild creatures in distress (especially seals) and to encourage visitors to help wildlife themselves. It acts as a sanctuary for seals, owls and kestrels, as well as lynx, wildcats, snowy owls and harvest mice.

LOCATION
Off the A1031 via the A1031, A104, A111 or A52

OPENING
29 Mar–8 Apr open daily 9am–4.30pm; 1 May–30 Sep; Oct open by demand Please phone for details

ADMISSION PRICES
Adult £4 Child £2 Concession £3

CONTACT
The Seal Sanctuary
North End
Mablethorpe
Lincolnshire LN12 1QG
Tel 01507 473346

Sibsey Trader Windmill

1 hr
Apr–Sep

An impressive six-storey tower mill, Sibsey Trader Windmill was built in 1877 and restored in 2001. It contains its original machinery for grinding corn, with milling artefacts on show and flour for sale.

★ Guided tours essential

LOCATION
½ mile west of Sibsey, off the A16, 5 miles north of Boston

OPENING
1 Apr–30 Sep open Sat & Bank holidays 10am–6pm; Open Sun 11am–5pm; Jul & Aug also open Tue 10am–6pm

ADMISSION PRICES
Adult £2 Child £1
Concession £1.50

CONTACT
Sibsey Trader Windmill, Sibsey Boston, Lincolnshire PE22 0SY
Tel 01205 460647
Web www.english-heritage.org.uk

Tattershall Castle

2 hrs
Mar–Dec

Tattershall is a vast **redbrick tower** with a moat, built in medieval times for Ralph Cromwell, Lord Treasurer of England. There are grand tapestries and four great chambers, each with spectacular views.

LOCATION
Off the A153

OPENING
Mar–Dec
Please phone for details

ADMISSION PRICES
Adult £3.20 Child £1.60
Family £8

CONTACT
Tattershall Castle
Tattershall
Lincoln
Lincolnshire LN4 4LR
Tel 01526 342543
Web www.nationaltrust.org.uk

155

Ancient House Museum

1 hr
All year

LOCATION
In Thetford town centre, south of Swafham. Reached by the A11, A134 or A1066

OPENING
All year open Mon–Sat 10am–12.30pm & 1pm–5pm; 27 May–30 Aug also open Sun 2pm–5pm

ADMISSION PRICES
Free except Jul & Aug
Fees Jul & Aug: Adult £1 Child 60p
Senior 80p Concession 80p

CONTACT
Ancient House Museum
White Hart Street
Thetford IP24 1AA
Tel 01842 752599
Web www.norfolk.gov.uk/tourism/museums

This **family attraction** is a magnificent fifteenth-century timber-framed merchant's house with a fine carved ceiling. Come and learn about local history and archaeology and enjoy displays on Thomas Paine, Maharajah Duleep Singh and the Vikings.

★ Tudor herb garden
★ Interactive displays
★ Family quizzes

Baconsthorpe Castle

1–2 hrs

All year

Baconsthorpe Castle is a fifteenth-century part-moated, semi-fortified house. The remains include the inner and outer gatehouse and curtain wall. The local post office sells guide books and postcards.

LOCATION
Off the A148 & B1149, ¾ mile north of the village of Baconsthorpe, off an unclassified road. 3 miles east of Holt

OPENING
All year open daily 10am–4pm

ADMISSION PRICES
Free

CONTACT
Baconsthorpe Castle
Baconsthorpe, Holt
Norfolk
Tel 01604 730325
Web www.english-heritage.org.uk

Banham Zoo

All day

All year

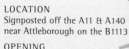

Enjoy a day of fun and education at this exciting wildlife attraction. The wildlife spectacular will take you on a journey to experience at close quarters some of the world's most exotic, rare and endangered animals.

LOCATION
Signposted off the A11 & A140 near Attleborough on the B1113

OPENING
All year open daily from 10am (seasonal closing times, please phone for details)

ADMISSION PRICES
Vary according to season

CONTACT
Banham Zoo
The Grove, Banham
Norfolk NR16 2HE
Tel 01953 887771
Web www.banhamzoo.co.uk

Bank Boats

2 hrs+

All year

Hire all-weather dayboats and take a trip on the beautiful River Ant. Canoes are also available.

LOCATION
On the slip road off the A149 between Stalham & Wroxham

OPENING
All year open daily 9am–5pm

ADMISSION PRICES
From £20 for 2 hrs

CONTACT
Bank Boats
Staithe Cottage
Wayford Bridge
Stalham
Norwich
Norfolk NR12 9LN

Barton House Railway

All day

2 hrs

Apr–Oct

Barton House has a miniature steam passenger railway and a steam and battery-electric railway. There are full-size M and GN accessories, including signals and signal boxes.

LOCATION
On the A1151 from Norwich

OPENING
Apr–Oct open 1 Sun per month 2.30pm–5.30pm
Please phone for details

ADMISSION PRICES
Adult 50p Child 25p

CONTACT
Barton House Railway
Hartwell Road, The Avenue
Wroxham, Norwich
Norfolk NR12 8TL
Tel 01603 782470

1–2 hrs

Varies

Bishops Boats Seal Trips

On this boat trip you will be able to see the seals and birds on Blakeney Point. There are many species of birds and both grey and common seals from a colony of approximately 500.

LOCATION	CONTACT
Trips depart from Blakeney Point reached by the A149	**Bishops Boats Seal Trips** Blakeney Point Blakeney, Holt Norfolk Tel 0263 740753 Email bishopsboats@bigfoot.com Web www.norfolksealtrips.co.uk
OPENING Please phone for details as times vary depending on the tides	
ADMISSION PRICES Adult £5.50 Child £4	

Blakeney Point

3 hrs+

All year

One of Britain's foremost bird sanctuaries, the point is noted in particular for its colonies of breeding terns and for the rare migrants that pass through in spring and autumn. Common and grey seals can also be seen.

LOCATION	ADMISSION PRICES
Follow the A149 from Sheringham or Wells-next-the-Sea	Free
	CONTACT
OPENING Please phone for details	**Blakeney Point** National Nature Reserve Blakeney, Holt Norfolk NR25 Tel 01263 740241

157

Bressingham Steam Experience & Gardens

2–3 hrs

All year

A working steam experience in a nationally-known garden setting with narrow-gauge railway rides, a Victorian steam roundabout, locomotive sheds, stationary engine displays, a royal coach, traction engines and gardens. The miniature steam-hauled trains run through 2½ miles of woodland in the beautiful Waveney Valley.

★ Dad's Army National Collection
★ Friends of Thomas the Tank Engine
★ Norfolk Fire Museum on site
★ Dell Garden with 5,000 species of perennials & alpines

LOCATION
3 miles west of Diss on the A1066 Diss–Thetford road

OPENING
Steam Experience & Garden open 31 Mar–31 Oct daily 10.30am–5.30pm Dad's Army National Collection open daily 1 Jan–31 Mar 10.30am–4pm; 1 Apr–30 Sep open daily 10.30am–5.30pm; 1 Oct–31 Dec open daily 10.30am–4pm

ADMISSION PRICES
Adult £7 Child £5 Family £23 Concession £6 Ride tickets £3.50

CONTACT
Bressingham Steam Experience & Gardens Bressingham, Diss Norfolk IP22 2AB Tel 01379 687386 Email info@bressingham.co.uk Web www.bressingham.co.uk

NORFOLK

Burgh Castle

1 hr+

All year

The remains of a third-century Roman fort, Burgh Castle is one of a chain built to defend the coast against the Saxon raiders. It has impressive walls with projecting bastions.

LOCATION
On the A143

OPENING
Open at any reasonable time; Please check website for details

ADMISSION PRICES
Free

CONTACT
Burgh Castle
Great Yarmouth
Norfolk NR31 9QG
Web www.english-heritage.org.uk

Caister Roman Site

2 hrs

All year

At Caister you can see the remains of a Roman commercial port which was possibly a fort. The footings of walls and buildings can be seen all along the main street.

★Educational visits welcomed

LOCATION
On the A1064 near Caister-on-Sea, 3 miles north of Great Yarmouth

OPENING
Open at any reasonable time; Please check website for details

ADMISSION PRICES
Free

CONTACT
Caister Roman Site
Great Yarmouth
Norfolk
Web www.english-heritage.org.uk

Caithness Crystal Visitor Centre

2-3 hrs

All year

Quality Assured Visitor Attraction
English Tourism Council

Glass-making is a magical craft that can transform sand into exquisite glassware using only the heat of a furnace and the skill of hand and eye. Witness it for yourself at the King's Lynn visitor centre and marvel at the demonstration of the skills of glass-making.

★ Guided tours available

★ Factory shop

LOCATION
Located off the A149, A47 & A10. Follow the brown tourist signs

OPENING
All year open Mon-Sat 9am-5pm, Sun 10.15am-4.15pm; Please phone for details of glassmaking demonstration times; Closed 31 Mar, 25, 26 Dec

ADMISSION PRICES
Free

CONTACT
Caithness Crystal Visitor Centre
Paxman Road, Hardwick Industrial Estate
King's Lynn
Norfolk PE30 4NE
Tel 01553 765111
Fax 01553 767628
Web www.caithnessglass.co.uk

Dinosaur Adventure Park

4 hrs+

Mar-Oct

Elephant Playbarn

Varies

All year

Come face-to-face with lifesize dinosaurs on the ultimate family adventure. The park includes a secret animal garden, adventure play areas, 'Climb-a-saurus', the 'Lost World Maze' and 'Raptor Racers'.

★ Dippy's Passport to Fun   ★ Country Capers

A converted Norfolk flint barn filled with bouncy castles, ball pools and toys suitable for the under-8s. There is also a fully enclosed courtyard with an adventure play area and lots of pedal toys.

LOCATION
9 miles from Norwich. Follow the brown tourist signs off the A47 or A1067

OPENING
Mar-Oct open daily 10am-5pm

ADMISSION PRICES
Please phone for details

CONTACT
Dinosaur Adventure Park
Weston Park, Lenwade, Norwich
Norfolk NR9 5JW
Tel 01603 870245
Email info@dinosaurpark.co.uk
Web www.dinosaurpark.co.uk

LOCATION
On the A149 south of Cromer

OPENING
All year open Wed, Thu, Fri
10am-4pm; School holidays
open Mon-Fri

ADMISSION PRICES
Adult Free Child £3

CONTACT
Elephant Playbarn
Mundesley Road, Knapton
North Walsham
Norfolk NR28 0RY
Tel 01263 721080
Fax 01263 722617

159

Fairhaven Woodland & Water Garden

½ day

All year

LOCATION
Follow the brown tourist signs off the A147 at the junction with the B1140 through South Walsham

OPENING
All year open daily 10am-5pm; 2 May-31 Aug open Wed, Thu 10am-9pm; Closed 25 Dec

ADMISSION PRICES
Adult £3.50 Child £1.25 Concession £3

CONTACT
Fairhaven Woodland & Water Garden
School Road
South Walsham
Norwich
Norfolk NR13 6DZ
Tel 01603 270449
Email fairhavengardens@norfolkbroads.com
Web www.norfolkbroads.com/fairhaven

These delightful woodland and water gardens have something of interest for everyone. There is a fantastic combination of plants and flowers, together with a separate wildlife sanctuary for bird-watchers and picturesque waterways spanned by small bridges.

1–2 hrs

Mar–Oct

Fenland & West Norfolk Aviation Museum

The Vampire T11 aircraft is one of the finest examples in the country and had a complete respray and airframe check. Visitors can sit in the cockpit and study the aircraft up close.

★ Guided tours for individuals

★ EE Lightning T5

★ Jet Provost

★ Shackleton Fuselage

★ Flight deck of a Boeing 747 jumbo jet

LOCATION
Take the old B198 to King's Lynn from Wisbech. The museum is ½ mile from the bypass

OPENING
2 Mar–27 Oct open Sat, Sun & Bank holidays 9.30am–5pm

ADMISSION PRICES
Adult £1.50 Child 75p

CONTACT
Fenland & West Norfolk Aviation Museum
Old Lynn Road, West Walton
Wisbech
Norfolk PE14 7DA
Tel 01945 584440
Email petewinning@btinternet.com
Web www.fawnaps.co.uk

Varies

All year

Funstop

Funstop is a children's indoor adventure centre with a giant slide, ball pond, tubes, scrambling nets, a special under-threes area and lots more.

★ Group visits available

LOCATION
From King's Lynn take the A148 to Cromer. Follow the one-way system. Funstop is on the left. From Norwich take the A140 round the one-way system

OPENING
All year open 10am–6pm
Please phone for details

ADMISSION PRICES
Under-3s £1.90 Over-3s £3

CONTACT
Funstop
Exchange House
Louden Road
Cromer, Norfolk NR27 9EF
Tel 01263 514976
Email denniscarroll@virgin.net

Great Yarmouth Sealife Centre

3 hrs

All year

Experience the spectacular eye-to-eye views of everything from shrimps and starfish to sharks and stingrays. The City of Atlantis has an underwater tunnel allowing visitors to walk on the seabed and encounter sharks and multi-coloured fish.

LOCATION
Take the A47 from Norwich, the A143 from Beccles or the A12 from Lowestoft

OPENING
All year open daily from 10am; Closed 25 Dec

ADMISSION PRICES
Adult £5.95 Child £3.95

CONTACT
Great Yarmouth Sealife Centre
Marine Parade, Great Yarmouth
Norfolk NR30 3AH
Tel 01493 330631
Fax 01493 330442
Web www.sealife.co.uk

Grimes Graves

2 hrs

All year

NORFOLK

i

LOCATION
7 miles north-west of Thetford off the
A134

OPENING
2 Jan–28 Mar open Wed–Sun 10am–1pm &
2pm–4pm; 1 Apr–30 Sep open daily
10am–1pm & 2pm–6pm; 1–31 Oct open
daily 10am–1pm & 2pm–5pm; 1 Nov–29
Dec open Wed–Sun 10am–1pm &
2pm–4pm; Closed 25, 26 Dec & 1 Jan

ADMISSION PRICES
Adult £2.10 Child £1.10 Concession £1.60

CONTACT
Grimes Graves
The Exhibition Building, Lynford
Thetford
Norfolk IP26 5DE
Tel 01842 810656
Web www.english-heritage.org-uk

**At Grimes Graves there is a
site** exhibition with remarkable
neolithic flint mines. The mines
are 4,000 years old and were first
excavated in the 1870s, with over
300 pits and shafts. One pit is
open to the public.

★ Safety helmets must be worn
★ Educational visits welcomed

161

High Lodge &
Thetford Forest Park

All day

All year

i

LOCATION
Midway between Brandon & Thetford, off
the B1107

OPENING
Visitor Centre open daily from Easter–end
Oct 10am–5pm plus winter weekends;
Forest Drive open all year 10am–8pm (or
dusk if earlier)

ADMISSION PRICES
Forest Drive: Summer weekdays £2.50,
weekends £3
Forest Drive: Winter weekdays £1,
weekends £2

CONTACT
High Lodge Forest Centre
Thetford Forest Park, Santon Downham
Brandon, Norfolk
Tel 01842 810271
www.forestry.gov.uk

Thetford Forest is Britain's largest lowland pine forest. High Lodge
Forest Centre is in the heart of the forest with walks, cycle hire, adventure
playground and a ropes course.

★ Largest maze in Europe
★ Bird walks
★ Deer safaris
★ Family Fun Walks

CENTRAL

Horsey Mere

2+ hrs
All year

A **large National Trust** property of 1,900 acres on the eastern edge of the Norfolk Broads. Ideal for a few hours' walking, it has sand dunes, farmland and reedbeds and is teeming with wildlife. The nearby Horsey Windpump windmill is open to visitors.

LOCATION
Off the B1159, 15 miles north of Great Yarmouth, between Martham & Stalham

OPENING
Please phone for details

ADMISSION PRICES
Free; Charge for car park & to the Windpump

CONTACT
Horsey Mere
Horsey, Great Yarmouth
Norfolk NR29 4EF
Tel 01493 393904

Hunstanton Sea Life Sanctuary

4 hrs
All year

Hunstanton has a breathtaking display of British marine life. Stroll around over 20 authentically recreated natural habitat settings as you view over 2,000 fish from 200 different species.

★ Otter sanctuary   ★ Seal sanctuary

LOCATION
On the A149 to Hunstanton from King's Lynn

OPENING
All year open daily from 10am; Closed 25 Dec

ADMISSION PRICES
Adult £4.99 Child £3.50 Family £14.50 Concession £3.95

CONTACT
Hunstanton Sea Life Sanctuary
Southern Promenade
Hunstanton
Norfolk PE36 5BH
Tel 01485 533576
Fax 01485 533531

162

ILPH Hall Farm

2–3 hrs
All year

Visit the centre for horses and learn more about the work of the International League for the Protection of Horses. Meet some of the horses and ponies in care, many of whom have been rescued from suffering caused by cruelty and neglect.

LOCATION
Off the A11, signposted between Attleborough & Thetford

OPENING
All year open Wed, Sat, Sun & Bank holidays 11am-4pm; Closed 25 Dec & 1 Jan

ADMISSION PRICES
Free

CONTACT
International League for the Protection of Horses
Snetterton, Norwich
Norfolk NR16 2LR
Tel 0870 8701927
Fax 0870 9041927
Email hq@ilph.org
Web www.ilph.org

Kool Kidz

Varies
All year

Kool Kidz is an indoor activity centre full of fun and fascination for children. There is a large soft play area, educational equipment and satellite television. Special needs children are welcome.

LOCATION
Turn off the A11 & take the exit at Breckland Lodge. Turn right into New Road

OPENING
All year open daily 10am-7pm; Closed 25, 26 Dec & 1 Jan

ADMISSION PRICES
Please phone for details

CONTACT
Kool Kidz
34-35 Haverscroft Industrial Estate, New Road, Attleborough
Norfolk NR17 1YE
Tel 01953 457333

Langham Glass

3–4 hrs

All year

NORFOLK

LOCATION
Follow the A148 from Holt to Fakenham
for 3 miles & then take the right turn on
to the B1156 & follow signs to Langham

OPENING
All year open daily 10am–5pm;
Closed 25, 26 Dec & 1 Jan

ADMISSION PRICES
Adult £3 Child £2 Family £8
Concession £2

CONTACT
Langham Glass
The Long Barn, North Street
Langham, Holt
Norfolk NR25 7DG
Tel 01328 830511
Fax 01328 830787
Email langhamglass@talk21.com
Web www.langhamglass.co.uk

Langham Glass is based in a large Norfolk barn complex that is pantiled and flint-faced. Teams of glassmakers can be seen working with molten glass using blowing irons and hand tools in a way that has been traditional for hundreds of years.

- ★ Bargain barn
- ★ Museum & video
- ★ Walled garden
- ★ Pottery throwing
- ★ Didgeridoo making
- ★ 6½-acre maze

163

3–4 hrs

Mar–Oct

Louis Tussauds House of Wax

A waxworks exhibition with torture chambers, a chamber of horrors, a hall of funny mirrors and a family amusement arcade.

LOCATION
Off the A143 to Great Yarmouth.
Follow the brown tourist signs

OPENING
1 Mar–30 Apr open daily
11am–4pm; 1 May–31 Aug open
daily 10.30am–6.30pm;
1 Sep–31 Oct open daily
11am–4pm

ADMISSION PRICES
Adult £3 Child £2 Family £9

CONTACT
Louis Tussauds House of Wax
18 Regent Road
Great Yarmouth
Norfolk NR30 2AF
Tel 01493 844851

The Mint

2 hrs+

All year

This family entertainment centre includes Quasar – the thrilling live action laser game.

LOCATION
Marine Parade is on the seafront
at Great Yarmouth

OPENING
All year open daily 9am–11pm

ADMISSION PRICES
Adult £2.99 Child £2.99

CONTACT
The Mint
31 Marine Parade
Great Yarmouth
Norfolk NR30 2EN
Tel 01493 842968
Email info@thurston.uk.com
Web www.thurston.uk.com

3 hrs+

All year

Norfolk Motor Cycle Museum

Young bike enthusiasts will enjoy the displays covering a wide collection of motor cycles dating from 1920–60.

★ Educational visits welcomed

LOCATION
Near the junction of the B1150 Norwich road & the A149 Great Yarmouth–Cromer road (the town bypass)

OPENING
All year; Closed 25 & 26 Dec & 1 Jan
Please phone for details

ADMISSION PRICES
Adult £2.50 Child £1.50
Concession £2

CONTACT
Norfolk Motor Cycle Museum
Railway Yard, North Walsham
Norfolk NR28 0DS
Tel 01692 406266

Norfolk Shire Horse Centre

2–3 hrs

Mar–Oct

Children can see Shire horses at work and learn about a bygone age when machinery was horse-powered. The centre also has a children's farm and riding school.

LOCATION
Off the A148 & the A149

OPENING
Mar–Oct; Please phone for details

ADMISSION PRICES
Adult £4.95 Child £2.95
Concession £3.95

CONTACT
Norfolk Shire Horse Centre
West Runton Stables
West Runton, Cromer
Norfolk NR27 9QH
Tel 01263 837339
Email bakewell@norfolkshire-horse.fsnet.co.uk
Web www.norfolk-shirehorse-centre.co.uk

164

All day

Seasonal

Pleasure Beach

The Pleasure Beach is situated on the seafront at the southern end of Great Yarmouth's Golden Mile and covers nine acres. As well as a main ride area with over 70 rides and the awe-inspiring Ejector Seat, there are two crazy golf courses and gardens.

★ Children's rides
★ Water attractions

LOCATION
Take the A12 from Lowestoft or the A47 from Norwich

OPENING
Please phone for details

ADMISSION PRICES
Free
Rides are paid for at reception or machines

CONTACT
Pleasure Beach
South Beach Parade
Great Yarmouth
Norfolk NR30 3EH
Tel 01493 844585
Fax 01493 853483
Email gypbeach@aol.com
Web www.pleasure-beach.co.uk

Redwings Visitor Centre

  2 hrs Mar–Oct

A sanctuary for more than 1,000 horses, ponies and donkeys that welcomes young visitors. It has talks and demonstrations on equine care, horse-drawn carriage rides and special events.

LOCATION
1 mile north-east of the village of Fritton on the A143 between Great Yarmouth & Beccles

OPENING
Mar–Oct; Please phone for details

ADMISSION PRICES
Adult £3.50 Child £1.50

CONTACT
Redwings Visitor Centre
Caldecott Hall, Fritton
Great Yarmouth
Norfolk NR31 9EY
Tel 01493 488531
Web www.redwings.co.uk

Roots of Norfolk at Gressenhall

   3 hrs Mar–Nov

This is a remarkable museum housed in a former workhouse and in an idyllic rural setting. It has displays on village and rural life plus a farm worked with horses and stocked with rare breeds.

★ Riverside trails   ★ Children's activities

LOCATION
3 miles north-west of East Dereham on the A47

OPENING
1 Mar–31 Oct open Tue–Sun & holidays 10.30am–5.30pm (last admission 4.45pm); Nov open Sun only
Please phone for details

ADMISSION PRICES
Adult £4.70 Child £3.30
Senior £4 Concession £4

CONTACT
Roots of Norfolk at Gressenhall
Gressenhall, Dereham
Norfolk NR20 4DR
Tel 01362 860563

Royal Norfolk Regimental Museum

   2 hrs All year

LOCATION
Take the A11 & follow signs for the city centre

OPENING
All year open Mon–Sat 10am–5pm; Closed 25, 26 Dec & 1 Jan

ADMISSION PRICES
Adult £1.80 Child 90p Concession £1.40

CONTACT
Royal Norfolk Regimental Museum
Shirehall, Market Avenue
Norwich
Norfolk NR1 3JQ
Tel 01603 493649
Email museums@norfolk.gov.uk
Web www.norfolk.gov.uk/tourism/museums

Children can have an interesting educational experience at this museum which has displays devoted to the social history of the county regiment from 1685. These include the daily life of a soldier, audio-visual displays and graphics, and a reconstructed World War I communication trench.

★ Educational visits welcomed
★ Please phone for details of current temporary displays

2 hrs+

Jul–Sep

South Creake Maize Maze

Looking for excitement and adventure? Then take the challenge of a seven-acre maze in a maize field. Set in 18 acres of unspoilt north Norfolk countryside, this is a chance to lose yourself in nature within the maze.

LOCATION
Between Fakenham & Burnham Market on the B1355, just off the A148 King's Lynn–Fakenham road

OPENING
20 Jul–15 Sep open daily 10am–6pm (last admission 5pm)

ADMISSION PRICES
Adult £3.50 Child £2.50
Family £10 Concession £2.50

CONTACT
South Creake Maize Maze
Compton Hall, South Creake
Fakenham
Norfolk NR21 9JD
Tel 01328 823224

3–4 hrs

All year

Thrigby Hall Wildlife Gardens

Visit a wide selection of Asian mammals, birds and reptiles, including tigers, crocodiles and storks. There are superb willow pattern gardens and a play area. There is also a dramatic swamp house for crocodiles and other tropical swamp dwellers.

LOCATION
Off the A1064 Caister–Acle road

OPENING
All year open daily 10am–5pm

ADMISSION PRICES
Adult £5.90 Child £3.90
Concession £4.90

CONTACT
Thrigby Hall Wildlife Gardens
Thrigby Hall, Filby
Great Yarmouth
Norfolk NR29 3DR
Tel 01493 369477
Fax 01493 368256
Email mail@thrigbyhall.co.uk
Web www.thrigbyhall.co.uk

1 hr+

Apr–Oct

The Tolhouse Museum

The Tolhouse Museum is one of the oldest prisons in the country. Explore the story of crime and punishment and discover what happened to smugglers, witches, pirates and murderers in Great Yarmouth.

★ Hands-on activities for all the family
★ Dressing up
★ Miniature brass rubbing
★ Photofit puzzle

LOCATION
Behind the Central Library in Great Yarmouth. Close to the South Quay & ½ mile from the railway station

OPENING
1 Apr–31 Oct open Mon–Fri 10am–5pm, Sat & Sun 1.15pm–5pm

ADMISSION PRICES
Adult £2.60 Child £1.30 Family £6
Concession £2

CONTACT
The Tolhouse Museum
Tolhouse Street
Great Yarmouth
Norfolk NR30 2SH
Tel 01493 858900/01493 745526
Email yarmouth.museums@norfolk.gov.uk
web www.norfolk.gov.uk/tourism/museums

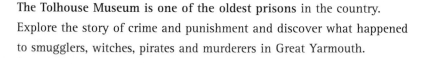

The Tropical Butterfly World

2–3 hrs

Feb–Oct

LOCATION
Signed from the A11 Attleborough bypass &
from the B1077 Attleborough–Watton road

OPENING
15 Feb–30 Oct open Mon–Sat 9am–6pm,
Sun 11am–4.30pm

ADMISSION PRICES
Butterfly garden & falconry: Adult £3.50
Child £2.50 Concession £3.50
Maze: Adult £3.50 Child £2.50 Concession
£3.50
Combined ticket: Adult £6 Child £4
Concession £6

CONTACT
The Tropical Butterfly World
Long Street, Great Ellingham
Attleborough
Norfolk NR17 1AW
Tel 01953 453175
Web www.gegc.co.uk

**Experience multi-coloured
butterflies in beautiful landscaped
gardens.** The fantastic 'Animagic'
contains a variety of animals and
birds from around the world. You
can visit the giant maze and treat
yourself to refreshments whilst the
children play on the caterpillar
climbing frame.

167

Wroxham Barns

2–3 hrs

All year

Quality Assured Visitor Attraction
The East of England Tourist Board

LOCATION
Approximately 10 miles from Norwich.
Follow the A1151 towards Wroxham & then
follow the brown tourist signs

OPENING
All year open daily 10am–5pm;
Closed 25, 26 Dec & 1 Jan

ADMISSION PRICES
Admission & car park Free
Junior farm £2.50
Under-3s Free

CONTACT
Wroxham Barns
Tunstead Road, Hoveton
Norfolk
NR12 8QU
Tel 01603 783762
Email info@wroxham-barns.co.uk
Web www.wroxham-barns.co.uk

Wroxham Barns will keep all the family happy. Watch traditional and
contemporary craft workers at work, indulge in a spot of shopping, feed
the friendly animals and have fun at the fair.

★ Traditional farm
★ Junior farm
★ Country food shop

3 hrs+

All year

Abington Museum

Billing Aquadrome

Varies

Mar–Nov

The museum includes social and military history. Displays show Northampton life, a Victorian cabinet of curiosities, the history of the building, Northamptonshire military history at home and abroad, and a nineteenth-century fashion gallery.

Billing Aquadrome is a leisure holiday park, set in 235 acres of parkland, woods and lakes. Facilities include an amusement centre, boating, coarse fishing and free children's play areas. There is also an outdoor swimming pool.

LOCATION
Approximately 1½ miles east of the town centre

OPENING
Please phone for details of timings
Closed 25, 26 Dec & 1 Jan

ADMISSION PRICES
Free

CONTACT
Abington Museum
Abington Park, Park Avenue
South Northampton
Northamptonshire NN1 5LW
Tel 01604 631454
Web
www.northampton.gov.uk/muse-ums

LOCATION
Off the A45, 3 miles from Northampton & 7 miles from the M1 exit at junction 15

OPENING
Mar–Nov open daily until 8pm; 24-hr access for caravans & tents

ADMISSION PRICES
Pedestrians £1 Cars £5

CONTACT
Billing Aquadrome
Crow Lane, Great Billing
Northampton
Northamptonshire NN3 9DA
Tel 01604 408181
Web www.aquadrome.co.uk

168

1–2 hrs

All year

Kirby Hall

Kirby Hall is one of the most outstanding Elizabethan mansions in the country. These peaceful ruins are home to peacocks, and the gardens now contain a fine parterre, with topiary.

★ Elizabethan festivals

★ Theatre productions

★ Free audio tour

LOCATION
On an unclassified road off the A43, 4 miles north-east of Corby

OPENING
1 Apr–31 Oct open daily 10am–6pm (5pm in Oct); 1 Nov–31 Mar open Sat & Sun 10am–4pm; Closed 24–26 Dec & 1 Jan

ADMISSION PRICES
Adult £3.50 Child £1.80 Family £8.80
Concession £2.60

CONTACT
Kirby Hall
Kirby Hall Deene
Nr Corby
Northamptonshire NN17 5EN
Tel 01536 203230
Web www.english-heritage.org.uk

1 hr

Apr–Oct

Rushton Triangular Lodge

Older children will enjoy this fascinating and puzzling building. Wander round the triangular rooms and try to decipher the Latin quotations. Then try to work out the mysterious numbers on the walls, whose meanings are still to be uncovered.

LOCATION	ADMISSION PRICES
1 mile west of Rushton, on an unclassified road, 3 miles from Desborough on the A6	Adult £2 Child £1 Concession £1.50
OPENING	**CONTACT**
1 Apr–31 Oct open daily 10am–6pm (5pm in Oct)	**Rushton Triangular Lodge** Rushton, Kettering Northamptonshire NN14 1RP Tel 01536 710761

Sulgrave Manor

2–3 hrs

Apr–Oct

A Tudor manor house and gardens, set within the heart of a peaceful Northamptonshire village, Sulgrave Manor hosts many special historical events and reconstructions, which are both educational and fun. Please phone for details.

LOCATION	ADMISSION PRICES
Sulgrave is just off the B4525 road from Banbury–Northampton, 7 miles from junction 11 off the M40	Adult £5 Child £2.50
OPENING	**CONTACT**
1 Apr–30 Oct open 2pm–5.30pm; Closed Mon & Fri	**Sulgrave Manor** Manor Road, Sulgrave Nr Banbury OX17 25D Tel 01295 760205 Web www.sulgravemanor.org.uk

169

Quality Assured Visitor Attraction

English Tourism Council

LOCATION
On the A6, 1 mile south of Kettering town centre & 1½ miles from the A14 at junction 10. Follow the signposts

OPENING
29 Mar–31 Oct open daily 9am–5.30pm

ADMISSION PRICES
Playground Free; Please phone for details of Park attractions

CONTACT
Wicksteed Park
Barton Road, Kettering
Northamptonshire NN15 6NJ
Tel 01536 512475
Email information@wicksteedpark.co.uk
Web www.wicksteedpark.co.uk

Wicksteed Park

All day

Mar–Oct

A large playground and an adventure park with over 30 different amusements including a miniature railway, petrol racing cars, Mautic Jets, cycle monorail and a water chute. The fun continues with round-abouts, dodgems and boats, canoes, a roller coaster, pirate ship and more.

★ Thrilling Toner Ride
★ 150 acres of parkland

1–2 hrs

All year

Brewhouse Yard Museum

This row of seventeenth-century cottages present a realistic glimpse of life in Nottingham over the last 100 years. Come and enjoy dug-out caves, 1920s shop windows, an air raid shelter and much more.

★ Hands-on activities

★ Events held throughout year

LOCATION
A 5-minute walk from Nottingham city centre & within easy access from train & bus stations

OPENING
Daily 10am–4.30pm (last admission 4pm)

ADMISSION PRICES
Weekends & Bank holidays: Adult £1.50
Child 80p
Weekdays: Free

CONTACT
Brewhouse Yard Museum
Brewhouse Yard
The Museum of Nottingham Life
Castle Boulevard,
Nottingham NG7 1FB
Tel 0115 9153600

170

1 hr

All year

The Caves of Nottingham

Discover subterranean Nottingham at this spectacular 750-year-old manmade sandstone cave system that lies beneath a modern-day shopping centre. Enjoy a glimpse of Nottingham's fascinating past with a 40-minute digital audio tour of the caves, explaining the various uses that the caves have been put to over the centuries.

★ Assistance for the hearing impaired

★ Audio guide available in 4 languages

★ Textual guide available in 6 languages

★ Evening visits

★ Victorian slum remains

★ Original air raid shelter

★ Natural water wells

LOCATION
Nottingham city centre. Inside the Broadmarsh shopping centre on the upper level

OPENING
All year open Mon–Sat 10am (last admission 4.15pm); Sun open 11am–4pm;
Closed 24, 25, 26, 31 Dec & 1 Jan

ADMISSION PRICES
Adult £3.75 Family £11.50
Concession £2.75

CONTACT
The Caves of Nottingham
Drury Walk
Broad Marsh Centre
Nottingham NG1 7LS
Telephone 0115 9241424
Email info@cavesofnottingham.co.uk

Galleries of Justice

3–4 hrs

All year

NOTTINGHAMSHIRE

Visitor Attraction of the Year 2002
Family Attraction of the Year 2002

LOCATION
Follow the brown tourist signs from
Nottingham city centre

OPENING
Tue–Sun (Bank holidays & Mon during
school holidays); Peak times 10am–5pm;
Off-peak 10am–4pm; Closed at Christmas;
Please phone for details

ADMISSION PRICES
Adult £6.95 Child £5.25 Family £19.95
Concession £5.95

CONTACT
Galleries of Justice
Shire Hall, High Pavement
Lace Market
Nottingham NG1 1HN
Tel 0115 9520555
Web www.galleriesofjustice.org.uk

Journey through 300 years of crime and punishment on this unique atmospheric site. Actors bring the experience to life as you discover first-hand what prison life was really like. Special family-based events are run throughout the school holidays.

★ Hands-on events in school holidays

★ Arts & crafts

★ Storytelling

171

Green's Mill

2 hrs

All year

Included in Best 50 Small Museums
The Independent

LOCATION
1 mile outside Nottingham city centre

OPENING
All year open Wed–Sun & Bank holidays
10am–4pm

ADMISSION PRICES
Free

CONTACT
Green's Mill
Windmill Lane, Sneinton
Nottingham NG2 4QB
Tel 0115 9156878
Web www.greensmill.org.uk

One of the few working inner city windmills in Britain, Green's Mill was once home to the nineteenth-century miller and mathematician George Green. Tour the mill and discover the fascinating process of turning grain into flour.

★ Hands-on experiments exploring
magnetism, electricity & light

★ Kite-making

★ Bread-baking

IBTE Telecommunications Museum

2 hrs

Varies

Children will enjoy the interactive approach of this museum, which explores the history and development of the telecommunications industry from the 1800s to the modern day.

LOCATION
Off the M1 on the A57 towards South Anston & Worksop

OPENING
For parties of 6 (minimum) to 40 (maximum) by appointment

ADMISSION PRICES
Free

CONTACT
IBTE Telecommunications Museum
Queen Street, Worksop
Nottinghamshire S8 7DR
Tel 01909 483680

Making It! Discovery Centre

4 hrs

May–Dec

A fun, engaging, entertaining and educational interactive, hands-on day out. The galleries celebrate the inventiveness of a variety of industries including shoe manufacture, brewing, soft drinks, textiles, printing, engineering and electronics.

LOCATION
Close to Mansfield town centre & Water Meadows leisure pool. Off the A60 & A617

OPENING
May–Dec open daily 10am–5.30pm; Closed 25, 26 Dec & 1 Jan

ADMISSION PRICES
Adult £5.95 Child £5.50
Family £19

CONTACT
Making It! Discovery Centre
Chadburn House, Weighbridge Road, Littleworth, Mansfield
Nottinghamshire NG18 1AH
Tel 01623 473273

172

Megazone

2 hrs

All year

Megazone is Nottingham's largest indoor laser game adventure centre. It also has video games, pool and football tables.

LOCATION
In central Nottingham within 5 minute walk of Market Square

OPENING
All year open daily 10am–5pm; Closed 24, 25 Dec

ADMISSION PRICES
1 game £3.80 2 games £6.50
3 games £8

CONTACT
Megazone
22 Cranbrook Street
Nottingham NG1 1ER
Tel 0115 9589178
Fax 0115 9243450

Museum of Costume & Textiles

2 hrs

All year

Costume displays from 1790 to the twentieth century are beautifully presented at this museum. There is also a fantastic collection of accessories including hats, shoes, bags and fans.

LOCATION
Off Maid Marion Way in Nottingham city centre

OPENING
All year open Wed-Sun & Bank holidays 10am–4pm; Closed 24–26 Dec & 1 Jan

ADMISSION PRICES
Free

CONTACT
Museum of Costume
51 Castlegate
Nottingham NG1 6AF
Tel 0115 915 3500
Web www.nottinghamcity.gov.uk

Nottingham Brass Rubbing Centre

1 hr

All year

LOCATION
In Nottingham city centre. Take the A52 from Derby, the M1 from Leicester or Sheffield, or the A46 from Lincoln

OPENING
All year open Mon–Sat 10am–4pm; Closed 25 Dec & 1 Jan

ADMISSION PRICES
Free

CONTACT
Nottingham Brass Rubbing Centre
St Mary's Church, High Pavement
The Lace Market
Nottingham NC1 1NF
Tel 0115 9582105

Children can enjoy brass rubbing with a selection of replica brasses moulded from originals from various churches.

★ Educational visits welcomed

Nottingham Castle

½ day

All year

LOCATION
10-minute walk from Nottingham city centre, within easy reach of Nottingham train & bus stations

OPENING
All year open daily 10am–5pm
(last admission 4.30pm)

ADMISSION PRICES
Weekdays & Bank holidays: Adult £2 Child £1 Concession £1
Weekdays: Free

CONTACT
Nottingham Castle
Off Friar Lane
Nottingham NG1 6EL
Tel 0115 9153700
Email marketing@ncmg.demon.co.uk

Nottingham Castle is a seventeenth-century mansion with a range of historical and contemporary art exhibitions. Interactive displays feature museum collections of silver, ceramics and Nottinghamshire treasures. Children can also explore the hidden passageways under the building.

★ Children's gallery
★ Lookout! playground
★ The Watchtower Trail
★ Sit on the Queen's throne
★ Events throughout the year

1–2 hrs
Mar–Oct

Sherwood Forest Fun Park

This small amusement park caters for families and children of all ages. Enjoy a fun-packed few hours sampling the Ghost Train, Dodgems, Giant Astroslide, Jumping Jack and Circus Train.

★ Games & prizes

LOCATION
At the entrance to Sherwood Country Park, 5 minutes walk from the Sherwood Forest Visitors Centre, just off the B6034

OPENING
Mar–end of Oct open daily 10am–dusk; Closed in winter (Nov–Feb)

ADMISSION PRICES
Free
Token system in operation

CONTACT
Sherwood Forest Fun Park
Sherwood Country Park, Edwinstowe
Nr. Mansfield
Nottingham NG21 9QA
Tel 01623 823536

174

4 hrs
All year

Sherwood Pines Forest Park

Situated in the centre of ancient Sherwood Forest, Sherwood Pines Forest Park is the largest woodland open to the public in the East Midlands. It offers interest and fun for all ages, whether it's a leisurely walk or off-road cycling that you enjoy. The visitor centre offers excellent refreshments, cycle hire and sales.

★ Variety of waymarked walks

★ Cycle hire

★ Cycle routes

★ Working forest

★ Visitor centre

★ Off-road area for mountain bikes

★ Wildlife haven

LOCATION
On the B6030 Clipstone–Ollerton Road, near the village of Edwinstowe in Nottinghamshire, 17 miles north of Nottingham

OPENING
Daily 8am–dusk; Closed 25 Dec

ADMISSION PRICES
Car park £2

CONTACT
Sherwood Pines Forest Park
Forestry Commission, Edwinstowe
Nottingham NG21 9JL
Tel 01623 822447
Email sherwoodfdo@forestry.gsi.gov.uk
Web www.forestry.gov.uk

Tales of Robin Hood

1½ hrs

All year

LOCATION
In Nottingham city centre, just 5 minutes walk from Nottingham Castle

OPENING
In summer open daily 10am–6pm (last admission 4.30pm); In winter open daily 10am–5.30pm (last admission 4pm)

ADMISSION PRICES
Adult £6.50 Child £4.50 Family £19.95 Senior & Student £5.25

CONTACT
Tales of Robin Hood
30–38 Maid Marion Way
Nottingham NG1 6GF
Tel 0870 7560440
Email robinhoodcentre@mail.com

Travel back in time as you discover the truth behind the legend of Robin Hood. Follow the Silver Arrow Trail and try your hand at archery and brass rubbing.

★ Events staged during school holidays

175

Wonderland Pleasure Park

4 hrs+

Apr–Oct

LOCATION
On the A614 at White Post Island, 12 miles from Nottingham & 8 miles from Ollerton

OPENING
1 Apr–30 Sep open daily 10.30am–6pm (last admission 5pm); 1–31 Oct open Sat, Sun & half-term 10.30am–4pm

ADMISSION PRICES
Adult £4.30 Child £4.30 Family £16.50 Concession £3.50

CONTACT
Wonderland Pleasure Park
White Post Island, Farnsfield
Newark
Nottinghamshire NG22 8XH
Tel 01623 882773
Email wonderland@btconnect.com
Web www.isipreview.co.uk/wonderland

A 30-acre safe, clean and secure park setting with a large tropical house – home to exotic butterflies, reptiles, birds and fish. There are also zip slides, trampolines, a drop, twist and astroslide complex, a roller coaster and a 7.25-gauge railway, taking trips around the park.

★ Soft play centre
★ Pets corner
★ Tennis & football
★ Massive maze
★ Fire engine & lightning jet

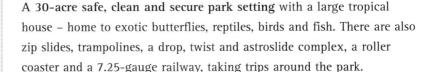

1 hr

Apr–Oct

Lyddington Bede House

Lyddington Bede House was the medieval palace of the bishops of Lincoln. The remaining building was converted into an almshouse in 1600. Discover the 'Bishop's Eye' and a mystery fire-fighting object!

★ Free educational leaflet

★ Legend of the Lludd & the plague of Albion events

★ Seventeenth-century Surgeon at Your Service

★ The Mummer's Return

★ Free audio tour

LOCATION
In Lyddington, 6 miles north of Corby, 1 mile east of the A6003. Next to the church in Lyddington

OPENING
1 Apr–30 Sept open daily 10am–6pm; Oct open daily 10am–5pm

ADMISSION PRICES
Adult £3.20 Child £1.60 Family £8

CONTACT
Lyddington Bede House
Blue Coat Lane, Lyddington
Uppingteam, Oakham
Rutland LE15 9LZ
Tel 01572 822438
Web www.english-heritage.org.uk

176

All day

All year

Rutland Water

The whole family can enjoy this 3,100 acre lake set in beautiful countryside, with over 20 miles of off-road cycling or walking. Spend time at the butterfly and aquatic centre, then take in the nature reserve or have a go on the climbing wall.

★ Fishing

★ Cycle hire

★ Museum on site

★ Watersports

LOCATION
Close to the A1 Grantham–Peterborough stretch & the A47 Leicester–Peterborough. The A606 Oakam–Stamford runs along the North Shore

OPENING
All year open daily dawn–dusk; Closed 25 Dec

ADMISSION PRICES
Please phone for details

CONTACT
Rutland Water
Sykes Lane, Empingham
Rutland LE15 8PX
Tel 01572 653026
Email tic@rutland-water.freeserve.co.uk
Web www.rutlandwater.net

Hawkstone Park
Historic Park & Follies

3–4hrs
Jan–Nov

At Hawkstone Park, the final resting place of King Arthur, you can explore a world of secret tunnels, concealed grotto caves and challenging woodland walks. Enjoy the Hawkstone Follies, including a 150-foot tower, the Narnia Arch and the Swiss Bridge. Themed events are held all year, including a Magical Narnia weekend, Circus Workshop, battle re-enactments, wildlife weekends and a Spooky Halloween Adventure!

★ Film location of the BBC production
Chronicles of Narnia
★ Panoramic views

177

Ironbridge
Gorge Museum

2–4 hrs
All year

The Ironbridge Gorge was the scene of a remarkable breakthrough in technology that led to the Industrial Revolution. Nine museums catalogue these events and the men who made them happen.

Quality Assured Visitor Attraction

English Tourism Council

Mythstories, Museum
of Myth & Fable

3 hrs+
Apr–Oct

Enjoy colourful displays of traditional stories from Shropshire and around the world, with illustrations, photographs and artefacts. There are things to touch and play with, puzzles to do and live storytelling in the inglenook fireplace.

4–5 hrs
All year

Park Hall Countryside Experience

This is an all-weather farm visitor attraction. Popular with young and old alike, Park Hall puts on regular activities where you can meet and feed the animals. This unique experience combines education, fun and adventure. An impressive 80 per cent of the activities are indoors.

- ★ Toy tractor circuit
- ★ Milking
- ★ Animal feeding
- ★ Lead the Shire horses
- ★ Soft play area
- ★ Playbus
- ★ Giant games area

- ★ Giant sandpits
- ★ Indoor & outdoor adventure areas
- ★ Children's driving school
- ★ Quad bikes
- ★ Animal trail
- ★ New nature trail
- ★ Pony grooming

LOCATION
In Oswestry, north Shropshire, 30 minutes from Chester. Take the A495 off the Oswestry bypass (A483)

OPENING
1 Apr–30 Sep open daily 10am–5pm; 1 Oct–31 Mar open Fri–Sun 10am–4pm; Open all school holidays & 1–24 Dec daily; Closed 25, 26, 31 Dec & 1 Jan

ADMISSION PRICES
Adult £4.60 Child £3.60
Family £17.50 Concession £3.60

CONTACT
Park Hall Countryside Experience
Park Hall, Oswestry
Shropshire SY11 4AS
Tel 01691 671123
Email rachel@parkhallfarm.co.uk
Web www.parkhallfarm.co.uk

178

3 hrs
Feb–Dec

Ray's Farm Country Matters

This attraction has unusual animals and birds, including red fallow Sika and Axis deer, Bagot, pygmy, angora and other goats. Come and visit the various owl species and the many other foreign breeds including llamas, horses, ponies and donkeys.

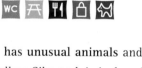

LOCATION
Signposted off the B4363 just south of Billingsley

OPENING
2 Feb–24 Dec open daily 10am–5.30pm

ADMISSION PRICES
Adult £4 Child £2.50
Concession £3.75

CONTACT
Ray's Farm Country Matters
Billingsley, Bridgnorth
Shropshire WV16 6PF
Tel 01299 841255
Email raysfarm@virtual-shropshire.co.uk
Web www.virtual-shropshire.co.uk/rays-farm/

Wonderland

2 hrs+
All year

Discover your favourite fairy-tale and nursery rhyme characters and their houses. Explore the Wonderland Maze, take a spin on the Mad Hatter's Tea Cup ride and enjoy playing in Dribble the Dragon's indoor soft play area.

LOCATION
Off the M54 at junctions 4 or 5. Follow the brown tourist signs for Town Park & Wonderland

OPENING
All year; Please phone for details

ADMISSION PRICES
Adult £3 Child £2.25
Under-3s Free Senior £2.25

CONTACT
Wonderland
Telford Town Park TF3 4AY
Tel 01952 591633
Web
www.wonderlandtelford.com

Alton Towers Theme Park

1 day

Mar–Nov

LOCATION
Travelling north take the M1 junction 23a, M6 junction 15, signposted from the motorway. Travelling south take the M1 junction 28, M6 junction 16, signposted from the motorway

OPENING
16 Mar–3 Nov open daily from 9.30am

ADMISSION PRICES
Adult £17 Child £14 Family £60

CONTACT
Alton Towers Theme Park
Alton, Stoke-on-Trent
Staffordshire ST10 4DB
Tel 0870 5204060
Web www.altontowers.com

This is a theme park with a blend of rides and attractions to suit every member of the family. It includes 200 acres of landscaped gardens, rides, live entertainment and the historic towers building. Come along and enjoy a fun-packed family day out.

★ Educational visits welcomed

Ash End Children's Farm

3 hrs

All year

LOCATION
In Middleton, near Tamworth in Staffordshire. Signposted off the A4091 & on the same road as Drayton Manor Park

OPENING
In summer open daily 10am–5pm; In winter open daily 10am–dusk; Closed 25, 26, 27 Dec & 1 Jan & weekdays in Jan

ADMISSION PRICES
Adult £2.10 Child £4.20

CONTACT
Ash End Children's Farm
Middleton Lane, Middleton
Nr Tamworth
Staffordshire B78 2BL
Tel 0121 3293240
Email
childrensfarm@ashendhouse.fsnet.co.uk
Web www.ashendhouse.fsnet.co.uk

This small family-owned farm has lots of friendly animals to feed and stroke. As well as outdoor activities and a play area, the farm offers lots of undercover attractions and some fascinating rare breeds.

★ Tours for groups
★ Birthday parties on the farm
★ Santa in December

All day

All year

Blackbrook Zoological Park

WC 🌲 🍴 📷

Blackbrook Zoological Park is a fun and educational day out. There is always something new to see at this constantly expanding attraction, from rare birds, unusual animals and reptiles, to insects and aquatics.

LOCATION
From Leek, take the A523 & the 1st right, signposted to the park, then the 1st right again

OPENING
In summer open daily 10.30am–5.30pm; In winter open daily 10.30am–4pm; Closed 25, 26, 31 Dec & 1 Jan

ADMISSION PRICES
Adult £6.25 Child £3.95
Family £18 Senior £5.25

CONTACT
Blackbrook Zoological Park
Winkhill, Staffordshire ST13 7QR
Tel 01538 308293
Web www.blackbrookzoological-park.co.uk

180

British Wildlife Rescue Centre

2 hrs

All year

The whole family will enjoy a visit to this refuge set up for the treatment of sick and injured British wildlife. The farm facilities are available to visitors.

★ Guided tours

LOCATION
On the A518 Stafford–Uttoxeter road, 1 mile from Weston

OPENING
All year open daily 10am–5pm; Apr–Sep open10am–6pm; Closed 25, 26 Dec & 1 Jan

ADMISSION PRICES
Adult £1.50 Child 50p

CONTACT
British Wildlife Rescue Centre
Amerton Working Farm
Stowe-by-Chartley, Stafford
Staffordshire ST18 0LA
Tel 01889 271308

2–3 hrs

All year

Churnet Valley Wildlife Park

WC 🌲

This wildlife park is set in natural grounds with large woodlands. There is a visitor and conservation centre and a walk to see various small animals and birds. There is also a nature reserve, which is part of the Churnet Valley, a Site of Special Scientific Interest.

★ Educational visits welcomed

LOCATION
From Cheadle & Stoke-on-Trent follow the A52, the A520 from Leek & the A50 from Uttoxeter

OPENING
29 Mar–31 Oct open daily 10am–dusk; 1 Nov–31 Mar open Sat & Sun 10am–dusk; Closed 25 Dec & 1 Jan

ADMISSION PRICES
Adult £3.50 Child £2

CONTACT
Churnet Valley Wildlife Park
Sprinks Lane, Kingsley
Stoke-on-Trent
Staffordshire ST10 2BX
Tel 01538 756702
Email info@churnetvalleywildlife.co.uk
Web www.churnetvalleywildlife.co.uk

Drayton Manor Family Theme Park

All day

Mar–Oct

LOCATION
On the A5 & A4091. On the M42 take junction 9 or 10

OPENING
23 Mar–27 Oct open daily 10.30am–6pm

ADMISSION PRICES
Adult £15 Child £11 Concession £6.50

CONTACT
Drayton Manor Family Theme Park
Tamworth
Staffordshire B78 3TW
Tel 01827 287979
Email info@draytonmanor.co.uk
Web www.draytonmanor.co.uk

Drayton Manor Family Theme Park offers a really fun day out that's a firm favourite with all the family. In over 250 acres of parkland and lakes you'll find no end of excitement and entertainment, with over 100 rides and attractions to enjoy.

★ Parties

★ Dancing

★ White knuckle rides

Etruria Industrial Museum

1–2 hrs

All year

Etruria Industrial Museum is situated on the Calden, Trent and Mersey Canals and includes the Etruscan Bone and Flint Mill. There is an interactive exhibition and a regular programme of events.

★ Craft workshops   ★ Steam-driven engines

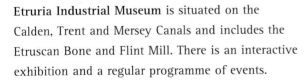

LOCATION
Signposted from the A500. The car park is off Etruria Vale Road

OPENING
All year open Sat–Wed 12pm–4.30pm; Closed weekends Jan–Mar

ADMISSION PRICES
Adult £2 Concession £1

CONTACT
Etruria Industrial Museum
Lower Bedford Street
Stoke-on-Trent ST4 7AF
Tel 01782 233144
Email etruria@swift.stoke.gov.uk
Web stoke.gov.uk.museums

Gladstone Pottery Museum

3 hrs

All year

A complete Victorian pottery factory where visitors can get to grips with the history and skills of the potteries. Throw your own pot or try your hand at a range of pottery crafts with our team of friendly expert presentation staff.

LOCATION
A50 from Stoke–Longton. Exit at junction 15 off the M6

OPENING
All year open daily 10am–5pm (last admission 4pm)

ADMISSION PRICES
Adult £3.95 Child £2.50
Concession £2.95

CONTACT
Gladstone Pottery Museum
Uttoxeter Road, Longton
Stoke-on-Trent ST3 1PQ
Tel 01782 319232
Email gladstone@stoke.gov.uk
Web www.stoke.gov.uk/gladstone

3-4 hrs

All year

Waterworld

Children will enjoy this wacky and wild water park. It has 19 exciting rides and attractions including wave machines, flumes, rapids and slides.

★ The Spacebowl

★ Aqua assault course

★ The Python

★ The Black Hole

★ Aquadisco parties available

LOCATION
Off Junction 16 of the M6. From the M1 follow the A50 to Stoke on Trent & then follow signs to Festival Park

OPENING
In summer open Mon & Tue 10am–6pm, Wed 10am–7pm, Thu 10am–8pm, Fri 10am–9pm, Sat & Sun 10am–6pm; In winter closed Mon & Tue, open Wed & Thu 1pm–7pm, Fri 1pm–9pm, Sat & Sun 10am–6pm

ADMISSION PRICES
Please phone for details

CONTACT
Waterworld
Waterworld Festival Park, Etruria
Hanley
Stoke on Trent ST1 5PU
Tel 01782 205747
Web www.waterworld.co.uk

1 hr+

All year

Bungay Castle

The remains of this large Norman castle contain many interesting features. The massive gatehouse towers still stand, as do the bridge pit and curtain walls. A mine tunnel is exposed along with the forebuilding with its latrine chamber (garderobe).

LOCATION
Off the A143 & A144

OPENING
5 Jan-23 Dec open daily 10am-4pm

ADMISSION PRICES
Adult £1 Child 50p Family £5 Concession 50p

CONTACT
Bungay Castle
Bungay
Suffolk
Tel 01986 896156

Bury St Edmunds Abbey

2 hrs

All year

Visit the remains of a Benedictine abbey, church and precinct with Norman tower, set in beautifully kept gardens. The two fourteenth-century gateways are the best preserved buildings. There is also a visitor centre with interactive displays.

LOCATION
Off the A14, at the east end of Bury St Edmunds

OPENING
All year open Mon-Fri 7.30am-dusk, Sat & Sun & Bank holidays 9am-dusk; Please phone for opening hours of visitor centre

ADMISSION PRICES
Free

CONTACT
Bury St Edmunds Abbey
Bury St Edmunds, Suffolk
Tel 01284 763110
Web www.english-heritage.org.uk

Clare Castle Country Park

3 hrs

All year

A **30-acre site** fronting onto the river Stour, combining the remains of a Norman motte-and-bailey castle and a Victorian railway station with natural history interest. There is also a visitor centre.

★ History & nature trail

LOCATION	ADMISSION PRICES
Signed off the A1092 in the centre of Clare	Free
	CONTACT
OPENING	**Clare Castle Country Park**
Park: All year open daily dawn–dusk	Malting Lane, Clare, Sudbury Suffolk CO10 8NW
Visitor centre: In the summer open daily 10am–5pm	Tel 01787 277491 Email john.laws@et.suffolkcc.gov.uk

Coastal Voyager

Varies

All year

Coastal Voyager offers a variety of sea trips and river cruises. There is a half-hour high speed blast trip and various tranquil river cruises along the beautiful River Blyth.

LOCATION	CONTACT
Trips depart from Southwold Harbour	**Coastal Voyager** 6 Strickland Place Southwold, Suffolk IP18 6HN
OPENING	Tel 07887 525082
Please phone for details	Fax 01502 723219
ADMISSION PRICES	Email thrills@southwold.ws
Please phone for details	Web www.blythweb.co.uk/sailsouthwold

183

Deben Cruises

2–3 hrs

May–Oct

LOCATION
From A12 from the Orwell Bridge follow signs to Lowestoft. Take the sign at the roundabout to Waldringfield & it will take you straight to the village
OPENING
May–Oct; Please phone for details
ADMISSION PRICES
Adult £5 Child £3 Concession £5
CONTACT
Deben Cruises Waldringfield Boatyard Ltd The Quay, Waldringfield Woodbridge Suffolk IP12 4QZ Tel 01473 736260 Fax 01473 736260

The Jahan cruises through 10 miles of lovely countryside, departing from the quay at Waldringfield Boatyard and returning to Waldringfield.

The cruises last two or three hours, depending on tides. Visit the picturesque port of Woodbridge or travel to Felixstowe Ferry.

★ Lunch or set tea & cruise packages

Golf FX

2–4 hrs

All year

The whole family can enjoy playing golf in this park. Children will have fun and surprises as they play a round on the 13-hole course.

LOCATION
Follow the A12 & A14, the amusement park is signposted within the town boundary

OPENING
In summer open daily 10am–9.30pm; In winter open daily 10am–6pm; Closed 25 Dec

ADMISSION PRICES
Over 3ft tall: £2
Under 3ft tall: £1.50

CONTACT
Golf FX
Manning's Amusement Park
Sea Road, Felixstowe
Suffolk IP11 2DW
Tel 01394 282370

Lowestoft & East Suffolk Maritime Museum

2–3 hrs

Mar–Oct

The museum houses models of fishing and commercial ships, shipwrights' tools, fishing gear, a lifeboat display, an art gallery and a drifter's cabin with models of fishermen.

LOCATION
Off the A12

OPENING
Easter & 28 Apr–6 Oct open daily 10am–4.30pm

ADMISSION PRICES
Adult 75p Child 25p
Concession 50p

CONTACT
Lowestoft & East Suffolk Maritime Museum
Sparrows Nest Park
Whapload Road
Lowestoft, Suffolk NR32 1XG
Tel 01502 561963

Manning's Amusement Park

3 hrs

Apr–Sep

This traditional children's amusement park has numerous rides and slides. There is also an amusement arcade, Sun market, bowling green, nightclub, sports bar and indoor Adventure Golf-FX.

LOCATION
Off the A14 & A12 on the seafront

OPENING
13 Apr–29 Sep open Sat & Sun & school holidays
Please phone for further details

ADMISSION PRICES
Free

CONTACT
Manning's Amusement Park
Sea Road, Felixstowe, Suffolk
IP11 2DW
Tel 01394 282370
Fax 01394 671622

Mid-Suffolk Light Railway Museum

2 hrs

Easter –Sep

The railway museum is dedicated to the Mid-Suffolk Light Railway. It shows restoration of the station and trackwork on part of the original route of the railway. Artefacts and memorabilia relating to the railway are preserved here.

LOCATION
About 1 mile from the A140 road in the village of Brockford-cum-Wetheringsett

OPENING
Good Fri–29 Sep open Sun & Bank holidays 11am–5pm

ADMISSION PRICES
Adult £1.50 Child 50p
Concession £1.50

CONTACT
Mid-Suffolk Light Railway Museum, Brockford Station Wetheringsett, Stowmarket Suffolk IP14 5PW
Tel 01449 766899

National Stud

Quality Assured Visitor Attraction
English Tourism Council

2 hrs

Mar–Sep

Horse-crazy children will enjoy this stable tour, which takes in the superb stallion unit, along with the stallions in residence, nursery yards and mares and foals in their paddocks.

LOCATION
Take the A11, A1304 & A1303. The stud is 2 miles south-west of Newmarket on the A1304

OPENING
1 Mar–30 Sep open Mon–Sat; Tours 11.15am, 2.30pm & Sun 2.30pm

ADMISSION PRICES
Adult £5 Child £3.50 Family £15 Concession £4

CONTACT
National Stud
Newmarket, Suffolk CB8 0XE
Tel 01638 663464
Email tours@nationalstud.co.uk
Web www.nationalstud.co.uk

New Pleasurewood Hills Leisure Park

All day

Easter –Oct

New Pleasurewood Hills has over 40 rides, shows and attractions set in 50 acres of lovely parkland. It is an ideal day out for families and young teens – whether your idea of fun is a thrilling ride or something much gentler.

LOCATION
Off the A12 between Great Yarmouth & Lowestoft

OPENING
Easter–Oct half-term; Please phone for specific opening dates; Opening hours 10am–4pm, 5pm or 6pm, depending on conditions

ADMISSION PRICES
Please phone for information

CONTACT
New Pleasurewood Hills Leisure Park, Leisure Way, Corton Lowestoft, Suffolk NR32 5DZ
Tel 01502 508200 (info line)
Web www.pleasurewoodhills.co.uk

Norfolk & Suffolk Aviation Museum

3 hrs

All year

This unique museum has 30 aircraft on display, from the early pioneers of flight up to the machines of the present day and Luftwaffe crash planes.

★ Royal Observer Corps Museum   ★ USAAF 8th Air Force displays
★ 446th Bomb Group Memorial

LOCATION
Off the B1062

OPENING
Jan–Mar open Tue, Wed, Sun, 10am–4pm (last admission 3pm); Apr–Oct Sun–Thu & Bank holidays 10am–5pm (last admission 4pm); Nov–Dec Tue, Wed, Sun 10am–4pm (last adm. 3pm)

ADMISSION PRICES
Free

CONTACT
Norfolk & Suffolk Aviation Museum
The Street, Flixton, Bungay Suffolk NR35 1NZ
Tel 01986 896644
Web www.aviationmuseum.net

Otter Trust

2–3 hrs

Apr–Sep

Many children love to watch these beautiful animals and will enjoy a visit to the Trust, which promotes the cause of otters and encourages the public to see, enjoy and learn about them at its centres.

LOCATION
Located off the A143, 1 mile west of Bungay

OPENING
1 Apr–30 Sep open daily 10.30am–6pm

ADMISSION PRICES
Adult £5 Child £3
Concession £4

CONTACT
Otter Trust
Earsham, Bungay
Suffolk NR35 2AF
Tel 01986 893470
Fax 01986 892461

Playworld Ocean Adventure

An indoor play area for children under 4ft 6in tall with ball ponds, scramble nets, slides, aerial glide and spooky room. There is also a toddler's area.

Varies

All year

LOCATION
Easy access from the A14 into Stowmarket. Signposted to the Leisure Centre from the town centre

OPENING
All year open Mon–Fri 9.30am–7pm, Sat & Sun 9am–6pm; Closed 25, 26 Dec & 1 Jan

ADMISSION PRICES
Child £2.85

CONTACT
Playworld Ocean Adventure
Mid Suffolk Leisure Centre
Gainsborough Road
Stowmarket, Suffolk IP14 1LH
Tel 01449 674980
Fax 01449 742815

Southwold Pier

Varies

All year

Visit this seaside pier and amusement centre. The new pier was completed in 2002 and is the first pier to be built in the UK for over 45 years. Additional attractions include a seaside holiday exhibition.

★ Educational visits welcomed

LOCATION
Off the A145, follow signs for Southwold

OPENING
Amusements open Jan–Jun Sat & Sun from 10am; Jun–Sep open daily from 9am; Sep–Dec open Sat & Sun from 10am
Please phone for specific dates

ADMISSION PRICES
Free

CONTACT
Southwold Pier
North Parade, Southwold
Suffolk IP18 6BN
Tel 01502 722105
Web
www.southwoldpier.demon.co.uk

Suffolk Horse Museum

2 hrs+

Apr–Sep

An indoor exhibition about the Suffolk Punch breed of heavy horse. This illustrates the history of the breed through paintings, photographs and exhibits and shows how the horse was used.

★ Shoeing   ★ The Life of the Horseman

LOCATION
In the centre of Market Hill in Woodbridge, off the A12 between Ipswich & Lowestoft

OPENING
Apr–Sep open Tue–Sun & Bank holidays 2pm–5pm
Please phone for details of dates

ADMISSION PRICES
Please phone for details

CONTACT
Suffolk Horse Museum
The Market Hill, Woodbridge
Suffolk IP12 4LU
Tel 01394 380643
Web www.btinternet.com/~suf-folkhs.horse.ht

Suffolk Owl Sanctuary

2–3 hrs

All year

The Suffolk Owl Sanctuary has a variety of animal attractions, including daily flying displays of different owls and raptors. There is also a woodland walk with a songbird hide and red squirrel enclosure with daily talks and feeding session.

LOCATION
On the A1120, 8 miles from Ipswich & Stowmarket

OPENING
In summer open 10am–5.30pm; In winter open 10am–4.30pm; Closed 25, 26 Dec & 1 Jan

ADMISSION PRICES
Free

CONTACT
Suffolk Owl Sanctuary
Stonham Barns, Pettaugh Road
Stonham Aspal, Stowmarket
Suffolk IP14 6AT
Tel 01449 711425
Fax 01449 710018
Email info@owl-help.org.uk
Web www.owl-help.org.uk

Suffolk Wildlife Park

All day

WC 🏕 🍴 🔒

All year

SUFFOLK

Let your children enjoy the ultimate African adventure set in 100 acres of coastal parkland. Embark on a thrilling journey through a wilderness of woods, lakeland and explorer trails to discover an abundance of wild animals from the African continent.

★ Safari train
★ Birds of prey display
★ Animal handling

187

West Stow Country Park & Anglo-Saxon Village

2 hrs+

All year

WC 🏕 🍴 🔒 🐾

West Stow is a reconstructed Anglo-Saxon village, built on the site of an original settlement and set in a 125-acre country park. Finds from the site are displayed in a specially built interpretation centre. Throughout the year, this unique village is brought to life when authentic costume groups host special events.

★ Nature trail
★ Woodland walks
★ River views
★ Lake
★ Anglo-Saxon costume events held throughout holiday periods

2 hrs

All year

Broomey Croft Children's Farm

Set in 600 acres of country park, Broomey Croft Children's Farm provides an opportunity for a family day of fun and a relaxing mixture of countryside walks and waterside activities.

★ Tractor & trailer rides

★ Lambing & bottle feeding lambs

★ Baby goats

★ Sheep shearing

★ Baby chicks

★ Bee display

★ Hand-feed the animals

LOCATION
10 minutes from junction 9 off the M42. Follow the A4091 towards Drayton Manor & follow the brown tourist signs

OPENING
Apr–Aug open daily 10am–5pm; Sep open weekends 10am–5pm; Oct–Mar open weekends 10am–4pm; Oct & Feb open daily half-terms

ADMISSION PRICES
Adult £3 Child £2.60 Senior £2.60

CONTACT
Broomey Croft Children's Farm
Bodymoor Heath Lane, Bodymore Heath
Kingsbury
North Warwickshire B76 0EE
Tel 01827 873844
Email info@childrens-farm.com
Web www.childrens-farm.com

188

3 hrs+

All year

Hatton Country World

Hatton Country World offers acres of fun for everyone, with a fun-packed day of events and activities, such as Farmyard Favourites and Adventure Land. Finish off your day with a relaxing browse round the unique shopping village or a trip to see the animals.

★ Daft Duck trials

★ Children's show

★ Bird-obatics

★ Soft play centre

★ Guinea pig village

★ Tristan the Runaway Tractor

★ Mini tractors

LOCATION
5 minutes from junction 15 off the M40. Take the A46 towards Coventry & turn onto the A4177 & follow the brown tourist signs

OPENING
In summer open daily 10am–5.30pm;
In winter open daily 10am–5pm; Closed Dec 25, 26

ADMISSION PRICES
Adult £8 Child £8 Under-3s Free

CONTACT
Hatton Country World
Hatton House
Warwickshire CV35 7LD
Tel 01926 843411
Email hatton@hattonworld
Web www.hattonworld.com

3 hrs

All year

Shakespeare's Birthplace

Each of the five Shakespeare houses on show has its own unique character and family connection to William Shakespeare, and offers a different insight into the world of the famous playwright.

LOCATION	CONTACT
Off the A439, the A3400, the A46 & M40 junction 15	**Shakespeare's Birthplace** Henley Street Stratford-upon-Avon
OPENING	Warwickshire CV37 6QW
Please phone for details	Tel 01789 204016 Web www.shakespeare.org.uk
ADMISSION PRICES	
Adult £6.50 Child £2.50 Concession £5.50	

Stratford-upon-Avon Butterfly Farm

1 hr+

All year

Wander through a tropical rainforest with a myriad multicoloured butterflies, birds and fish. See fascinating animals in Insect City and view deadly spiders in perfect safety in Arachnoland.

★ Expert staff   ★ Wildlife video shows

LOCATION	ADMISSION PRICES
On the River Avon, opposite the Royal Shakespeare Theatre. Easily accessible from the town centre	Adult £4.25 Child £3.25 Family £12.50 Senior & Student £3.75
	CONTACT
OPENING	**Stratford Butterfly Farm**
In summer open daily 10am–6pm; In winter 10am–dusk; Closed 25 Dec	Traway Walk, Swan's Nest Lane Stratford-upon-Avon CV37 7LS Tel 01789 299288 Web www.butterflyfarm.co.uk

3–4 hrs

All year

Twycross Zoo

Twycross is the leading primate zoo in the country, where children can see wildlife from around the world.

★ Seal & penguin feeding times   ★ Rare breeds

★ Pets corner

LOCATION	ADMISSION PRICES
On the A444 in Leicestershire, within easy reach of all the midland counties	Adult £6.50 Child £4.50 Senior £5
	CONTACT
OPENING	**Twycross Zoo**
In summer open daily 10am–5.30pm; In winter open daily 10am–4pm; Closed 25 Dec	Burton Road, Atherstone Warwickshire CV9 3PX Tel 01827 880250 Web www.twycrosszoo.com

Warwick Castle

Quality Assured Visitor Attraction

English Tourism Council

2 hrs

All year

Experience 1,000 years of history at Warwick Castle. See the medieval preparation for battle in Kingmaker, join a Victorian Royal Weekend Party and enjoy special events throughout the year.

LOCATION	ADMISSION PRICES
2 miles from junction 15 off the M40, Warwick Castle is easily accessible by road or rail	Please phone for details
	CONTACT
OPENING	**Warwick Castle**
Apr–Sep open daily 10am–6pm; Oct–Mar open daily 10am–5pm	Warwick Warwickshire CV34 4QU Tel 0870 4422000 Web www.warwick-castle.co.uk

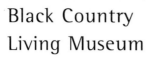

Black Country Living Museum

4 hrs

All year

Discover a fascinating world where an old-fashioned village has been created beside the canal. Wander around original shops and houses, ride on a tramcar or fairground swingboat, go down the mine or just soak up the atmosphere.

LOCATION	ADMISSION PRICES
On the Tipton road, the A4037 in Dudley. 3 miles from junction 2 off the M5 via the A4123	Adult 8.50 Child £5 Family £23 Concession £7
	CONTACT
OPENING	**Black Country Living Museum**
1 Mar–31 Oct open daily 10am–5pm; 1 Nov–28 Feb open Wed–Sun 10am–4pm; Closed 23-25 Dec	Tipton Road, Dudley West Midlands DY1 4SQ Tel 0121 5579643 Web www.bclm.co.uk

Cadbury World

3 hrs+

All year

Fun for all ages with Cadabra, a magical Cadbury journey, and the Cadbury Fantasy Factory. Children can learn all about chocolate: where it came from, who first drank this mysterious potion and when it was first eaten.

LOCATION	ADMISSION PRICES
Off the A38 Bristol road, along the A4040, 1 mile south of the Bristol road	Adult £8.50 Child £6.50 Family £26 Concession £7
	CONTACT
OPENING	**Cadbury World**, Linden Road
Please phone for details and to make reservations	Bournville, Birmingham West Midlands B30 2LD Tel 0121 4514180 Web www.cadburyworld.co.uk

Critters Farm

½ day

All year

Enjoy close encounters with over 300 animals, including birds of prey, reptiles, rabbits and chickens. Children can try bottle-feeding baby lambs, watch the duck racing and greet the goats.

LOCATION	ADMISSION PRICES
Take the A463 or A459 or A457 into Sedgley. Signposted from Cotwall End Road or Catholic Lane	Adult £2.50 Child £1.75 Concession £1.75
	CONTACT
OPENING	**Critters Farm**, Cotwall End,
1 Nov–28 Feb open daily 9.30am–4pm; 1 Mar–31 Oct 9.30am–5pm; Closed 25 Dec	Catholic Lane, Sedgley, Dudley West Midlands DY3 3YE Tel 01902 674668 Email dawn.laycock@talk21.com

Dudley Zoo & Castle

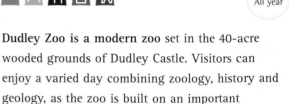

3 hrs+

All year

Dudley Zoo is a modern zoo set in the 40-acre wooded grounds of Dudley Castle. Visitors can enjoy a varied day combining zoology, history and geology, as the zoo is built on an important limestone escarpment.

LOCATION	CONTACT
On the A459 in Dudley	**Dudley Zoo & Castle**
	2 The Broadway, Dudley
OPENING	West Midlands DY1 4QB
1 Mar–31 Oct open daily 10am–4pm; 1 Sep–31 Mar 10am–3pm; Closed 25 Dec	Tel 01384 215313 Email marketing@dudleyzoo.org.uk Web www.dudleyzoo.org.uk
ADMISSION PRICES	
Adult £6.75 Child £4.50 Family £23	

Lapworth Museum of Geology

2 hrs
All year

For an educational few hours, take the children to visit one of the oldest specialist geological museums in the UK. Dating back to 1880, Lapworth has an extensive and fascinating collection of fossils, minerals and rocks.

LOCATION	ADMISSION PRICES
On the A38 into Birmingham	Free
OPENING	**CONTACT**
All year open Mon-Fri 9am–5pm; Sat & Sun 2pm–5pm; Closed 29 Mar–1 Apr, 24 Dec–2 Jan	**School of Earth Sciences** Birmingham University Edgbaston, Birmingham West Midlands B15 2TT Tel 0121 4147294 Email lapmus@bham.ac.uk

Lunt Roman Fort

1 hr
Apr–Aug

Enjoy an educational visit to Lunt Roman Fort. A unique Roman fort, it features a reconstructed cavalry training circle and holds re-enactments of Roman history with the XIV Legion.

LOCATION	ADMISSION PRICES
In Baginton Village, near Coventry. It can be approached from the A45 & the A46	Adult £2 Child £1
OPENING	**CONTACT**
Apr–Aug open daily 10am–5pm	**Lunt Roman Fort** Coventry Road Bagington CV8 3AG Tel 024 76832565/ 024 76303567

National Sea Life Centre

3 hrs+
All year

LOCATION
In the heart of Birmingham city centre at Brindleyplace, next to the National Indoor Arena & International Convention Centre

OPENING
All year open daily 10am–5.30pm; Closed 25 Dec

ADMISSION PRICES
Adult £8 Child £5.50 Family £24 Concession £5.95

CONTACT
National Sea Life Centre
The Water's Edge
Brindleyplace, Birmingham
West Midlands B1 2HL
Tel 0121 6334700
Email slcbirmingham@merlin-entertainments.co.uk
Web www.sealife.co.uk

This sea life centre has over 55 fascinating displays. Children can come face-to-face with literally hundreds of amazing sea creatures, from sharks to shrimps.

★ Claws exhibition
★ Transparent underwater tunnel

4 hrs

All year

Ryton Organic Gardens

Ryton Organic Gardens is the UK's national centre for organic gardening, set within 10 acres of glorious gardens. A fantastic interactive visitors centre is opening in May 2003. Brilliant for children, The Vegetable Kingdom is an exciting addition to this family day out.

★ Parking on site
★ Children's garden

LOCATION
Off the A45 on the road to Wolston, 5 miles south-east of Coventry

OPENING
All year open daily 9am–5pm; Closed Christmas week

ADMISSION PRICES
Adult £3.95 Child £1.50

CONTACT
Ryton Organic Gardens
Ryton on Dunsmore
Coventry CU8 3LG
Tel 02476 303517
Email enquiry@hdra.org.uk
Web www.hdra.org.uk

192

2 hrs

Feb–Dec

Broadway
Magic Experience

The Broadway Magic Experience has displays of new and old teddy bears, toys and magical animated scenes.

LOCATION
In Broadway just off the main A44 bypass road

OPENING
1 Feb–31 Dec open Tue–Sun 10am–5pm; Closed 25, 26 Dec

ADMISSION PRICES
Please phone for details

CONTACT
Broadway Magic Experience
76 High Street
Broadway
Worcestershire WR12 7AJ
Tel 01386 858323
Email bearsand
dolls@hotmail.com

The Hop Pocket
Craft Centre

4 hrs

All year

The Hop Pocket Craft Centre is situated in the beautiful Frome Valley. See over 300 different craftsmen's work on display, including pottery, glass engraving, jewellery, soft toys, paintings, and woodturning-gifts to suit every pocket.

LOCATION
On the B4214 just off the A4103 Worcester–Hereford road

OPENING
All year; Please phone for details

ADMISSION PRICES
Free

CONTACT
The Hop Pocket Craft Centre
New House Farm
Bishops Frome
Worcester WR6 5BT
Tel 01531 640323
Email jpfpudge@aol.com

3 hrs

All year

Mamble Craft Centre Limited

Mamble Craft Centre is housed in seventeenth-century barns on an ancient medieval site, with stunning views to the Clee Hills. It offers an insight into past and present crafts through its four craft workshops where you can see items being made.

LOCATION
Off the A456 in the village of Mamble, midway between Bewdley & Tenbury Wells

OPENING
All year open Tue–Sun & Bank holidays 10.30am–5pm; Oct–Dec open Mon 10.30am–5pm; Closed 25 Dec–1 Jan

ADMISSION PRICES
Free

CONTACT
Mamble Craft Centre Ltd
Church Lane, Mamble
Kidderminster
Worcestershire DY14 9JY
Tel 01299 832834

Upton Heritage Centre

2 hrs

Apr–Sep

This restored bell tower is the oldest surviving building in the town and is a local landmark. It tells the story of the battle of Upton in 1651 during the Civil War. There are also exhibits on local history and the development of Upton-upon-Severn.

LOCATION
On the B4211 from Great Malvern & the A38 & A4104 from Worcester

OPENING
1 Apr–30 Sep open daily 1.30pm–4.30pm; Open some mornings
Please phone for details

ADMISSION PRICES
Free

CONTACT
Upton Heritage Centre
Church Street, Upton-upon-Severn, Worcester
Worcestershire WR8 0HT
Tel 01684 592679

193

West Midland Safari & Leisure Park

3 hrs

Mar–Nov

This park is set in 200 acres comprising a drive-through animal safari with exotic species such as rhinos, lions, tigers, giraffes, wolves, emus, wallabies and many more. Come and see the Pets Corner, the reptile house, the sea lion show and Hippo Lakes!

LOCATION
On the A456 between Kidderminster & Bewdley

OPENING
16 Mar–3 Nov open daily 10am–5pm (last admission 4pm)

ADMISSION PRICES
Adult £5.95 Child £5.95

CONTACT
West Midland Safari & Leisure Park
Spring Grove, Bewdley
Worcestershire
DY12 1LF
Tel 01299 402114
Web www.wmsp.co.uk

Worcestershire County Museum

1–1½ hrs

Feb–Nov

Housed in the north wing of the Bishop's Palace, exhibits include a restored cider mill, costumes and horse-drawn vehicles. There are also gypsy caravans, crafts and examples of industries of the county.

LOCATION
On the B4193 road from Stourport-Kidderminster. 4 miles south of Kidderminster on the A449 to Worcester

OPENING
1 Feb–30 Nov open Mon–Thu 10am–5pm, Fri & Sun 2pm–5pm; Closed 29, 31 Mar

ADMISSION PRICES
Adult £2.50 Child £1.20
Family £6.50 Concession £1.20

CONTACT
Worcestershire County Museum
Hartlebury Castle, Hartlebury
Kidderminster
Worcestershire DY11 7XZ
Tel 01299 250416

W. MIDLANDS/WORC

North-east

The North-east of England encompasses Yorkshire to its south, Durham in its heart and Northumberland to the north. All three counties are bordered to the east by the North Sea, and the Pennines run through the centre of the region.

The wild beauty of the Yorkshire moors and one of the most varied coastlines in the country make this a county of contrasts. Spend a day enjoying nature at the Wildfowl & Wetlands Trust of Washington or get right up to date with a visit to Eureka! – Britain's first interactive museum, designed especially for children. York is a city of living history and one of the best examples of this is Jorvik Viking Centre, a celebrated museum which transports you back to the sights, sounds and smells of the Viking era. Durham boasts some of the most dramatic natural splendours in the country. High Force Waterfall is the highest waterfall in England. Far to the north, Northumberland is dotted with castles and ruins. Boats leave the town of Seahorses for the Farne Islands, which are home to seals, puffins and other seabirds.

Much of Northumberland is part of the National Park and it offers amazing views of the far-reaching Cheviot Hills. At its heart is Kielder Water, a vast man-made lake. From here, the River Tyne flows through Tyne and Wear where you can visit a cheese farm, enjoy an undersea safari at the Blue Reef Aquarium or spend a day at the Hancock Museum, with its extensive wildlife collections and interactive displays.

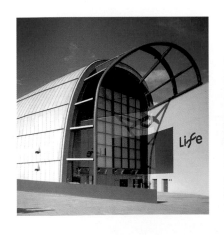

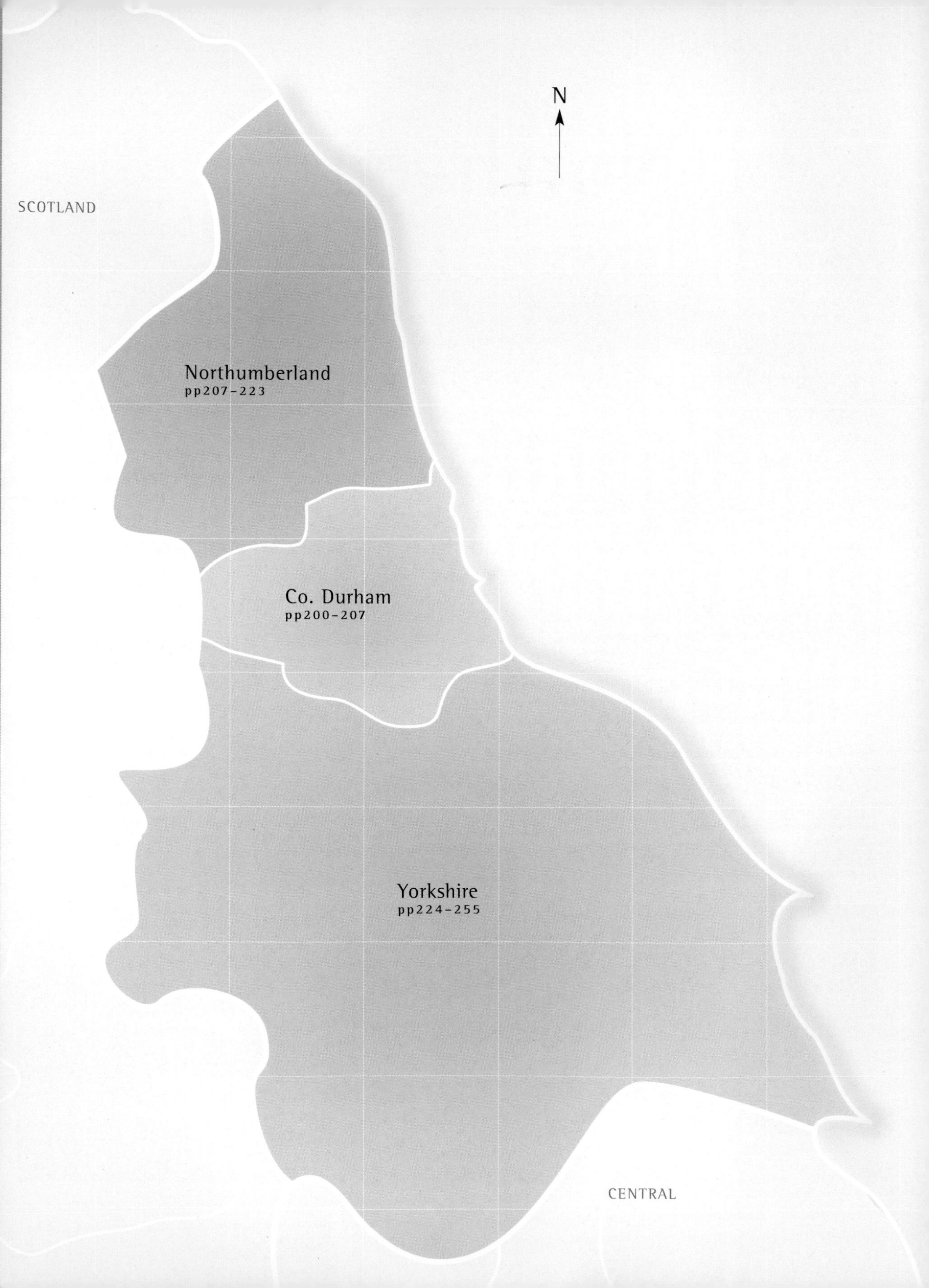

N

SCOTLAND

Northumberland
pp207–223

Co. Durham
pp200–207

Yorkshire
pp224–255

CENTRAL

Below is a list of places in the North-east, organised by county and type.

Durham

HISTORIC BUILDINGS

MUSEUMS & EXHIBITIONS

SPORT & LEISURE

ANIMAL ATTRACTIONS

BOAT & TRAIN TRIPS

PARKS, GARDENS & NATURE TRAILS

THEME PARKS & ADVENTURE PLAYGROUNDS

HERITAGE & INDUSTRIAL

Northumberland

HISTORIC BUILDINGS

MUSEUMS & EXHIBITIONS

SPORT & LEISURE

ANIMAL ATTRACTIONS

BOAT & TRAIN TRIPS

PARKS, GARDENS & NATURE TRAILS

Yorkshire

198

3 hrs+

All year

Allensford Park

Barnard Castle

2 hrs

All year

Allensford is a picnic park in a sheltered riverside setting, with a children's play park and shop. There is a nature trail in Deneburn Wood and beautiful riverside woodland walks, as well as magnificent views of the Derwent Valley.

Barnard Castle was built in 1125 and the impressive ruins are on the banks of the River Tees in some of the most beautiful scenery in the country. Barnard Castle is a must-see on any day trip to Durham.

LOCATION
From Consett take the A692 to the A68; from Durham take the A691 to Consett; from Newcastle take the A692 to the A68

OPENING
Park: All year open daily dawn–dusk; Shop: 1 Mar–31 Oct open daily 10am–5pm

ADMISSION PRICES
Free

CONTACT
Allensford Park
Consett
Durham DH8 9BA
Tel 01207 505572
Web
www.virtualtourismcentre.com

LOCATION
Off the A688 or A67

OPENING
All year open Apr–Sep 10am–6pm; Nov–Mar open Wed–Sun 10am–4pm; Closed 1–2pm & 24, 25, 26 Dec & 1 Jan

ADMISSION PRICES
Adult £2.40 Child £1.20
Under-5s Free Concession £1.80

CONTACT
Barnard Castle
Newgate
Barnard Castle
Durham DL12 8NP
Tel 01833 638212

All day

All year

Beamish, The North of England Open Air Museum

Living Museum of the Year 2002
Northumbria Family Attraction of the Year 2002

Beamish is an extraordinary day out for the whole family. Touch, taste and experience the past at Beamish. This is a living open air museum which vividly illustrates life in the Great North in the early 1800s and early 1900s.

★ Meet the Animals at Home Farm

★ Discover a real 'drift' mine

★ Enjoy a ride on the trams

★ Special events throughout the summer

LOCATION
Located in County Durham, between Durham City & Newcastle upon Tyne & 4 miles from the A1(M) junction 63

OPENING
In summer open daily 10am–5pm (last admission 3pm); In winter 10am–4pm (last admission 3pm); Closed Mon & Fri; Please check Christmas opening times

ADMISSION PRICES
Summer: Adult £12 Child £6 Senior £9
Winter: Adult £4 Child £4 Senior £4

CONTACT
Beamish, The North of England Open Air Museum
Durham DH9 0RG
Tel 0191 3704000
Fax 0191 3704001
Email museum@beamish.org.uk
Web www.beamish.org.uk

Bear Bottoms

2 hrs

WC

All year

LOCATION
Within easy reach of the Prince Bishops car park & shopping centre in Durham

OPENING
All year open Mon–Fri 10am–5.30pm, Sat 9.30am–5.30pm; 1 Jun–31 Aug, 1 Oct, 1–31 Dec open Sun 10am–4pm; Closed 25, 26 Dec & 1 Jan

ADMISSION PRICES
Free

CONTACT
Bear Bottoms
12 Elvet Bridge Durham
Durham DH1 3AA
Tel 0191 3832922
Email bearbotts@aol.com
Web www.bearbottoms.co.uk

A teddy bear business in the heart of historic Durham. Visitors can see workshops for designing and making bears and an exhibition of bears from around the world. Different themed exhibitions are run monthly.

★ Educational visits welcomed

201

Bowes Museum

2–3 hrs

All year

WC

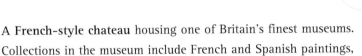

LOCATION
¼ mile from Market Place in Barnard Castle

OPENING
All year open daily 11am–5pm

ADMISSION PRICES
Adult £4 Child £3 Family £12 Senior £3

CONTACT
Bowes Museum
Newgate
Barnard Castle
Durham DL12 8NP
Tel 01833 690606
Fax 01833 637163
Email info@bowesmuseum.org.uk
Web www.bowesmuseum.org.uk

A **French-style chateau** housing one of Britain's finest museums. Collections in the museum include French and Spanish paintings, furniture and ceramics. There are beautiful gardens for children to wander through and fascinating exhibitions throughout the year.

★ Silver swan automaton
★ Exhibits excavated from Roman forts

½ day

All year

Bowlees Picnic Area

This picnic area is in a sheltered side valley of Teesdale. There are four beautiful waterfalls in the site and more falls alongside a footpath that leads to Gibsons Cave.

LOCATION
On the B6277, 2½ miles north-west of Middleton-in-Teesdale

OPENING
All year open daily 24 hrs

ADMISSION PRICES
Free

CONTACT
Bowlees Picnic Area
Middleton-in-Teesdale
Barnard Castle
Durham DL12 0XF
Tel 0191 3833594
Email andy.niven@durham.gov.uk
Web www.durham.gov.uk

3 hrs

All year

Bowlees Visitor Centre

Part of Durham Wildlife Trust, the centre displays exhibitions of food and farming, geology, flora and fauna. One of the highspots of a visit is the amazing High Force Waterfalls.

★ Test out the Feely Box
★ Make your mark with Footprints in Sand
★ Close to the amazing High Force Waterfalls
★ Guided walks by arrangement
★ Close to the River Tees
★ Near to Bowlees Beck

LOCATION
Signposted from the B6277, between Middleton in Teesdale & High Force in Durham, or from Alston–Middleton in Teesdale

OPENING
Easter or the last week in Mar–end of Oct open daily 10.30am–5pm; Nov–Mar open Sat & Sun 10.30am–4pm; Other times by appointment

ADMISSION PRICES
Adult 50p Child 20p Family £1

CONTACT
Bowlees Visitor Centre
Bowlees
Middleton
Durham DL12 0XE
Tel 01833 622292

Varies

All year

Carricks Picnic Area

Castle Eden Dene National Nature Reserve

4 hrs+

All year

Bring the whole family to enjoy this beautiful picnic area alongside the River Derwent, near the head of the stunning Derwent Reservoir.

At **Castle Eden Dene National Nature Reserve** you can enjoy 12 miles of walks through wooded valley owned and managed by English Nature. Parts of the reserve remain almost unaltered since the Ice Age.

★ Enjoy the woodland birds   ★ Spot a red squirrel

LOCATION
On the B6306, 2 miles north-east of Blanchland

OPENING
All year open daily 24 hrs

ADMISSION PRICES
Free

CONTACT
Carricks Picnic Area
Edmundbyers
Derwent Reservoir
Consett
Durham DH8 9NL
Tel 0191 3833594
Email
andy.niven@durham.gov.uk
Web www.durham.gov.uk

LOCATION
Situated on the southern side of Peterlee from the A19, signposted Shotton & Peterlee. Drive to Passfield Way then take the 1st right to Durham way for ¾ mile

OPENING
All year open daily at any reasonable time

ADMISSION PRICES
Free

CONTACT
Castle Eden Dene National Nature Reserve, Oakerside Dene Lodge, Stanhope Chase Peterlee, Durham SR8 1NJ
Tel 0191 5860004
Fax 0191 5182403

203

All day

All year

Consett–Sunderland Railway Path

Diggerland

3 hrs+

All year

The railway path offers a 20-mile traffic-free cycle route, using former railway lines. It is suitable for pedestrians, cyclists, people with disabilities and horse riders (on some lengths). The path is abundant with flora and fauna and works of public art.

A **unique adventure park based on** the world of construction machinery, where children and adults can ride and drive real JCBs and dumpers in safety.

★ Adventure playground

LOCATION
On the A692, off the A68 & A691

OPENING
All year open daily at all times

ADMISSION PRICES
Free

CONTACT
Consett–Sunderland Railway Path
Consett
Durham DH8 9EH
Tel 0117 9290888
Web www.c2c-guide.co.uk

LOCATION
Exit the A1(M) at junction 62 & head west towards Consett. After 6 miles turn left at the roundabout to Langley Park

OPENING
All year open weekends, Bank holidays & school holidays 10am–5pm

ADMISSION PRICES
Adult £2.50 Child £2.50
Under-2s Free Senior £1.25
Extra payment required to drive motorised vehicles

CONTACT
Diggerland
Langley Park
Durham DH7 9TT
Tel 08700 344437
Web www.diggerland.com

2–3 hrs

All year

The DLI Museum

Enter the world of **County Durham Light Infantry** soldiers and their families. Dramatic and interactive displays let you see for yourself what their lives were like.

★ Dress up as a soldier
★ Hands-on experience of exhibits
★ Durham Art Gallery included in price
★ View hundreds of medals
★ Beautiful views of DLI grounds
★ Find out how the soldiers lived in the trenches

LOCATION
½ mile north-west of Durham city centre, off the A691, near the railway station

OPENING
Apr–Oct open 10am–5pm; Nov–Mar open 10am–4pm; Closed 25 Dec

ADMISSION PRICES
Adult £2.50 Family £6.25
Concession £1.25

CONTACT
The DLI Museum
Aykley Heads
Durham DH1 5TU
Tel 0191 3842214
Email dli@durham.gov.uk
Web www.durham.gov.uk

204

---

2 hrs

Apr–Oct

Durham Heritage Centre

This **museum of local history** tells the story of Durham from the tenth century to the present-day, using videos, displays, models and artefacts to make history come alive for people of all ages.

LOCATION
On the centre of Durham off the A690, A177 or A691

OPENING
Apr–May open Sat, Sun, Bank holidays 2pm–4.30pm; Jun open daily 2pm–4.30pm; Jul–Sep open daily 11am–4.30pm; Oct open Sat & Sun 2pm–4.30pm
Please phone for specific dates

ADMISSION PRICES
Adult £1 Child (5–16 years) 30p
Concession 75p

CONTACT
Durham Heritage Centre
Saint Mary-le-Bow
North Bailey
Durham DH1 3ET
Tel 0191 3845589

Hamsterley Forest

2–4 hrs

All year

Hamsterley **has exhibits** on forestry and wildlife in its visitor centre. There are also fascinating walks and a forest drive.

LOCATION
From the A68 at Witton-le-Wear follow the brown tourist signs to the forest

OPENING
Forest: All year open daily 7.30am–9pm
Visitor Centre: Mar–Oct open Mon–Fri 10am–4pm, Sat & Sun 11am–5pm
Please phone for details of specific dates

ADMISSION PRICES
Free
Car park charge

CONTACT
Hamsterley Forest
Forest Enterprise, Redford
Hamsterley Forest
Bishop Auckland
Durham DL13 3NL
Tel 01388 488312
Web www.forestry.gov.uk

Kascada Leisure Complex

Killhope Lead Mining Museum

Situated in the heart of historic Durham, the Kascada Leisure Complex has excellent leisure facilities, with 20 bowling lanes using the latest computerised technology.

LOCATION
From the A1(M) take the A690 towards Durham, take last right at Gilesgate roundabout, into Claypath, right at traffic lights then left into The Sands

OPENING
All year open Mon–Fri 11am–11pm, Sat & Sun open 10am–11pm; Closed 25, 26 Dec & 1 Jan

ADMISSION PRICES
Please phone for details

CONTACT
Kascada Leisure Complex
Walkergate
Durham DH1 1SQ
Tel 0191 3830300
Fax 0191 3844440
Web www.kascadabowl.com

Find out about the working conditions of lead miners. Visitors can explore deep within the mines which have been restored to look as they would have done in the 1870s. There is an exhibition about the lives of the miners and their families.

LOCATION
Between Stanhope & Alston beside the A689

OPENING
Apr–Sep open daily, Oct weekends & half-term week 10.30am–5pm (last admission 4.30pm)

ADMISSION PRICES
Adult £3.40 Child £1.70
Senior £2.40 Concession £1.70
Additional charge for mine visit

CONTACT
Killhope Lead Mining Museum
Cowhill, Durham DL13 1AR
Tel 01388 537505
Email killhope@durham.gov.uk

205

Meet the Middletons

Mister Twisters

This is an exciting visitor attraction for all ages. There are family-friendly indoor activities and displays centred on life in this rural 'company town' in the mid nineteenth century.

LOCATION
B6277 to Middleton-in-Teesdale. 10 miles west of Barnard Castle

OPENING
All year open daily 11am–5pm; Closed 25, 26 Dec & 1 Jan

ADMISSION PRICES
Free
Please phone for activity prices

CONTACT
Meet the Middletons
Chapel Row
Middleton-in-Teesdale
Barnard Castle
Durham DL12 0SN
Tel 01833 641000
Web
www.meetthemiddletons.co.uk

This exciting indoor play and party centre includes a multi-level soft play climbing frame, Aztec tower, inflatable temple and spooky tomb. There is a separate under-5s play village with a baby crawling pit and activity room.

LOCATION
From the A1(M) take the A691 to Consett; from Gateshead take the A692 to Consett

OPENING
All year open Sun–Thu 9am–8pm; Fri & Sat open 9am–9pm; Closed 25, 26 Dec

ADMISSION PRICES
Adult Free Under-5s £2.50/1½ hrs 5–12 years £2.95/1½ hrs

CONTACT
Mister Twisters, No1 Industrial Estate, Medomsley, Consett Durham DH8 6TW
Tel 01207 500007
Web www.mistertwisters.co.uk

2 hrs+

Apr–Oct

Otter Trust's North Pennines Reserve

This reserve has many unusual birds including five nesting species of waders. You will see wildfowl including widgeon, mallard, teal and pintail. There are Asian and British otters, red and fallow deer, Exmoor ponies and rare breeds of domestic livestock.

LOCATION
On the main A66 Scotch Corner–Penrith road; 3 miles west of Bowes village

OPENING
1 Apr–31 Oct open daily 10.30am–6pm

ADMISSION PRICES
Adult £4.50 Child (4–16) £2.50

CONTACT
Otter Trust's North Pennines Reserve, Vale House Farm Bowes, Barnard Castle Durham DL12 9RH
Tel 01833 628339
Fax 01986 892461

Prince Bishop River Cruiser

1 hr

All year

The Prince Bishop river cruiser sails on the River Wear. It offers the best views of Durham Cathedral, Durham Castle and the bridges. The trip includes a commentary that will suit children of all ages.

★ Sun deck   ★ 1 hour Santa Cruises in Dec

LOCATION
The cruiser is found below the Prince Bishop shopping centre in Durham

OPENING
By prior arrangement
Please phone in advance for sailing times

ADMISSION PRICES
Adult £4 Child £2
Santa Cruises: £3

CONTACT
Durham River Trips Ltd
The Boathouse
Elvet Bridge
Durham DH1 3AH
Tel 0191 3869525

---

3 hrs+

May–Sep

Raby Castle

Raby Castle is a magnificent example of a medieval castle in Teesdale. A wonderful day out for the family, with stunning rooms to wonder at.

★ High Force Waterfall nearby   ★ Extensive gardens

★ Deer park   ★ Adventure playground

LOCATION
On the A688, 8 miles north east of Barnard Castle

OPENING
Jun, Jul, Aug open daily except Sat; May & Sep Wed & Sun only; Bank holidays open Sat–Wed; Please phone for details of Christmas opening

ADMISSION PRICES
Adult £6 Child £2.50 Senior £5

CONTACT
Raby Castle
Staindrop, Darlington
Durham,
DL2 3AH
Tel 01833 660202
Web www.rabycastle.com

Top Gear Indoor Karting

Varies

All year

Top Gear is a leisure karting centre. It provides indoor karting fun for everyone aged 8–88 and is a great place for family birthdays.

LOCATION
Follow tourist signs from the A690 from Sunderland

OPENING
All year open Mon–Fri 12pm–8pm, Sat & Sun 10am–6pm; Closed 25–26 Dec & 1 Jan

ADMISSION PRICES
Adult £12   Child £12

CONTACT
Top Gear Indoor Karting
13 Renny's Lane, Gilesgate Moor
Durham DH1 2RS
Tel 0191 3860999
Email info@durhamkarting.co.uk
Web www.durhamkarting.co.uk

Whitworth Hall Country Park

3 hrs

All year

Hand-feed the red and fallow deer in this 73-acre historic parkland. There is also an ornamental lake, a Victorian walled garden, a woodland garden and indoor and outdoor play facilities for children.

★ Feed the ducks
★ Frequent events
★ Explore the walled garden
★ Bobby Shafto's Playbarn

LOCATION
7 miles west of Durham & the A1. At A1 junction 61 join the A688 'Spennymoor'. Continue following signs for Whitworth Hall Hotel

OPENING
All year open daily noon–dusk

ADMISSION PRICES
Free

CONTACT
Whitworth Hall Country Park
Nr Spennymoor
Durham DL16 7QX
Tel 01388 811772
Web www.whitworthhall.co.uk

Allenheads Heritage Centre

1–2 hrs

Apr–Oct

Set in the centre of the village, at the heart of the North Pennines, this heritage centre brings to life the lead-mining past of the village of Allenheads.

★ Armstrong water engine
★ Nature trail
★ Restored blacksmith's shop
★ Lead mining exhibition

LOCATION
Off the A69 at Hexham

OPENING
Apr–Oct open daily 10am–5pm
Please phone for specific dates

ADMISSION PRICES
Adult £1   Child (7–16) 50p

CONTACT
Allenheads Heritage Centre
Allenheads
Hexham
Northumberland NE47 9UQ
Tel 01434 685395
Fax 01434 685301

Alnwick Castle

1–2 hrs

Apr–Oct

This medieval castle has wonderful Renaissance furnishings inside its walls. The Regiment Museum of Royal Northumberland Fusiliers is housed in the Abbott's Tower along with the museum of local archaeology and the Percy Tenantry volunteers.

LOCATION
Off the A1 or A697 on the out-skirts of Alnwick town

OPENING
Apr–Oct open daily 11am–5pm
(last admission 4.15pm)

ADMISSION PRICES
Adult £6.74   Child £3.50
Concession £5.75

CONTACT
Alnwick Castle
Alnwick
Northumberland NE66 1NQ
Tel 01665 510777
Email
enquiries@alnwickcastle.com

Bailiffgate Museum

3 hrs

All year

Presenting north Northumberland and the old county town of Alnwick in exciting, interactive style, the museum covers everything from border warfare to the old shops and trades of Alnwick.

LOCATION
Take the A1(M) to Alnwick; 30 miles south of Berwick-upon-Tweed; 35 miles north of Newcastle upon Tyne

OPENING
All year open daily 10am–5pm

ADMISSION PRICES
Adult £2   Child £1.50   Family £5
Concession £1.75

CONTACT
Baliffgate Museum
Baliffgate
Alnwick
Northumberland NE66 1LU
Tel 01665 605847
Fax 01665 605394
Email museumalnwick@btcon-nect.com

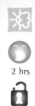

2 hrs

Mar–Oct

Bamburgh Castle

Quality Assured Visitor Attraction
English Tourism Council

This magnificent coastal castle contains collections of furniture, paintings, arms and armour. A royal centre by AD 547, the rocky outcrop has been occupied since the prehistoric period. The present fortress has a museum room, grand kings hall, cross hall, armoury and the Victorian scullery for children to explore.

★ Guided tours for individuals

LOCATION
From the A1 Belford bypass take either the B1341 or the B1342 to Bamburgh

OPENING
17 Mar–31 Oct open daily 11am–5pm (last admission 4.30pm)

ADMISSION PRICES
Adult £4.50 Concession £3.50

CONTACT
Bamburgh Castle
Bamburgh
Northumberland NE69 7DF
Tel 01668 214515
Fax 01668 214060
Email bamburghcastle@aol.com
Web www.bamburghcastle.com

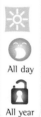

All day

All year

Bedlington Country Park

A delightful country park on the north side of the River Blyth with a picnic and barbecue area, paddling pool, children's play area, as well as pleasant horse and nature trails. There is a variety of wildlife within the park.

LOCATION
Via the A1068 or A189 from north or south

OPENING
All year open daily dawn-dusk

ADMISSION PRICES
Free

CONTACT
Bedlington Country Park
Humford Mill
Church Lane
Bedlington
Northumberland NE22 5RT
Tel 01670 829550
Fax 01670 834484

Bill Quay Farm

2 hrs

All year

LOCATION
Take the A185 from Heworth interchange,
turn left down Station Road (¼ mile from
Hurworth) & take 1st left at crossroads

OPENING
All year open daily 10am–5pm

ADMISSION PRICES
Free

CONTACT
Bill Quay Farm
Hainingwood Terrace
Bill Quay
Gateshead
Tyne and Wear NE10 0TE
Tel 0191 4385340

Bring your children to Bill Quay Farm to experience farm livestock, from the traditional to the bizarre. There is also an abundance of artworks and a green retreat for wildlife, as well as a family picnic area.

★ Panoramic views of the Tyne

209

Blue Reef Aquarium

2–3 hrs

All year

LOCATION
From the A19, follow the signs to
Tynemouth; from the A1058 follow the
signs to Tynemouth

OPENING
All year open daily 10am–6pm (last
admission 5pm); Closed 25 Dec

ADMISSION PRICES
Adult £4.95   Child (4–16) £3.25
Family £14.50   Concession £4.25

CONTACT
Blue Reef Aquarium
Grand Parade
Tynemouth
Tyne and Wear NE30 4JF
Tel 0191 2581031
Fax 0191 2572116
Email info@bluereefaquarium.co.uk
Web www.bluereefaquarium.co.uk

The ultimate undersea safari, Blue Reef brings the magic of the undersea world alive. Explore the drama of the North Sea and the dazzling beauty of a spectacular coral reef. This giant tropical ocean tank, with its own underwater tunnel and more than 30 living displays, provides a truly unforgettable experience for parents and children.

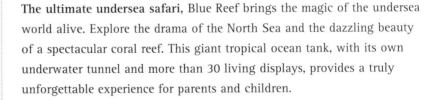

2–4 hrs

All year

Bolam Lake Country Park

Bolam Lake Country Park has everything for a family day out. There is a lake surrounded by beautiful woodland and meadows with paths and picnic areas. It is ideal for bird-watching.

LOCATION
Take the C155 from Belsay or Morpeth

OPENING
All year open daily (car park closes at dusk); Visitor centre open daily during busy periods
Please phone for details

ADMISSION PRICES
Free

CONTACT
Bolam Lake Country Park
Site Office, Belsay
Newcastle upon Tyne
Northumberland NE20 0HE
Tel/Fax 01661 881234

2 hrs

All year

Borough Woods Local Nature Reserve

This ancient wild woodland nature reserve has a round walk of about two miles, including footways along the steep slopes of the River Wansbeck valley.

LOCATION
Follow the B6343 road (sign-posted Mitford, Cambo) from Morpeth for 1 mile, turn left onto High House Road

OPENING
All year open daily at all times

ADMISSION PRICES
Free

CONTACT
Borough Woods Local Nature Reserve
High House Road
Morpeth
Northumberland NE61 2YU
Tel 01670 514351
Email
CMarlee@castlemorpeth.gov.uk
Web www.castlemorpeth.gov.uk

2 hrs+

All year

Bowes Railway

The Bowes Railway is the only preserved rope-hauled railway in the world. Visitors are given a unique insight into how coal was moved from local collieries to the Tyne at Jarrow for shipment. Children will be fascinated by the two steam engines, diesel locomotives, old colliery wagons, historic workshops and the educational historical exhibition.

★ Guided tours for individuals

LOCATION
Drive to Springwell Village from the A194 (M) or from Washington turn off on the A1 (M) from the north

OPENING
Museum: All year open Mon–Fri 8.30am–4pm. Please phone for train operating times

ADMISSION PRICES
Adult £1 Under-16s 50p Concession £1
Free admission when trains are not operating

CONTACT
Bowes Railway
Springwell Village, Gateshead
Tyne and Wear NE9 7QJ
Tel 0191 4161847
Web www.bowesrailway.co.uk

Brigantium

1 hr
All year

This **archaeological reconstruction** centre has plenty to stimulate the young explorer. Wander round the Roman British farm, roundhouse, mesolithic hunting camp, Roman defences and road, and marvel at the Bronze Age burial and stone circle.

LOCATION
On the A68 from Jedburgh or Corbridge or the A696 from Newcastle

OPENING
All year open daily
9.30am–4.30pm

ADMISSION PRICES
Adult £2.50   Child £1.50
Family £7   Concession £1.50

CONTACT
Brigantium
Rochester Cafe
Rochester
Newcastle upon Tyne
Tyne and Wear NE19 1RH
Tel 01830 520801

Carlisle Park & Castle Woods

Quality Assured Visitor Attraction
English Tourism Council

2 hrs+
All year

Carlisle Park is a fun-packed park with historic architectural remains. There are Riverside and woodland walks, an aviary, tennis courts, bowling greens, a paddling pool and boating lake.

★ Guided tours for individuals

LOCATION
From the A1 follow the signs to Morpeth town centre

OPENING
All year open daily at all times

ADMISSION PRICES
Free

CONTACT
Carlisle Park & Castle Woods
Morpeth
Northumberland NE61 1YD
Tel 01670 512807
Fax 01670 516866
Email carlislepark@castlemor-peth.gov.uk
Web www.castlemorpeth.gov.uk

Centre For Life

3 hrs+
All year

There's always something new at the Centre for Life. Meet your four billion-year-old family, explore what makes us all different, test your brain power and enjoy the thrill of the crazy motion ride.

★ Escape from Dino Island 3D ride
★ Adventure playground
★ Weird Science@Life
★ Open-air ice rink in Times Square during Christmas period

LOCATION
From the south take the A19, A184, A69 or A1 into Newcastle upon Tyne; from the north take the A69 into Newcastle upon Tyne

OPENING
All year open Mon–Sat 10am–6pm, Sun 11am–6pm (last admission 4.30pm); Closed 25 Dec & 1 Jan

ADMISSION PRICES
Adult £6.95   Child (5–16) £4.50
Family £19.95

CONTACT
Centre For Life
Times Square
Newcastle upon Tyne
Tyne and Wear NE1 4EP
Tel 0191 2438210
Fax 0191 2438201
Email general@centre-for-life.co.uk
Web www.centre-for-life.co.uk

1 hr

May-Sep

Chillingham Castle

This medieval fortress has Tudor additions, a torture chamber and dungeon, and a woodland walk. It has beautifully furnished rooms and an Italian topiary garden with herbaceous borders.

LOCATION
From Newcastle upon Tyne take the A1 & then the A697, then follow signs from Wooler; from the north take the A1 south & follow the brown tourist signs

OPENING
May-Sep open daily except Tue 12pm-5pm; Jul-Aug daily 12pm-5pm
Please phone for specific dates

ADMISSION PRICES
Adult £5 Child (3-13) £1
Concession £4

CONTACT
Chillingham Castle
Chillingham
Wooler
Northumberland NE66 5NJ
Tel 01668 215359
Web www.chillingham-castle.com

Conundrum Farm

2 hrs

Feb-Dec

England's most northerly farm visitor centre, Conundrum Farm offers a farm trail, a fun barn and indoor and outdoor play areas. Children will love the farm animals and well designed play areas.

★ Animals galore   ★ Pet barn
★ Feed the fish   ★ Pedal tractors

LOCATION
Conundrum Farm is ½ mile north of Berwick-upon-Tweed, just off the A1

OPENING
In summer open daily 10am-5pm; In winter open daily 10am-4pm; Closed 25 Dec-1 Feb

ADMISSION PRICES
Adult £2.95 Child £1.95

CONTACT
Conundrum Farm
Berwick upon Tweed
Northumberland
Tel 01289 308000
Web
www.conundrumfarm.co.uk

212

2-4 hrs

All year

Cresswell Pond Nature Reserve

Positioned in a beautiful area of the bay, the lagoon offers a fascinating and fun day out with all the family. It is popular with bird enthusiasts for its rare bird sightings. There is access to the nearby dunes where you can enjoy the flowers and wildlife.

LOCATION
From the A1068, turn east at Widdrington roundabout. The reserve is 6 miles south of Amble

OPENING
All year open daily at all times

ADMISSION PRICES
Free

CONTACT
Cresswell Pond Nature Reserve
Blakemoor Farm, Cresswell
Morpeth
Northumberland NE61 5EH
Tel 0191 2846884
Email mail@northwt.org.uk
Web
www.wildlifetrust.org.uk/northumberland/index.htm

Farne Islands

2 hrs

Varies

Take the whole family on a boat trip to the Farne Islands. They house a bird reserve holding around 70,000 pairs of breeding birds, from 21 different species. They are also home to a large colony of grey seals.

LOCATION
The islands are 2-5 miles off the north Northumberland Coast. Take the B1340 & then a boat from Seahouses harbour

OPENING
Please phone for details

ADMISSION PRICES
Adult £3.40-£4.40

Under-16s £1.70-£2.20
Boat fees are extra

CONTACT
The Farne Islands
Seahouses
Northumberland
Tel 01665 721099

Hancock Museum

4 hrs

WC 🛏 🍴

All year

i

LOCATION
Follow signs for the city centre north from the A167 & the motorway

OPENING
All year open Mon-Sat 10am-5pm,
Sun open 2pm-5pm;
Closed 25, 26 Dec & 1 Jan

ADMISSION PRICES
Adult £4.50 Child (5-16) £2.95
Family £12.95 Concession £2.95

CONTACT
Hancock Museum
Barras Bridge
Newcastle upon Tyne
Tyne and Wear NE2 4PT
Tel 0191 2227418
Fax 0191 2226753
Email hancock.museum@ncl.ac.uk
Web www.twmuseums.org.uk

The North's premier natural history museum, the Hancock Museum has extensive wildlife collections and challenging displays including The Magic of Birds and Abel's Ark. Take a closer look at the world in The Living Planet, a hands-on environmental gallery, and Earthworks, an exciting, interactive geology experience.

★ Land of the Pharaohs exhibition
★ World premier exhibitions

Heritage Centre

2 hrs

WC 🛏 🐕

Mar-Sep

i

LOCATION
Follow the B6320 from Hexham-
Bellingham (17 miles). The Heritage Centre is in Woodburn Road, in Station Yard opposite the Hillside Estate

OPENING
Mar-Sep open Fri-Mon 10.30am-4.30pm
Please phone for specific dates

ADMISSION PRICES
Adult £1 Child (5-16) 50p
Concession 50p

CONTACT
Heritage Centre
Station Yard
Woodburn Road
Bellingham
Hexham
Northumberland NE48 2DF
Tel 01434 220050

This small folk museum situated in the old railway station yard houses photographs, artefacts and memorabilia recording the life and times of the people in the North Tyne Valley and Redewater Valley.

★ Guided tours for individuals
★ Photographic exhibitions
★ Toy, embroidery, farm and mining exhibitions
★ Family tree tracing
★ Special attractions for children

1 hr+

All year

Housesteads Roman Fort Hadrian's Wall

Children will be fascinated to encounter life as it was on Rome's northernmost frontier at Housesteads – a jewel in the crown of Hadrian's Wall and the most complete Roman fort in Britain.

LOCATION
Take the B6318 2¾ miles north east of Bardon Mill

OPENING
Mar–Sep open daily 10am–6pm; Oct open daily 10am–5pm; Nov–Mar open daily 10am–4pm; Closed 24–26 Dec & 1 Jan

ADMISSION PRICES
Adult £3   Child (5–16 years) £1.50   Concession £2.30

CONTACT
Housesteads Roman Fort
Haydon Bridge, Hexham
Northumberland NE47 6NN
Tel 01434 344363

3 hrs

Mar–Dec

Kielder Castle Forest Park Centre

Kielder Castle is the visitor centre for Britain's biggest forest. The centre is an ideal starting point for a family forest visit. A guided walks programme, forest trails, cycle routes and Britain's longest forest drive all start from the castle.

LOCATION
From Hexham take the B6074 to Chollerford, the B6320 to Bellingham & the C200 to Kielder

OPENING
28 Mar–31 Oct open daily 10am–5pm; 1–31 Aug open daily 10am– 6pm; 1 Nov–24 Dec open Sat & Sun 11am–4pm

ADMISSION PRICES
Free

CONTACT
Kielder Castle
Kielder, Hexham
Northumberland NE48 1ER
Tel 01434 250209
Web www.forestry.gov.uk

All day

All year

Kielder Water Leaplish Waterside Park

Situated in the north Tyne Valley, this waterside park is set in breathtaking scenery and has a 27-mile shoreline. There are facilities and activities to suit all ages.

★ Birds of Prey Centre
★ Lake cruises
★ Heated indoor swimming pool
★ Cycling trails
★ Water sports
★ Crazy golf
★ Adventure playground

LOCATION
3 miles from the Scottish border, 20 miles north of Bellingham at the top of the Kielder Reservoir. 1 hour north of Hexham

OPENING
All year open daily; Some facilities are seasonal
Please phone for details

ADMISSION PRICES
Free

CONTACT
Kielder Water
Falstone
Hexham
Northumberland
Tel 0870 2403549
Web www.kielder.org

2–3 hrs

Feb–Oct

Marine Life Centre & Haunted Kingdom

The museum and aquarium are set out on four levels. There is an exhibition with audio-visual conversations between fishing families. The centre also houses Northumbria's Haunted Kingdom, an adventure for children.

LOCATION
Off the B1340 on the coast

OPENING
28 Feb–31 Oct open daily
10.30am–5pm

ADMISSION PRICES
Prices depend on venue
Please phone for details

CONTACT
Marine Life Centre & Haunted Kingdom
8–10 Main Street
Seahouses
Northumberland NE68 5RG
Tel 01665 721257
Web www.marinelifecentre.co.uk

New Metroland

3 hrs+

All year

Among the many children's attractions are a roller coaster, a pirate ship, swinging chairs, dodgem cars, a children's railway, a Ferris wheel, airplanes, helicopters, slides and climbing nets.

LOCATION
Take the A1(M) to Gateshead
MetroCentre

OPENING
All year open Mon–Sat
10am–8pm, Sun 11am–6pm;
Mon–Fri 12pm–8pm during term
time; Closed 25 Dec

ADMISSION PRICES
Please phone for details

CONTACT
New Metroland
39 Garden Walk, Gateshead
Metro Centre, Gateshead
Tyne and Wear NE11 9XY
Tel 0191 4932048
Web www.metroland.uk.com

215

Northumberland Cheese Farm

2 hrs+

All year

LOCATION
1 mile north of Dinnington, across the C356, then 1 mile down the road, following the brown tourist signs

OPENING
All year open daily 10am–5pm (please ring for details of moulding time); Closed 25–28 Dec, 1–3 Jan

ADMISSION PRICES
Free

CONTACT
Northumberland Cheese Farm
The Dairy, Make Me Rich Farm
Blagdon
Seaton Burn
Newcastle upon Tyne
Tyne and Wear NE13 6BZ
Tel 01670 789798
Fax 01670 789644
Email enquiries@northumberland-cheese.co.uk
Web www.northumberland-cheese.co.uk

Children will be fascinated to see cheeses made in a traditional way. A viewing window in the wall allows visitors to look into the dairy from the outside to see for themselves how each cheese is made.

★ Cheese-making days
★ Tasting sessions

4 hrs+

All year

Otterburn Hall

At **Otterburn Hall** the whole family can enjoy the 400 acres of gardens, forest walks, lakes, nature trails and canoeing, as well as the fascinating rare breeds collection.

★ Guided tours
for individuals

LOCATION
Take the A696. Otterburn Hall is 30 miles north of Newcastle upon Tyne

OPENING
All year open daily 9am–5pm

ADMISSION PRICES
Free

CONTACT
Otterburn Hall
Otterburn
Newcastle upon Tyne
Northumberland NE19 1HE
Tel 01830 520663
Fax 0191 3852267
Email enquiries@otterburn.hall.com

216

2 hrs

Varies

Pier Amusements Centre

At the **Pier Amusements Centre** you can play Quasar, a futuristic game where each player is armed with a laser gun and shoots the opposition to win points.

LOCATION
On the pier front at South Shields. Reached via the A183, A1018 or A185

OPENING
Please phone for details

ADMISSION PRICES
Prices depend on activities
Please phone for details

CONTACT
Pier Amusements Centre
South Shields
Tyne and Wear NE33 2JS
Tel 0191 4553885

Planetarium South Tyneside College

Children can learn about the stars at this planetarium and observatory.

★ Guided tours compulsory for individuals

2 hrs+

Varies

LOCATION
Please phone for details

OPENING
Planetarium: Adult £3
Child (5–18) £1.50
Observatory: Adult £1
Child (5–18) £1

ADMISSION PRICES
Please phone for details

CONTACT
Planetarium South Tyneside College, St George's Avenue
South Shields
Tyne and Wear NE34 6ET
Tel 0191 4273589
Web www.stc.ac.uk

All day

All year

Plessey Woods Country Park

Children will burn off lots of energy on a day trip to Plessey Woods. There are riverside walks and woodland areas with nature trails and picnic sites.

★ Children's play area ★ Visitor centre with displays

LOCATION
On the A192; just off the A1068, (coastal route) & close to the A1

OPENING
All year open daily 8am–dusk

ADMISSION PRICES
Free

CONTACT
Plessey Woods Country Park
Shields Road, Hartford
Bedlington
Northumberland NE22 6AN
Tel 01670 824793
Email plesseywoods@northumberland.gov.uk
Web
www.northumberland.gov.uk

Pot-a-Doodle-Do

2 hrs

All year

An oasis of creativity for all to enjoy. There is a wide range of art and craft activities to try at Pot-a-Doodle-Do, as well as a large children's play area. Friendly staff are on hand to help make sure your day is the best it can be.

LOCATION
South of Berwick-upon-Tweed on the A1

OPENING
All year open daily 10am–5pm

ADMISSION PRICES
Free

CONTACT
Pot-a-Doodle-Do
Borewell Farm
Scremerston
Berwick-upon-Tweed
Northumberland TD15 2RJ
Tel 01289 307507
Email
christine.whiteford@rdplus.net

217

3 hrs

All year

Prudhoe Waterworld

Prudhoe Waterworld has a leisure pool incorporating a wave machine, 130-ft aquaslide, jacuzzi and other fun-packed water features.

★ Soft play area ★ Bowling green
★ Fitness gym ★ Play area

LOCATION
Signposted from the A695 between Hexham & Newcastle

OPENING
All year open Mon–Fri 7.15am–10pm, Sat & Sun 8am–5pm; Some sessions are reserved for schools, so it is advisable to phone in advance

ADMISSION PRICES
Please phone for details

CONTACT
Prudhoe Waterworld
Front Street
Prudhoe
Northumberland NE42 5DQ
Tel 01661 833144

Saltwell Park

1–3 hrs

All year

At Saltwell Park you can enjoy bedding displays, a rose garden, a wooded dene, a children's play area and a boating lake. There are brass bands and bowls during the summer.

LOCATION
Off the A184 or A692 south of Newcastle upon Tyne

OPENING
All year open daily 7.30am–dusk

ADMISSION PRICES
Free

CONTACT
Saltwell Park
Saltwell Road
Gateshead
Tyne and Wear NE8 4SF
Tel 0191 4333000
Web www.gateshead.gov.uk

2 hrs+

All year

Scotch Gill Wood
Local Nature Reserve

All day
All year

Silksworth
Sports Complex

Come to this ancient wild woodland nature reserve to enjoy a round ¾-mile walk including footways along the steep slopes of the River Wansbeck valley. There is abundant wildlife and flora to enjoy here.

At Silkworth there are three ski slopes, along with a water sports lake, fishing lake, entertainment bowl, athletics track, BMX track, adventure playground and much more for children of all ages.

LOCATION
Follow the B6343 from Morpeth for ½ mile, turn right into the car park at the 1st bridge over the river

OPENING
All year open daily at all times

ADMISSION PRICES
Free

CONTACT
Scotch Gill Wood Local Nature Reserve
Mitford Road
Morpeth
Northumberland NE61 1RG
Tel 01670 514351
Email
CMarlee@castlemorpeth.gov.uk
Web www.castlemorpeth.gov.uk

LOCATION
To the east of the A690 Durham–Sunderland road, approx 2 miles south-west of Sunderland

OPENING
All year open Mon–Fri 1pm–9pm, Sat & Sun 10am–5pm; Ski slopes open at different times; Please phone for details; Closed Easter & Christmas

ADMISSION PRICES
Please phone for details

CONTACT
Silksworth Sports Complex
Silksworth Lane
Silksworth
Sunderland
Tyne and Wear SR3 2AN
Tel 0191 5535785
Fax 0191 5535789
Web www.sunderland.gov.uk

1 hr+

Feb–Nov

Souter Point Lighthouse

The lighthouse and associated buildings were built in 1871 and contained the most advanced lighthouse technology of their day. The lighthouse is full of interest for children. They can see the engine room, the battery room, the Victorian keeper's cottage and the light tower.

LOCATION
Take the A183 coast road from Sunderland to South Shields

OPENING
Feb & Mar–Nov open daily, except Fri, 11am–5pm (last admission 4.30pm); Open Good Fri 11am–5pm
Please phone for details

ADMISSION PRICES
Adult £3 Child (5–16) £1.50
Family £7.50 National Trust members Free

CONTACT
Souter Point Lighthouse
Coast Road
Whitburn
South Shields
Tyne and Wear SR6 7NH
Tel 0191 5293161
Fax 0191 5290902
Web www.ntnorth.demon.co.uk

★ Compass room with hands-on activities

★ Rock pool fish tank shows

★ Creatures from the Coast activity

★ Ship to Shore Communication activity

★ Pirates & Smugglers activity

★ Lighthouses & Lighthouse Life exhibition

South Tyne Trail

Varies

All year

LOCATION
Take the A689 south from Haltwhistle to the South Tyne Trail

OPENING
All year open daily at all times

ADMISSION PRICES
Free

CONTACT
South Tyne Trail
Haltwhistle
Northumberland

This former railway line is open to walkers of all ages, and for much of its length to cyclists and horse-riders. The trail has excellent views of the South Tyne Valley and it includes the spectacular Lambley Viaduct.

★ Interpretation displays near Coanwood
★ Self-guided trail
★ Disabled access to viaduct
★ Information boards & leaflets
★ Trail shared with South Tynedale Railway between Kirkhaugh & Alston

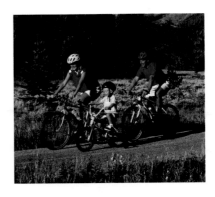

Tanfield Railway

2 hrs+

All year

LOCATION
Located off the A68 on the A6299

OPENING
All year open daily (viewing only); Trains operate all year 11am–4pm
Please phone for specific dates

ADMISSION PRICES
Adult £4 Child (5–14) £2 Family £10
Concession £2

CONTACT
Tanfield Railway
Old Marley Hill
Sunniside
Gateshead
Tyne and Wear NE16 5ET
Tel 0191 3887545
Email tanfield@ingsoc.demon.co.uk
Web www.tanfield-railway.co.uk

Tanfield is a three-mile steam railway and the oldest existing railway in the world. Travel into the scenic Causey Woods where the 1727 Causey Arch bridge is the centrepiece in a deep valley with many walks and display boards giving the eighteenth-century railway history of the area.

★ Guided tours for individuals
★ The oldest working engine shed in Britain
★ Large collection of locally built locomotives

2–3 hrs

Mar–Oct

Tower Knowe Visitor Centre

Amongst the many facilities and exhibitions at the Tower Knowe Visitor Centre, The First 500 Million Years exhibition interprets the history of the valley from beyond the Ice Age to the present day and will fascinate children and adults alike.

★ Comprehensive information on Western Europe's largest artificial lake
★ Activities
★ Fishing permits
★ Cruises

LOCATION
From the A68 from Horsley or the A69, at Hexham, follow the brown tourist signs to Kielder

OPENING
Mar–Oct open daily 10am–4pm; Please phone for extended summer opening times & precise opening dates

ADMISSION PRICES
Free

CONTACT
Tower Knowe Visitor Centre
Kielder Water
Hexham
Northumberland NE48 1BX
Tel 0870 2403549
Fax 01434 250806
Email kielder.water@nwl.co.uk
Web www.kielder.org

2–5 hrs

All year

Wansbeck Riverside Park

An award-winning country park with a delightful camping and caravan site. A wide range of water activities is available and other activities are on hand close by. The park is easily accessible and ideal for family fun, whether you are staying for an afternoon or a week.

LOCATION
Take the A1068. The park is located between Ashington & Bedlington

OPENING
All year open daily 8am–dusk

ADMISSION PRICES
Free

CONTACT
Wansbeck Riverside Park
Green Lane
Ashington
Northumberland NE63 8TX
Tel/Fax 01670 812323

Wet 'N' Wild

3 hrs+

All year

LOCATION
1 mile from the Tyne Tunnel northern entrance

OPENING
All year open daily 10am–9.30pm
Please ring for winter opening times

ADMISSION PRICES
Adult £4.75–£6.95 Child (under 1.2m)
£2.95–£3.85 Concession £2.95–£3.85

CONTACT
Wet 'n' Wild
Rotary Way
Royal Quays
North Shields
Tyne and Wear NE29 6DA
Tel 0191 2961333
Fax 0191 2965790
Email bookings@wetnwild.co.uk
Web www.wetnwild.co.uk

A tropical indoor water park providing a mix of water-based fun activities for all the family, where you pay once and play all day.

★ Double twister flume
★ Outdoor lagoon
★ 4 fast flumes
★ Wave canyon
★ The Black Hole
★ Kamikaze
★ The Abyss tyre ride
★ Lazy river
★ 9 flumes

Whickham Thorns Outdoor Activity Centre

Varies

All year

LOCATION
Off the A184 on the way into Newcastle upon Tyne

OPENING
All year open daily Mon–Fri 11am–10pm,
Sat 11am–6.30pm, Sun 12pm–3pm; Closed during certain holidays
Please phone for details

ADMISSION PRICES
Free
Please phone for activity prices

CONTACT
Whickham Thorns
Outdoor Activity Centre
Market Lane
Dunston
Gateshead
Tyne and Wear NE11 9NX
Tel 0191 4335767
Fax 0191 4335766

This activity centre offers plenty of excitement, including an assault course, a climbing wall, cycle hire, a ski slope, archery and orienteering. There is also a snowboarding club and a parent and toddler club.

★ Duke of Edinburgh Award scheme
★ First Boulder Park in the North-East

½ day

All year

Whitehouse Farm Centre

Whitehouse Farm Centre, the all-weather fun attraction, is a great day out in the country. You will find everything from traditional farm animals to cuddly pets and baby animals.

★ Craft workshops
★ Tractor & trailer rides
★ Seasonal events
★ Children's party venue
★ Face painting

★ Candle-making
★ Craft activities
★ Soft play area
★ Adventure playground

LOCATION
Just off the A1, south-west of Morpeth

OPENING
All year open 10am–5pm
Please phone for details of specific dates

ADMISSION PRICES
Adult £3.50 Child (3–16) £2.60
Concession £2.60

CONTACT
North White House Farm
Morpeth
Northumberland NE61 6AW
Tel 01670 789998
Fax 01670 789113
Email linda@w-centre-demon.co.uk
Web www.whitehousefarmcentre.co.uk

222

½ day

All year

Whitley Bay Ice Rink

Whitley Bay Ice Rink offers something for everyone. Come and enjoy a morning of tenpin bowling and then have a brisk swim or a leisurely paddle in the swimming pool. The ice rink is also a concert venue.

LOCATION
From the south take the A1 through the Tyne Tunnel, then the A1085; from Newcastle upon Tyne take the A1085

OPENING
All year open daily; Closed 25 Dec
Please phone for details

ADMISSION PRICES
Adult £3 Child £3

CONTACT
Whitley Bay Ice Rink
Hillheads Road
Whitley Bay
Tyne and Wear NE25 8HP
Tel 0191 2911000
Fax 0191 2911001
Email icerink@ukonline.co.uk

Wildfowl & Wetlands Trust Washington

3 hrs+

All year

LOCATION
Signposted from the A195 & the A1231.
The Trust is 4 miles from the A1(M) & 1
mile from the A19

OPENING
All year open daily 9.30am–5pm (4pm in
winter); Closed 25 Dec

ADMISSION PRICES
Adult £4.90 Child (4–16) £2.90
Family £12 Concession £3.90

CONTACT
Wildfowl & Wetlands Trust Washington
District 15
Washington
Tyne and Wear NE38 8LE
Tel 0191 4165454
Fax 0191 4165801
Email wetlands@euphony.net
Web www.wwt.org.uk

The trust is home to over 900 ducks, geese, swans and flamingos. Many birds will take food from your hand. The annual highlight is the downy duckling days (May to July) when visitors can see young birds take their first wobbly steps in the nursery. The spring highlight is the nesting colony of the Grey Heron, and the winter highlight is the feeding station with woodland birds such as the Great Spotted Woodpecker and Bullfinch.

★ Play area for children
★ Wetland Discovery Centre
★ 100 acres of wetland & woodland
★ Over 900 rare wildfowl
★ Special events & activities throughout
the year

223

Woodhorn Colliery Museum

2 hrs

All year

LOCATION
Ashington is 15 miles north of Newcastle &
5 miles east of Morpeth. Follow the A189
Coastal Route from Newcastle/Alnwick or
the A1 & A197 from Morpeth

OPENING
May–Aug open Wed–Sun 10am–5pm;
Sep–Apr open Wed–Sun 10am–4pm

ADMISSION PRICES
Free

CONTACT
Woodhorn Colliery Museum
QEII Country Park
Ashington
Northumberland NE63 9YF
Tel 01670 856968
Fax 01670 810958
Email woodhron@wansbeck.gov.uk

Woodhorn Colliery Museum is one of the most important preserved collieries in England, set within a country park. It offers excellent facilities for a great family day out. Highlights include original pit buildings, social history displays and a narrow-gauge railway.

★ Workshops
★ Special exhibition programme
★ Adventure playground

Varies

All year

Apollo Canal Cruises

Both Water Prince, **a traditional Leeds and Liverpool** wide canal barge, and Apollo, a traditional canal narrow boat, will take you on a fantastic cruise through the beautiful Saltaire and Pennine hills.

★ Luxury cruises all season

★ Superbly refurbished historic vessels

★ See locks, aquaducts, industrial heritage & countryside

★ Children's cruises

★ Santa cruises

LOCATION
In central Shipley, off the junction of the A657 & A6038

OPENING
Operates daily; As per booking for restaurant boats; Waterbus runs during school holidays & weekends

ADMISSION PRICES
Please phone for details

CONTACT
Apollo Canal Cruises
Shipley Wharf
Wharf Street
Shipley
West Yorkshire BD17 7DW
Tel 01274 595914
Fax 01274 588653
Web www.apollocanalcruises.co.uk

224

3 hrs

School hols

Archaeological Resource Centre

Become an archaeological detective! Visitors follow clues to piece together the past and find out what life was like in Viking times. Guided by an archaeologist, you will handle 1,000-year-old bones, pottery and even ancient ice-skates.

LOCATION
Take the A19 or the A64 into the centre of York

OPENING
School holidays open for independent visitors Mon–Sat 11am–3pm; Closed Dec & Jan

ADMISSION PRICES
Adult £4.50
Child (5–15 years) £4
Family £15 Concession £4

CONTACT
Archaeological Resource Centre
St Saviourgate, York YO1 8NN
Tel 01904 643211
Web www.vikingjorvik.com

Atlantis

3 hrs+

May–Sep

Atlantis water theme park has two of the world's largest water slides, a river rapids run, a whirlpool bath and lots of water-based activities!

★ Ice cream parlour   ★ Waveball

★ Sunbathing area

LOCATION
Follow the A64 into Scarborough

OPENING
May–Sep open daily 10am–6pm
Please phone for details

ADMISSION PRICES
Adult £5.50 Child (5–15 years)
£4.20

CONTACT
Atlantis
North Bay
Scarborough
North Yorkshire YO12 7TU
Tel 01723 372744

Bagshaw Museum

3-4 hrs

WC 🚻 🔒

All year

YORKSHIRE

LOCATION
The A652, A62 & M62 are all nearby &
within easy access

OPENING
All year open Mon–Fri 11am–5pm; Sat &
Sun open 12pm–5pm; Closed Good Fri,
24–26 Dec & 1 Jan

ADMISSION PRICES
Free

CONTACT
Bagshaw Museum
Wilton Park
Batley
West Yorkshire WF17 0AS
Tel 01924 326155
Fax 01924 326164
Email bagshaw.museum@kirkleesmc.gov.uk
Web www.kirkleesmc.gov.uk

Bagshaw Museum surrounds you with the sights and sounds of past
times and faraway places. Time and space mean nothing when you can
step straight from an Egyptian tomb into the enchantment of the tropical
rainforest. On the way, journey through the vibrant colours of the Orient
and tame the mythical beasts of four continents.

★ Wonder at the gothic decor of the mansion
★ Butterfly centre open in summer
★ Enchanted Forest
★ Follow the fortunes of the Bagshaws
★ Travel through Asia, Africa & the Americas
★ Glimpse the Kingdom of Osiris

225

---

3 hrs

All year

Barlow Common
Local Nature Reserve

 WC 🚻 🐾

Enjoy a family day out walking in a variety of
wildlife habitats including woodland, meadow,
ponds, a small lake and reedbed. Barlow Common is
notable for its birdlife, wildflowers and butterflies.

★ Coarse fishing facilities   ★ Nature trail
★ Information centre   ★ Bird-watching hide

LOCATION
Take the A1041 Selby–Snaith
road

OPENING
All year open daily dawn–dusk

ADMISSION PRICES
Free

CONTACT
Barlow Common
Local Nature Reserve
Barlow Road
Barlow
Selby
North Yorkshire YO8
Tel/Fax 01757 617110

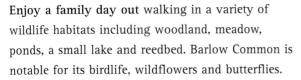

Barnsley Metrodome
Leisure Complex

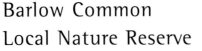

WC 🍴

½ day

All year

Barnsley Metrodome has a super pool complex
offering a total water experience, including the
Space Adventure, a fabulous new water theme park.

★ Bowls & karate available   ★ Holiday activities

LOCATION
Via the A61/A628 interchange.
Also signposted from the M1 at
junction 37

OPENING
All year open daily 9am–10pm;
Closed 25 Dec & 1 Jan
Pools are open various hours
Please phone for details

ADMISSION PRICES
Please phone for details

CONTACT
**Barnsley Metrodome Leisure
Complex**, Queens Ground
Queens Road, Barnsley
South Yorkshire S71 1AN
Tel 01226 730060
Web www.themetrodome.co.uk

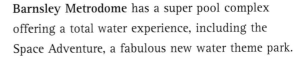

Beck Isle Museum of Rural Life

2 hrs
Mar–Oct

WC

Come and see bygones of the Victorian age, with something to interest all ages. There are many rooms, including a grocer's shop, children's room, printer's workshop, costume room, kitchen and new display area in operation.

LOCATION
Reached from the A170 & A169

OPENING
5 Mar–5 Oct open daily
10am–5pm

ADMISSION PRICES
Adult £2.50 Child £1.20
Family £6 Concession £2

CONTACT
Beck Isle Museum of Rural Life
Bridge Street
Pickering
North Yorkshire YO18 8DU
Tel/Fax 01751 473653
Web www.beckislemuseum.co.uk

Beech End Model Village

1–2 hrs
All year

WC

At this fascinating model village, children can enjoy interactive fun controlling scale model boats and vehicles. They can push buttons for light and sound effects and peep inside the model houses.

LOCATION
In the centre of Leyburn,
Wensleydale

OPENING
Easter–end Oct open Mon–Fri;
School holidays & Sat & Sun
open 10.30am–5pm; Other
months open Mon, Wed & Fri
2pm–5pm

ADMISSION PRICES
Adult £1.90 Child £1.30
Senior £1.60

CONTACT
Beech End Model Village
Commercial Square, Leyburn
North Yorkshire DL8 5BP
Tel 01969 625400
Web www.beech-end.co.uk

226

Betton Farm Visitor Centre & Animal Farm

3 hrs
All year

Betton Farm offers an animal farm, a pets corner with a toy tractor area and a play area. There is also an indoor sand-pit and a honey bee exhibition.

★ Farm shop with own bakery

★ Meet farmyard friends

LOCATION
On the A170, a few miles west
of Scarborough

OPENING
All year open 10am–5pm; Closed
25, 26 Dec

ADMISSION PRICES
Adult £1 Child £1
Family £3.50

CONTACT
Betton Farm Visitor Centre &
Animal Farm
Racecourse Road
East Ayton
Scarborough
North Yorkshire YO13 9HT
Tel 01723 863143

Bolton Abbey Estate

Quality Assured Visitor Attraction
English Tourism Council

2 hrs+
All year

You can enjoy nature trails, woodland walks, a tithe barn and picnic areas in this beautiful country estate alongside the River Wharfe.

★ Strid Wood nature trails

★ 80 miles of footpaths

LOCATION
On the B6160, off the A59
Skipton–Harrogate road

OPENING
Estate & priory: All year open
daily dawn–dusk
Car park: Locked at 9pm in
summer & 6pm in winter

ADMISSION PRICES
Free

CONTACT
Bolton Abbey
Skipton
North Yorkshire BD23 6EX
Tel 01756 718009
Web www.boltonabbey.com

Bolton Castle

 1 hr+
All year

Bring the family along to this fascinating and historical castle. Bolton Castle has dominated its beautiful Yorkshire Dales setting since its completion in 1399. One of the country's best preserved castles, it is the site where Mary Queen of Scots was imprisoned.

i

LOCATION
6 miles west of Leyburn, just off the A648. Signposted from Wensley

OPENING
Mar–Nov open daily 10am–5pm; Dec–Feb open daily 10am–4pm Please phone for details

ADMISSION PRICES
Adult £4 Child/Senior/Student £3
Family £10

CONTACT
Bolton Castle
Leyburn
North Yorkshire DL8 4ET
Tel 01969 623981
Web www.boltoncastle.co.uk

Bondville Miniature Village

 2 hrs
May–Sep

Town and countryside in miniature – Bondville is a masterpiece in landscape. Bondville gives lasting pleasure for young and old, complemented by hundreds of handmade model figures and buildings.

i

LOCATION
The village is on the A165

OPENING
1 May–30 Sep open daily from 10am

ADMISSION PRICES
Adult £2.50   Child £1.50
Family £6

CONTACT
Bondville Miniature Village
Sewerby Road
Sewerby
Bridlington
Yorkshire YO15 1EL
Tel 01262 401736

227

Bradford Industrial Museum & Horses at Work

 2 hrs
All year

The museum has an original nineteenth-century spinning mill complex, complete with mill owner's house, back-to-back cottages and job masters' stables with working Shire horses. There are spinning, weaving and horse demonstrations every day.

i

LOCATION
Take the A658 (Harrogate road), A6177 (ring road)

OPENING
All year open Tue–Sat 10am–5pm, Sun 12pm–5pm; Closed Mon, except Bank holidays, Good Fri & 25, 26 Dec

ADMISSION PRICES
Free

CONTACT
Bradford Industrial Museum & Horses at Work, Moorside Mills Moorside Road, Bradford West Yorkshire BD2 3HP
Tel 01274 631756
Web www.bradford.gov.uk

Bretton Country Park

 ½ day
All year

Come to Bretton Country Park and enjoy 100 acres of parkland. There are three colour trails in the country park for families to follow, enabling children to learn as they have fun.

i

LOCATION
Leave the M1 at junction 38 & take the A637 to Wakefield

OPENING
Park: All year open daily dawn–dusk
Visitor centre: Open Sat & Sun 11am–4pm

ADMISSION PRICES
Free

CONTACT
Bretton Country Park
West Bretton
Wakefield
West Yorkshire S73 4BX
Tel 01924 830550

All day

All year

Bridlington Leisure World

New attractions at Bridlington Leisure World include a wave pool with tropical rainstorm and a water slide. There are main and learner swimming pools, a family entertainment centre, and for the children – Kiddies Kingdom and skating.

LOCATION
Off the A165 (off the M62). The nearest town is Scarborough

OPENING
Varies, depending on activity
Please phone for details

ADMISSION PRICES
Please phone for details

CONTACT
Bridlington Leisure World
The Promenade
Bridlington
Yorkshire YO15 2QQ
Tel 01262 606715
Web
www.bridlington.net/leisureworld

Brockholes Farm Visitor Centre

2 hrs

All year

This visitor centre includes traditional farm buildings, housing a selection of farm animals and including a pedigree herd of Limousin cattle. You can also see small animals, including rabbits, guinea pigs and hamsters.

LOCATION
Take the A638 from Doncaster towards Bawtry & turn onto the B1396

OPENING
All year open daily
10am–4.30pm; Closed 25 Dec

ADMISSION PRICES
Adult £3.50 Under-14s £2.75
Concession £2.75

CONTACT
Brockholes Farm Visitor Centre
Brockholes Lane, Branton
Doncaster
South Yorkshire DN3 3NH
Tel 01302 535057

228

1–2 hrs

All year

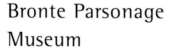

Bronte Parsonage Museum

The home of the Bronte sisters, Haworth Parsonage is now a museum containing displays of the sisters' personal treasures, pictures, clothes and manuscripts, and an exhibition interpreting their lives and works.

LOCATION
12 miles north of Halifax. Via the M62 or A629

OPENING
Please phone for details

ADMISSION PRICES
Adult £4.80 Child £1.50

CONTACT
Bronte Parsonage Museum
Church Street
Haworth
Keighley
West Yorkshire BD22 8DR
Tel 01535 642323
Fax 01535 647131

Calder Valley Cruising

1–2 hrs

By appt

Calder Valley offers motorboat and horse-drawn cruises on the Rochdale Canal with a visitor centre in a converted barge. Travel up and down locks and be legged through a tunnel by our crew.

★ Special theme cruises   ★ Daily summer waterbus

LOCATION
On the A646 in the middle of Hebden Bridge, 7 miles from Halifax

OPENING
Open by appointment only

ADMISSION PRICES
Please phone for details

CONTACT
Calder Valley Cruising
Barge Branwell
The Marina, New Road
Hebden Bridge
West Yorkshire HX7 8AD
Tel/Fax 01422 845557

Cannon Hall Open Farm

2 hrs

All year

This working farm is now open to visitors. Come and enjoy exhibits of cattle, pigs and sheep, as well as rabbits, ponies and horses. There are also exotic animals such as chinchillas, wallabies and llamas.

★ Adventure playground   ★ Baby animals

LOCATION
Take the A635 from Barnsley just after Cawthorne village. Signposted on right

OPENING
All year open Apr–Aug Mon–Sat 10am–4.30pm; Sep–Mar open Mon–Sat 10.30am–4.30pm, Sun & Bank holidays 10.30am–5pm

ADMISSION PRICES
Adult £2.25 Child £1.75

CONTACT
Cannon Hall Open Farm
Cawthorne, Barnsley
South Yorkshire S75 4AT
Tel 01226 790427
Fax 01226 792511
Web www.cannonhallfarm.co.uk

Captain Cook Memorial Museum

1–2 hrs
Mar–Oct

This fascinating museum is housed in a harbourside house with a ship-timbered attic where the young James Cook lodged as an apprentice. Learn all about his ships, his explorations, his companions and his amazing discoveries.

LOCATION
In Grape Lane, Whitby. It is 100 yards from the swing bridge in the town centre

OPENING
Mar open weekends only 11am–3pm; Apr–Oct open daily 9.45am–5pm

ADMISSION PRICES
Adult £3 Child £2 Senior £2.50

CONTACT
Captain Cook Memorial Museum, Grape Lane, Whitby
North Yorkshire YO22 UBA
Tel 01947 601900
Web
www.cookmuseumwhitby.co.uk

229

Colour Museum

½ day

All year

The Colour Museum is unique. Dedicated to the history, development and technology of colour, it is the only museum of its kind in Europe. A truly colourful experience for both kids and adults, it's fun, it's informative and it's well worth a visit.

LOCATION
The B6144 (Westgate) is the nearest main road. Signposted

OPENING
All year open Tue–Sat 10am–4pm; Closed Sun, Mon & Bank holidays; Closed 23 Dec–1 Jan, 29 Mar–1 Apr

ADMISSION PRICES
Adult £1.75 Child £1.25
Concession £1.25 Family £4

CONTACT
Colour Museum
PO Box 244, Perkin House
Providence Street, Bradford
West Yorkshire BD1 2PW
Tel 01274 390955

Dalby Forest Drive & Visitor Centre

2 hrs+
All year

Come and enjoy this 9-mile scenic drive with car parks, picnic places and waymarked walks ranging from 2–7 miles. There is also a Habitat Trail and an orienteering course.

LOCATION
Leave the A170 at Thornton Dale & head for Low Dalby

OPENING
All year, weather permitting; Visitor centre open daily Apr & Oct 11am–4pm; May, Jun & Sep 10am–5pm; Jul & Aug 10am–5.30pm

ADMISSION PRICES
Price per car £4

CONTACT
Dalby Forest Drive
& Visitor Centre
Low Dalby
Pickering
North Yorkshire YO18 7LT
Tel 01751 460295

1 hr+

All year

Dales Countryside Museum Centre

This wonderful museum tells the story of the Yorkshire Dales – its people and environment. There is a steam locomotive and carriages with video displays and an interactive area for all the family.

★ Guided tours for individuals

LOCATION
Off the A684 in the Old Station Yard

OPENING
All year open daily 10am–5pm

ADMISSION PRICES
Adult £3 Family £8
Concession £2

CONTACT
Dales Countryside Museum Centre
Station Yard
Yorkshire DL8 3NT
Tel 01969 667450
Email hawes@ytbtic.co.uk

Dobsons Sweets

1 hr

By appt

Dobsons Sweets will show you the traditional manufacturing of confectionery. See boiled sweets being made by this small family firm, established in 1850.

★ Video presentation

LOCATION
Elland town centre. Leave the M62 at junction 24 to reach Elland

OPENING
By appointment only

ADMISSION PRICES
Adult £3.50 Child £3.50

CONTACT
Dobsons Sweets
Northgate
Elland
West Yorkshire HX5 0RU
Tel 01422 372165
Fax 01422 310902
Email sales@dobsons.co.uk
Web www.dobsons.co.uk

1–2 hrs

All year

Doncaster Aeroventure South Yorkshire Aircraft Museum

A fascinating day out for any budding plane enthusiast. Come and see this collection of British jets and helicopters. Occupying the last part of the former Doncaster airfield, the site also features other buildings of the wartime period which are part of a long-term restoration scheme to return them to use.

★ Guided tours for individuals

★ D.H. Vampire 11, D.H. Chipmunk T10 & D.H. Dove

★ Westland Scout, Whirlwind H.A.R. 9, Wessex & Bell Sioux

LOCATION
Leave the M18 at junction 3 & turn into the A6182. Also reached via the A638 Doncaster–Bawtry road

OPENING
All year open Thu–Sun including Bank holidays 10am–5pm

ADMISSION PRICES
Adult £3 Child £1 Family £7
Concession £1

CONTACT
Doncaster Aeroventure South Yorkshire Aircraft Museum
Sandy Lane
Doncaster
South Yorkshire DN4 5EP
Tel 01302 761616
Web www.syam.freehosting.net

The Earth Centre

3 hrs+

All year

LOCATION
Off the M18 at junction 36, then follow the A630

OPENING
Daily open 10am–5pm; Closed 25 Dec

ADMISSION PRICES
Adult £4.50 Child £4.50

CONTACT
The Earth Centre
Denaby Main
Doncaster
South Yorkshire DN12 4EA
Tel 01709 513933
Fax 01709 512010
Email info@earthcentre.org.uk
Web www.earthcentre.org.uk

The Earth Centre is a 400-acre ecology park with something for all the family. It includes showcased buildings, exhibitions, landscaping and gardens. Green gardens now cover an ex-coalmine where a coal-spoil has been planted with over 1,000 trees.

★ Guided tours for individuals
★ Nature trails
★ Educational hands-on exhibitions
★ Aquatic ecology
★ Film show
★ Play areas

231

3–4 hrs

All year

Eden Camp

1998 winner
The England for Excellence Awards

Eden Camp is the only modern history theme museum of its kind in the world. A visit to this museum will transport you back to wartime Britain. You will experience the sights, the sounds and even the smells of those historic years.

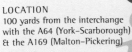

LOCATION
100 yards from the interchange with the A64 (York–Scarborough) & the A169 (Malton–Pickering)

OPENING
2nd Mon in Jan–23 Dec open daily 10am–5pm

ADMISSION PRICES
Adult £4 Child £3 Senior £3

CONTACT
Eden Camp Modern History Theme Museum
Malton
North Yorkshire
Tel 01653 697777
Email admin@edencamp.co.uk
Web www.edencamp.co.uk

Eureka!

All day

All year

Eureka! is Britain's first interactive museum designed for children. It opens up an amazing world of hands-on exploration. There are over 400 exhibits and activities to encourage children to use their senses and imagination.

LOCATION
Next to Halifax railway station. M62 junction 24 follow signs to Halifax & then the brown tourist signs to Eureka!

OPENING
All year open daily 10am–5pm; Closed 24, 25, 26 Dec

ADMISSION PRICES
Adult £5.50 Over-3s £5.50
Family £25

CONTACT
Eureka!
Discovery Road
Halifax, West Yorkshire HX1 2NE
Tel 07626 983191
Web www.eureka.org.uk

Varies

Falconry UK Bird of Prey & Conservation Centre

Mar–Oct   WC 🏕 🍴

Enjoy the thrills and excitement of falconry at the Birds of Prey centre in the picturesque grounds of Sion Hill Hall. Come close to the flight and power of some of the world's most beautiful birds of prey.

★ Breathtaking displays
★ Eagles & hawks fly around you
★ Sit in the English Garden
★ Falcons & owls swoop around
★ Explanations from skilled handlers

LOCATION
On the A167, 6 miles south of Northallerton. Take the A61 west from Thirsk, then the A167 north for 3 miles, or the A61 east from the A1 then the A167 north for 3 miles

OPENING
Mar–Oct open daily 10.30am–5.30pm

ADMISSION PRICES
Adult £4.50 Child £2.50 Family £12

CONTACT
Falconry UK Centre
Sion Hill Hall
Kirby Wiske
Thirsk
North Yorkshire YO7 4EU
Tel 01845 587522
Email mail@falconrycentre.co.uk
Web www.falconry.co.uk

232

2 hrs+

Apr–Sep

Farming Flashback

WC 🏕 🍴

This working farm has a large vintage machinery collection – a must-see for every mechanically-minded child. Come and see the traction engines, tractors, harvesters and fire engines.

LOCATION
1½ miles from Ampleforth. Follow signs

OPENING
Apr–Sep open Mon–Sat 10am–6pm

ADMISSION PRICES
Adult £2.50 Concession £2.50

CONTACT
Farming Flashback
Thorpe Hall Farm
Ampleforth
York
North Yorkshire YO62 4DL
Tel 01439 788793

Flamingo Land Theme Park & Zoo

WC 🏕 🍴

All day

Apr–Dec

Flamingo Land offers a great family day out, with something for everyone. The park has attractions for all ages, with thrilling rides such as the Magnum Force, triple-looping roller coaster and the free-falling Cliff Hanger. There's also a zoo!

LOCATION
In North Yorkshire, off the A64 Scarborough–York road on the A169 Malton–Pickering road

OPENING
Apr–Nov open daily 10am–5pm or 6pm; Zoo only open Nov–Dec 10am–5pm too

ADMISSION PRICES
Adult £13.50 Child £13.50
Under-3s Free Family £50
Senior £6.75

CONTACT
Flamingo Land, Kirby Misperton, Malton YO17 6UX
Tel 01653 668287
Web www.flamingoland.co.uk

The Foundry Climbing Centre

Varies

All year

The Foundry Climbing Centre provides indoor climbing experience for anyone of any age – from novices to experts. Instruction is available on request and children's climbing clubs are run regularly.

★ Activities also run in the Peak District National Park

233

Goodalls of Tong – Working Farm & Countryside Visitor Centre

2–3 hrs

All year

This visitor centre can be used as a base to explore the farm, Tong village and the extensive network of footpaths and bridleways. Children will love the home-made dairy ice cream.

★ 80 different flavours of ice cream available

★ Cheeses, preserves, teas & coffee manufactured on site

★ Wildlife garden

★ Collection of old dairy machinery

★ Viewing galleries

2 hrs+

Mar–Nov

The Grainary Wildlife Farm

The farm welcomes less able people as well as able people to enjoy the countryside. There are seven walks, both modern and traditional, taking in farming, friendly animals, lakeside trails, forest walks and indoor and outdoor play areas.

★ Guided tours for individuals
★ Education centre
★ Beautiful views
★ Plant sales
★ Wildflower trails

LOCATION
Via the A165, A171 or the A64

OPENING
Mar–Nov
Please phone for details

ADMISSION PRICES
Please phone for details

CONTACT
The Grainary Wildlife Farm
Keassbeck Hill Farm
Harewood Dale
Scarborough
North Yorkshire YO13 0DT
Tel 01723 870026
Email thesimpsons@grainary.co.uk
Web www.grainary.co.uk

234

2 hrs+

All year

Hands On History –
The Old Grammar School

WC

This building houses The Story of Hull and its People exhibition. The attraction is a schools curriculum resource centre, created with children in mind, and features the Victorians and Egyptians. It is open to the public at weekends and during school holidays.

LOCATION
Take the A63 to the town centre & the A1079 from York

OPENING
All year open weekends & school holidays
Sat 10am–5pm, Sun 1.30pm–4.30pm;
Closed Good Fri
Please phone for opening times over Christmas

ADMISSION PRICES
Free

CONTACT
Hands on History – The Old Grammar School
South Church Side
Hull HU1 1RR
Tel 01482 613902
Fax 01482 613710
Email museums@hullcc.gov.uk

Harewood House & Bird Garden

2 hrs+
Mar–Dec

This fine Yorkshire home contains wonderful fine furniture, paintings and porcelain. The grounds have stunning lakeside and woodland walks and the bird garden has over 150 species of birds.

★ Free audio tour

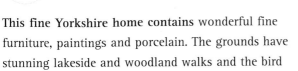

LOCATION
On the junction of the
A61/A659 Leeds–Harrogate road

OPENING
Mar–Nov open daily; Bird garden open from 10am; House open from 11am. Grounds & bird garden open weekends in Nov & Dec

ADMISSION PRICES
Full ticket: Adult £8 Child £5
Please phone for details of other ticket prices

CONTACT
Harewood House & Bird Garden
Harewood LS17 9LQ
Tel 0113 2181010
Email business@harewood.org

Hatfield Water Park

Varies
All year

YORKSHIRE

This all-round watersports centre offers canoeing, kayaking, sailing, windsurfing and powerboating activities. The site also includes a 3-star rated caravan and campsite and residential visitor centre.

★ Adventure playground

LOCATION
Off the A18, just outside
Hatfield Village on the road to Thorne

OPENING
In summer open daily
9am–5.30pm; In winter open
Mon–Fri 9am–4.30pm

ADMISSION PRICES
Free
Activity prices vary
Please phone for details

CONTACT
Hatfield Water Park
Old Thorne Road, Doncaster
South Yorkshire DN7 6EQ
Tel 01302 841572

235

Hazel Brow Visitor Centre

2 hrs+
Mar–Sep

LOCATION
From Richmond take the A6108 signposted Leyburn for approx 5 miles; branch off onto the B6270 to Reeth; continue for 9 miles to Low Row

OPENING
Mar–Sep open Sun, Wed & Thu 11am–6pm;
School & Bank holidays open Mon & Tue
Please phone for details

ADMISSION PRICES
Adult £4 Child (2–16 years) £3.50
Family £14

CONTACT
Hazel Brow Visitor Centre
Low Row
Richmond
North Yorkshire DL11 6NE
Tel 01748 886224
Email hazelbrowfarm@aol.com
Web www.yorkshirenet.co.uk/hazelbrow

Hazel Brow is an award-winning 200-acre organic livestock farm in the heart of Swaledale. Farming in the Dale is portrayed through displays, exhibitions and a farm video. Find out about organic food production, walk along the riverside nature trail or take the paths through the hay meadows, herb-rich pastures and wild heather moorland.

★ Guided tours for individuals
★ Lambing time visits in April
★ May–Sep crafts & skills demonstrations
★ Sheepdog training
★ Woolcraft & butter making
★ Spinning & quilting demonstrations

3 hrs
All year

Heeley City Farm

Come and meet the farmyard animals at this community-based family attraction, housed in a mini-farm and environmental centre.

★ Garden centre

★ Educational displays

★ Adventure playground

LOCATION
1½ miles south of Sheffield city centre, just beyond the end of Bramall Lane (the home of Sheffield United F.C.)

OPENING
In summer open daily 9am–5pm; In winter open daily 9am–4.30pm

ADMISSION PRICES
Free
Donations welcomed

CONTACT
Heeley City Farm
Richards Road, Sheffield
South Yorkshire S2 3DT
Tel 0114 2580482
Email farm@heeleyfarm.org.uk

All day
All year

Highland Adventure Playground

Highfield Adventure Playground has lots of things for children to do. They can choose what to do from games, trips, art and craft, sport and climbing.

★ Play Staff on hand

★ Football

★ Woodwork

★ Swimming

LOCATION
Mount Pleasant Park, just off the A621 Abbeydale road, 1 mile from the city centre of Sheffield

OPENING
All year open daily except Wed & Sun; Closed for Christmas

ADMISSION PRICES
Free

CONTACT
Highfield Adventure Playground
Mount Pleasant Park
Sheffield
Yorkshire
Tel 0114 203720

1–2 hrs
All year

The Honey Farm

This is a working honey farm with a very extensive exhibition of live honey-bees. All visitors get a guided tour with a full description of the life and history of bees.

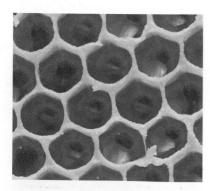

★ Farm shop

★ Farmyard animals

★ Craft workshops

★ Children's play area

LOCATION
Off the A64 then along the A170 & the A171

OPENING
All year open daily 10am–5pm; Closed 25, 26 Dec

ADMISSION PRICES
Adult £2.95   Child £1.50

CONTACT
The Honey Farm
Racecourse Road
East Ayton
Scarborough
North Yorkshire YO13 9HT
Tel 01723 864001
Fax 01723 862455
Email beehealth@aol.com

Island Heritage

2–3 hrs

All year

LOCATION
From Masham take the A6108 towards Middleham then the 1st left to Fearby, Healey & Leighton

OPENING
Apr–Oct open Tue–Sun 10am–6pm & Bank holidays only; Nov–Mar open Tue–Sun 11am–4pm; Closed 25, 26 Dec & 1 Jan

ADMISSION PRICES
Free

CONTACT
Island Heritage
Pott Hall Farm
Healey
Ripon
North Yorkshire HG4 4LT
Tel 01765 689651
Fax 01765 689350
Email islandheritage@hotmail.com
Web www.islandheritage.co.uk

A working farm producing natural, undyed woollen products from its own flock of rare breed, primitive sheep. Watch the lambs being born from mid-April to May, the sheep being sheared in June and the fleeces being sorted for spinning from August to late October.

★ Guided tours for individuals
★ Working craft demonstrations
★ Viewing window
★ Rare breed woollen goods

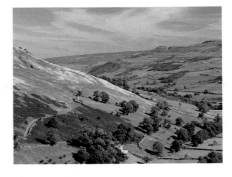

Quality Assured Visitor Attraction
English Tourism Council

Jorvik – The Viking City

4 hrs+

All year

LOCATION
Follow the A19 or A64 into the city centre & follow the signs to Coppergate shopping centre

OPENING
All year open Apr–Oct daily 9am–5.30; Nov–Mar open daily 10am–4.30pm; Closed 25 Dec

ADMISSION PRICES
Adult £6.95 Child (5–15 years) £5.10
Concession £6.10 Family £21.95

CONTACT
The Viking City
Jorvik
Coppergate
York
Yorkshire YO1 9WT
Tel 01904 543403
Email enquiries@vikingjorvik.com
Web www.vikingjorvik.com

Journey back to the heart of York as it would have been in AD975, on the very site where archaeologists discovered the preserved remains of the Viking-age city. Experience the sights, sounds and even smells of the Viking era, faithfully recreated following archaeological research.

★ Artefact gallery
★ 800 artefacts on display
★ Models recreate craftsmen, traders & merchants

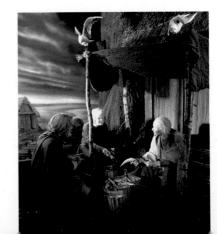

Varies

All year

Keighley & Worth Valley Railway

This fully-operational, preserved railway branch line is five miles long and runs from Keighley to Oxenhope. Along the line are six award-winning stations.

238

2 hrs

Apr–Sep

Kinderland

Kinderland is a play and activity park full of exciting things to do. It is mainly traditional, but has up-to-date design. Essentially for under-12s.

Langdale Quest

Various

Feb–Oct

Langdale Quest is the ideal family adventure. Drive, navigate and seek clues along 50 miles of forest tracks in Langdale Forest near Pickering.

Laser Arena

2 hrs+
All year

Lightwater Valley Theme Park

3 hrs+
Easter–Oct

A futuristic wasteland filled with sounds, FX lights and enemies! Stalk opponents equipped with state of the art laser hardware. Use stealth, cunning, strategy and skill to score points.

Lightwater Valley Theme Park features a number of white-knuckle rides including The Ultimate Roller coaster, Beaver Rapids Log Flume, Go-Karting and the Falls of Terror.

LOCATION
In Sheffield city centre on the corner of Snig Hill & Bank Street

OPENING
All year open daily 11am–9pm; Closed 25 Dec

ADMISSION PRICES
1 game £3.50 2 games £6
3 games £7.50 Family £10

CONTACT
Laser Arena
4 Bank Street
Sheffield
Yorkshire S1 2DS
Tel 0114 2721400
Web www.laserarena.co.uk

LOCATION
Take the A6108, or follow the signs from the A1 & A61

OPENING
Easter–October 10am–5pm

ADMISSION PRICES
Height over 4ft 3in: £9.95
Height under 4ft 4in: £7.95

CONTACT
Lightwater Valley Theme Park
North Stainley
Ripon
North Yorkshire HG4 3HT
Tel 0870 4580060
Fax 01765 635359
Email
leisure@lightwatervalley.co.uk
Web www.lightwatervalley.net

239

Millennium Galleries

3 hrs
All year

LOCATION
In the centre of Sheffield by Arundel Gate. Follow signs from city centre

OPENING
All year open daily Mon–Sat 10am–5pm, Wed 10am–9pm, Sun 11am–5pm

ADMISSION PRICES
Adult £4 Child £2 Family £9
Concession £3

CONTACT
Millennium Galleries
Arundel Gate
Sheffield
Yorkshire S1 2PP
Tel 0114 2782600
Email info@sheffieldgalleries.org.uk

This new museum has four galleries: Special Exhibitions, Metalwork, Craft & Design and the Ruskin Gallery. Many of the exhibitions have hands-on elements that will appeal to children, and exhibitions in other galleries change regularly, keeping the galleries up-to-date.

3-4 hrs

May-Oct

Monk Park Farm Visitor Centre

This open farm in Hambleton Hills has indoor and outdoor viewing and feeding areas, a wildfowl lake and animal attractions. Meet breeds such as wallabies, rheas, llamas, lambs, piglets, goats, deer, ponies ducks, geese, hens, swans and pheasants.

LOCATION
Bagby, just off the A19 south of Thirsk

OPENING
1 May–31 Oct open daily 11am–5.30pm

ADMISSION PRICES
Adult £3.50 Child £2.50
Concession £2.50

CONTACT
Monk Park Farm Visitor Centre
Monk Park
Bagby
Thirsk
North Yorkshire
Tel 01845 597730

240

2 hrs

Feb-Dec

Mother Shipton's Cave & the Petrifying Well

First opened in 1630, Mother Shipton's Cave and Petrifying Well are the oldest tourist attractions in Britain. Children will particularly enjoy the cave, petrifying well, museum, playground and 12 acres of riverside grounds.

★ Guided tours compulsory for individuals
★ Mother Shipton's Kitchen
★ Barbecue during children's holidays

LOCATION
On the A59 from Harrogate or York, the cave is in the centre of Knaresborough

OPENING
1 Mar–1 Nov open 9.30am–5.30pm;
1 Nov–20 Feb weekends only
10am–4.30pm; Closed Jan

ADMISSION PRICES
Adult £4.95 Child £3.95 Concession £3.50
Family £13.50

CONTACT
Mother Shipton's Cave & Petrifying Well
Prophesy House
High Bridge
Knaresborough
North Yorkshire HG5 8DD
Tel 01423 864600
Web www.mothershipton.co.uk

All day

All year

National Museum of Photography, Film & TV

National Railway Museum

2–5 hrs

All year

Take a voyage of discovery at the National Museum of Photography, Film & Television. Explore the eight free interactive galleries where you can ride on a magic carpet, read the news or look back at your TV favourites from the past.

There's plenty to entertain the children at the National Railway Museum. Discover the story of the train in a great day out for all the family. This museum has three huge galleries packed with fun and knowledge.

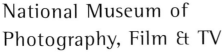

LOCATION City centre location, follow the brown signs	**ADMISSION PRICES** Free
OPENING All year open Tue–Sun 10am–6pm; Open Mon during school & Bank holidays; Closed 24–26 Dec, Open 31 Dec, 1 Jan Please phone to confirm	**CONTACT** National Museum of Photography, Film & TV Bradford West Yorkshire BD1 1NQ Tel 01274 202030 Web www.nmpft.org.uk

LOCATION 540 metres from York railway station. Signposted from the city centre & from York's ring road	Charges may apply for special events **CONTACT** National Railway Museum Leeman Road, York
OPENING All year open daily 10am–6pm; Closed 24–26 Dec	Yorkshire YO26 4XJ Tel 01904 621261/ 01904 686286
ADMISSION PRICES Free	Email nrm@nmsi.ac.uk Web www.nrm.org.uk

241

2 hrs+

All year

Nidderdale Museum

North Yorkshire Moors Railway

Quality Assured Visitor Attraction

English Tourism Council

Varies

Mar–Nov

The museum covers all aspects of Nidderdale life in the past. The displays bring history to life for children. They include a complete cobbler's shop, a Victorian sitting-room and kitchen, a school-room, a general store, a joiner's shop and a solicitor's office.

The North Yorkshire Moors Railway runs between the historic market town of Pickering and Grosmont near Whitby and is one of the world's oldest railway lines. Trains also call at the picturesque stations of Levisham and Goathland.

LOCATION Take the B6265 from Harrogate & the B6165 from Ripon & Grassington	**ADMISSION PRICES** Adult £1.50 Child 75p **CONTACT** Nidderdale Museum
OPENING Easter–end Oct open daily 2pm–5pm; Aug open daily 11am–5pm; Nov–Apr Sat & Sun 2pm–5pm; Closed 23, 24 Dec	Council Offices, Pateley Bridge Harrogate North Yorkshire HG3 5LE Tel 01423 711225 Web www.nidderdale.co.uk

LOCATION Take the A169 or A170 to Pickering	**CONTACT** North Yorkshire Moors Railway Pickering Station Park Street
OPENING 23 Mar–3 Nov open daily; Times vary; 9 Nov–29 Dec open week-ends only	Pickering North Yorkshire YO18 7AJ Tel 01751 472508 Email admin@nymr.demon.co.uk
ADMISSION PRICES Please phone for details	Web www.nymr.demon.co.uk

2-4 hrs

All year

Oakwell Hall & Country Park

History comes alive at Oakwell Hall. This beautiful Elizabethan manor house has delighted visitors for centuries. Stroll round the delightful period garden or check out the wild and wonderful inhabitants of the wildlife access garden.

★ Adventure playground

★ Visitor centre

★ Discover Oakwell! interactive exhibition

★ Waymarked nature trails

LOCATION
Take the A652 Batley–Bradford road; the park is signed along this road. Take the M62 exit at junction 26/27

OPENING
All year open Mon–Fri 11am–5pm, Sat & Sun 12pm–5pm; Closed Good Fri, 24–26 Dec & 1 Jan

ADMISSION PRICES
Adult £1.40 Child (5–13 years) 50p
Concession 50p Family £3

CONTACT
Oakwell Hall & Country Park
Nutter Lane
Birstall
Batley
West Yorkshire WF17 9LG
Tel 01924 326240
Fax 01924 326249
Email oakwell.hall@kirkleesmc.gov.uk
Web www.kirkleesmc.gov.uk

242

Varies

Jul–Sep

Orchard Farm Steam Railway

Orchard Farm Railway is a 10¼ gauge miniature steam railway set in landscaped grounds. The whole family will enjoy the miniature Victorian station with a tunnel, bridges, a lake and boats.

LOCATION
On the A165 Bridlington–Scarborough road, turn off for Hunmanby. The railway is on the right

OPENING
Bank holidays & Jul–Sep open daily 11am–4pm; Santa Claus run in Dec

ADMISSION PRICES
Adult £1 Child £1

CONTACT
Orchard Farm Steam Railway
Hunmanby
Filey
North Yorkshire YO14 0PU
Tel 01723 891582

Ormesby Hall

This eighteenth-century mansion is full of fascination for everyone of all ages. You can wander round the gardens and enjoy the beautiful house and its famous stables.

2 hrs+

Apr–Nov

LOCATION
3 miles south-east of Middlesborough & west of the A19. Take the A174, the A172 & follow the signs

OPENING
Apr–Nov open Tue–Thu, Sun, Bank holidays & Good Friday 2pm–5pm

ADMISSION PRICES
Adult £3.50 Child £1.70
Family £8.50

CONTACT
Ormesby Hall
Ormesby
North Yorkshire TS7 9AS
Tel 01642 324188
Email yorkor@smtp.ntrust.org.uk

Park Rose Owl Sanctuary

3 hrs

All year

LOCATION
On the A165/A166, 2 miles south of Bridlington

OPENING
All year open daily 10am–5pm;
Closed 25–31 Dec

ADMISSION PRICES
Adult £1.75 Child (3–16 years) £1.25
Family £5.50

CONTACT
Park Rose Owl Sanctuary
Carnaby Covert Lane
Bridlington
Yorkshire YO15 3QF
Tel 01262 606800
Fax 01262 400202

The owl sanctuary is set in natural woodland. There are 15 aviaries along a woodland walk displaying 48 owls and birds of prey. There are guided information tours and flying displays daily in summer season.

★ Honey bee exhibition
★ Pottery seconds shop

Pickering Trout Lake

Varies

Mar–Oct

LOCATION
Signposted 'Fun Fishing' from Pickering, 400 yds past North Yorkshire Moors Railway Station

OPENING
Mar–Oct open daily 10am–5pm

ADMISSION PRICES
Please phone for details

CONTACT
Pickering Trout Lake
Newbridge Road
Pickering
North Yorkshire YO18 8JD
Tel 01751 474219
Email pickeringtroutlake@talk21.com

Pickering lake is stocked with rainbow trout so that you can try fishing by float or fly methods. This is an ideal place for children to learn the art of angling – 99 per cent of our visitors catch a fish!

★ Guided tours for individuals
★ Tackle available for hire or sale
★ Courses available

2 hrs

All year WC

Pontefract Museum

Discover the events that took place in Pontefract. Personal accounts provide an insight of the sieges of the castle during the Civil War, what it was like to work in the town's liquorice factories and how people survived the workhouse 100 years ago.

LOCATION
In Pontefract town centre, next to the library

OPENING
All year open Mon–Fri 10am–4.30pm, Sat 10.30am–4.30pm

ADMISSION PRICES
Free

CONTACT
Pontefract Museum
Salter Row
Pontefract
West Yorkshire WF8 1BA
Tel 01977 722740
Fax 01977 722742

The Quad Squad

Varies

All year

Enjoy the Quad Squad's trekking facility around the more scenic parts of Pheasant Hill Farm and parts of Dalby Forest. Children will be enthralled by this fun-packed and exhilarating adventure.

LOCATION
On the A170 west of Scarborough & east of Pickering

OPENING
Please phone for details

ADMISSION PRICES
Adult £15 per hour
Child £15 per hour

CONTACT
The Quad Squad
Pheasant Hill Farm, Ebberston
Scarborough
North Yorkshire YO13 9PB
Tel/Fax 01723 859041
Web www.quadbikes.fsnet.co.uk

244

4–5 hrs

Mar–Sep

Renishaw Hall Gardens

Renishaw Hall gardens, museum and galleries are set in 300 acres of parkland with nature trails, reserves and a sculpture park. Children's events are organised regularly and there is a children's play area.

★ Special events
★ Adventure playground

LOCATION
2 miles from junction 30 off the M1, between Ecrington & Renishaw on the A6135

OPENING
Mar–Sep open Thu–Sun & Bank holidays 10.30am–4.30pm
Please phone for details of separate events

ADMISSION PRICES
Adult £5 Child Free Concession £4

CONTACT
Renishaw Hall Gardens
Renishaw Hall
Sheffield
South Yorkshire
Tel 01246 432310
Fax 01246 430760
Email info@renishawhall.free-online.co.uk
Web www.sitwell.co.uk

2 hrs

All year

Richard III Museum

Was Richard III guilty of the brutal murder of the Princes in the Tower? Or was he just a loyal ruler? The museum allows you to decide by reconstructing a trial, presenting the case and passing sentence.

LOCATION
Access York via the A19, A59 or A64. The museum has a town-centre location

OPENING
Nov–Feb open daily 9.30am–4pm; Mar–Oct open daily 9am–5pm; Closed 25, 26 Dec & 1 Jan

ADMISSION PRICES
Adult £2 Child £1

CONTACT
Richard III Museum
Monk Bar
York YO1 7LQ
Tel 01904 634191
Web
www.richardiiimuseum.co.uk

Richmond Castle

1–2 hrs

All year

One of the most imposing Norman remains in England, Richmond Castle towers over the town. The rectangular keep is 100ft high and is one of the finest in the country.

LOCATION
In Richmond town centre, on the A6108

OPENING
1 Apr–16 Jul open 10am–6pm; 9 Feb–16 Feb 10am–5pm; 17 Jul–31 Aug 9.30am–7pm; Closed 24–26 Dec & 1 Jan

ADMISSION PRICES
Adult £2.90 Child £1.50

CONTACT
Richmond Castle (EH)
Richmond
North Yorkshire DL10 4QW
Tel 01748 822493
Web
www.english-heritage.org.uk

245

Rievaulx Abbey

4–5 hrs

All year

LOCATION
3 miles north-west of Helmsley on minor road off the B1257

OPENING
1 Apr–30 Sep open daily 10am–6pm; 9–16 Feb 10am–5pm; 17 Jul–31 Aug 9.30am–6pm; Oct open daily 10am–5pm; 1 Nov–31 Mar open daily 10am–4pm; Closed 24–26 Dec & 1 Jan

ADMISSION PRICES
Adult £3.60 Child £1.80 Concession £2.70

CONTACT
Rievaulx Abbey (EH)
Rievaulx
York
North Yorkshire YO62 5LB
Tel 01439 798228
Fax 01439 798450

Discover the spectacular and extensive remains of the first Cistercian monastery in northern England. Experience the unrivalled peace and serenity of this twelfth-century site in the beautiful valley of the River Rye. Trace the past glories and splendours of the thriving community of monks who lived and worked here.

Ripley Castle

2 hrs+
All year

Ripley Castle has been the Ingilby family home since 1345. It is full of fine armour, furniture, chandeliers and panelling, as well as a priests' hiding hole. There are beautiful walled gardens, a deerpark that is guaranteed to thrill the children and an extensive tropical plant collection in hothouses.

★ Guided tours compulsory for individuals
★ Capability Brown deerpark
★ Lakeside walk

LOCATION
On the A61 3½ miles north of Harrogate

OPENING
Jun–Aug open daily 10.30am–3pm;
Sep–May Tue, Thu, Sat & Sun
10.30am–3pm

ADMISSION PRICES
Castle & Gardens: Adult £5.50 Child £3
Gardens only: Adult £3 Child £1.50

CONTACT
Ripley Castle
Ripley
Harrogate
North Yorkshire HG3 3AY
Tel 01423 770152
Fax 01423 771745
Web www.ripleycastle.co.uk

246

Rotunda Museum

2 hrs+
All year

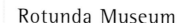

The finest purpose-built museum of its age in the country, the museum includes displays from the internationally important mesolithic site of Star Carr, Gristhorpe Man, a Bronze Age tree trunk burial and items of Victorian Scarborough.

LOCATION
Foreshore, less than 100yds from the south bay beach & 5 minutes from the town centre

OPENING
1 Jun–30 Sep open daily, except Mon, 10am–5pm; 10 Oct–31 May open Tue, Sat & Sun 11am–4pm; Closed 25 Dec–1 Jan

ADMISSION PRICES
Adult £2 Child £1.50
Family £5 Concession £1.50

CONTACT
Rotunda Museum
Vernon Road
Scarborough
North Yorkshire YO11 2NN
Tel 01723 374839

RHS Garden Harlow Carr

½ day
All year

There is something of interest for people of all ages at RHS Garden Harlow Carr. Educational and leisure courses are run all year and there are special days themed around family activities. There is also an open-air theatre.

LOCATION
Situated on Crag Lane, off Otley road (B6162) about 1½ miles from the centre of Harrogate

OPENING
All year open daily 9.30am–6pm (or dusk if earlier)

ADMISSION PRICES
Adult £4.50 Child (11–16) £1
Under-11s Free Senior £3.50
RHS Members Free

CONTACT
RHS Garden Harlow Carr
Crag Lane, Harrogate HG3 1QB
Tel 01423 565418
Web www.rhs.org.uk

Ryedale Folk Museum

2–3 hrs

Mar–Nov

LOCATION
Take the A170 from Helmsley into Hutton-le-Hole

OPENING
10 Mar–3 Nov open daily 10am–5.30pm (last admission 4.30pm)

ADMISSION PRICES
Adult £3.25 Child £1.75 Family £8.25
Concession £2.75

CONTACT
Ryedale Folk Museum
Hutton-le-Hole
York
North Yorkshire YO62 6UA
Tel 01751 417367
Fax 01751 417367

Ryedale Folk Museum contains reconstructed local buildings including long-houses, an Elizabethan manor house, furnished cottages, craftsmen's tools and household and agricultural implements. You can also see the oldest daylight photographic studio in the country, along with archaeological displays from pre-history to the tenth century.

YORKSHIRE

247

2 hrs

Feb–Oct

St Leonard's Farm Park

Come and meet friendly farmer James and his family on their award-winning farm. The farm has rare and modern breeds of animals (some of which you can feed), play areas, nature footpaths and listed barns and buildings.

LOCATION
A6038 from Otley/Ilkley, A6038 from Shipley/Bradford

OPENING
Feb–Mar open Sat & Sun 10am–4pm; Mar–Sep Tue–Sun 10am–6pm; Sep–Oct Sat & Sun 10am–4pm; Open Bank holidays & summer holidays

ADMISSION PRICES
Adult £2.25
Child (2–16 years) £1.75

CONTACT
St Leonard's Farm Park
Chapel Lane, Esholt, Shipley
West Yorkshire BD17 7RB
Tel 01274 598795
Email farmerjames1@aol.com

Sandal Castle

1 hr+

All year

Sandal Castle is an excavated medieval castle overlooking the site of the Battle of Wakefield in 1460 and the scene of the Civil War siege. It has beautiful views of the Calder Valley.

★ Displays & models on site in centre

LOCATION
On the A61, 2 miles from the city centre in the direction of Barnsley

OPENING
All year open daily dawn–dusk; Please phone 01924 305903 for centre times

ADMISSION PRICES
Free

CONTACT
Sandal Castle
Manygates Lane, Sandal
Wakefield, West Yorkshire
Tel 01924 305352
Fax 01924 305770

Sea Life & Marine Sanctuary

2-3 hrs

All year

At the **Sea Life Centre** you have the opportunity to meet creatures that live in and around the oceans of the British Isles, ranging from starfish and crabs to rays and seals.

★ Marine sanctuary

★ Otters, sharks & sea-horses

LOCATION
Follow signs to North Bay Leisure Park, situated on Whitby Road, beyond Atlantis & Kinderland; look for white pyramids

OPENING
All year open daily from 10am; Closed 25 Dec

ADMISSION PRICES
Adult £5 Child £3.50 Senior £4

CONTACT
Sea Life & Marine Sanctuary
Scalby Mills, Scarborough
North Yorkshire YO12 6RP
Tel 01723 376125
Fax 01723 376285
Web www.sealife.co.uk

Sheffield Cycle Speedway Club

1-2 hrs

All year

Sheffield Cycle Speedway Club is a British Cycling 'improve' club. It provides cycling experience for children of all ages and abilities.

★ Free loan of equipment

★ Experienced coach in attendance

LOCATION
Bochum Parkway, Sheffield

OPENING
In summer (Mar-Oct) open Mon or Wed until 7.30pm; In winter (Nov-Feb) open Sun fortnightly. Please phone before travelling

ADMISSION PRICES
Adult £1.50 Child £1.50

CONTACT
Graves Tennis & Leisure Centre
Bochum Parkway, Sheffield
Tel 01246 824220
Email martin-gamble@hotmail.com

Sheffield Ski Village

3½ hrs

All year

If you are looking for a totally unique and exhilarating day out, the Ski Village at Sheffield is the perfect destination. Here at Europe's largest all-season ski resort, you can learn to ski, play in the Penguin Park club or just relax in the authentic Swiss atmosphere!

★ White Rock Mountain Bar
★ Thunder Valley Toboggan Run
★ Authentic mountain lodge
★ Video games arcade
★ BBQ shack
★ Four Mammoth ski lifts
★ Ski & snowboard school
★ Children's parties
★ Evening parties
★ Equipment hire
★ Adventure playground

LOCATION
The village is 5 minutes from Sheffield city centre. Follow the brown tourist signs

OPENING
In summer open Mon-Fri 11am-10pm, Sat & Sun 10am-8pm, Bank holidays 10am-10pm; In winter open Mon-Fri 10am-10pm, Sat & Sun & Bank holidays & 26 Dec-2 Jan 9am-10pm; Closed 25 Dec

ADMISSION PRICES
Please phone for details

CONTACT
Sheffield Ski Village
Vale Road
Sheffield S3 9SJ
Tel 0114 2769459
Email info@sheffieldskivillage.co.uk
Web www.sheffieldskivillage.co.uk

Skipton Castle

2 hrs+

All year

Skipton Castle is one of the best-preserved and most complete medieval castles in England, despite enduring a three-year siege during the Civil War. After the Battle of Marston Moor it was the only Royalist stronghold left in the north. Today we can see in the castle's stones the story of this period of English history and of many earlier ones too.

249

Staintondale Shire Horse Farm Visitor Centre

2 hrs+

Jun–Sep

Shire horse and Shetland pony lovers will love Staintondale. Live shows are a regular feature and include the Shire horses and Shetland ponies in full western roping rig. You can even learn how to spin a lariat, whatever the weather!

★ Cart rides usually available
★ Period museum portraying rural history
★ Static displays
★ Breathtaking scenery

1-2 hrs

All year

Streetlife – Hull Museum of Transport

Streetlife has some of the finest period displays on railways, horse-drawn carriages, cycles, cars and trams. Come and meet the animated horses and experience a simulated carriage ride. Costumed figures and smells add to the visual display.

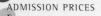

LOCATION
Take the A63 to the town centre, turn left into Old Town & the High Street

OPENING
Mon-Sat open 10am-5pm, Sun 1.30pm-4.30pm; Closed Good Friday; Please phone for details of specific dates

ADMISSION PRICES
Free

CONTACT
Streetlife – Hull Museum of Transport
6 High Street, Hull HU1 1PS
Tel 01482 613956
Email museums@hull.gov.uk
Web www.hullcc.gov.uk

3 hrs

All year

Thackray Medical Museum

This award-winning, interactive museum offers serious family fun. Explore the slums of Victorian Leeds as one of the city 'characters' and discover some of the weird treatments available.

LOCATION
Next to St James's Hospital, 2 miles east of city centre; follow signs for St James's Hospital

OPENING
All year open Tue-Sun, including Bank holidays 10am-5pm (last admission 3pm); Closed 24, 25, 26 Dec &1 Jan

ADMISSION PRICES
Adult £4.40   Child £3.30
Family £14   Concession £3.60

CONTACT
Thackray Museum
Beckett Street
Leeds, West Yorkshire LS9 7LN
Tel 0113 244 4343
Web www.thackraymuseum.org

250

1 hr

Varies

Thorne Memorial Park Railway

Thorne Memorial Park Railway Society operates the miniature railway. The members build and maintain the railway. Juniors, retired and people with disabilities are welcome.

LOCATION
1-2 miles from the M18 motorway, depending on whether you use junctions 5 or 6. Next to Stainforth & Keadby Canal on the A614 into the town centre

OPENING
Sun open 12pm-4.30pm, subject to weather
Please phone for details

ADMISSION PRICES
25p for all Under-3s Free

CONTACT
Thorne Memorial Park Railway
South Parade
Thorne
Doncaster
South Yorkshire DN8
Tel 01302 842948
Web www.thornerailway.org.uk

3 hrs

All year

Tropical World

Visitors can walk in the tropical atmosphere among exotic trees, waterfalls, rockpools and pools containing terrapins and carp. There are also reptiles, insects and butterflies as well as a re-created South American Rainforest and a Desert House.

LOCATION
3 miles north of Leeds city centre, off the A58 at Oakwood

OPENING
All year open daily 10am-early evening or dusk; Closed 25 Dec

ADMISSION PRICES
Adult £1.50 Child 75p Under-8s Free

CONTACT
Tropical World
Canal Gardens
Roundhay Park
Leeds
Yorkshire LS8 2ER
Tel 0113 2661850

Walkley Canalside Mill & Rosehip Valley Railway

2–3 hrs

All year

LOCATION
On the A646 at Hebden Bridge

OPENING
All year open Wed–Sun 10am–5pm

ADMISSION PRICES
Free

CONTACT
Walkley Canalside Mill &
Rosehip Valley Railway
Canal Wharf Sawmill
Hawkesclough
Hebden Bridge
West Yorkshire HX7 8NH
Tel 01422 842061

Come and enjoy a family day out experiencing living history, woodland walks, waxworks, a miniature railway and a riverside restaurant.

★ See clogs being made
★ World of the Honey Bee
★ Factory outlet mall

251

Wensleydale Experience

1 hr
All year

A working dairy with viewing gallery and museum. Learn about the history of Wensleydale cheese and see milk being made into cheese – then taste the finished product!

LOCATION
From the A1 to Richmond follow signs to Leyburn & then to Hawes

OPENING
In summer open Mon–Sat 9am–5pm, Sun 9.30am–4.30pm
Times may vary in winter
Please phone for details

ADMISSION PRICES
Adult £2 Child £1.50

CONTACT
Wensleydale Experience
Gayle Lane, Hawes
North Yorkshire DL8 3RN
Tel 01969 667664
Email creamery@wensleydale.co.uk
Web www.wensleydale.co.uk

White Scar Cave

2 hrs
All year

White Scar is the longest show cave in Britain. You can see underground waterfalls, thousands of stalactites, and the massive 330-ft Battlefield Cavern. Take the 80-minute guided tour which covers over one mile of underground adventure.

LOCATION
17 miles east of the M6 junction 35. In the Yorkshire Dales National Park, 1½ miles from Ingleton on the B6255 road to Hawes

OPENING
Daily, weather permitting, 10am–5.30pm; Closed 25 Dec

ADMISSION PRICES
Adult £6.50 Child £3.60
Family £18.50

CONTACT
White Scar Cave, Ingleton
North Yorkshire LA6 3AW
Tel 01524 241244
Email info@wscave.co.uk
Web www.wscave.co.uk

Wykeham Lakes

Varies

All year

Come to Wykeham Lakes to enjoy **fishing, sailing,** windsurfing, boat hire, scuba diving and canoeing! There are also nature trails and bird-watching facilities.

★ Guided tours compulsory for individuals

★ Picnic hampers, barbecues or cold lunches

★ Pike fishing during winter

★ Two trout fishing lakes

★ One coarse fishing lake

★ Watersports lake

★ Sailing & watersports tuition

★ Car parks

LOCATION
Situated 6 miles west of Scarborough off the A170 between West Ayton & Wykeham

OPENING
Boating & watersports lake open all year daily dawn–dusk; Fishing available all year; Nature trails & bird-watching available all year

ADMISSION PRICES
Prices vary according to activity/duration
Please phone for details

CONTACT
Wykeham Lakes
Charm Park
Wykeham
Scarborough
North Yorkshire
Tel 01723 866600
Fax 01723 864329

YorkBoat River Trips

1 hr

Feb–Nov

YorkBoat Guided River Trips and Evening Cruises are a must during your visit to historic York. Enjoy the modern river-boats and be amazed as the captains share their knowledge and stories of York in an entertaining live commentary.

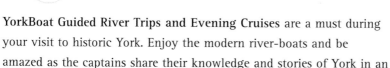

★ Guided tours compulsory for individuals

★ Floodlit evening cruises

★ Themed summer nights

★ Barbecue cruises

★ Ghost cruises with costumed storyteller

LOCATION
In York city centre, next to Museum Gardens (Lendl Bridge), or at Kings Staith near Cliffords Tower & Castle Museum

OPENING
Guided river trips Feb–Nov from 10.30am; Ghost cruise Mar–Oct 7pm–8pm; Floodlit cruise Mar–Oct 9.15pm–10.30pm; Closed 24 Dec–3 Jan
Please phone for precise dates

ADMISSION PRICES
Adult £6–£7.50 Under-15s £3–£5
Family £18 Concession £5.50–£6.50

CONTACT
Yorkboat River Trips
The Boatyard
Lendal Bridge
York YO1 7DP
Tel 01904 628324
Fax 01904 647204
Email info@yorkboat.co.uk
Web www.yorkboat.co.uk

Yorkshire Air Museum & Allied Air Forces Memorial

2 hrs
All year

LOCATION
Off the A64, the B1228 or A1079, then the B1228

OPENING
From last weekend in Mar–Remembrance Sun open Mon–Fri 10.30am–4pm, Sat & Sun 10.30am–15pm, plus Bank holidays 10.30am–5pm; Nov–end Mar open daily 11am–3pm; Closed Christmas & New Year

ADMISSION PRICES
Adult £5 Child £3 Family £14

CONTACT
Yorkshire Air Museum & Allied Air Forces Memorial
Halifax Way
Elvington
York YO41 4AU
Tel 01904 608595
Web www.yorkshireairmuseum.co.uk

This museum is inside part of an original World War II bomber command station. There are aircraft workshops and a Halifax and Mosquito rebuild project on show. Static displays include Meteors, Lightning, Canberra, Buccaneers, Hunters and Victor tanker. See the Barnes Wallis Collection, Blackburn Heritage display, Royal Observer Corps room and much more. Guaranteed to thrill all plane enthusiasts – whatever their age.

★ Archive films shown
★ Volunteer aircrew stewards give tours

Yorkshire Dales Falconry & Conservation Centre

2 hrs+
All year

LOCATION
Take the A65 bypass from Settle–Kendal

OPENING
All year open daily 10am–5pm; Closed 25 Dec

ADMISSION PRICES
Adult £4.50 Child £2.95 Family £12.95

CONTACT
Yorkshire Dales Falconry & Conservation Centre
Crows Nest
Giggleswick
Settle
North Yorkshire LA2 8AS
Tel 01729 822832
Fax 01729 825160

This award-winning falconry centre has many species of birds of prey from around the world including vultures, eagles, hawks, falcons and owls, plus Great Britain's only free-flying condor.

★ Guided tours for individuals
★ All-weather facility
★ Handling courses
★ Flying displays

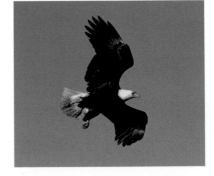

York Dungeon

Catch the plague at **York Dungeon** and take a spine-tingling tour through the plague-ravaged streets of fourteenth-century York.

York Model Railway

Come and enjoy this marvellous collection of model railway engines situated next to the railway station in the historic city of York.

LOCATION
York city centre

OPENING
Oct–Mar open daily 10.30am–4.30pm; Apr–Sep open daily 10am–5.30pm; Closed 25 Dec

ADMISSION PRICES
Adult £7.50 Child (6–15 years) £5.50 Family £22 Concession £5.50

CONTACT
York Dungeon
12 Clifford Street
York YO1 9RD
Tel 01904 632599
Fax 01904 612602
Email yorkdungeons@merlin-entertainments.com
Web www.thedungeons.com

LOCATION
Next to York station in the city centre

OPENING
Mar–Oct open 9.30am–6pm; Nov–Feb open 10.30am–5pm; Closed 25, 26 Dec

ADMISSION PRICES
Please phone for details

CONTACT
York Model Railway
Tearoom Square
York Station
York YO2 2AB
Tel 01904 630169

Yorkshire Museum

The European award-winning Yorkshire Museum is set in 10 acres of botanical gardens located in the historic centre of York. It displays some of the finest Roman, Anglo-Saxon, Viking and medieval treasures ever discovered in Britain and is a fascinating place for the whole family.

★ Home of the Middleham Jewel

★ The Hunters and the Hunted gallery

★ Special exhibitions throughout the year

LOCATION
Town centre location, within walking distance of rail station & bus stops

OPENING
All year open daily 10am–5pm; Closed 25, 26 Dec & 1 Jan

ADMISSION PRICES
Adult £4.50 Under-16s £2.95
Family £14 Concession £2.95

CONTACT
Yorkshire Museum
Museum Gardens
York YO1 7FR
Tel 01904 551800
Fax 01904 551802
Email yorkshire.museum@york.gov.uk
Web www.york.gov.uk

Yorkshire Museum of Farming

2 hrs+

All year

The Yorkshire Museum of Farming has tools and machinery of a bygone age, reconstructions of James Herriot's Surgery, a blacksmith's shop, a chapel, a hardware shop and a Land Army display. Paddocks and pens hold rare breeds farm animals and poultry, and there is much more too.

★ Guided tours for individuals
★ Replica Dark Ages & Roman fort
★ Educational projects
★ Home to Derwent Valley Light Railway
★ York bee pavilion
★ Play area

255

Yorvik Brass Rubbing Centre

2 hrs

WC

All year

Yorvik offers visitors a unique English pastime that is creative, educational and fun. Brass rubbing appeals to all ages and it is easy to do. Using paper and coloured metallic waxes, you can create your own beautiful wall hangings. Come to Yorvik and bring history alive.

★ Situated in a delightful old cottage

North-west

The Lake District, Cheshire, Merseyside and Lancashire are included in this region. Each is very different, with its own historical and industrial heritage, ranging from Lancashire's cotton mills to Liverpool's shipping and cultural past. North Wales is known for its wild landscape and Cheshire for its rich Roman heritage. Cumbria is, of course, best known for the Lake District National Park, and Lancashire has, among other things, the traditional seaside resort of Blackpool.

In Cheshire, you can visit Chester Zoo which has over 7,000 animals and many special activities for children, and get a taste of Roman life at the Dewa Roman Experience, where visitors can walk along reconstructions of Roman streets. In Cumbria, along with the many countryside and lakeside activities, there are some surprising attractions for families, such as The Cars of the Stars Museum, which has a collection of TV and film vehicles. Lancashire has much to offer, including Blackpool with its Pleasure Beach and Sea Life Centre. It also has remnants of its industrial past, such as the Ellenroad Engine House, the oldest complete steam cotton-mill engine in the country. In North Wales, you can enjoy the wildlife at the Welsh Mountain Zoo, as well as take a trip on the Snowdon Mountain railway, transporting you up to the top of the tallest mountain in England and Wales.

N

Cumbria
pp272–287

NORTH–EAST

Lancashire
pp287–300

● MANCHESTER
pp300–302

Merseyside
pp303–308

Flintshire

Anglesey

Cheshire
pp262–271

Gwynedd

Denbighshire

NORTH WALES
pp309–317

Powys

CENTRAL

Below is a list of places to visit in the North-west, organised by county and type.

Cheshire

HISTORIC BUILDINGS

MUSEUMS & EXHIBITIONS

SPORT & LEISURE

ANIMAL ATTRACTIONS

PARKS, GARDENS & NATURE TRAILS

THEME PARKS & ADVENTURE PLAYGROUNDS

MISCELLANEOUS

Cumbria

HISTORIC BUILDINGS

MUSEUMS & EXHIBITIONS

SPORT & LEISURE

ANIMAL ATTRACTIONS

BOAT & TRAIN TRIPS

PARKS, GARDENS & NATURE TRAILS

HERITAGE & INDUSTRIAL

Merseyside

North Wales

Air Raid Shelters

These **air raid shelters** were carved into the cliffs in the town centre. Now a visitor attraction, children can experience the sights and sounds of the Blitz and life in general in 1940s Britain.

★ Guided tours compulsory

LOCATION
In Stockport town centre. Leave the M63 at junction 12 & take the A6 to Stockport

OPENING
All year open Mon–Sat 11am–5pm & Sun 1–5pm

ADMISSION PRICES
Adult £3.50 Child (5–16) £2.25
Family £10 Concession £2.75

CONTACT
Air Raid Shelters
61 Chestergate
Stockport
Cheshire SK1 4AR
Tel 0161 4741940
Fax 0161 4741942

Alphabet Zoo

An **adventure playground** that provides a real challenge for children, with the emphasis on purposeful play in a safe environment. Children must be accompanied by an adult, although supervision is available on site.

LOCATION
Leave the M60 at junction 1

OPENING
All year open daily 10am–7pm;
Closed 25, 26, 31 Dec & 1 Jan

ADMISSION PRICES
£2.79 per 1½ hrs
Weekends & holidays £3.29 per hour

CONTACT
Alphabet Zoo
Mentor House
King Street West
Stockport
Cheshire SK3 0DY
Tel 0161 4772225

Blue Planet Aquarium

County Family Attraction
Good Guide to Britain 1999

The Blue Planet Aquarium has one of the largest collections of sharks in Europe. These amazing creatures pass only inches from visitors' faces in the underwater safari tunnel.

★ Interactive exhibits

LOCATION
Take junction 10 off the M53 & follow the brown tourist signs. 8 miles from Chester Railway Station

OPENING
In summer open daily 10am–6pm; In winter open daily 10am–5pm; Closed 25 Dec

ADMISSION PRICES
Adult £7.25 Child £4.95

CONTACT
Blue Planet Aquarium
Cheshire Oaks, Ellesmere Port
Cheshire CH65 9LF
Tel 0151 3578804
Email info@blueplanetaquari-um.co.uk

Bollin Valley

All day

All year

The Bollin Valley is served by a network of over 100 miles of waymarked footpaths. These link the valley's often historic towns and villages with farmland, woodland, ponds and manmade features.

★ Programme of activities
★ Visitor centre

LOCATION
Access points to the whole valley are numerous but visitors can phone for directions

OPENING
All year open daily except 25 Dec

ADMISSION PRICES
Free

CONTACT
Bollin Valley County Offices
Chapel Lane
Wilmslow
Cheshire SK9 1PU
Tel/Fax 01625 534790
Email bollin@cheshire.gov.uk

Brookside Miniature Railway

1–2 hrs

All year

An extensive miniature railway layout that runs through the grounds of a large garden centre. There are lots of features of interest on the journey such as the river bridges, a pond filled with koi carp and a craft centre.

★ Railway museum
★ Steam & diesel locomotives
★ Santa Specials at Christmas

LOCATION
On A523 midway between Hazel Grove & Poynton. Follow the brown tourist signs

OPENING
In summer open daily 10.45am–4.30pm;
In winter open daily 10.45am–4pm
(Apr–Sep open weekends & Weds & all Bank & school holidays); Closed 25 Dec & Easter Sun

ADMISSION PRICES
Adult £1 Child 50p

CONTACT
Brookside Miniature Railway
Macclesfield Road
Poynton
Cheshire
Tel 01625 872919

2 hrs

Apr–Oct

Capesthorne Hall

Capesthorne Hall is a much-loved home where the Bromley-Davenports and their ancestors have lived since Domesday times. It contains a great variety of treasures including fine paintings, furniture, marbles and Greek vases. It lies in gardens, lakes and parkland extending over 100 acres. There are enjoyable woodland walks for all the family.

LOCATION
On the A31, about 6 miles south of Wilmslow & 7 miles north of Congleton

OPENING
Gardens: 1 Apr–31 Oct open Wed, Sun & Bank holiday Mon 12pm–5pm
Hall: 1 Apr–31 Oct open Wed & Sun 1.30pm (last admission 3.30pm); Closed Easter Sat

ADMISSION PRICES
Hall, chapel & gardens: Adult £6.50
Child £3 Family £12 Concession £5.50

CONTACT
Capesthorne Hall
Siddington
Macclesfield
Cheshire SK11 9JY
Tel 01625 861221
Fax 01625 861619
Email info@capesthorne.com
Web www.capesthorne.com

264

3 hrs

All year

Catalyst: Science Discovery Centre

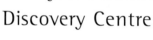

At Catalyst, science and technology really come alive through a host of interactive exhibits and hands-on displays. Children and adults alike can tug, tease and test over 100 different exhibits as they walk through four action-packed galleries.

LOCATION
Follow the road signs to Widnes (south) & then the brown tourist signs

OPENING
Please phone for details

ADMISSION PRICES
Adult £4.65 Child £3.40
Family £13.95

CONTACT
Catalyst: Science Discovery Centre
Gossage Building
Mersey Road, Widnes
Cheshire WA8 0DF
Tel & Fax 0151 4201121
Web www.catalyst.org.uk

Cheshire Blue Lavender

2 hrs

Jul–Aug

A garden of lavender growing a number of varieties of this beautiful scented plant. Families can spend a tranquil few hours in this rural setting, rich in bees and butterflies, as they pick their own bunches of lavender.

LOCATION
7 miles east of Chester, 1 mile from Tarvin village & 3 miles from Tarporley

OPENING
Jul & Aug–Bank holiday Mon open Wed–Sun 12–5pm

ADMISSION PRICES
Free

CONTACT
Cheshire Blue Lavender
Burton Road
Duddon, Tarporley
Cheshire CW6 0ET
Tel & Fax 01829 741099
Email sarah.evens@bluelavender.co.uk
Web www.bluelavender.co.uk

Cheshire Military Museum

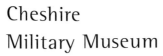

1–2 hrs

All year

Children will enjoy this museum, which houses an interactive Soldiers of Cheshire exhibition, telling the story of Cheshire's military history.

★ Guided tours (pre-book)
★ Tableaux
★ Interactive computer displays
★ Hands-on exhibits

LOCATION
Close to the city centre

OPENING
All year open daily 10am–5pm (last admission 4.30pm); Closed 22 Dec–2 Jan

ADMISSION PRICES
Adult £2 Concession £1

CONTACT
Cheshire Military Museum
The Castle
Chester CH1 2DN
Tel 01244 403933
Web www.chester.ac.uk\military-museum

Chester Visitor Centre

½ day

All year

The ideal starting point for exploring Chester, activities include guided walks, brass rubbing, candle-making and hands-on activities for children.

★ History of Chester displays
★ World of Names
★ Video show

LOCATION
Accessible from the A483, A56, A51, A41, A55 & M53. Follow signs for the city centre

OPENING
All year; Please phone for details

ADMISSION PRICES
Free

CONTACT
Chester Visitor Centre
Vicars Lane
Chester
Cheshire CH1 1QZ
Tel 01244 402111
Web www.chestertourism.com

265

Chester Zoo

All day

All year

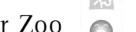

LOCATION
Easily accessible from the M53 junction 12. Follow the brown tourist signs

OPENING
All year open daily from 10am; Closed 25 Dec

ADMISSION PRICES
All year; Please phone for details

CONTACT
Chester Zoo
Upton-by-Chester
Chester CH2 1LH
Tel 01244 380280
Web www.chesterzoo.org
Email info@chesterzoo.co.uk

The UK's largest zoological gardens, Chester Zoo has over 7,000 animals housed in spacious enclosures. The zoo is set in 100 acres of beautiful landscaped gardens and has many attractions directed towards children.

★ Monkey Islands
★ Children's Farm
★ Zoofari
★ Overhead railway & waterbus
★ Face painting
★ Brass rubbing
★ Let's Make craft centre

2 hrs

All year

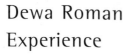

Dewa Roman Experience

An **educational few hours** can be spent here, discovering what life was like in Roman Britain. Children can step aboard a Roman galley and stroll along reconstructions of Roman streets, experiencing the sights, sounds and smells of Roman Chester.

LOCATION
Accessible from all major road routes; follow signs for Chester city centre

OPENING
All year open daily 9am–5pm, except in Dec & Jan when open 10am–4pm; 24 Dec open am only; Closed 25, 26 Dec

ADMISSION PRICES
Adult £3.95 Child £2.25
Family £11 Concession £3.50

CONTACT
Dewa Roman Experience
Pierpoint Lane, Bridge Street
Chester, Cheshire CH1 1NL
Tel 01244 343407
Fax 01244 347737

Gulliver's World

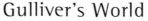

All day

Apr–Sep

A **theme park for families** with children from two to 13 years of age. It has over 50 rides, attractions and shows.

LOCATION
Take junction 9 off the M62 & follow the signposts

OPENING
Apr–Sep open daily
10.30am–5pm

ADMISSION PRICES
Please phone for details

CONTACT
Gulliver's World
Old Hall
Warrington
Cheshire WA5 9YZ
Tel 01925 444888
Web www.gulliversfun.co.uk

266

2 hrs

Jan–Nov

Hack Green Secret Nuclear Bunker

A **real government** nuclear war headquarters, this place was a secret for over 50 years. Built in the 1950s and rebuilt in the 1980s, it contains decontamination facilities, a Minister of State's office, life support systems and more. There are two cinemas, audio-visual presentations, and many hands-on activities for all age groups.

★ Soviet Spy Mouse Trail for children
★ World War II Radar Station
★ Military vehicle collection
★ Blind/partially sighted facilities
★ Deaf/hearing impaired facilities
★ Wheelchair access to 1st floor & bunker bistro

LOCATION
From junction 16 on the M6 take the signs to Nantwich, then to Whitchurch on the A530. Follow the Secret Bunker signs

OPENING
From 3rd Sat in March–31 Oct open daily from 10.30am–5.30pm; Nov, Jan & Feb open Sat & Sun only from 11am–4pm

ADMISSION PRICES
Adult £5.30 Child £3.30 Family £16
Senior £4.30
Reduced charge for wheelchair users

CONTACT
Hack Green Secret Nuclear Bunker
PO Box 127, Nantwich
Cheshire CW5 8AQ
Tel 01270 629219
Email coldwar@hackgreen.co.uk
Web www.hackgreen.co.uk

Macclesfield Riverside Park

All day

All year

Take the whole family to enjoy this pretty country park with woodland, wetland, ponds and a wild flower meadow.

★ Visitor centre

LOCATION
Between Macclesfield &
Prestbury. Take the A538 out of
Macclesfield

OPENING
All year open daily 9am–4pm
except 25 Dec

ADMISSION PRICES
Free

CONTACT
Macclesfield Riverside Park
Beechwood Mews
Macclesfield
Cheshire SK10 2SL
Tel 01625 511086
Email bollin@cheshire.gov.uk

Marbury Country Park

All day

All year

Set in 200 acres of woodland, this park has self-guided trails and orienteering and is ideal for walkers and picnickers.

LOCATION
Leave the M56 at junction 10 &
take the A523 & A559

OPENING
May–Sep open daily 8am–8pm;
Oct–Apr open daily 8am–5pm

ADMISSION PRICES
Free
Car park charge

CONTACT
Marbury Country Park
Comberbach, Northwich
Cheshire CW9 6AT
Tel/Fax 01606 77741
Email marbury@cheshire.gov.uk

Mouldsworth Motor Museum

2 hrs

Feb–Nov

LOCATION
Follow the B5393 into Ashton &
Mouldsworth

OPENING
3 Feb–end Nov open Sun, Bank holiday
Mon 12pm–5pm; Jul & Aug open Wed, Sat
& Sun 12pm–5pm

ADMISSION PRICES
Adult £3 Child £1.50 Concession £2.50

CONTACT
Mouldsworth Motor Museum
Smithy Lane
Mouldsworth
Chester
Cheshire CH3 8AR
Tel 01928 731781

Mouldsworth Motor Museum was built in 1937, set in its own grounds in the heart of the Cheshire countryside. It has over 60 veteran and classic cars and motorcycles. The museum is also home to a 1920s replica garage, toys and pedal cars.

★ Free quiz with prizes for children

All day

Apr–Oct

Oulton Park

Watch spectacular car and bike racing with British superbikes, Formula 3s and British touring cars. One-to-one instruction at the Escort Cosworth Rally School and safe training at the Early Drive School are both on offer.

★ Family fun days

★ Children's entertainers

★ Fairground rides

★ Circus workshops

★ Bouncy castle

LOCATION
Take junction 18 off the M6 & follow the A54 to Chester for 12 miles. Turn left onto the A49 to Whitchurch & follow the signposts

OPENING
Apr–Oct open Sat for minor meetings; Sun or Bank holidays open for major meetings

ADMISSION PRICES
Please phone for details

CONTACT
Oulton Park Race Circuit
Octagon Motorsports Limited
Little Budworth
Tarporley
Cheshire CW6 9BW
Tel 01829 760301
Web www.octagonmotorsports.com

268

1 hr

All year

Paradise Mill & Silk Museum

Set in a real restored mill with 26 Jacquard hand looms, this venue gives an idea of working conditions during the 1930s. It includes a design room and manager's office.

★ Guided tours for individuals

LOCATION
Take the A523 & follow signs for Macclesfield town centre

OPENING
Apr–Oct open Tue–Sun 1pm–5pm;
Mar–Nov open Tue–Sun 1pm–4pm; Closed Good Fri, 23 Dec–2 Jan

ADMISSION PRICES
Mill & Silk Museum: Adult £5.10
Under-16s £2.90 Family £11.15
Concession £2.90

CONTACT
Paradise Mill & Silk Museum
Park Lane
Macclesfield
Cheshire SK11 6UT
Tel 01625 612045
Fax 01625 612048
Email postmaster@silk-macc.u-net.com
Web www.silk-macclesfield.org

Reddish Vale Country Park

All day

WC All year

LOCATION
Take the B6167 Reddish road from Stockport

OPENING
Park: All year open daily
Visitor centre: All year open Wed 1pm–4pm & Thu–Sun 10am–4pm; Closed 25 Dec

ADMISSION PRICES
Free

CONTACT
Reddish Vale Country Park
Reddish Vale Visitor Centre
Mill Lane, Reddish, Stockport
Cheshire SK5 7HE
Tel 0161 4775637
Fax 0161 4779296

A beautiful country park offering walks, trails, special events and task days. It also features displays on the area's heritage, wildlife and future. Fishing is available on two large mill ponds.

★ Orienteering course
★ Cycle trail
★ Butterfly park

269

Rivacre Valley Local Nature Reserve

All day

All year

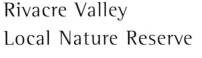

A natural area which has been landscaped with an orienteering trail, waymarked art and nature trail and guided walks.

★ Guided tours
★ Occasional events

★ Disabled access to certain areas

LOCATION
Leave the M53 at junction 17;
Take the A41 to the town centre

OPENING
All year open daily 24 hrs

ADMISSION PRICES
Free

CONTACT
Rivacre Valley Local Nature Reserve
Rivacre Road
Ellesmere Port
South Wirral
Cheshire CH64 2UQ
Tel 0151 3571991
Fax 0151 3550508

Salt Museum

1–2 hrs

All year

The museum covers the fascinating story of Cheshire's oldest industry, with temporary exhibitions from early times to the present day.

LOCATION
Take the A533 northbound to Northwich & follow signs for the Salt Museum

OPENING
All year open Tue–Fri 10am–5pm, Sat & Sun 2pm–5pm; Aug open Mon 10am–5pm; Bank holiday Mon open 10am–5pm; Closed 24–26 Dec & 1 Jan

ADMISSION PRICES
Adult £2.25 Child £1.15 Family £5.65 Concession £1.95

CONTACT
Salt Museum
162 London Road
Northwich
Cheshire CW9 8AB
Tel 01606 41331
Fax 01606 350420
Web www.saltmuseum.org.uk

Stapeley Water Gardens

3 hrs

All year

A **garden centre** specialising in water gardening with display pools, pet centre and angling superstore. The Palms Tropical Oasis is a huge glass pavilion housing exotic plants, fish and animals, including sharks and toucans.

★ Pet centre

★ Santa in his Grotto at Christmas

LOCATION
1 mile south of Nantwich on the A51. Head towards Stone (junction 16 on the M6)

OPENING
All year open daily except 25 Dec & Easter Sun
Please phone for details

ADMISSION PRICES
The Palms Tropical Oasis:
Adult £4.35 Child £2.50
Family (2+2) £11.65 Senior £3.90

CONTACT
Stapeley Water Gardens
London Road
Stapeley
Nantwich
Cheshire CW5 7LH
Tel 01270 623868
email stapeleywg@btinternet.com

270

Stockley Farm

2 hrs+

Mar–Oct

Stockley Farm is a modern working dairy farm. It comprises 500 acres on the Arley Estate in the glorious Cheshire countryside. Visitors can watch a herd of 150 British Friesians being milked in one of the most modern computerised milking parlours in the country.

★ Play area

★ Birds of prey display

★ Pony rides

★ Tractor & trailor rides

LOCATION
Leave the M56 at junction 10, the M6 at junction 19/20 & follow the signs

OPENING
24 Mar–6 Oct open Sat–Sun 11am–5pm, Bank holiday Mon & school holidays Tue–Fri

ADMISSION PRICES
Adult £4.50 Child (3–16) £3.50 Family £15
Concession £3.50

CONTACT
Stockley Farm
Arley
Northwich
Cheshire CW9 6LZ
Tel 01565 777323
Email mark.walton@farming.co.uk
Web www.stockleyfarm.co.uk

Styal Country Park

All day

All year

LOCATION
Leave the M56 at junction 5 & take the B5166

OPENING
All year open daily 7am–dusk

ADMISSION PRICES
Adult £5

CONTACT
Styal Country Park (NT)
Quarry Bank Mill
Quarry Bank Road
Styal, Wilmslow
Cheshire SK9 4LL
Tel 01625 527468
Fax 01625 527139

A country park set in a wooded river valley, with many miles of beautiful walks through woods and along the riverside.

★ Circular wheelchair route from Twinnies Bridge car park

271

Walton Hall & Gardens

2 hrs+

Apr–Oct

LOCATION
Leave the M56 at junction 11 & follow the A56. Located 2 miles from Warrington town centre on the A56

OPENING
Parkland: Open daily 8am–dusk
Other facilities: Open Oct–Apr Sat, Sun, Bank holiday Mon & school holidays 10.30am– 4.30pm; May–Sep open daily 10.30am–5pm

ADMISSION PRICES
Free

CONTACT
Walton Hall & Gardens
Walton Lea Road
Higher Walton
Warrington WA4 6SN
Tel 01925 261957
Fax 01925 861868
Email waltonhall@warrington.gov.uk
Web www.warrington.gov.uk

An ideal place for a family day out with many attractions including extensive lawns, picnic areas, ornamental gardens and woodland trails.

★ Guided tours
★ Children's zoo
★ Pitch & putt
★ Paths accessible to wheelchair users
★ Park ranger service & heritage centre

1 hr+

Apr-Oct

Appleby Castle

An eleventh-century castle and Norman keep with pleasant grounds. Climb the stairs to the top and see the magnificent views.

★ Children's playground   ★ River walks

★ Brass rubbing

LOCATION
Take the A66 & B260. Follow the M6 for 13 miles to junction 38 northbound or junction 40 southbound

OPENING
Apr-Oct

ADMISSION PRICES
Please phone for details

CONTACT
Appleby Castle
Appleby-in-Westmorland
Cumbria CA16 6XH
Tel 017683 53823
Fax 017683 51082

Aquarium of the Lakes

Quality Assured Visitor Attraction

English Tourism Council

2 hrs+
All year

Over 30 spectacular naturally themed displays cleverly recreate the journey of a Lakeland river from mountain-top to the open sea.

★ Audio-visual theatre   ★ Interactive displays

LOCATION
Take the A590 to Newby Bridge & follow the signs for the Aquarium & Lakeside which is at the southern tip of Lake Windermere

OPENING
1 Feb-3 Mar & 4 Nov-31 Dec open Mon-Sun 9am-4pm;
4 Mar-3 Nov open Mon-Sun 9am-5pm

ADMISSION PRICES
Adult £4.25 Child (3-15) £3
Concession £3.95

CONTACT
Aquarium of the Lakes
Lakeside, Newby Bridge
Ulverston, Cumbria LA12 8AS
Tel 015395 30153
Email aquariumofthelakes@real-live.co.uk
Web
www.aquariumofthelakes.co.uk

272

All day

All year

Bardsea Country Park

A beautiful coastal country park with lovely sea views over Morecambe Bay. The large woodland area is ideal for walking. Seawood, a Site of Special Scientific Interest, is located next to the park and is owned by the Woodland Trust.

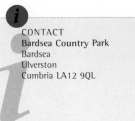

LOCATION
Take the A5087
Ulverston-Barrow road

OPENING
All year open daily

ADMISSION PRICES
Free

CONTACT
Bardsea Country Park
Bardsea
Ulverston
Cumbria LA12 9QL

The Beacon

Quality Assured Visitor Attraction

English Tourism Council

2 hrs+
All year

Discover the fascinating history of Whitehaven, West Cumbria's Georgian Port. Situated on the harbourside, audio-visual, graphic and interactive presentations tell the story of the town's maritime, social and industrial heritage.

LOCATION
Follow the A595 to Whitehaven & then the town centre signs to south harbour

OPENING
Open all year Tue-Sun from 10am; Closed during school holidays; Please phone for details

ADMISSION PRICES
Adult £4 Child (5-16) £2.75
Family £12 Concession £3.30

CONTACT
The Beacon
West Strand, Whitehaven
Cumbria CA28 7LY
Tel 01946 592302
Web www.copelandbc.gov.uk

Blackwell

1–2 hrs

WC   Feb–Dec

CUMBRIA

i

LOCATION
Follow the A5074 from Bowness (Lyth Valley Road). Located 1 mile from Bowness

OPENING
14 Feb–22 Dec open daily 10am–5pm (closing 4pm in Feb, Mar, Nov & Dec)

ADMISSION PRICES
Adult £4.50 Child £2.50 Family £12

CONTACT
Blackwell, the Arts & Craft House
Lakeland Arts Trust
Bowness-on-Windermere
Windermere, Cumbria LA23 3JR
Tel 01539 446139
Fax 01539 488486
Email info@blackwell.org.uk
Web www.blackwell.org.uk

Inspired by lakeland wild flowers, trees, berries and birds, Baillie Scott designed every last detail of this house, as can be seen in the beautifully restored interiors. Outside from the garden terraces, there are wonderful views of Windermere. Children can have a go at the Blackwell quiz.

273

Borders Regiment & King's Own Royal Border Regiment Museum

2 hrs
WC   All year

i

LOCATION
Near Carlisle city centre

OPENING
1 Apr–30 Sep open daily 9.30am–6pm; Oct 9.30am–5pm; 1 Nov–31 Mar 10am–4pm; Closed 24–26 Dec & 1 Jan

ADMISSION PRICES
Adult £3.20 Child (5–15) £1.60
Concession £2.40

CONTACT
Borders Regiment & King's Own Royal Border Regiment Museum
Queen Mary's Tower
The Castle, Carlisle
Cumbria CA3 8UR
Tel 01228 532774
Fax 01228 521275
Email rhq@kingsownborder.demon.co.uk

This museum has a large collection of uniforms, weapons, medals, field and anti-tank guns, trophies, models, silver and pictures. Audio-visual and video displays depict the 300-year history of Cumbria's County Infantry Regiment. It is located within Carlisle Castle, the regiment's home since 1873.

Varies
All year

Brewery Arts Centre

Open all-year-round, this venue has a family theatre, music events, cinema, visual arts and arts and crafts workshops.

LOCATION	CONTACT
In the centre of Kendal, 10 minutes walk from the bus & train stations	**Brewery Arts Centre** 122A Highgate Kendal Cumbria LA9 4HE
OPENING	Box office tel 01539 725133
All year open from 10am	Email admin@breweryarts.co.uk
ADMISSION PRICES	Web www.breweryarts.co.uk
Please phone for details	

Carlisle Castle

2 hrs
All year

A **great medieval fortress** with a thrilling past. Today visitors can explore fascinating and ancient chambers, stairways and dungeons.

★ Kings Own Regimental Museum located here

★ Lively exhibitions

★ Guided tours available

LOCATION	ADMISSION PRICES
On the north side of the city, beyond the cathedral	Adult £3.20 Child (5–16) £1.60 Concession £2.40
OPENING	CONTACT
29 Mar–30 Sep open daily 10am–6pm; 1–31 Oct open daily 10am–5pm; 1 Nov–31 Mar open daily 10am–4pm; Closed 24–26 Dec & 1 Jan	**Carlisle Castle** Carlisle, Cumbria CA3 8UR Tel 01228 591922 Fax 01228 514880

274

1 hr

Feb–Nov

Cars of the Stars Motor Museum

Featuring celebrity TV and film vehicles including Chitty Chitty Bang Bang, the Batmobile and Del Boy's Robin Reliant van, this is one for both film and car lovers.

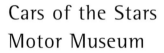

LOCATION	ADMISSION PRICES
Leave the M6 at junction 40 & follow the A66 to Keswick. Located 100 yards from Keswick's main street	Adult £3.50 Child (3–14) £2.50
	CONTACT
OPENING	**Cars of the Stars**
11–22 Feb & 24 Mar–30 Nov open daily 10am–5pm; 1–31 Dec open Sat & Sun 10am–5pm	**Motor Museum** Standish Street, Keswick Cumbria CA12 5LS 017687 73757 Email cotsmm@aol.com Web carsofthestars.com

Cumberland Pencil Museum

2 hrs

All year

Cumberland Pencil Museum traces the history of pencil-making from the discovery of graphite to present-day methods of pencil manufacture. Children can see the world's largest pencil here.

★ Brass rubbing

★ Children's drawing area

LOCATION	ADMISSION PRICES
Follow the A66 to Keswick. Located 300 yards west of Keswick town centre	Adult £2.50 Child £1.25 Family £6.25 Concession £1.25
OPENING	CONTACT
All year open daily 9.30am–4pm (last admission 4pm); Closed 25, 26 Dec & 1 Jan	**Cumberland Pencil Museum** Southey Works, Keswick Cumbria CA12 5NG Tel 017687 73626 Web www.pencils.co.uk/

Cumberland Toy & Model Museum

2 hrs

WC

All year

LOCATION
Follow the A66 to Cockermouth

OPENING
All year open daily 1 Feb–30 Nov
10am–5pm; Dec–Jan times may vary
Please phone for details

ADMISSION PRICES
Adult £3 Child (4–14 years) £1.50
Family £8 Concession £2.60

CONTACT
Cumberland Toy & Model Museum
Banks Court
Market Place
Cockermouth
Cumbria CA13 9NG
Tel 01900 827606
Email Rod@toymuseum.co.uk
Web www.toymuseum.co.uk

The museum features toys dating from 1900 to the present day. The collection includes Scalextric cars, a battery-powered model helicopter, dolls houses and prams, a 1930s Hornby O-gauge tinplate railway laid out in a garden shed, Lego models, and 24 hidden teddy bears to discover.

★ Worksheets & quizzes for children

Dalemain Historic House & Garden

WC

½ day

Mar–Oct

LOCATION
On the A592 Penrith–Ullswater road, 3
miles from junction 40 of the M6

OPENING
Park: 23 Mar–13 Oct open daily
10.30am–5pm
House: 23 Mar–13 Oct open daily
11am–4pm

ADMISSION PRICES
House & Gardens: Adult £5 Child (6–16)
£3.50 Family £14.50
Gardens only: Adult £5 Child Free (if
accompanied)

CONTACT
Dalemain Historic House & Garden
Dalemain Estates
Dalemain
Penrith
Cumbria CA11 0HB
Tel 017684 86450

Dalemain is a beautiful Tudor and Georgian house with fascinating interiors set among several fine gardens, parkland with red squirrels and fallow deer and the Lakeland Fells. Children love the nursery, Mrs Mouse House on the back stairs and the hiding hole in the housekeeper's room.

★ Children's garden
★ Footpathed walks
★ Cruises available on nearby Ullswater

Varies

All year

Derwentwater Marina

Eden Ostrich World

2 hrs+

All year

The marina specialises in watersports with RYA sailing courses, windsurfing courses, canoe, kayak and dinghy hire available. Other activities include ghyll scrambling, abseiling, climbing and walking.

Come face-to-face with African black ostriches, rare breeds of cattle, donkeys, Shire horses, pigs, goats, red deer, ducks and geese.

★ Soft play area   ★ Tractor & Trailer rides

LOCATION
From Keswick take the A66 &
follow the signs for Portinscale

OPENING
All year open daily 9am–5pm;
Closed 20 Dec–3 Jan

ADMISSION PRICES
Please phone for details

CONTACT
Derwentwater Marina
Portinscale, Keswick
Cumbria CA12 5RF
Tel 017687 72912
Email
derwentwater.marina@ken-comp.net
Web
www.derwentwatermarina.co.uk

LOCATION
In the Eden Valley, 5 miles east
of Penrith on the A686 towards
Alston. Take junction 40 on the
M6

OPENING
Mar–Oct open daily 10am–5pm;
Nov–Feb open Wed–Mon
10am–5pm

ADMISSION PRICES
Adult £4.50 Child £3 Family
(2+2) £13 Concession £3.25

CONTACT
Eden Ostrich World
Langwathby Hall Farm
Langwathby, Penrith
Cumbria CA10 1LW
Tel 01768 881771
Web www.ostrich-world.com

276

½ day

Apr–Oct

The Edward Haughey Aviation Heritage Centre

Young people interested in civil and military aviation history will be fascinated by this museum. Among the items on display are aircraft from the 1950s and 1960s and the Blue Streak Rocket Program. Visitors can sit in the pilot's seat of the Vulcan B2.

★ Mock-up control tower
★ Engine room
★ Vulcan B2, Canberra T4 & Sikorsky S-55a
among aircraft on display

LOCATION
3½ miles east of Carlisle on the A69

OPENING
Apr–Oct open Fri, Sat & Sun

ADMISSION PRICES
Please phone for details

CONTACT
**The Edward Haughey Aviation
Heritage Centre**
Aviation House
Crosby-on-Eden, Cumbria
Tel 01228 573823
Email
info@solway-aviation-museum.co.uk
Web www.solway-aviation-museum.co.uk

Florence Mine Heritage Centre

3 hrs

Apr–Sep

Explore this mine museum and simulated underground workings. Go underground to visit Europe's last working, deep iron ore mine.

★ Guided tours compulsory for individuals

LOCATION	**ADMISSION PRICES**
The mine is clearly visible from the A595 Egremont bypass; follow the brown tourist signs towards Wilton	Adult £6.50 Child £4.50
	CONTACT
	Florence Mine Heritage Centre
	Florence Mine, Egremont
OPENING	Cumbria CA22 2NR
Apr–Sep open weekends & Bank holidays 10am–4pm	Tel/Fax 01946 820683
	Web www.florencemine.com

Hawkshead Trout Farm

½ day+

All year

A well-stocked lake where you can fish by boat or from the shore. Suitable for inexperienced, intermediate and expert anglers. Tuition is available and children can feed and catch their own fish.

★ Shop selling tackle & bait   ★ Barbecues

LOCATION	£7 per rod including 2 fish
1½ miles south of Hawkshead, on the road to Newby Bridge	**CONTACT**
	Hawkshead Trout Farm
OPENING	Hawkshead, Ambleside
All year open daily 9am–6pm	Cumbria LA22 0QF
	Tel 015394 36541
ADMISSION PRICES	Web www.fishlink.com/esthwaite-organicfish.com
Cost for fishing: Adult £18 Child £9 Concession £16 Catch your own enclosure:	

CUMBRIA

277

Honister Slate Mine

Quality Assured Visitor Attraction

English Tourism Council

1½ hrs

Feb–Nov

An opportunity to see ancient craftsmanship and to learn the history and feel the atmosphere of bygone years as you take an underground tour of this working mine.

★ Guided tours compulsory   ★ Disabled access to visitor centre

LOCATION	**ADMISSION PRICES**
From Keswick take the B5289 through Borrowdale & Rosthwaite for 9 miles; From Cockermouth follow the B5292 & B5289 for 14 miles	Mine tour: Adult £7 Child £4
	CONTACT
	Honister Slate Mine
	Honister Pass, Borrowdale
	Keswick
OPENING	Cumbria CA12 5XN
1 Feb–30 Nov open daily 9am–5pm	Tel 017687 77230
	Web www.honister

Kendal Museum

1½ hrs

Feb–Dec

Displays of the archaeology and natural history of the Lake District sit alongside a world wildlife exhibition. There are free quizzes, worksheets and activities for children and events throughout the summer holidays.

LOCATION	**ADMISSION PRICES**
On the A6 North of Kendal, opposite the railway station	Adult £3.50 Child £1.75
	Family £9
OPENING	**CONTACT**
In summer open Mon–Sat 10.30am–5pm; In winter open Mon–Sat 10.30am–4pm; Closed Christmas–mid Feb	**Kendal Museum**, Morag Clement Station Road
	Kendal LA9 6BY
	Tel 01539 721374
	Web www.kendalmuseum.org.uk

1–3 hrs

All year

Keswick Holiday Arts Studio

Come and enjoy the activities at this craft centre. You can paint on ceramics, slate or glass, print your own postcards or t-shirt, learn how to throw a pot or paint in watercolours.

LOCATION
3 minutes walk from Keswick town centre, on the Penrith road

OPENING
All year open Mon, Wed, Fri & Sun 10am–1pm, 12pm–5pm & 7pm–10pm; Tue & Thur open 10am–1pm & 2pm–5pm; Closed 25 & 26 Dec

ADMISSION PRICES
Please phone for details

CONTACT
Keswick Holiday Arts Studio
1 Wordsworth Street, Keswick
Cumbria CA12 4HU
Tel 017687 75990
Fax 017687 80087
Email info@keswickstudio.co.uk
Web www.keswickstudio.co.uk

The Lake District Coast Aquarium

1 hr+

All year

This independently-owned aquarium has a comprehensive collection of native marine species. Exciting displays recreate natural habitats, including a 'walk-over' raypool and 'hands-in' rock pool. Tickets are valid for re-entry on same day.

LOCATION
Take junction 40 on the M6 & the A594 to Maryport or junction 44 & the A595 south to connect with the A596 coastal route

OPENING
1 Mar–31 Oct open daily 10am–5pm; 1 Nov–28 Feb open daily 11am–4pm; Closed 25 & 26 Dec

ADMISSION PRICES
Adult £4.50   Child (4–18) £2.95
Family £13.30   Concession £3.80

CONTACT
The Lake District Coast Aquarium
South Quay, Maryport
Cumbria CA15 8AB
Tel 01900 817760

278

---

2 hrs+

Feb–Nov

The Lake District Visitor Centre

This visitor centre is located in an Edwardian house on the shores of Windermere. It has landscaped gardens and superb views.

★ Guided walks
★ Lake cruises
★ Adventure playground
★ Interactive exhibitions

LOCATION
On the A591 between Ambleside & Windermere

OPENING
9 Feb–17 Feb & 23 Mar–3 Nov open daily; Garden & grounds open all year; Please phone for details of winter opening

ADMISSION PRICES
Free

CONTACT
The Lake District Visitor Centre
Brockhole, Windermere
Cumbria LA23 1LJ
Tel 015394 46601
Web www.lake-district.gov.uk

Lakeland Bird of Prey Centre

2 hrs+
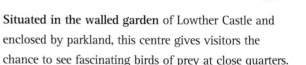

Mar–Oct

Situated in the walled garden of Lowther Castle and enclosed by parkland, this centre gives visitors the chance to see fascinating birds of prey at close quarters.

★ Daily flying demonstrations

LOCATION
From the north take the A6, approximately 5 miles south of Penrith; from the south leave the M6 at junction 39 taking the A6 through Shap, about 15 miles north of Kendal

OPENING
23 Mar–31 Oct 10.30am–5pm

ADMISSION PRICES
Adult £5   Child £2.50
Concession £4

CONTACT
Lakeland Bird of Prey Centre
Old Walled Garden, Lowther
Penrith, Cumbria CA10 2HH
Tel/Fax 01931 712746

Lakeland Equestrian

1 hr+

WC

All year

LOCATION
On the A591 Windermere–Ambleside road.
The gateway is on the right, immediately
after the roundabout sign

OPENING
All year open daily 10am–4pm;
Closed 25 Dec

ADMISSION PRICES
Short ride: Adult £18 Child £13
Phone for details of other prices

CONTACT
Lakeland Equestrian
Wynlass Beck
Windermere
Cumbria LA23 1EU
Tel 015394 43811
Email info@lakelandequestrian.co.uk
Web www.lakelandequestrian.co.uk

This centre offers horse-riding for all ages and abilities including short,
hill, farm, pub and trail rides. All are undertaken with qualified staff and
on suitable mounts, ranging from ex-competition horses to native breeds.

★ Packed lunches available

★ Treks from 1 hr to all day

Lakeland Miniature Village

2 hrs

All year

Visit Lakeland in a day at Cumbria's only
miniature village. It has over 100 buildings made
from local Coniston slate, handmade by Edward
Robinson. They include houses, farms, barns and
tiny wishing wells.

LOCATION
From Grange-over-Sands take
the B5277 to Flookburgh, follow
the signs to Ravenstown & turn
left after the post office

OPENING
All year open daily 10am–dusk

ADMISSION PRICES
Adult £2.50 Child (5+) 50p
Concession £2

CONTACT
Lakeland Miniature Village
The Coach House, Winder Lane
Flookburgh, Grange-over-Sands
Cumbria LA11 7LE
Tel 015395 58500
Web www.lakelandminiature
village.com

Lakeland Wildlife Oasis

2 hrs+

All year

Enjoy a fascinating journey through the animal
kingdom, from microbes to monkeys, in this unique
wildlife exhibition.

★ Animal handling sessions   ★ Interactive displays

LOCATION
On the A6, 2½ miles south of
Milnthorpe, near junction 35 on
the M6

OPENING
All year open daily 10am–5pm
(last admission 4pm); Closed 25
& 26 Dec

ADMISSION PRICES
Adult £5.50 Child £3
Under-4s Free Senior £4

CONTACT
Lakeland Wildlife Oasis
Milnthorpe,
Cumbria LA7 7BW
Tel 015395 63027
Web www.wildlifeoasis.co.uk

Varies

Mar–Oct

Lakeside & Haverthwaite Railway

Take an enjoyable steam train ride from Haverthwaite to Lakeside through the beautiful Leven Valley.

LOCATION
On the A590

OPENING
Open 23 Mar–7 Apr, 4 May–27 Oct, also 13, 14, 20, 21, 27, 28 Apr & Sats & Suns; Santa specials only 7, 8, 14, 15, 21, 22 Dec

ADMISSION PRICES
Single Journey: Adult £2.30 Child £1.65

Return Journey: Adult £3.90 Child 1.95

CONTACT
Lakeside & Haverthwaite Railway, Haverthwaite Station Ulverston, Cumbria LA12 8AL Tel 015395 31594 Fax 015395 30503

Laserquest

1 hr

All year

Unleash a volley of laser fire in the battle zone – the ultimate sci-fi action adventure for the over-7s. Each game lasts for 20 minutes. Book in advance.

★ Party package available

★ Play solo or in a team

★ Simple or complex games

LOCATION
In Carlisle city centre

OPENING
In summer open 10am–9pm Mon–Sat & Sun 10am–7pm; In winter open Mon–Fri 11am–9pm, Sat 10am–9pm, Sun 10am–7pm; Closed 25, 26 Dec & 1 Jan

ADMISSION PRICES
£3.50 per game £5.50 for 2 games £7 for 3 games

CONTACT
Laserquest, Bush Brow Victoria Viaduct Carlisle CA3 8AN Tel 01228 511155

All day

Varies

Llama Treks

Come llama-trekking in the spectacular surroundings of the North Pennines. You lead the friendly llamas, who carry your gear, including any refreshment you many want along the way. A guide leads the way and helps with the llamas. Children over 12 manage the experience quite easily.

LOCATION
From Penrith follow the A686 & take a right turn to Garrigill

OPENING
Please phone for details

ADMISSION PRICES
Treks: Adult £10–£35 Under-12s £7–£23

CONTACT
Llama Treks
Ivy House
Garrigill
Alston
Cumbria CA9 3DU
Tel 01434 382501
Email llmas@garrigill.com
Web www.garrigill.com

Lonscale Sheepdogs
& Farm Visits

1 hr

May–Sep

Low Sizergh Barn

1 hr+

Mar–Dec

Experience at first-hand the magic of the working collie. Groups of school children with teachers are welcome for educational visits.

Walk on the new farm trail and enjoy the beautiful countryside around this organic dairy farm. See the cows and hens, and watch out for wildlife and birds in the fields, pond and woods.

LOCATION
Take the A66 to the Keswick bypass roundabout, then the 1st left and after ½ mile the 1st left into Brundholme Road; From the A591 turn right into Station Street & go straight on to Brunholme Road

OPENING
1 May–26 Sep open daily
4pm–5.30pm

ADMISSION PRICES
Adult £2 Child (5+) 50p

CONTACT
**Lonscale Sheepdogs
& Farm Visits**
Lonscale Farm, Threlkeld
Keswick, Cumbria CA12 4TB
Tel 017687 79603
Email
ad.scrimgeour@talk21.com

LOCATION
Situated 4 miles south of Kendal on the A591. From junction 36 off the M6 take the A591 & follow signs for Sizergh Castle & Low Sizergh Barn

OPENING
22 Mar–31 Dec open Mon–Sun 9am–5.30pm; 2 Jan–21 Mar open Mon–Sun 9.30am–5pm; Closed 25, 26 Dec & 1 Jan

ADMISSION PRICES
Free

CONTACT
Low Sizergh Barn
Sizergh, Kendal
Cumbria LA8 8AE
Tel 015395 60426
Email apark@low-sizergh-barn.co.uk
Web www.low-sizergh-barn.co.uk

Maryport
Maritime Museum

2 hrs

All year

LOCATION
Follow the brown tourist signs from the A596

OPENING
All year open daily; In winter closed Sun

ADMISSION PRICES
Free

CONTACT
Maryport Maritime Museum
1 Senhouse Street
Maryport
Cumbria
CA15 6AB
Tel 01900 813738
Email maryport.maritime.museum@allerdale.gov.uk
Web www.allerdale.gov.uk

A wealth of objects, pictures, models and paintings illustrate Maryport's fascinating maritime past and the story of the docks. Maryport was the birthplace of the infamous 'Bounty' mutineer Fletcher Christian and the museum highlights this along with the town's links with 'The White Star Line' and the ill-fated Titanic.

2 hrs+

Feb–Oct

Mirehouse Historic House & Gardens

A **comparatively small historic house,** given to the Spedding family in 1802. Standing between mountains and lake, it is a living home with a tradition of relaxed welcome. It has an interesting history and links with many famous writers.

★ Poetry walk with changing displays
★ Nature walks with children's notes
★ Woodland adventure playground

LOCATION
On the A591, 3 miles north of Keswick

OPENING
Grounds & tearoom: 16 Feb–24 Mar open daily
House: 24 Mar–31 Oct open Sun & Wed & various dates in Aug
Please phone for details

ADMISSION PRICES
House & Gardens: Adult £4   Child £2
Family £11.75
Gardens only: Adult £2   Child £1

CONTACT
Mirehouse Historic House & Gardens
Underskiddaw, Keswick
Cumbria CA12 4QE
Tel 017687 72287
Email info@mirehouse.com
Web www.mirehouse.com

½ day

All year

Muncaster Castle

Family Attraction of the Year
Good Britain Guide 2001

A **historic castle (allegedly haunted)** and headquarters of the World Owl Centre, it has 70 acres of gardens, a meadow vole maze and children's play area.

LOCATION
On the A595 1 mile south of Ravenglass.
Take junction 40 off the M6 southbound & junction 36 off the M6 northbound

OPENING
Castle & Maze: Mar–Nov open daily
Gardens & World Owl Centre: All year open daily
Please phone for details

ADMISSION PRICES
Castle, gardens & owl centre: Adult £7.80
Child £5   Family £21   Under-5s Free

CONTACT
Muncaster Castle
Ravenglass
Cumbria CA18 1RQ
Tel 01229 717614
Email info@muncaster.co.uk
Web www.muncaster.co.uk

Museum of Lakeland Life

2 hrs

Feb–Dec

LOCATION
Take the A6 or M6 from Lancaster & follow signs for town centre. At the southern end of Kendal, follow the brown tourist signs for Abbot Hall

OPENING
14 Feb–24 Dec open Mon–Sat; Early closing at 4pm in Feb, Mar, Nov & Dec

ADMISSION PRICES
Adult £3.50 Child (5–16) £1.75
Family £9

CONTACT
Museum of Lakeland Life
Abbot Hall, Kendal
Cumbria LA9 5AL
Tel 01539 722464
Fax 01539 722494
Email info@lakelandmuseum.org.uk
Web www.lakelandmuseum.org.uk

The Museum of Lakeland Life shows how the Cumbrian people worked, lived and entertained themselves in the changing social climate of the past 200 years. Exhibits include a street scene, reconstructed workshops and a Victorian bedroom and parlour.

★ Postman Pat room
★ Headquarters of the Arthur Ransome Society
★ Special events & activities

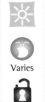

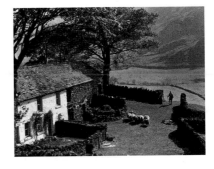

National Trust Fell Foot Country Park

All day

All year

These 18 acres of lakeside parkland provide an area for bathing, fishing and boating.

★ Adventure playground
★ Boat hire

LOCATION
At the extreme southern end of Lake Windermere, on the east shore

OPENING
Open all year daily 9am–7pm or dusk if earlier; 31 Mar–4 Nov tearoom, shop & boat hire available

ADMISSION PRICES
Free
Pay & Display car park

CONTACT
National Trust Fell Foot Country Park, Newby Bridge
Ulverston, Cumbria LA12 8NN
Tel 015395 31273
Email fellfootpark@ntrust.org.uk
Web www.nationaltrust.org.uk

Platty+

Varies

Mar–Oct

A family-based business offering canoeing, kayaking, dinghy sailing, dragonboating and rowing on Derwentwater. Children and adults with special needs are welcomed.

LOCATION
From Keswick take the B5289 (Borrowdale road) for about 3 miles. Park in the Stakis Lodore Hotel car park & walk down to the boat landing

OPENING
1 Mar–31 Oct open daily 10am–6pm

ADMISSION PRICES
Please phone for prices of various activities

CONTACT
Platy+
Lodore Boat Landings
Derwentwater, Borrowdale
Keswick
Cumbria CA12 5UQ
Tel 017687 77282
Web www.plattyplus.co.uk

2 hrs+

All year

Ravenglass & Eskdale Railway

Take a gentle steam-train ride from the coast at Ravenglass to the foot of England's highest mountain at Eskdale, through the beautiful Lake District landscape. Depending on the weather visitors can travel in open or cosy covered carriages.

★ Frequent appearances of La'al Ratty, water vole stationmaster, in the summer holidays

★ Children's guide to the line

LOCATION
On the A595 western Lake District coastal road

OPENING
Late Mar–early Nov open daily 9am–5.30pm; Winter open weekends 10am–4.15pm; Open Feb half-term, Christmas & New Year

ADMISSION PRICES
All-day ticket: Adult £7.80 Child (5–15) £3.90 Under-5s Free
Family tickets available

CONTACT
Ravenglass & Eskdale Railway Ltd
Ravenglass
Cumbria CA18 1SW
Tel 01229 717171

2 hrs+

All year

Rheged

Quality Assured Visitor Attraction
English Tourism Council

Rheged is a dramatic visitor attraction in Cumbria. Named after a Celtic kingdom, it is Britain's largest grass-covered building and contains seven levels of attractions and entertainments and a six-storey-high cinema screen.

★ Children's Corner
★ Children's competitions
★ Special events
★ Ball pool
★ Soft play area

LOCATION
Leave the M6 at junction 40 near Penrith. Rheged is ¾ mile further on the A66 in the direction of Keswick

OPENING
All year open daily 10am–5.50pm

ADMISSION PRICES
Free; Charge per activity or event

CONTACT
Rheged – The Village in the Hill
Redhills, Penrith
Cumbria CA11 0DQ
Tel 01768 868000
Email enquiries@rheged.com
Web www.rheged.com

Sellafield Visitor Centre

2 hrs+

All year

LOCATION
11 miles South of Whitehaven, on the A595

OPENING
May–Oct open 10am–6pm; Nov–Mar open 10am–4pm; Closed 25 Dec

ADMISSION PRICES
Free

CONTACT
Sellafield Visitor Centre
Sellafield, Seascale
Cumbria CA20 1PG
Tel 019467 27027
Web www.sparkingreaction.info

Ten zones outline what the nuclear industry is all about. There are hands-on interactive scientific experiments, intriguing shows and displays. For a closer look, take a tour of the Sellafield site on one of the sightseer coaches, where your host will explain the facts about the site operations in more detail and answer any questions.

South Lakes Wild Animal Park

2 hrs+

All year

One of Europe's leading conservation zoos. The rolling 17 acres are home to the rarest animals on earth. Many, such as lemurs, exotic parrots, kangaroos and wallabies, have complete freedom to wander at will.

LOCATION
Take junction 36 off the M6 & follow the signs on the A590. At Dalton turn right at Tudor Square & continue for 1 mile

OPENING
All year open daily 10am–5pm (4.30pm in winter);
Closed 25 Dec

ADMISSION PRICES
Adult £7 Child (3–15) £5
Concession £5

CONTACT
South Lakes Wild Animal Park
Crossgates, Dalton-in-Furness
Cumbria LA15 8JR
Tel 01229 466086
Web www.wildanimalpark.co.uk

South Tynedale Railway

Varies

Apr–Oct

Take a leisurely ride through the beautiful scenery of the South Tyne valley. The trains are hauled by preserved steam and diesel engines. The station at Kirkhaugh has no road access, but may be reached via the lineside footpath from Alston.

LOCATION
On the A686 north of Alston centre

OPENING
29 Mar–27 Oct open selected days
Please phone or visit the website for details

ADMISSION PRICES
Alston–Kirkhaugh return:
Adult £4 Child (3–16) £2

CONTACT
South Tynedale Railway
Railway Station, Alston
Cumbria CA9 3JB
Tel 01434 381696
Web www.strps.org.uk

All day

All year

Talkin Tarn Country Park

Varies

All year

Ullswater 'Steamers'

Get active when you visit this 65-acre lake set amid 120 acres of farmland and woodland.

★ Sailing, boating, canoeing & windsurfing

★ Coarse fishing available on a day ticket basis

★ Play area for children

LOCATION
On the B6413, 9 miles east of Carlisle & 2 miles south of Brampton

OPENING
Park: open all year daily dawn–dusk
Please phone for opening details of other facilities

ADMISSION PRICES
Free

CONTACT
Talkin Tarn Country Park
Brampton
Cumbria CA8 1HN
Tel 016977 41050

Cruises between Glenridding, Howtown and Pooley bridge are run daily from March to October, weather permitting. There is access to a variety of walks including Howtown to Glenridding and spectacular picnic spots in unspoilt scenery.

LOCATION
Accessible off junction 40 of the M6 at Penrith or over Kirkstone Pass from Windermere & Ambleside

OPENING
All year open daily; Sailing times vary so please phone for details or look at the website

ADMISSION PRICES
Return ticket: Adult £5.80 Child (5–16) £2.90 Family £16

CONTACT
Ullswater 'Steamers', 13 Maude Street, Kendal, Cumbria LA9 4QD
Tel 017684 82229
Web www.ullswater-steamers.co.uk

286

1 hr

All year

Ulverston Heritage Centre

2 hrs+

All year

Whinlatter Forest Park & Visitor Centre

An old spice warehouse that contains historical artefacts from Ulverston and reconstructions of old Ulverston shops and houses.

★ Guided tours available

LOCATION
The centre is clearly signposted in Ulverston city centre

OPENING
All year open Mon–Sat 9.30am–4.30pm; Closed 25 Dec & 1 Jan

ADMISSION PRICES
Please phone for details

CONTACT
Ulverston Heritage Centre
Hannover House
Victoria Road, Ulverston
Cumbria LA12 0BY
Tel 01229 580820
Email heritage@tower-house.demon.co.uk

Nestling in England's only mountain forest, Whinlatter Forest Park offers a wide variety of activities, from waymarked walks and orienteering courses, for all abilities and ages.

★ Adventure playground

LOCATION
Signed on the A66 from Keswick

OPENING
All year open Mon–Fri 9.30am–6pm, Sat 9am–6pm, Sun 11am–5pm

ADMISSION PRICES
Free; Car park charge

CONTACT
Whinlatter Forest Park & Visitor Centre, Braithwaite Keswick, Cumbria CA12 5TW
Tel 017687 78469
Fax 01768 778049
Email whinlatter@forestry.gsi.gov.uk
Web www.nwefd.co.uk

Windermere Lake Cruises

1 hr+

All year

Cumbria Large Visitor
Attraction of the Year (2001)
Cumbria Tourist Board

LOCATION
Take junction 36 off the M6. Follow the brown tourist signs along the A590 to Lakeside or the A591 to Windermere for Bowness & Ambleside

OPENING
All year open every day; In summer open during daylight hours; In winter open 9.45am–4.30pm

ADMISSION PRICES
Adult £5 Child (5–15) £2.50
Family £13.50

CONTACT
Windermere Lake Cruises
Tel 015395 31188
Email w.lakes@virgin.net
Web www.windermere-lakecruises.co.uk

Steamers and launches sail daily throughout the year between Ambleside, Lakeside and Bowness. In both winter and summer the scenery is breathtaking, encompassing mountains, secluded bays and wooded islands.

Varies

All year

Anderton Outdoor Centre

Enjoy a range of watersports, including sailing, canoeing, and kayaking. Outdoor activities include climbing and abseiling, orienteering, environmental education, mountain biking and archery.

LOCATION
Accessible via the M61 & M6, on the A673

OPENING
All year open daily 9.30am–dusk

ADMISSION PRICES
Please phone for details

CONTACT
Anderton Outdoor Centre
New Road, Anderton, Chorley Lancashire PR6 9HG
Tel 01257 474341
Fax 01257 474320
Email anderton@airtime.co.uk

Animal World

2 hrs

All year

From farmyard animals to chipmunks and wildfowl, to tropical birds and the sights and sounds of a tropical rainforest, Animal World opens a window into the natural world.

★ Guided tours

LOCATION
Off the northern ring road, Moss Bank Way (A58)

OPENING
Apr–Sep open daily 10am–4.30pm; Oct–Mar open Mon–Thu & Sat & Sun 10am–3.30pm & Fri 10am–2.30pm; Closed 25, 26 Dec & 1 Jan

ADMISSION PRICES
Free

CONTACT
Animal World
Moss Bank Park
Moss Bank Way, Bolton
Lancashire BL1 5SN
Tel 01204 846157
Fax 01204 365034

All day

All year

Beacon Country Park

Beacon Fell Country Park

½ day

All year

A **picturesque country park** that stages events and activities throughout the year.

★ Orienteering course

★ Heritage trail

★ Ranger services

Spend a relaxing few hours walking in this country park with 185 acres of extensive conifer woods and moorland.

LOCATION
Leave the M6 at junction 27;
Leave the M58 at junction 5

OPENING
All year open daily

ADMISSION PRICES
Free

CONTACT
Beacon Country Park
Beacon Lane, Upholland
Skelmersdale
Lancashire WN8 7RU
Tel 01695 622794
Email beacon.park@westlancs-dc.gov.uk

LOCATION
Signposted from the A6

OPENING
Please phone for details of opening dates & times

ADMISSION PRICES
Free

CONTACT
Beacon Fell Country Park
Goosnargh, Preston
Lancashire PR3 2NL
Tel 01995 640557
Email judy.campbell-ricketts@env.lancscc.gov.uk
Web
www.lancashire.com/icc/env/cs

20 mins

All year

Blackburn Karting

An **'Arrive and Drive'** go-kart session takes about 20 minutes and is open to over-12s. Younger children will be thrilled to have a go on the children's quad bikes.

★ Children's parties

★ Karting School

★ Grand Prix (1½ hrs+)

LOCATION
Blackburn town centre, behind the railway station

OPENING
All year open daily

ADMISSION PRICES
Free; Charge for each activity

CONTACT
Blackburn Karting
East Lancs Warehouse
Bridge Street, Blackburn
Tel 07970 200801
Email nigel@blackburnkarting.com
Web www.blackburnkarting.com

The Blackpool Piers

All day

WC ‖ 🔒

Mar–Nov

LANCASHIRE

LOCATION
North Pier is located on the North Promenade; South Pier on the South Promenade & Central Pier on Central Promenade

OPENING
Mar–Nov daily from 10am

ADMISSION PRICES
Free; Charge for individual rides

CONTACT
The Blackpool Piers
Tel 01253 621452
Fax 01253 752308
Web www.blackpoollive.com

Each pier has its own unique attractions and atmosphere. North Pier provides an atmosphere of romantic nostalgia with an original Venetian carousel ride, South Pier is home to heart-stopping daredevil rides, while Central Pier offers gentler fairground rides and games.

★ Children's play areas (South & Central Pier)
★ Fairground rides (South & Central Pier)
★ Amusement arcades (South & Central Pier)
★ Children's entertainer (North & South Pier)

289

Blackpool Pleasure Beach

All day

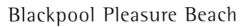

Mar–Nov   WC 🏕 ‖ 🔒

Blackpool Pleasure Beach lies on 42 acres and offers more than 145 rides, attractions and shows for children of all ages.

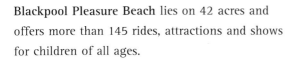

LOCATION
Take junction 32 on the M6. Follow the brown tourist signs on the M55

OPENING
12 Mar–2 Nov open daily
Open some winter weekends

ADMISSION PRICES
Unlimited wristband £26

CONTACT
Blackpool Pleasure Beach
Ocean Boulevard
Blackpool FY4 1EZ
Tel 0870 4445566
Web www.blackpoolpleasure-beach.com

Blackpool Sea Life Centre

2 hrs

All year

WC ‖

The Sea Life Centre houses one of Europe's largest marine collections. It has over 40 fascinating displays, allowing exciting close-up encounters with marine life, including sharks.

LOCATION
Leave the M55 at junction 4 into Blackpool

OPENING
All year open daily from 10am;
Closed 25 Dec

ADMISSION PRICES
Adult £7   Child (4–14) £5

Family £20   Concession £6

CONTACT
Blackpool Sea Life Centre
The Promenade
Blackpool FY1 5AA
Tel 01253 622445
Fax 01253 751647
Web www.sealife.co.uk

2-3 hrs

All year

WC

Bolton Museum, Art Gallery & Aquarium

The museum contains permanent displays of Egyptology, natural and local history, geology, archaeology, art and sculpture and has an exciting programme of changing exhibitions. Children particularly enjoy the aquarium.

LOCATION
Accessible from the A666

OPENING
All year open Mon–Sat 10am–5pm; Closed Bank holiday Mon

ADMISSION PRICES
Free

CONTACT
Bolton Museum, Art Gallery & Aquarium
Le Mans Crescent, Bolton
Lancashire BL1 1SE
Tel 01204 332211
Fax 01204 332241
Email museum@bolton.gov.uk
Web www.boltonmuseums.org.uk

290

2 hrs

Apr–Sep

WC

British in India Museum

An interesting museum full of artefacts relating to the British in India. On display are Indian regimental ties, paintings, photographs of military and civilian subjects, model soldiers, medals, coins, toys and examples of Indian dress.

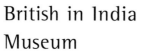

LOCATION
Take the A56/A6068 from Burnley–Keighley

OPENING
Apr–Sep open Wed & Sat 2pm–5pm

ADMISSION PRICES
Adult £3 Child 50p

CONTACT
British in India Museum
Newtown Street
Colne
Lancashire BB8 0JJ
Tel & Fax 01282 870215

Burrs Activity Centre

Varies

All year

Children will have fun at this outdoor activity centre, where they can try canoeing, climbing, orienteering, hiking, kayaking and abseiling.

LOCATION
Leave the M66 at junction 2, follow the A58 to Bolton & then take the B6214

OPENING
All year open daily

ADMISSION PRICES
Free; Charge for activities

CONTACT
Burrs Activity Centre
Woodhill Road, Bury
Lancashire BL8 1DA
Tel 0161 764 9649
Email
burrs@activity_centre.freeserve.co.uk
Web www.activity@centre.freeserve.co.uk

Bury Art Gallery & Museum

1 hr

All year

Highlights of the collection include paintings by Turner and Lowry and a lively programme of contemporary art exhibitions. Paradise Street recreates Bury life of the 1950s – children of all ages can ring the tram bell and send the model trains running through Bury's two stations.

★ Children's activities

★ Guided tours

LOCATION
In the centre of Bury, a few yards from the bus/train interchange

OPENING
All year open Tue–Sat 10am–5pm; Closed Mon, Sun, Easter

ADMISSION PRICES
Free

CONTACT
Bury Art Gallery & Museum
Moss Street
Bury
Lancashire BL9 0DR
Tel 0161 2535878
Fax 0161 2535915
Email artgallery@bury.gov.uk
Web www.bury.gov.uk

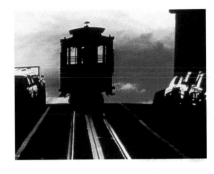

Camelot Theme Park

Lancashire's Family Attraction of the Year 2002

Good Britain Guide

All day

Mar–Oct

Five magical lands full of thrilling rides for all ages, such as Excalibur 2 a fearsome ride that spins you two ways simultaneously at over 75 feet in the air.

★ Rollercoasters

★ Water slides

★ Shows

★ Jousting tournament

LOCATION
Leave the M6 at junction 27/28 & the M61 at junction 8

OPENING
23 Mar–27 Oct open 10am–5pm; Please phone 01257 452100 for opening details

ADMISSION PRICES
Adult £13.50 Child £13.50
Family £45 Concession £9

CONTACT
Camelot Theme Park
Park Hall Road, Charnock Richard, Chorley
Lancashire PR7 5LP
Tel 01257 453044
Email kingarthur@camelotthemepark.co.uk
Web
www.camelotthemepark.co.uk

Cedar Farm Galleries

½ day

All year

There are contemporary crafts, farm animals and a funky playground at these galleries.

LOCATION
Accessible via the M6. At the crossroads in Mawdesley Village turn into Gorsey Lane & then into Back Lane

OPENING
All year open Tue–Sun & Bank holiday Mon 10am–5pm; Closed 25–27, 30, 31 Dec & 1 Jan

ADMISSION PRICES
Free

CONTACT
Cedar Farm Galleries
Back Lane
Mawdesley, Ormskirk
Lancashire L40 3SY
Tel 01704 822616
Web www.cedarfarm.net

1 hr

Feb–Dec

Clitheroe Castle Museum

2 hrs+

All year

Docker Park Farm Visitor Centre

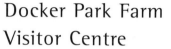

Clitheroe Castle Museum brings to life the history and geology of the Ribble Valley. It has an Edwardian kitchen, cloggers shop and an eighteenth-century mine, all complete with sound effects.

A **working livestock farm** with horses, pigs, sheep, goats and poultry.

★ Feed the baby animals & goats

★ Lakeside walk

★ Tractor & trailor rides, weather permitting (extra charge)

★ Pony rides, weather permitting (extra charge)

LOCATION
Off the A59 Preston–Skipton by-pass. Follow the brown tourist signs. The museum is situated alongside the castle keep

OPENING
Feb–mid Dec open 11am–5pm (to 4.30pm in winter); Closed Jan; Please phone for details

ADMISSION PRICES
Adult £1.60 Child 25p
Family (2+2) £3.40 Senior 75p

CONTACT
Clitheroe Castle Museum
Tel 01200 424635
Email
museum@ribblevalley.gov.uk
Web www.@ribblevalley.gov.uk

LOCATION
Exit the M6 at junction 35 onto the B6254

OPENING
1 Mar–31 Oct open daily 10.30am–5pm; 1 Nov–28 Feb open Sun–Mon 10.30am–4pm; Closed 24 Dec–1 Jan

ADMISSION PRICES
Adult £3.50 Child £2.50
Family £11 Concession £3

CONTACT
Docker Park Farm Visitor Centre, Arkholme, Carnforth
Lancashire LA6 1AR
Tel 01524 221331

Varies

All year

East Lancashire Railway

This **mainly steam-hauled service** runs between Bury, Ramsbottom and Rawenstall every weekend. Visitors can break up the journey at any station to visit the shops in quaint Ramsbottom and stalls at Bury market.

★ Year-round activities & events

★ Guided tours

★ Teddy Bears Picnic on August Bank holidays

★ Sculpture trail on route

★ Picnic sites in areas of scenic interest

LOCATION
Accessible from the A56 & A58

OPENING
All year open Sat & Sun 9am–5pm; Jul & Aug open Sat & Sun 10am–3.30pm; Nov open Sat & Sun 9am–4pm

ADMISSION PRICES
Please phone for details

CONTACT
East Lancashire Railway
Bolton Street Station
Bury, Lancashire BL9 0EY
Tel 0161 7647790
Fax 01772 685984
Email loisvevers@aol.com
Web www.east-lancs-rly.co.uk

2 hrs

Feb–Dec

Ellenroad Engine House

A fascinating engine house which contains the only surviving complete working steam cotton-mill engine, together with its original steam-raising plant.

★ Guided tours

LOCATION	CONTACT
Leave the M62 at junction 21	**Ellenroad Engine House**
	Elizabethan Way, Milnrow
OPENING	Rochdale
Feb–Dec open 1st Sun of each	Lancashire OL16 4LG
month 12pm–4pm; 3 engines in	Tel 01706 881952
steam 1st Sun of the month;	Fax 01706 641203
Closed 7 Jan	Email ellenroad@aol.com
	Web www.ellenroad.org.uk
ADMISSION PRICES	
Steaming: Adult £2 Child (2–16)	
£1 Family £5 Concession £1	

Farmer Parr's Animal World

2 hrs+

All year

Over 20 acres of farmland with a large and fascinating collection of farm and rare breed animals, including poultry and pets.

★ Indoor barn
★ Fylde Country Life Museum

LOCATION	CONTACT
Follow the M55 to Fleetwood &	**Farmer Parr's Animal World &**
then take the A585	**Fylde Country Life Museum**
	Wyrefield Farm
OPENING	Rossall Lane, Fleetwood
All year open daily 10am–5pm;	Lancashire FY7 8JP
Closed 25, 26 Dec	Tel 01253 874389
ADMISSION PRICES	
Adult £3.25 Child £2.50 Family	
£10 Concession £3	

293

Haigh Country Park

2–3 hrs

All year

LOCATION
From the M6 take the A49 to Standish,
then the B5239 to Haigh
OPENING
All year open daily except 25, 26 Dec
ADMISSION PRICES
Charge per activity
Car park £1 per day
CONTACT
Haigh Country Park
Haigh
Wigan WN2 1PE
Tel 01942 832985
Email hhgen@wiganmbc.co.uk
Web www.haighhall.net

Explore and enjoy this country park which offers woodland trails and a wide variety of events and activities including archery, rock climbing and abseiling.

★ Free Sunday afternoon entertainment
★ Outdoor theatre productions
★ Miniature railway
★ Children's craft workshops
★ Putting green

All day

All year

Hollingworth Lake Country Park

A **country park consisting of lake** and surrounding countryside, with boating, nature reserve, trails, events, guided walks, visitor centre, play areas and picnic sites.

LOCATION
Leave the M62 at junction 21 & take the B6225 onto the A58

OPENING
Please phone for details

ADMISSION PRICES
Free

CONTACT
Hollingworth Lake Country Park
Rakewood Road, Littleborough
Lancashire OL15 0AQ
Tel 01706 373421
Web www.rochdale.gov.uk

All day

All year

Jumbles Country Park

A **network of footpaths** radiating up the valley and across adjacent hills. The visitor centre holds displays, exhibitions and events all-year-round.

LOCATION
Off the A676

OPENING
Park: All year open daily 24 hrs
Visitor centre: Times restricted
Please phone for details

ADMISSION PRICES
Free

CONTACT
Jumbles Country Park
Bradshaw Road, Bradshaw
Bolton
Lancashire BL2 4JS
Tel 01204 853360
Fax 01204 852728

Leighton Hall

2 hrs

May–Sep

This **interesting historical building** has large grounds with a maze, woodland walk and a collection of birds of prey.

★ Guided tours compulsory

LOCATION
Leave the M6 at junction 35 & follow the signs on the A6

OPENING
May–Sep open Sun, Tue–Fri & Bank holiday Mon from 2pm

ADMISSION PRICES
Adult £4 Child (5–16) £2.70
Family £12

CONTACT
Leighton Hall
Lancaster LA5 9ST
Tel 01524 734474
Email leightonhall@yahoo.co.uk

All day

All year

Leisure Lakes

Spend a relaxing day out at a 30-acre lake with sandy beaches, walks and outdoor activities.

- ★ Golf driving range
- ★ Jet-ski centre
- ★ Mountain bike centre
- ★ Windsurf centre

LOCATION
Off the A565, 6 miles from Southport & 10 miles from Preston

OPENING
All year open daily 9am–7pm

ADMISSION PRICES
Adult £2.50 Child £2

CONTACT
Leisure Lakes
Mere Brow
Tarleton, Preston
Lancashire PR4 6JX
Tel 01772 813446
Fax 01772 816250

Louis Tussauds Waxworks

2 hrs

All year

Louis Tussauds Waxworks has five floors packed with over 150 models of some of the heroes and villains of stage and screen, music and sport, history and royalty.

LOCATION
Blackpool Promenade, opposite Central Pier

OPENING
In summer open daily 10am–6pm; In winter open Mon–Fri 10am–5pm, Sat–Sun 10am–6pm

ADMISSION PRICES
Phone for details

CONTACT
Louis Tussauds Waxworks
87–89 Central Promenade
Blackpool FY1 5AA
Tel 01253 625953
Email chriswalne@leisure-parcs.co.uk
Web www.blackpoollive.com

295

Oswaldtwistle Mills

All day

All year

LOCATION
Accessible from the M65 junction 7, the M62, A58 & the M6 junction 29

OPENING
All year open Mon–Wed & Fri–Sat 9am–5pm, Thu open 9am–8pm & Sun open 11am–5pm; Closed Easter Sun, 25, 26 Dec & 1 Jan

ADMISSION PRICES
Stockley Sweets: Adult £1 Child 50p
Concession 50p
Time Tunnel: Adult £1 Child 50p
Concession 50p

CONTACT
Oswaldtwistle Mills Shopping Village
Moscow Mill, Colliers Street
Oswaldtwistle
Accrington
Lancashire BB5 3DE
Tel 01254 871025
Email info@o-mills.co.uk
Web www.o-mills.co.uk

A family attraction, set within a working mill and its grounds, Oswaldtwistle Mills offers an interesting range of facilities and shopping.

- ★ Guided tours
- ★ Wendy House Village
- ★ Nature Trail
- ★ Sweet factory
- ★ Cloth weaving display

2–3 hrs

All year

Pendle Heritage Centre

Enjoy a pleasant few hours at this seventeenth-century farm manor house. It has a walled garden, barn, cobbled farmyard and attractive picnic area.

LOCATION
Leave the M65 at junction 13 & take the A682 onto the B6247

OPENING
All year open daily 10am–5pm; Closed 25 Dec

ADMISSION PRICES
Adult £2.75 Child £1.50 Family £5.50

CONTACT
Pendle Heritage Centre
Park Hill, Barrowford
Nelson
Lancashire BB9 6JQ
Tel 01282 661701
Fax 01282 611718
Email tic@htnw.co.uk
Web www.htnw.co.uk

All day

All year

Pennington Flash Country Park

World-renowned as a bird-watcher's paradise, this is a popular beauty spot, lake and nature reserve.

★ Mobile refreshment vehicle
★ 7 viewing hides
★ 9-hole golf course (charge)
★ Fishing
★ Sailing
★ Footpaths

LOCATION
Take the A572 from Leigh town centre & the A580 from Manchester & Liverpool

OPENING
All year open daily 24 hrs

ADMISSION PRICES
Free; Pay & Display car park

CONTACT
Pennington Flash Country Park
St Helens Road
Leigh
Lancashire WN7 3PA
Tel/Fax 01942 605253

All day

Mar–Nov

Pleasureland

Pleasureland has over 100 rides, attractions and games. There is something for everyone, from the white knuckle thrills of the Traumatizer to the gentler junior rides. Phone for information on special events such as the circus schools, educational tours and parties.

★ Rollercoaster rides
★ Junior rides
★ Go-karts
★ Bumper boats
★ Children's quad bikes
★ Waterboggan

LOCATION
On Southport seafront

OPENING
Mar–5 Nov open daily from 11am
Late Sep–Oct open weekends from midday

ADMISSION PRICES
All-day wristband £16 Junior wristband £11 Supersaver (any 4 bands) £50

CONTACT
Pleasureland
Marine Drive, Southport
Lancashire PR8 1RX
Tel 08702 200204 (general info)
Tel 08702 200205 (group booking)
Web www.pleasureland.uk.com

Rumble Tumble

1 hr+

All year

Children can have fun and be challenged in this giant indoor adventure zone.

Sandcastle Tropical Waterworld

Quality Assured Visitor Attraction
English Tourism Council

½ day

All year

A water-based leisure complex with four pools, it offers a variety of thrills including cascading water slides and white-knuckle water chutes.

★ Wave pool   ★ Adventure playground
★ Children's pool   ★ Children's entertainer

LOCATION	CONTACT
Off the A49, in Wallgate town centre	**Rumble Tumble** 10 Tower Enterprise Park Great George Street Wigan Lancashire WN3 4DP Tel 01942 494922
OPENING All year open daily 10am–7pm; Closed 25, 26 Dec & 1 Jan	
ADMISSION PRICES Child (1–12): Giant Playzone from £2.50; Pre-school Playzone from £1.25	

LOCATION	CONTACT
On South Promenade	**Sandcastle Tropical Waterworld** South Promenade Blackpool FY4 1BB Tel 01253 343602 Fax 01253 406490
OPENING Please phone for details	
ADMISSION PRICES Please phone for details	

Ski Rossendale

All day

All year

LOCATION
Follow the M65 to Rawtenstall. The centre is located on the town's outskirts
OPENING Please phone for details
ADMISSION PRICES Please phone for details
CONTACT **Ski Rossendale** Haslingden Old Road Rawtenstall, Rossendale Lancashire BB4 8RR Tel 01706 226457 Fax 01706 831294

Ski Rossendale is the North's premier ski centre. Open all year round, the centre is ideal for beginners and expert skiers alike. Set amidst trees and parkland, Ski Rossendale commands a superb view over the Rossendale Valley.

★ Ski School
★ 190-yard main slope
★ 80-yard intermediate slope
★ 30-yard nursery slope
★ Individual or group lessons

½ day+

All year

Three Sisters Racing Circuit

Karting, motorcycle racing, cycle racing and canoeing are just some of the motor sports offered at this recreation centre.

★ Model boats

★ Surfing

★ Pony trail

★ Nature trail

★ Orienteering

LOCATION
Leave the M6 at junction 24 southbound & junction 25 northbound

OPENING
Please phone for details

ADMISSION PRICES
Please phone for details

CONTACT
Three Sisters Racing Circuit
Bryn Road, Ashton-in-Makerfield
Wigan
Lancashire WN4 8DD
Tel 01942 270230
Fax 01942 270508
Email info@racing-school.co.uk
Web www.racing-school.co.uk

298

½ day+

All year

Twine Valley Country Park & Fishery

Twine Valley offers trout fishing, coarse fishing and fun fishing for children. There is also an animal park with llamas, rheas, Shire horses, ponies, pygmy goats and a small herd of red deer.

★ Feed the fish   ★ Many walks

LOCATION
Leave the M6 at junction 1 & take the A56

OPENING
All year open daily 10am–11pm except 25 Dec

ADMISSION PRICES
Coarse fishing per day:
Adult £10 Child £5

CONTACT
Twine Valley Country Park & Fishery
The Fishermans Retreat
Riding Head Lane, Bye Road
Ramsbottom, Bury
Lancashire BL0 0HH
Tel 01706 825314
Email
fishermans@twinevalley.fsnet.co.uk

West Lancashire Light Railway

Varies

All year

Ride on a narrow-gauge steam railway and visit a historic collection of locomotives and rolling stock at this light railway centre.

LOCATION
Leave M6 at junction 31 & head for Preston; take the A59 to Tarleton, then the unclassified road to Hesketh Bank

OPENING
Apr–Oct & Bank holiday Mon open 12pm–5.30pm; Nov–Mar open Sun 12.30pm–5pm; Closed Easter Sat, 25, 26 Dec & 1 Jan; Steam trains operate in Apr–Oct only

ADMISSION PRICES
Adult £1.75 Child £1 Family £4

CONTACT
West Lancashire Light Railway
Station Road
Hesketh Bank, Preston
Lancashire PR4 6SP
Tel 01772 815881
Fax 0870 4443245
Email publicity@westlancs.org
Web www.westlancs.org

Whitworth Water Ski & Recreation Centre

All day

All year

LOCATION
Take the A671 from Rochdale

OPENING
1 Apr–31 Oct open daily 9am–dusk; 1 Nov–28 Mar open daily 9.30am–dusk (weather permitting); Closed 25, 26 Dec & 1 Jan

ADMISSION PRICES
Please phone for details

CONTACT
Whitworth Water Ski & Recreation Centre
Cowm Reservoir, Tong Lane, Whitworth
Rochdale
Lancashire OL12 8BE
Tel 01706 852534
Email andynflo@whitworthwaterski.co.uk
Web www.whitworth-waterski.co.uk

The aim of the centre, which is run in conjunction with an able-bodied ski club, is to teach people of all disabilities how to water-ski and to help them to integrate with able-bodied members. Full instruction and equipment are provided.

★ Water-skiing
★ Banana rides
★ Ringo rides
★ Disabled bikes

299

Williamson Park

2 hrs

All year

Take the family to visit the Ashton Memorial, a Victorian folly, a conservation garden and a tropical butterfly house.

★ Minibeast cave   ★ Small mammal enclosure
★ Free flying bird enclosure

LOCATION
Follow the Lancaster signs from junction 33 or 34 of the M6. Follow the brown tourist signs from the city

OPENING
Please phone for details

ADMISSION PRICES
Adult £3.25 Child £1.75 Family £11 Concession £2.75

CONTACT
Williamson Park
Quernmore Road
Lancaster
Lancashire LA1 1UX
Tel 01524 33318

Windmill Animal Farm

2 hrs

All year

Children can watch, feed and play with farm animals – sheep, rabbits, pigs and goats – in the barn where they live. There are also Shetland ponies, cows and deer.

★ Adventure playground   ★ Miniature railway
★ Indoor play barn

LOCATION
Follow signs from the A59 at Burscough & Rufford

OPENING
Easter–mid-Sep open daily 10am– 5pm; Oct–Easter open weekends & school holidays

ADMISSION PRICES
Adult £3.50 Child £2.75

Family £10 Concession £2.50

CONTACT
Windmill Animal Farm
Redcat Lane
Burscough, Ormskirk
Lancashire L40 1UQ
Tel 01704 892282
Fax 01704 896282

2 hrs+
All year

Worden Arts & Crafts Centre

Set in 157 acres of parkland, this arts and crafts centre has a fully-equipped theatre, six craft workshops and an exhibition display room.

★ Miniature railway

★ Garden for the blind

★ Maze

★ Children's play area

LOCATION
Leave the M6 at junction 28 & follow the signs for Worden Arts Centre

OPENING
Open daily 8am–dusk

ADMISSION PRICES
Free

CONTACT
Worden Arts & Crafts Centre
Worden Park, Leyland
Preston
Lancashire PR25 1DJ
Tel 01772 455908
Fax 01772 624733
Website www.worden-arts.co.uk

Wyreside Ecology Centre

All day
All year

A visitor centre set in the heart of the Wyre Estuary Country Park, the Wyreside Ecology Centre provides an excellent base for nature trails and riverside walks.

★ Riverside path suitable for blind visitors

★ Cycles available for hire for disabled visitors

LOCATION
Follow the M55, then the A585 & B5268

OPENING
Jan–Mar & Nov–Dec open daily 11am–3pm; Apr–Oct open daily 10.30am–4.30pm; Closed 25 Dec

ADMISSION PRICES
Free

CONTACT
Wyreside Ecology Centre
Wyre Estuary Country Park
River Road, Thornton
Blackpool
Lancashire FY5 5LR
Tel/Fax 01253 857890
Email rreeves@wyrebc.gov.uk
Web www.wyrebc.gov.uk

300

2 hrs+
All year

The Adventures of Dreamieland

Children will enjoy this spooky interactive ride.

★ Children's activity centre

★ Parent & toddler education sessions

★ Special events

★ Arts & crafts sessions

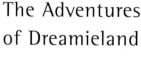

LOCATION
At junction 9 & 10 off the M60

OPENING
Jan–Nov open Mon–Fri 10am–9pm, Sat 9am–7pm, Sun 12pm–6pm; Nov–Jan open Mon–Fri 10am–10pm, Sat 9am–8pm, Sun 12pm–6pm; Closed 25 Dec

ADMISSION PRICES
Adult £3.95 Child £3.25
Family £13.75

CONTACT
The Adventures of Dreamieland
203 The Dome, The Trafford Centre, Manchester M17 8DF
Tel 0161 7497490
Web www.dreamieland.com

The Airport Tour Centre

2 hrs+
All year

Children interested in airplanes will love this trip to the airport. Trained guides explain in detail the inner workings of the airport's various departments. Pre-booking is essential.

LOCATION
Leave the M56 at junction 5

OPENING
All year open daily 10am–8pm; Closed 25, 26 Dec & 1 Jan

ADMISSION PRICES
Adult £5 Child (5–15) £3
Concession £5

CONTACT
The Airport Tour Centre
Terminal 1, Manchester Airport
Manchester M90 1QX
Tel 0161 4892442
Email tourcentre@tasmanchester.com
Web webmaster@tasmanchester.com

Castlefield Urban Heritage Park

½ day

All Year

LOCATION
Follow the signs from the M602, M61, M62, M56 & all radial routes serving Manchester city centre

OPENING
All year open daily
Please phone for details

ADMISSION PRICES
Free

CONTACT
Castlefield Urban Heritage Park
Castlefield Visitor Centre
Castlefield
Manchester M3 4JN
Tel 0161 8344026
Email enquiries@castlefield.org.uk
Web www.castlefield.org.uk

A **historic, restored canal basin,** home to Britain's first man-made canal, its first passenger railway station and the site of the Roman settlement of Mamucium. The history of the site has been preserved and now accommodates award-winning attractions and museums.

★ Museum of Science & Industry
★ Granada Studios Tour
★ Towpath walks & trails
★ Weekend boat trips

Gallery of Costume

2 hrs

All year

An **elegant early Georgian house,** containing one of the finest costume collections in the country. It includes clothes worn by men, women and children from the seventeenth century to the present day.

★ Programme of events for all ages

LOCATION
Accessible from all major routes; Follow the signs to Rusholme

OPENING
In summer open daily 10am–5.30pm; In winter open daily 10am–4pm

ADMISSION PRICES
Free

CONTACT
Gallery of Costume
Platt Hall, Wilmslow Road
Rusholme
Manchester M14 5LL
Tel 0161 2245217
Web
www.manchestergalleries.org

Heaton Park Farm Centre

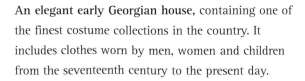

3 hrs

All year

A **hall and gallery** with grounds offering many activities for children.

★ Children's playground
★ Boating lake
★ 18-hole golf course
★ Bowling green
★ Farm centre
★ Pets corner
★ Pitch & Putt
★ Horse riding

LOCATION
Leave the M60 at junction 19 & take the A576

OPENING
All year open Mon–Thu & Sat–Sun 10am–3pm

ADMISSION PRICES
Free

CONTACT
Heaton Park Farm Centre
Prestwich
Manchester M25 2SW
Tel 0161 7731085
Fax 0161 7980107

Ordsall Hall Museum

2 hrs

All year

Dating back over hundreds of years, Ordsall Hall is a very fine example of an Elizabethan black-and-white half-timbered manor-house.

★ Family events & exhibitions programme

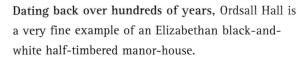

LOCATION	ADMISSION PRICES
Signposted from the A57 & A5063	Free
	CONTACT
OPENING	**Ordsall Hall Museum**
All year open Mon–Fri 10am–4pm, Sun 1pm–4pm; Closed Good Friday, Easter Sun, 25, 26 Dec & 1 Jan	Ordsall Lane Salford Manchester M5 3AN Tel 0161 8720251 Email admin@ordsallhall.org Web www.ordsallhall.org

People's History Museum

2 hrs

All year

Displays document such topics as the lives of coal miners, cotton mill workers and the first professional footballers. Interactive exhibits help children to have a greater understanding of social history.

LOCATION	ADMISSION PRICES
Via the A6, M602, M62, A56; Follow the signs to Castlefield	Adult £1 Child £1
	CONTACT
OPENING	**People's History Museum**
All year open Tue–Sun 11am–4.30pm; Closed Good Fri, 24–26 Dec, 1 Jan	The Pump House, Bridge Street Manchester M3 3ER Tel 0161 8396061 Web www.peopleshistorymuse-um.org.uk

302

Trafford Ecology Park

2 hrs

All year

Trafford Ecology Park is a peaceful oasis in the middle of Trafford Park Industrial Estate. Visitors can come to the centre to see the displays, take part in the special events, or simply discover the wealth of wildlife that lives there.

LOCATION	CONTACT
Leave the M602 at junction 2 & follow the A576; Leave the M60 at junction 9 & follow the A5081	**Trafford Ecology Park** Lake Road Trafford Park Manchester M17 1TU Tel 0161 8737182 Fax 0161 8760523 Email st@groundwork.org.uk Web www.groundwork.org.uk
OPENING	
All year open Mon–Fri 8am–5pm	
ADMISSION PRICES	
Free	

Wythenshawe Park

All day

All year

Wythenshawe Park has a seventeenth-century hall set in 275 acres of parkland. It offers a range of leisure facilities, including football, orienteering and pony rides.

LOCATION	CONTACT
Leave the M53 at junction 3. The park is located 7 miles from the town centre	**Wythenshawe Park** Wythenshawe Road Northenden Manchester M23 0AB Tel 0161 9982117 Fax 0161 9451743
OPENING	
All year open daily with 24-hour access to the park	
ADMISSION PRICES	
Free	

2 hrs+

All year

The Cavern Quarter

The Cavern Quarter is the cultural birthplace of the Beatles. Its main attractions are the Cavern Club, Yellow Submarine and Dooley Statue. Within the Quarter are numerous features which, when viewed in sequence, create the Beatles Village.

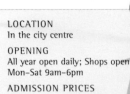

LOCATION	CONTACT
In the city centre	**The Cavern Quarter**
OPENING	Liverpool
All year open daily; Shops open Mon–Sat 9am–6pm	Merseyside L2 6RE
	Tel 0151 2271963
ADMISSION PRICES	
Free	

2 hrs+

Mar–Oct

Croxteth Hall & Country Park

An Edwardian stately home set in 500 acres of countryside, featuring a Victorian walled garden and a visitor farm.

★ Miniature railway ★ Rare breeds of livestock

★ Adventure playground

LOCATION	CONTACT
Leave the M57 at junction 4 & take the A580 towards Liverpool	**Croxteth Hall & Country Park** Croxteth Hall Lane
OPENING	Liverpool
Mar–Oct open daily 11am–5pm	Merseyside L12 0HB
ADMISSION PRICES	Tel 0151 2285311
Hall, farm & garden: Adult £3.80	Fax 0151 2282817
Child £1.90 Family £9.40	Web www.croxteth.co.uk
Concession £1.90	

303

2 hrs+

All year

Historic Warships at Birkenhead

Visitors to HMS Plymouth will experience what life is like on the high seas, whilst on Onyx visitors can imagine they are stalking their prey while looking through the periscope.

LOCATION	CONTACT
Follow the signs from the M53	**Historic Warships at Birkenhead**
OPENING	East Float
Apr–Aug open daily 10am–5pm; Sep–Mar open daily 10am–4pm; Closed 24–26 Dec & 7–17 Feb Mon–Fri	Dock Road Birkenhead Merseyside CH41 1DJ Tel 0151 6501573
ADMISSION PRICES	Web
Adult £5.50 Child (5–16) £3.50 Family £15 Concession £4.50	www.warships.freeserve.co.uk

Knowsley Safari Park

All day

All year

Knowsley Safari Park has a five-mile drive through 500 acres of rolling countryside, where some of the world's wildest animals roam free.

LOCATION	CONTACT
Leave the M62 at junction 2, the M57 at junction 2 & follow the signs	**Knowsley Safari Park** Prescot Merseyside L34 4AN
OPENING	Tel 0151 4309009
1 Mar–31 Oct open daily 10am–4pm; Nov–28 Feb open daily 11am–3pm; Closed 25 Dec	Fax 0151 4263677 Email safari.park@knowsley.com Web www.knowsley.com
ADMISSION PRICES	
Adult £8 Child (up to 15) £5	

Liverpool Planetarium

1 hr

All year

WC

Enjoy an exciting visual experience of space in a domed auditorium at this planetarium. The support programme 'Nightwatch' takes a look at the night sky.

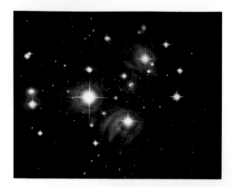

★ 40-minute performance

LOCATION
Follow the signs from the M62. In Liverpool city centre

OPENING
All year open Tue–Fri at 3.15pm, Sat & Sun at 1.15pm, 2.15pm, 3.15pm & 4.05pm; Closed 23–26 Dec & 1 Jan

ADMISSION PRICES
Adult £1 Child 50p

CONTACT
Liverpool Planetarium
Liverpool Museum
William Brown Street
Liverpool
Merseyside L3 8EN
Tel 0151 4784235
Fax 0151 4784390
Web www.nmgm.org.uk

Mersey Ferries River Explorer Cruise

1–2 hrs

All year

WC

This cruise along the Mersey takes 50 minutes and has a recorded commentary. A stop-off at the Wirral Terminal allows for a visit to an aquarium, children's play area, shop and café.

★ Pirate-themed children's play area at Seacombe (2-9 years)

★ Aquarium at Seacombe

★ Free children's activity pack with return child explorer tickets & family tickets

★ Children's birthday parties catered for

LOCATION
Pier Head Liverpool is signposted from Albert Dock. Follow the signs on the M53 for Seacombe & Woodside on Wirral

OPENING
All year open daily Mon–Fri 10am–3pm, Sat, Sun & Bank holidays 10am–6pm; Closed 25, 26 Dec & 1 Jan

ADMISSION PRICES
Adult £4.30 Child £2.40 Family £11.30

CONTACT
Mersey Ferries River Explorer Cruise
Mersey Ferries Ltd
Victoria Place
Seacombe
Wallasey CH44 6QY
Tel 0151 3301444

Model Railway Village

2 hrs

Mar–Oct

Museum of Liverpool Life

1 hr+

All year

MERSEYSIDE

Set within 1½ acres of sheltered gardens, this beautiful miniature village has over 200 1:18 scale models including watermills, churches, shops and houses. There is also a garden gauge railway.

The museum celebrates the unique character of the vibrant city of Liverpool, with galleries depicting various aspects of city life, including Mersey Culture, Making a Living, the River Mersey and City Soldiers, which tells the story of the King's Regiment.

i

LOCATION
Northbound on the M6 take junction 26, the M58 & A570. Southbound on the A59 take junction 31. Signposted

OPENING
23 Mar–31 Oct open daily 10am–5pm (last entry 4pm); Jul–Aug 10am–6pm (last entry 5pm)

ADMISSION PRICES
Adult £3.50 Child (2–16) £2
Family £9 Concession £2

CONTACT
Model Railway Village
Lower Promenade, Kings Gardens
Southport, Merseyside PR8 1RB
Tel/Fax 01704 214266
Web www.visit.southport.org.uk

i

LOCATION
Follow the A565

OPENING
All year open daily 10am–5pm (last admission 4.30pm); Closed 23–26 Dec & 1 Jan

ADMISSION PRICES
Free

CONTACT
Museum of Liverpool Life
Albert Dock
Liverpool
Merseyside L3 1PZ
Tel 0151 4784499
Email liverlife@nmgm.org
Web www.museumofliverpool-life.org.uk

305

National Wildlife Centre

2–3 hrs

Apr–Sep

i

LOCATION
Junction 5 off the M62. Follow the brown tourist signs

OPENING
Apr–Sep open daily 10am–5pm (last admission 4pm)

ADMISSION PRICES
Adult £3 Under-5s Free Concession £1.50
Season & Family tickets available

CONTACT
National Wildlife Centre
Court Hey Park
Roby Road
Liverpool L16 3NA
Tel 0151 7371819
Email info@nwc.org.uk
Web www.nwc.org.uk

A family-friendly visitor attraction that promotes the creation of new places for wildflowers and their importance to the environment. There are demonstration gardens, a plant nursery and a rooftop walkway.

★ Exhibition barn with activities for children
★ Brass rubbing
★ Children's play area
★ Wall with climbing handles

Port Sunlight Village Trust

1 hr+

All year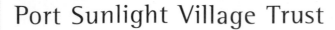

A **picturesque nineteenth-century** garden village on the Wirral, founded by William Hesketh Lever for his factory workers and named after his famous Sunlight soap. Now a designated conservation area, it features beautiful open spaces and floral displays.

★ Guided tours
★ Heritage centre with displays

LOCATION
Leave the M53 at junction 5. Follow the signs on the A41

OPENING
Apr–Oct open daily 10am–4pm; Nov–Mar open Mon–Fri 10am–4pm, Sat & Sun 11am–4pm; Closed 24 Dec–1 Jan

ADMISSION PRICES
Adult 70p Child (5–16) 40p
Concession 60p

CONTACT
Port Sunlight Village Trust
95 Greendale Road
Port Sunlight
Wirral
Merseyside CH62 4XE
Tel 0151 6444803
Fax 0151 6458973
Web www.portsunlightvillage.com

Southport Zoo

3 hrs

All year

A **small zoo with a good variety of animals** including chimps, lions, snow leopards, lynx, capbybara, parrots, reptiles and fish.

★ Pets corner barn
★ Children's play area
★ Quiz trails
★ Schoolroom & natural history museum
★ Book in advance for talks

LOCATION
From the outskirts of Southport follow the brown tourist signs. The zoo entrance is next to Pleasureland & opposite the Dunes Leisure Centre

OPENING
In summer open daily 10am–6pm; In winter open daily 10am–4pm; Closed 25 Dec

ADMISSION PRICES
Adult £4 Child £3 Senior £3.50 Group rates available

CONTACT
Southport Zoo
Princes Park
Southport
Merseyside PR8 1RX
Tel 01704 548894
Email info@southportzoo.co.uk
Web www.southportzoo.co.uk

Speke Hall, Gardens & Woodland

2 hrs+

All year

LOCATION
Leave the M62 at junction 6 & the M56 at junction 12; Follow the brown tourist signs on the A5300

OPENING
23 Mar–31 Oct open Wed–Sun 1pm–5pm;
2 Nov–8 Dec open Sat & Sun 1pm–4pm;
Open Bank holiday Mon; Closed 24, 25, 26, 31 Dec & 1 Jan

ADMISSION PRICES
House, Garden & Grounds: Adult £5
Child (5–18) £3 Concession £14

CONTACT
Speke Hall, Gardens & Woodland (NT)
The Walk
Liverpool
Merseyside L24 1XD
Tel 0151 4277231
Email mspsxc@smtp.ntrust.org.uk
Web www.spekehall.org.uk

One of the most famous half-timbered houses in the country, dating from 1530. A fully-equipped Victorian kitchen and servants' hall enables visitors to see behind the scenes.

★ Woodland walks

307

Tate Liverpool

All day

All year

Take the children for a cultural day out at Tate Liverpool, the home of the National Collection of modern art in the North of England. Part of the historic Albert Dock, it has four floors of art, free daily talks and a shop and cafe.

LOCATION
In Liverpool city centre, beside the river

OPENING
All year open Tue–Sun & Bank holiday Mon 10am–5.30pm;
Closed 24–26 Dec, 1 Jan & Good Fri

ADMISSION PRICES
Charges for special exhibitions:
Adult £4 Child Free
Family £8 Concessions £3

CONTACT
Tate Liverpool, Albert Dock
Liverpool, Merseyside L3 4BB
Tel 0151 7027400
Web www.tate.org.uk/liverpool/

Western Approaches

1 hr+

Mar–Oct

Visit the former top-secret underground headquarters for the Battle of the Atlantic. Restored with original artefacts, children will enjoy the guided tour and audio-visual display which help to bring a dramatic period of history vividly to life.

LOCATION
In the city centre

OPENING
1 Mar–31 Oct open Mon–Thu & Sat 10.30am–4.30pm (last adm. 3.50pm); Closed Good Friday

ADMISSION PRICES
Adult £4.75 Child (under 16) £3.45 Family £39.95

CONTACT
Western Approaches
1 Rumford Street
Liverpool
Merseyside L2 8SZ
Tel 0151 2272008
Fax 0151 2366913

45 mins

Winter WC

Williamson Tunnels

When you enter Williamson Tunnels, you enter a strange underground kingdom which has lain beneath the city of Liverpool since the early 1800s. Visitors can see and touch the brick and sandstone workings of this key section of the tunnels, whilst enjoying entertaining commentary from an expert guide.

LOCATION
From the M62 follow the motorway into Liverpool & look for the brown tourist signs for Town Centre/Cathedrals until you reach Smithdown Lane. The heritage centre is on the left after the police station

OPENING
In winter open daily 10am–5pm

ADMISSION PRICES
Adult £3.50 Child £2 Family £10
Concession £3

CONTACT
Williamson's Tunnels, FOWT
15–17 Chatham Place
Liverpool
Merseyside L7 7HD
Tel 0151 7096868
Email info@willliamsontunnels.com

308

2 hrs

All year

World of Glass

Take a journey of discovery into one of the most common substances on earth. See live demonstrations of glass-blowing by resident artists and wander through a maze of tunnels which are the remains of the oldest glass-making tank furnace in the world.

★ Underground maze of tunnels to explore
★ Fun zone with distorting mirrors & kaleidoscopes
★ Special effects

LOCATION
Leave the M62 at junction 7 & the M6 at junction 24 & head into the town centre

OPENING
All year open daily 10am–5pm; Closed 25, 26 Dec & 1st Jan

ADMISSION PRICES
Adult £5 Child (5–16) £3.60 Family £15
Concession £3.60

CONTACT
World of Glass
Chalon Way
St Helens
Merseyside WA10 1BX
Tel 01744 22766
Email info@worldofglass.com
Web www.worldofglass.com

1 hr

May–Sep

Amgueddfa Syr Henry Jones Museum

This **fascinating museum** of Welsh rural life is set in a nineteenth-century workman's cottage. It includes displays on Victorian life in a typical Welsh community.

Anglesey Angora Bunny Farm

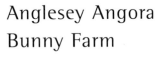

3 hrs

All year

A **hands-on farm experience** is available at the Bunny Farm with over 500 animals and birds to see. Many wander freely to be stroked and fed.

★ Special activities on Sundays & school holidays

LOCATION
On the A548 Abergele–Llanrwst road in Llangernyw. Follow the signs from the car park

OPENING
May–Sep open Tue–Fri & Bank holidays 10.30am–1pm & 2pm–5pm, Sat & Sun 2pm–5pm

ADMISSION PRICES
Please phone for details

CONTACT
Amgueddfa Syr Henry Jones Museum, Y Cwm, Llangernyw Abergele LL22 8PR
Tel 01745 860661

LOCATION
On the A5104, 2 miles from Corwen

OPENING
Please phone for details

ADMISSION PRICES
Please phone for details

CONTACT
Anglesey Angora Bunny Farm Corwen LL21 9BY
Tel/Fax 01490 413180

Anglesey Sea Zoo

½ day

Mar–Nov

LOCATION
Follow the Lobster signs from the Britannia Bridge onto Anglesey

OPENING
Mar–Nov open 10am–6pm (last admission 5pm)

ADMISSION PRICES
Adult £5.95 Child £4.95 Family ticket From £14.95 Senior £5.50

CONTACT
Anglesey Sea Zoo
Brynsiencyn LL61 6TQ
Tel 01248 430411
Email fishandfun@seazoo.demon.co.uk
Web angleseyseazoo.co.uk

Underwater and undercover, this sea zoo offers much to see and do. On display are many fascinating sea creatures such as sea-horses, conger eels, octopuses and sharks. There is also a shipwreck.

★ Crab fishing (small charge)

★ Fish feeding displays

★ Staffed touch tank during school holidays

★ Pearl fishing

★ Wave tank

Beaumaris Gaol & Courthouse

1 hr+
Easter–Sep

This courthouse was built in 1614 and was renovated in the nineteenth century. Its treadmill and grim cells bring the harsh realities of prison to life.

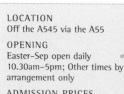

LOCATION
Off the A545 via the A55

OPENING
Easter–Sep open daily
10.30am–5pm; Other times by arrangement only

ADMISSION PRICES
Gaol: £2.75 Courthouse: £1.50
Combined family ticket £7.75

CONTACT
Beaumaris Gaol & Courthouse
Steeple Lane
Anglesey LL58 8EW
Tel 01248 810921
Fax 01248 750282

Beaumaris Marine Services

Varies
Varies

Cruise down the Menai Strait to Puffin Island, passing the old quarry workings and Penmon Lighthouse, to view the many species of seabird and, maybe, catch a glimpse of the seals. Fishing trips for experienced anglers or beginners are available.

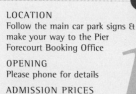

LOCATION
Follow the main car park signs & make your way to the Pier Forecourt Booking Office

OPENING
Please phone for details

ADMISSION PRICES
Please phone for details

CONTACT
Beaumaris Marine Services
The Anchorage
Rosemary Lane
Beaumaris LL58 8ED
Tel/Fax 01248 810746

310

Bryn Bras Castle

2 hrs
Apr–Sep

Built in 1830, Bryn Bras Castle is set against the backdrop of Snowdonia mountains. It has elegant rooms with richly carved furniture. There are historic gardens, woodland and many fine walks.

LOCATION
4 miles east of Caernarfon, off the A4086

OPENING
Open for pre-booked groups only

ADMISSION PRICES
Please phone for details

CONTACT
Bryn Bras Castle
Llanrug
Caernarfon
LL55 4RE
Tel 01286 870210

Erdigg Hall

1 hr+
Mar–Oct

A family home that captures the life of a bustling household both above and below stairs in the early twentieth century.

★ Woodland walks   ★ Children's guide

LOCATION
2 miles south of Wrexham, sign-posted off the A483 & A525

OPENING
House: 23 Mar–3 Nov open Sat–Wed

ADMISSION PRICES
Adult £6.60 Child £3.30
Family £16.50

CONTACT
Erdigg Hall
Gardens & Country Park
Erddig
Wrexham LL13 0YT
Tel 01978 355314
Infoline 01978 557019
Email erdigg@ntrust.org.uk
Web www.nationaltrust.org.uk

Ffestiniog Railway

½ day+

All year

LOCATION
At the south-east end of town, on the A487

OPENING
All year open weekends; Trains run daily from Mar–Nov; Closed 25 Dec

ADMISSION PRICES
Day ticket £14

CONTACT
Ffestiniog Railway
Harbour Station
Porthmadog
North Wales LL94 9NF
Tel 01766 516073
Email info@festrail.co.uk
Web www.festrail.co.uk

Take a trip on the world's oldest independent railway company. The track runs through 13 miles of spectacular scenery from the sea up to the mountains. Special events are held throughout the year.

311

Great Orme Mines

1 hr

Feb–Oct

The whole family can enjoy this fascinating underground tour of a large Bronze Age mine. There is also a surface archaeological site and a visitor centre.

LOCATION
In the Great Orme Country Park. Follow the 'Copper Mine' signs from Llandudno Promenade

OPENING
Feb–Oct open daily 10am–5pm

ADMISSION PRICES
Adult £4.50 Child £3 Family (2+2) £12.50 Under-5s Free

CONTACT
Great Orme Mines
Great Orme, Llandudno
Conwy LL30 2XG
Tel 01492 870447
Web
www.greatorme.freeserve.co.uk

Greenfield Valley Heritage Park

1 hr+

All year

This is an award-winning heritage park of renovated Welsh buildings with seven scheduled Ancient Monuments.

★ Adventure playground   ★ Farm museum with livestock

LOCATION
Follow the A548 coast road to Greenfield where there is a free coach & car park

OPENING
Farm museum: 1 Apr–31 Oct
Rest of site: All year

ADMISSION PRICES
Adult £2.50 Child £1.50
Under-5s Free

CONTACT
Greenfield Valley Heritage Park
Administration Centre
Greenfield
Holywell CH8 7GH
Tel 01352 714172
Web www.greenfieldvalley.com

2–4 hrs

Mar–Oct

Greenwood Forest Park

From traditional crafts such as papermaking and wool spinning to zooming 70 yards down the Great Green Run sledge slide, there is a wide range of entertainment on offer at this award-winning adventure park.

★ Sledge rides
★ Inflatable slide
★ Archery
★ Jungle boats
★ Toddler's play area

LOCATION
1 mile off the B4366 between Caernarfon & the A5/A55 junction close to Bangor. Located between Bethel & Y Felinheli

OPENING
Mid Mar–31 Aug open daily 10am–5.30pm; Sep & Oct open Mon–Sat 10am–5pm & Sun 11am–5pm

ADMISSION PRICES
Please phone for details

CONTACT
Greenwood Forest Park
Y Felinheli
Gwynedd LL56 4QN
Tel 01248 670076 (information line)
Tel 01248 671493

312

All day

All year

Henblas Country Park

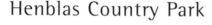

There are **30 attractions** on this site including falconry displays, sheep shearing and indoor and outdoor adventure playgrounds.

LOCATION
Take the B4422 from the A5, 10 miles from Britannia Bridge

OPENING
Please phone for details

ADMISSION PRICES
Please phone for details

CONTACT
Henblas Country Park
Bordorgan
Wales LL62 5DL

Horse Drawn Boats Centre

Varies

Mar–Oct

Enjoy a horsedrawn boat trip along the beautiful Vale of Llangollen. There is also a museum with working models, murals and slides.

LOCATION
On the A5

OPENING
Apr–Oct open daily; Mar open Sat & Sun

ADMISSION PRICES
Adult £3.50 Child £2.50

CONTACT
Horse Drawn Boats Centre
The Wharf
Wharf Hill
Llangollen LL20 8TA
Tel 01978 840697

Inigo Jones Slateworks

1 hr

All year

LOCATION
On the A487, 6 miles from Caernarfon

OPENING
In summer open 9am–5pm; In winter open 10am–5pm

ADMISSION PRICES
Entry to showroom Free
Self-guided tour £3.80

CONTACT
Inigo Jones
Groeslon
Caernarfon
Gwynedd LL54 7ST
Tel 01286 830242
Email slate@inigojones.co.uk
Web www.inigojones.co.uk

See Welsh craftsmanship at first-hand on a tour of the Inigo Jones slateworks and learn about the development of the Welsh slate industry in the historical exhibition. The self-guided tour, in which you record your own commentary, starts with a film on how slate is mined.

★ Children's quiz with slate prize
★ Engraving & calligraphy workshops

313

Llanberis Lake Railway

1 hr+

Mar–Oct

Take a leisurely ride in a quaint historic steam engine along the shores of beautiful Padarn Lake. Break your journey to visit the Welsh Slate Museum or to enjoy a lakeside picnic.

★ Adventure playground & woodland centre at the half-way station

LOCATION
Just off the A4086
Caernarfon–Capel Curig road, at Llanberis. Follow the Padarn Country Park signs

OPENING
Mar–Oct open most days from 11am–4pm; Check the website for the timetable

ADMISSION PRICES
Adult £5 Child £3.50
Family tickets available

CONTACT
Llanberis Lake Railway
Llanberis Gwynedd LL55 4TY
Tel 01286 870579
Email info@lakrailway.co.uk
Web www.lake-railway.co.uk

Llangollen Exhibition Centre

½ day

All year

Best Value Family Day Out
GRANADA TV (1998)

Dr Who fans will enjoy meeting Daleks and Cybermen at the Dr Who Experience in this varied exhibition centre.

★ Model Railway World   ★ Strobe lighting effects
★ Llangollen Museum

LOCATION
On the A539 from Chester & Wrexham

OPENING
All year open daily; Closed Wed in Nov, Jan & Feb, except during school half-term & 25, 26 Dec & 1 Jan

ADMISSION PRICES
Single Attraction: Adult £5.95
Child (5+) £3.95 Family £15.95

CONTACT
Llangollen Exhibition Centre
Mill Street, Llangollen
Denbighshire LL20 8RX
Tel 01978 860584
Web www.dapol.co.uk

1 hr

Mar–Oct

Llangollen Motor Museum

Museum of Childhood Memories

1 hr

Mar–Nov

This small **museum** houses a collection of cars, motorcycles and memorabilia. The owners are ready to answer individual questions.

A **multiple award-winning museum** that celebrates the magic of childhood with thousands of toys, nursery furniture, games, money boxes, arcade machines and other ephemera. It is a nostalgic experience for adults and lots of fun for children.

LOCATION
1 mile from Llangollen on Horseshoepass Road & 10 miles from Wrexham

OPENING
Mar–Oct open Tue–Sun

ADMISSION PRICES
Adult £2.50 Family (2+3) £6
Senior £2

CONTACT
Llangollen Motor Museum
Llangollen
Pentrefelin
Denbighshire LL20 8EE
Tel 01978 860324
Web www.llangollenmotormuseum.co.uk

LOCATION
Leave the A55 after crossing Britannia Bridge. Turn right on the A545 & drive for 3 miles. Located opposite the castle

OPENING
Mar–Nov open 10.30am–5pm

ADMISSION PRICES
Adult £3.25 Child £2
Family £9.50

CONTACT
Museum of Childhood Memories, 1 Castle Street Beaumaris, Anglesey LL58 8AP
Tel 01248 712498

314

½ day

All year

Palace Fun Centre

Experience all the fun of the fair at the Palace Fun Centre.

★ Astroslide (25-ft drop slide)
★ Climbing canyon
★ Ballpond
★ Maze

LOCATION
From the A55 follow the signs for Rhyl. On the promenade opposite the paddling pool

OPENING
All year open daily 10am–10pm

ADMISSION PRICES
Please phone for details

CONTACT
Palace Fun Centre
38–45 West Parade
Rhyl LL18 1NG
Tel 01745 344446
Fax 01745 336502
Email palacefun@hbleisure.co.uk
Web www.hbleisure.co.uk

Penrhyn Castle

½ day

Mar–Nov

LOCATION
At the junction of the A55/A5 near Bangor, Gwynedd

OPENING
Jul & Aug castle open 11am–5pm, grounds & tearoom open 10am–5pm
Mar–Jun & Sep–Nov castle open 12pm–5pm, grounds & tearoom open 11am–5pm

ADMISSION PRICES
Adult £6 Child £3 Family (2+3) £15
National Trust members Free

CONTACT
Penrhyn Castle
Bangor
Gwynedd LL57 4HN
Tel 01248 353084
Email penrhyncastle@ntrust.org.uk

This fairy-tale castle will delight adults with its fine art collection, spectacular grand staircase and neo-Norman architecture. For children there is a wealth of special activities and events throughout the season, ranging from archery lessons to the Cowboys and Indians Fun Day.

★ Doll museum
★ Train museum
★ Family events
★ Children's guidebook
★ Touch screen computer quizzes
★ Orienteering course

Portmeirion

3 hrs

All year

A private village created by Clough Williams Ellis on the coast of Snowdonia with extensive woodland gardens. Built in a romantic, fairy-tale style, it has grottoes and cobbled squares. There is a sandy beach and playground for children.

LOCATION
Signposted from the A487 at Minffordd village between Penrhyndeudraeth & Porthmadog in Gwynedd

OPENING
All year open daily from 9.30am–5.30pm

ADMISSION PRICES
Adult £5.50 Child £2.70 Family (2+2) £13 Concession £4.40

CONTACT
Portmeirion
Gwynedd LL48 6ET
Tel 01766 772311
Web www.portmeirion-village.com

Rhiw Goch Ski Centre

Varied

All year

Children can learn to dry-ski at the Rhiw Goch Ski Centre. Mountain-biking is also available.

LOCATION
Take the A470 between Dolgellau & Porthmadog

OPENING
All year open daily except 25 Dec

ADMISSION PRICES
Please phone for details

CONTACT
Rhiw Goch Ski Centre
Bronabe, Trawsfynydd
Blaenau Ffestiniog LL41 4UR
Tel 01766 540578
Fax 01766 540305
Web www.logcabin-skiwales.co.u

2-3 hrs

All year

RSPB South Stack Nature Reserve

This popular reserve has a stunning coastline and rare maritime heathland. Seabirds can be viewed from Ellins Tower. Binoculars and telescopes are available for visitors to use.

★ Restaurant open in summer

★ Children's activities in Ellis Tower including underwater artwork, velcro fun-board and RSPB Wildlife Explorers Club

★ Events programme throughout the summer; Please contact the reserve for details

LOCATION
Three km west of Holyhead. Signposted from Holyhead & Trearddur Bay

OPENING
Reserve & car park: All year open daily
Ellins Tower: Easter–Sep open 11am–5pm

ADMISSION PRICES
Free

CONTACT
RSPB South Stack Cliffs Nature Reserve
Plas Nico, South Stack
Holyhead
Anglesey LL65 1YH
Tel 01407 764973
Email caroline.bateson@rspb.org.uk
Web www.rspb.org.uk

316

2½ hrs

Mar–Nov

Snowdon Mountain Railway

Travel on the only public rack and pinion railway in Britain to the summit of Snowdon – the tallest mountain in England and Wales. For those wishing to walk down, a single ticket to the summit station is available.

LOCATION
Operates from Llanberis station on the A4086, 7½ miles from Caernarfon

OPENING
Mid-Mar–first week of Nov open daily 9am–5pm

ADMISSION PRICES
Please phone for details

CONTACT
Snowdon Mountain Railway
Llanberis, Gwynedd LL55 4TY
Tel 0870 4580033
Web www.snowdonrailway.co.uk

Talyllyn Railway

2½ hrs

Easter–Nov

The railway operates a daily steam service from Easter to November and at Christmas. Its original locomotives still operate today. It climbs the steep Fathew Valley and stops at Dolgoch Falls and the Nant Gwernol Forest.

LOCATION
On the A493 at Tywyn

OPENING
Please phone for timetable

ADMISSION PRICES
Day rover ticket £9

CONTACT
Talyllyn Railway
Wharf Station, Neptune Road
Tywyn LL36 9EY
Tel 01654 710472
Fax 01654 711755
Email enquiries@talyllyn.co.uk
Web www.talyllyn.co.uk

Varies

May–Oct

Traws Pleasure Cruises

Traws Pleasure Cruises run cruises on Trawsfynydd Lake using an Amsterdam Water Bus with an experienced commentator on board for every trip.

LOCATION
10 miles south of Porthmadog on the A470. Traws & the Lake Visitor centre are signposted

OPENING
May–Oct; Please phone for details

ADMISSION PRICES
Please phone for details

CONTACT
Traws Pleasure Cruises
Rhyd-y-Felin, Trawsfynydd
Blaenau Ffestiniog LL41 4UU
Tel & Fax 01766 540375

The Welsh Mountain Zoo

All day

All year

A wildlife collection maintained in a natural environment. It has many attractions and activities for children.

★ Some disabled access
★ Children's farm
★ Jungle Adventureland
★ Sea lion feeding shows
★ Penguin Parade
★ Chimp Encounter Show

LOCATION
3 minutes from the A55 express-way Rhos-on-Sea exit. Signposted

OPENING
In summer open 9.30am–6pm (last admission 4.50pm); In winter open 9.30am–5pm (last admission 4pm)

ADMISSION PRICES
Adult £6.85 Child (3 yrs+) £4.60
Family £19.75 Student £4.60
Senior £5.60

CONTACT
Welsh Mountain Zoo
Old Highway, Colwyn Bay
Conwy LL28 5UY
Tel 01492 532938

317

Wepre Country Park

All day

All year

LOCATION
Signposted by brown tourist signs from the centre of Connah's Quay on the old A548 coast road

OPENING
Visitor centre open all year daily 9am–5pm

ADMISSION PRICES
Free

CONTACT
Flintshire Countryside Service – South Wepre Country Park Visitor Centre
Wepre Drive, Connah's Quay
Flintshire CH5 4HL
Tel 01244 814931
Email countryside@flintshire.gov.uk
Web www.flintshire.gov.uk

Recorded as 'forest' in the Doomsday Book, this country park is 1,000 years old and is a wonderful place to explore. Its visitor centre is open all year.

★ Guided walks
★ Family activities
★ Adventure playground

Scotland

With a mountainous, sparsely populated land, Scotland has Edinburgh as its historic capital and Glasgow as its largest city. To the north lie the Highlands, the Western Isles and Orkney, and to the west the large area known as Strathclyde. Fife and Aberdeenshire are to the east and to the south you'll find the Lothians, Dumfries and Galloway, and the Scottish Borders.

Edinburgh has many notable attractions, varying from Edinburgh Zoo, with over 1,000 animals, to the internationally acclaimed Royal Botanic Gardens. In Glasgow, you can visit the Clydebuilt Scottish Maritime Museum, where you can steer your own virtual ship. In Aberdeenshire, enjoy admiring Balmoral Castle, the Royal Family's holiday home. The Borders has the fascinating Satrosphere, a fun scientific exhibition with interactive displays for all the family. In Dumfries and Galloway, there is the fabulous Creetown Gemrock Museum, with it extensive display of gems, crystals and fossils, and a fascinating Camera Obscura. The Highlands celebrate their countryside and wildlife with attractions such as the Bella Jane Boat Trips off the Isle of Skye and the Highland Wildlife Park. In Strathclyde, you can take your family skiing at the Newmilns Dry Slope or visit country parks such as the Calderglen Country Park which has a children's zoo and playground.

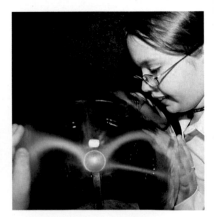

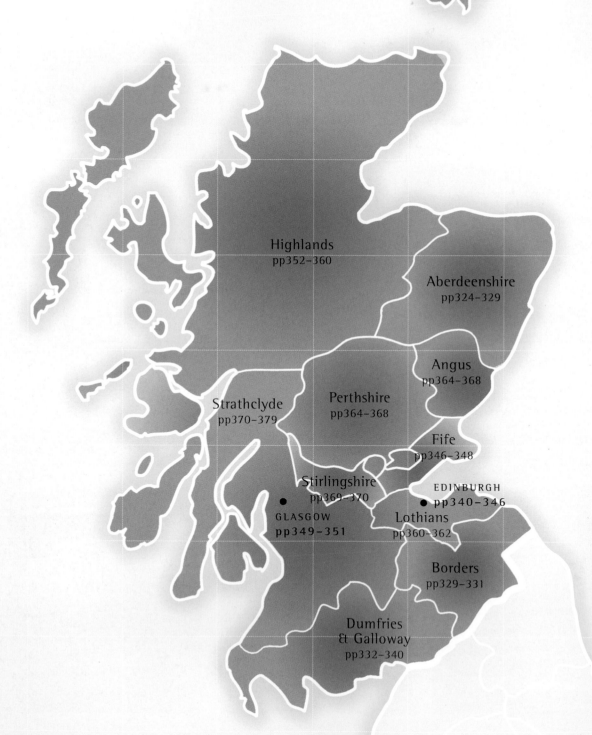

Orkney
pp362–364

Highlands
pp352–360

Aberdeenshire
pp324–329

Angus
pp364–368

Strathclyde
pp370–379

Perthshire
pp364–368

Fife
pp346–348

Stirlingshire
pp369–370

EDINBURGH
pp340–346

GLASGOW
pp349–351

Lothians
pp360–362

Borders
pp329–331

Dumfries
& Galloway
pp332–340

Below is a list of places to visit in the Scotland organised by county and type.

Aberdeenshire

HISTORIC BUILDINGS

MUSEUMS & EXHIBITIONS

SPORT & LEISURE

ANIMAL ATTRACTIONS

THEME PARKS & ADVENTURE PLAYGROUNDS

Borders

MUSEUMS & EXHIBITIONS

ANIMAL ATTRACTIONS

PARKS, GARDENS & NATURE TRAILS

Dumfries & Galloway

HISTORIC BUILDINGS

MUSEUMS & EXHIBITIONS

ANIMAL ATTRACTIONS

BOAT & TRAIN TRIPS

PARKS, GARDENS & NATURE TRAILS

THEME PARKS & ADVENTURE PLAYGROUNDS

Edinburgh

HISTORIC BUILDINGS

Fife

Glasgow

Highlands

Aberdeenshire Farming Museum

2 hrs

May–Oct

This farming museum is situated in a nineteenth-century farmhouse. Its collection of artefacts gives an insight into 200 years of farming and family life in Aberdeenshire.

★ Sensory garden   ★ Guided tours

LOCATION
1 mile west of Mintlaw on the A950

OPENING
May–Sep open daily 11am–4.30pm; Apr & Oct weekends only 12pm–4.30pm
Park open all year; Please phone for details

ADMISSION PRICES
Free

CONTACT
Aberdeenshire Farming Museum, Aden Country Park
Nr Mintlaw
Aberdeenshire AB42 5FQ
Tel 01771 622906

Balmoral Castle

3 Star Historic Attraction
Aberdeen and Grampian Tourist Board

1–2 hrs

Apr–Jul

For seven generations since 1852, Balmoral has been the Royal Family's holiday home. The public are invited to view certain areas including the ballroom, carriage room and art gallery.

LOCATION
Entrance to the driveway is off the A93 between Ballater & Braemar at Crathie on Royal Deeside

OPENING
Apr–Jul open daily 10am–5.30pm (last recommended admission 4pm)

ADMISSION PRICES
Adult £4.50 Child £1
Senior £3.50

CONTACT
Balmoral Estates
Crathie, Nr Ballater
Aberdeenshire AB35 5TB
Tel 01339 742334
Web www.balmoralcastle.com

Banff Museum

2 hrs

Jun–Sep

Silver, arms, armour, natural history and geology are all on display here. There are special exhibits on the nineteenth century and Thomas Edward, the Banff naturalist, as well as the eighteenth-century astronomer James Ferguson.

LOCATION
Located in Banff town centre off the A98

OPENING
Jun–Sep open Mon–Sat 2pm–4.30pm

ADMISSION PRICES
Free

CONTACT
Banff Museum
High Street
Banff AB45 1AE
Tel 01771 622906
Email andrew.hill@aberdeenshire.gov.uk

Beach Leisure Centre

All day

Varies

Relax at this leisure centre with pool and flumes, fitness studio, health suite, climbing wall and sports hall. There is also an adjoining ice arena.

LOCATION
Next to the beach at Aberdeen

OPENING
Please phone for details

ADMISSION PRICES
Please phone for details

CONTACT
Beach Leisure Centre
Beach Promenade
Aberdeen AB24 5NR
Tel 01224 647647
Fax 01224 648693
Web www.aberdeen.net.uk/fun-beach

Codona's Pleasure Fair

Varies

All year

Codona's amusement park is packed with over 30 sensational rides and attractions for all the family. There are fun children's rides and, for the white-knuckle fans, there's the giant Log Flume and 360 degree Looping Star Roller Coaster.

★ Dodgems

★ Guest rides

★ Indoor entertainment complex

★ Waltzers

★ Haunted house

5 Star Museum Attraction

Aberdeen and Grampian Tourist Board

Gordon Highlanders Museum

2 hrs+

All year

Relive the dramatic story of the Gordon Highlanders through the lives of the outstanding kilted soldiers of north-east Scotland.

★ Interactive displays

★ Handling areas

★ Gardens

★ Audio-visual displays

Varies

All year

Hayfield Riding Centre

Perfectly situated within the beautiful grounds of Hazlehead Park, Hayfield Riding Centre provides pleasure riding and tuition for riders of all standards.

★ Horses to ride

★ Two indoor schools

★ Cross-country course

★ Beautiful beach for horse-riding

★ Clubroom & gallery

★ Riding for the disabled centre

LOCATION
In the grounds of Hazlehead Park, close to Aberdeen

OPENING
Closed 24, 25, 26 Dec
Please phone for course details

ADMISSION PRICES
Please phone for details

CONTACT
Hayfield Riding Centre
Hazlehead Park
Aberdeen AB15 8BB
Tel 01224 315703
Fax 01224 313834
Email info@hayfield.com
Web www.hayfield.com

½ day

Apr–Sep

Leith Hall

The home of the Leith family from 1650, the mansion house contains interesting personal possessions and a military exhibition. The estate has a garden with two ponds, a bird hide, ice house, stables and several waymarked trails.

★ Guided ranger walks for children

★ Halloween events

★ Easter egg hunt

★ 'Build a scarecrow' sessions

LOCATION
On the B9002, 1 mile west of Kennethmont & 34 miles north-west of Aberdeen. Signposted off the A96

OPENING
Apr–Sep open Fri–Tue 12pm–5pm (last admission 4.15pm)

ADMISSION PRICES
Varies according to ticket type
Please phone for details

CONTACT
Leith Hall
Kennethmont
Huntly
Aberdeenshire AB54 4NQ
Tel 01464 831216
Web www.nts.org.uk

Macduff Marine Aquarium

2 hrs+

All year

ABERDEENSHIRE

LOCATION
A short walk from Macduff town centre, just east of the harbour. Reached via the A98, A947 or A96

OPENING
Please phone for details

ADMISSION PRICES
Please phone for details

CONTACT
Macduff Marine Aquarium
11 High Shore
Macduff
Banffshire AB44 1SL
Tel 01261 833369
Web www.marine-aquarium.com

Macduff Marine Aquarium is the most northerly of Scotland's aquaria and has several unique features, including the main tank which is open to the air.

★ Come & watch feeding times

★ Watch dive sessions

★ Children's quizzes

★ Audio-visual theatre

327

2 hrs

Bank hols

Maud Railway Museum

Northfield Farm Museum

1–2 hrs

May–Sep

Learn about the Great North of Scotland Railway in this interesting railway museum.

Come and enjoy looking at exhibits such as tractors, motor bikes, farm implements, household items and a Smiddy engineer's workshop.

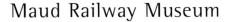

LOCATION
In the village of Maud on the B9029

OPENING
Open Bank holiday Mon
12.30pm–5pm

ADMISSION PRICES
Please phone for details

CONTACT
Maud Railway Museum
Maud
By Peterhead
Aberdeen AB42 5LY
Tel 01771 622906
Email andrew.hill@aberdeen-shire.gov.uk

LOCATION
10 miles south-west of Fraserburgh, just off the A98

OPENING
May–Sep open daily
11am–5.30pm

ADMISSION PRICES
Adult £1.50 Child £1.50
Senior £1.50

CONTACT
Northfield Farm Museum
New Pitsligo
Nr Fraserburgh
Aberdeenshire
Tel 01771 653504

The Old Royal Station

3 hrs
All year

This renovated railway station features royalty and railway exhibitions with commentary and audio-visual presentations about Royal Deeside.

4 Star Speciality Attraction
Aberdeen and Grampian Tourist Board

LOCATION
In the centre of the picturesque Deeside village of Ballater, on the A93 Aberdeen–Braemar road

OPENING
Please phone for details

ADMISSION PRICES
Please phone for details

CONTACT
The Aberdeen & Grampian Tourist Board
27 Albyn Place
Aberdeen AB10 1YL
Tel 01224 288817
Fax 01224 581367
Email ballater@agtb.ossian.net

Peterhead Maritime Heritage Centre

1–2 hrs
Jun, Jul, Aug

This maritime heritage centre offers a historic look back in time at the Peterhead experience of Whaling and gives an insight into the oil industry.

4 Star Speciality Attraction
Aberdeen and Grampian Tourist Board

LOCATION
Overlooking Peterhead Bay & beside the beach and marina. Reached via the A90 or A950

OPENING
Please phone for details

ADMISSION PRICES
Please phone for details

CONTACT
Peterhead Maritime Heritage Centre
South Road
Peterhead
Aberdeenshire AB42 2YP
Tel 01779 473000

Satrosphere

2 hrs+
All year

4 Star Speciality Attraction
Aberdeen and Grampian Tourist Board

Fun for families and for grown-ups who love to explore, experiment and find out how the world works. Look into infinity, light up a plasma dome, step inside a bubble or see pink elephants – it's all possible at Satrosphere.

★ Find out about food & farming
★ Milking exhibit
★ Visit the wormery
★ Explore the world of ants, slugs & snails
★ Interactive shows
★ Workshops
★ Special events

LOCATION
Off Beach Boulevard & Links Road near to the Patio Hotel

OPENING
All year open Mon–Sat 10am–5pm, Sun 11.30am–5pm

ADMISSION PRICES
Adult £5 Child £3 Under-3s Free
Concession £3

CONTACT
Satrosphere
The Tramsheds
179 Constitution Street
Aberdeen AB24 5TU
Tel 01224 640340
Email Satrosphere@satrosphere.net
Web www.satrosphere.net

Storybook Glen

All day

All year

This **28-acre family theme park** has over 100 life-sized models set in beautifully landscaped gardens.

★ 20 acres of scenic beauty

★ Old Macdonald's farmhouse

★ Wildlife nature study

LOCATION
In Maryculter, just off South Deeside Road, 5 miles west of Aberdeen

OPENING
1 Mar–31 Oct open daily 10am–6pm (last admission 4pm); Nov–28 Feb open Sat & Sun 11am–4pm

ADMISSION PRICES
Please phone for details

CONTACT
Storybook Glen
South Deeside Road
Aberdeen
Tel 01224 732941
www.activitypoint.co.uk

Coldstream

½ day
All year

The seat of the Home family, it has interesting grounds with a museum, craft centre and nature trails along a lake and into woodland.

LOCATION
15 miles from Berwick-upon-Tweed on the A698

OPENING
Garden & Grounds: Open all year dawn–dusk
Museum: Open all year Mon–Fri 10am–5pm, Sat-Sun 12pm–5pm

ADMISSION PRICES
Free; Car park charge

CONTACT
Coldstream
Douglas & Angus Estates
Horsel TD12 4LP
Tel 01890 882834

Devil's Porridge Exhibition

3 hrs

All year

An amazing exhibition that tells the secret story of a great munitions factory and the people involved in its fascinating history.

★ Not suitable for children under 7 years

★ Working model locomotive

★ Simulated military entrenchment

LOCATION
Heading south from Glasgow, leave the A74 (M) motorway at Eaglesfield & follow signs for Annan & Eastriggs

OPENING
All year open Wed–Sat 10am–4pm & Sun 12pm–4pm

ADMISSION PRICES
Adult 70p Child Free

CONTACT
Devil's Porridge Exhibition
St John's Church, Dunedin Road
Eastriggs, Annan
Tel 01461 40460
Web devilsporridge.co.uk

Drumlanrig's Tower

2 hrs
All year

4 Star Museum
Scottish Borders Tourist Board

Drumlanrig's Tower interprets Hawick's turbulent history from medieval times, using the latest audio-visual technology. The exhibition is housed in beautifully restored period building.

LOCATION
South of Selkirk on the A7 & west of Jedburgh on the A698

OPENING
Please phone for details

ADMISSION PRICES
Under-16s Free; Please phone for details

CONTACT
Drumlanrig's Tower
Wilton Lodge
Wilton Lodge Park
Hawick
Roxburgh TD9 7JL
Tel 01450 373457

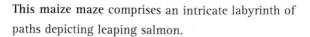

Fishwick Mains Amazing Maize Maze

2 hrs+
Varies

This maize maze comprises an intricate labyrinth of paths depicting leaping salmon.

★ Bouncy castle
★ Outdoor play area
★ Jungle theme puzzle

LOCATION
On the north bank of the River Tweed, 4 miles west of the Berwick-upon-Tweed bypass. 1 mile off the B6461

OPENING
Please phone for details

ADMISSION PRICES
Under-5s Free; Please phone for details of other prices

CONTACT
Fishwick Mains, Nr Paxton Berwick-upon-Tweed Berwickshire TD15 1XQ
Tel 01289 386111
Email fish@fishwickmaze.com

Halliwell's House Museum & Robson Gallery

1 hr+
Easter–Oct

This museum has an interesting permanent exhibition of a recreated ironmonger's shop, as well as temporary exhibitions of visual arts and crafts and local history.

★ Guided tours   ★ Video presentations

LOCATION
On the main A7 south of Edinburgh

OPENING
Easter–31 Oct open Mon–Sat 10am–5pm, Sun 2pm–4pm; Jul–Aug open Mon–Sat 10am–5.30pm, Sun 2pm–5pm

ADMISSION PRICES
Please phone for details

CONTACT
Halliwell's House Museum & Robson Gallery
High Street, Selkirk Selkirkshire TD7 4JX
Tel 01750 20096
Fax 01750 23282
Email iabrown@scotborders.gov.uk

Harestanes Visitor Centre

3 hrs
All year

This visitor centre has lots of events, exhibitions and walks for all the family and the biggest playpark in the Borders.

LOCATION
5 km north of Jedburgh. Well-signposted from the A68, A698 & B6400

OPENING
Please phone for details

ADMISSION PRICES
Please phone for details

CONTACT
Harestanes Countryside Visitor Centre
Ancrum
Jedburgh TD8 6UQ
Tel 01835 830306
Email harestanes@scotborders.gov.uk

Jedburgh Castle Jail & Museum

1–2 hrs
Easter–Oct

3 Star Museum Attraction
Scottish Borders Tourist Board

A nineteenth-century reform prison with displays interpreting the history of Jedburgh.

★ Guided tours   ★ Outdoor play area

LOCATION
On the A68, south-east of Selkirk

OPENING
Please phone for details

ADMISSION PRICES
Please phone for details

CONTACT
Jedburgh Castle Jail & Museum
Wilton Lodge
Wilton Lodge Park
Hawick
Roxburgh TD9 7JL
Tel 01450 373457

Jedforest Deer & Farm Park

3 hrs+

WC

May–Oct

LOCATION
5 miles south of Jedburgh on the A68

OPENING
May–Aug open 10am–5.30pm; Sep–Oct
open 11am–4.30pm

ADMISSION PRICES
Please phone for details

CONTACT
Jedforest Deer & Farm Park
Mervinslaw Estate
Jedburgh
Roxburghshire TD8 8PL
Tel 01835 840364
Fax 01835 840362
Web www.aboutscotland.com/jedforest/

At this modern working farm
you can see deer herds and rare
breeds as well as your favourite
farm animals.

★ Hands-on interpretation barn
★ Birds of prey displays & tuition
★ Ranger-led activities & walks
★ Nature trails
★ Crazy golf
★ Feeding the animals

331

---

2 hrs

Mar–Nov

Mary Queen of Scots Visitor Centre

This visitor centre tells the story of the life of
the tragic Queen, who herself visited Jedburgh in
1556, staying in Wilton Lodge formerly owned by
the Kerr Family.

LOCATION
On the A7 south of Selkirk

OPENING
Mar–mid Nov open daily
10am–5pm

ADMISSION PRICES
Under-16s Free; Phone for
details of other prices

CONTACT
Mary Queen of Scots
Visitor Centre
Wilton Lodge
Wilton Lodge Park
Hawick
Roxburgh TD9 7JL
Tel 01450 373457

Three Hills Roman Heritage Centre

2 Star Historic Attraction
Scottish Borders Tourist Board

2 hrs

Apr–Oct

A modern exhibition of life on the Scottish Roman
frontier. There are artefacts, models, replicas, an
audioguide and guided site walks.

LOCATION
In Melrose on the A6091

OPENING
Apr–31 Oct open daily
10.30am–4.30pm

ADMISSION PRICES
Under-5s Free; Please phone for
details of other prices

CONTACT
Three Hills Roman
Heritage Centre
Cockleroi Newstead
Melrose
Roxburghshire TD6 9DE
Tel 01896 822651/822463
Email secretary@trimontium.
freeserve.co.uk

Barholm Mains Open Farm

2 hrs

Varies

Castledykes Park & Gardens

Varies

All year

At **Barholm Farm** there are lots of animals on show, from traditional farm animals to rheas, water buffalo and llamas.

2 Star Wildlife & Nature Attraction
Dumfries and Galloway Tourist Board

A **public park and gardens** with a children's play area.

LOCATION
In Creetown on the A75 south of Newton Stewart

OPENING
Please phone for details

ADMISSION PRICES
Please phone for details

CONTACT
Barholm Mains Open Farm
Barholm Mains
Creetown
Dumfries & Galloway DG8 7EN
Tel 01671 820346

LOCATION
Next to the River Nith in Dumfries

OPENING
Please phone for details

ADMISSION PRICES
Please phone for details

CONTACT
Mr Chris Cook
Municipal Chambers
Buccleuch Street
Dumfries
Dumfries & Galloway DG1 2AD
Tel 01387 245916
Fax 01387 267225

4 hrs

All year

Cream O'Galloway

A **natural experience for the whole family,** in which you can enjoy the adventure playground, nature trails, beautiful scenery and dog walk.

★ Stray Play straw bale play area

★ Family activity days

★ Guided walks

★ Education programmes

★ Children's club

★ Farm tours

LOCATION
In the south-west of Scotland. From the A75 near Gatehouse-of-Fleet, take the road to Sandgreen. Turn left after 1½ miles

OPENING
Apr–Oct open daily; Nov–Mar open weekends only
Please phone for details

ADMISSION PRICES
Adventure playground £2

CONTACT
Cream O'Galloway
Rainton
Gatehouse-of-Fleet
Castle Douglas DG7 2DR
Tel 01557 814040
Email info@creamogalloway.co.uk
Web www.creamogalloway.co.uk

Creetown Exhibition Centre

DUMFR'S & GALLOWAY

2 hrs

Easter–Oct

WC

LOCATION
500 yards off the A75 between Gatehouse-of-Fleet & Newton Stewart

OPENING
Easter–Oct open 11am–4pm
Opening days vary; please phone for details

ADMISSION PRICES
Please phone for details

CONTACT
Creetown Exhibition Centre
16 St John Street
Creetown
Dumfries & Galloway DG8 7JF
Tel 01671 820343
Web www.scotland-creetown.com/

An exhibition of Creetown past and present, shown through a large collection of historical photographs, artefacts, audio and video presentations and hands-on activities.

★ History of the quarries
★ Sculptures
★ Fishing, mining & farming exhibitions
★ War-time memorabilia

★ Wigtown Bay nature reserve
★ Local arts & crafts
★ Activities to suit children of all ages

333

Creetown Gemrock Museum

2 hrs

WC

Feb–Dec

4 Star Museum
Scottish Tourist Boards

LOCATION
7 miles from Newton Stewart, 11 miles from Gatehouse-of-Fleet, just off the A75

OPENING
Open all year except Jan
Please phone for details

ADMISSION PRICES
Adult £3.25 Child £1.75 Family £8.25
Senior £2.75

CONTACT
Creetown Gemrock Museum
The Stephenson Family
Chain Road
Creetown DG8 7HJ
Tel 0845 4560245
Email gem.rock@btinternet.com

Creetown Gemrock Museum has a fantastic collection of gemstones, crystals, minerals and fossils. There is a fascinating volcanic eruption display, a fossilised dinosaur egg and meteorites from outer space. Visitors can watch experts cutting stones in the lapidary workshop.

1 hr

Apr–Sep

Dalbeattie Museum Trust

This museum gives an insight into what we used in the past. Visitors can view and handle household utensils, agriculture, quarrying and bobbin-making tools. Historic industries are depicted in pictures and old-fashioned children's games can be enjoyed by the family.

LOCATION
Just off the High Street, Dalbeattie is on the corner of Southwick Road & High Street in the town centre

OPENING
Apr–Sep open Mon–Sat 10am–4pm, Sun 2pm–4pm

ADMISSION PRICES
Adult £1 Accompanied Child Free
Senior 50p

CONTACT
Dalbeattie Museum Trust
231 High Street
Dalbeattie
Dumfries & Galloway DG5 4DW
Tel 01556 610437

1 hr+

Varies

David Coulthard Museum & Pitstop Diner

An exhibition of David Coulthard memorabilia from his go-karting days through to Formula 1. The collection includes cars, trophies, race-suits and more.

LOCATION
In the village of Twynholm, near Kirkcudbright just off the A75

OPENING
Please phone for details

ADMISSION PRICES
Please phone for details

CONTACT
David Coulthard Museum
Burnbrae
Twynholm
Kirkcudbright
Dumfries & Galloway
DG6 4NU
Tel 01557 860050

Dock Park

½ day

All year

Enjoy this public park with children's play area and recreation facilities.

LOCATION
Next to the River Nith in Dumfries

OPENING
Please phone for details

ADMISSION PRICES
Free

CONTACT
Dock Park
Municipal Chambers
Buccleuch Street
Dumfries
Dumfries & Galloway DG1 2AD
Tel 01387 245916

Dumfries & Galloway Aviation Museum

3 hrs

WC

Easter–Oct

A fascinating collection of aircraft and memorabilia reaching back to the golden era of flight.

★ 3-storey wartime control tower
★ Garden
★ Huge collection of artefacts
★ Aircraft engine collection
★ Video presentations
★ Guided tours

335

---

4 Star Award
Scottish Tourist Board

Dumfries Museum & Camera Obscura

1–2 hrs

WC

All year

Set in its own gardens, Dumfries Museum and Camera Obscura is situated in a converted windmill. From the camera you can see a panoramic view of Dumfries. The museum is a treasure house of history in Dumfries and Galloway.

★ Children's worksheets available

Galloway Deer Range

1–2 hrs
All year

Visitors can walk amongst and handle the red deer, as well as taking close-up photographs.

LOCATION	CONTACT
On the outskirts of New Galloway	**Galloway Deer Range**
	Laggan O Dee
OPENING	New Galloway
Please phone for details	Dumfries & Galloway DG7 3SQ
	Tel 0860 853351
ADMISSION PRICES	
Please phone for details	

King Robert The Bruce's Cave

1 hr
Varies

This world-famous ancient monument marks the site where King Robert The Bruce hid in a cave during the wars of independence.

★ Children's play area   ★ Fishing

★ Cycling   ★ Walking

LOCATION	ADMISSION PRICES
Turn off the A74, 3 miles north of Gretna at a sign for Kirkpatrick Fleming turn into the village & follow all signs to Bruce's Cave	Under-5s Free
	Please phone for other prices
	CONTACT
	King Robert The Bruce's Cave
	Cove Lodge, Kirkpatrick Fleming
OPENING	Dumfries & Galloway DG11 3AT
Please phone for details	Tel 01461 800285

Kirkcudbright River Trips

Varies
Spring–Sum

Take a trip on the Lovely Nellie, a specially designed river trip vessel equipped with all necessary safety equipment. Take in views of the local landscape and the bay and travel up the river and enjoy a varied selection of wildlife.

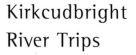

LOCATION	ADMISSION PRICES
In Kirkcudbright Harbour, off the A75	Prices vary
	Please phone for details
OPENING	**CONTACT**
Trips daily in spring & summer	**Kirkcudbright River Trips**
Times vary according to tides	10 Holroyd Road, Kirkcudbright
Please phone for details	Dumfries & Galloway DG6 4HR
	Tel 01557 331684

Monreith Animal World

3 hrs
Mar–Oct

A wildlife haven, this park has Asian otters, beavers, reptiles, degu guinea pigs, rabbits, rheas, poultry, ducks, pygmy goats, cattle, sheep and chipmunks.

★ Not suitable for under-14s   ★ Feed the beavers

★ Hands-on talks

LOCATION	CONTACT
On the A747 between Port William & Whithorn	**Monreith Animal World**
	Monreith
OPENING	Newton Stewart
End Mar–Oct open 10am–5pm	Wigtownshire DG8 8NQ
	Tel 01988 700217
ADMISSION PRICES	
Please phone for details	

Moonstone Miniatures

A **display of model** stately homes, houses and shops built to 1:12 scale, all imaginatively and lavishly furnished.

Neverland Adventure Play Centre

Neverland is a children's adventure play centre for children up to age 10. Themed on J. M. Barrie's story of Peter Pan, children can meet all their favourite characters.

LOCATION
Near the crossroads of Kirkpatrick Durham, 1½ miles from Springholm Village on the A75 & 4 miles from Castle Douglas

OPENING
1 May–17 Sep open Wed–Fri 10am–9pm
At other times please phone first

ADMISSION PRICES
Under-5s Free
Please phone for other prices

CONTACT
Moonstone Miniatures
4 Victoria Street
Kirkpatrick Durham
Castle Douglas
Kirkcudbrightshire DG7 3HQ
Tel 01556 650313

LOCATION
In Dumfries town centre, reached via the A75, A76, A701 or the A74 (M)

OPENING
Please phone for details

ADMISSION PRICES
Please phone for details

CONTACT
Neverland Adventure
Play Centre
Park Lane
Dumfries
Dumfriesshire DG1 2AX
Tel 01387 249100

337

Old Bridge House Museum

3 Star Award
Scottish Tourist Board

Visit Dumfries' oldest house, now a museum of everyday life. You can see the family kitchen, nursery and bedroom of a Victorian home and pay a visit to an early dentist's surgery.

★ Worksheets for children

Robert Burns Centre

4 Star Award
Scottish Tourist Board

Situated in an old mill building, this museum is dedicated to the poet Robert Burns.

★ Worksheets for children with small reward on completion
★ Children's play area
★ Film theatre

LOCATION
At the end of the Old Bridge on the Maxwelltown bank of the River Nith

OPENING
Apr–Sep open Mon–Sat 10am–5pm & Sun 2pm–5pm

ADMISSION PRICES
Free

CONTACT
Old Bridge House Museum
Mill Road
Dumfries DG2 7BE
Tel 01387 256904
Web www.dumgal.gov.uk/museum

LOCATION
On Mill Road by the River Nith at the Old Wear on Maxwelltown Bank

OPENING
In summer open Mon–Sat 10am–8pm & Sun 2pm–5pm;
In winter open Tue–Sat 10am–1pm & 2pm–5pm

ADMISSION PRICES
Free; Audio-visual show £1.50
Concession 75p

CONTACT
Robert Burns Centre
Mill Road
Dumfries DG2 7BE
Tel 01387 264808
Web www.dumgal.gov.uk

1 hr

All year

Robert Burns House

This is the house in which the famous poet Robert Burns died. It has been preserved in its original condition and contains many original artefacts and manuscripts.

★ Children's worksheets available, with reward given for completion

★ Audio tour available

LOCATION
Burns Street, off Shakespeare Street, next to Brooms Road car park

OPENING
In summer open Mon–Sat 10am–5pm & Sun 2pm–5pm; In winter open Tue–Sat 10am–1pm, 2pm–5pm

ADMISSION PRICES
Free

CONTACT
Robert Burns House
Burns Street
Dumfries DG1 2PS
Tel 01387 255297

3 hrs

Apr–Oct

Shambellie House Museum of Costume

4 Star Museum Attraction
Dumfries and Galloway Tourist Board

Step back in time and experience Victorian and Edwardian grace, elegance and refinement in this museum of costume. Original costumes are displayed in appropriate room settings.

★ Regular events for children   ★ Bridal bedroom exhibition

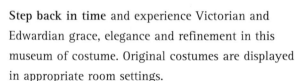

LOCATION
7 miles south of Dumfries on A710, Solway Coast Road

OPENING
Apr–Oct open Mon–Sun 11am–5pm

ADMISSION PRICES
Adult £2.50 Under-16s Free
Concession £1.50

CONTACT
Shambellie House Museum of Costume
New Abbey
Dumfries
Dumfriesshire DG2 8HQ
Tel 01387 850375
Fax 01387 850461
Web www.nms.ac.uk

Sophie's Puppenstube & Doll's House Museum

3 Star Museum
Dumfries and Galloway Tourist Board

2 hrs

All year

This museum houses an exhibition of over 50 doll houses and their inhabitants, from home and abroad. The shop sells miniatures, gifts and collectable porcelain dolls.

LOCATION
In Newton Stewart on the A714, about ½ mile from the A75

OPENING
Please phone for details

ADMISSION PRICES
Adult £2.50 Child £1.50

Family £6.50 Senior £2

CONTACT
Sophie's Puppenstube & Doll's House Museum
29 Queen Street
Newton Stewart
Wigtownshire DG8 6JR
Tel & Fax 01671 403344

2 hrs

All year

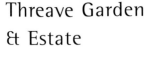

Threave Garden & Estate

A **garden for all seasons**, best known for its spring-time display of daffodils. Herbaceous beds are colourful in summer and the trees and heather striking in autumn.

★ Visitor centre with exhibitions

LOCATION	CONTACT
Castle Douglas	**Threave Garden & Estate**
OPENING	Castle Douglas
All year open Mon–Sun	Tel 0131 2439300
9.30am–5.30pm	Fax 0131 2439302
ADMISSION PRICES	
Please phone for details	

Tolbooth Museum

1 hr

Apr–Sep

A **museum that charts** the life of ordinary Upper Nithsdale people. It has an exhibition recreating life in a local jail and displays tell the story of the mines and the local knitting tradition of Sanquhar.

★ Audio-visual presentation   ★ Museum trail

LOCATION	CONTACT
At the end of the High Street in	**Tolbooth Museum**
St. Sanquhar town centre	High Street
OPENING	St Sanquhar GD4 6BN
Apr–Sep open Tue–Sat	Tel 01659 50186
10am–1pm, 2pm–5pm & Sun	Web www.dumgal.gov.uk/muse-ums
2pm–5pm	
ADMISSION PRICES	
Free	

339

Wildfowl & Wetlands Trust, Caerlaverock

1 day

All year

LOCATION
Located 9 miles south-east of Dumfries along the Solway Coast Heritage Trail
OPENING
Open all year daily 10am–5pm; Closed 25 Dec
ADMISSION PRICES
Adult £4 Child £2.50 Under-4s Free
CONTACT
WWT Caerlaverock
Eastpark Farm
Caerlaverock
Dumfriesshire DG1 4RS
Tel 01387 770200
Email caerlaverock@wwt.org.uk
Web www.wwt.org.uk

Caerlaverock has a 1,400 acre wild nature reserve with modern hides and observation towers linked by a network of screened approaches. There are seasonal nature trails.

★ Barnacle geese & whooper swans in winter
★ Migrating songbirds in summer
★ Rare amphibians
★ Summer & evening events
★ Guided walks
★ Binocular hire
★ Self-catering accommodation available
★ Badger watching

2 hrs

All year

The World Famous Old Blacksmiths Shop Centre

4 Star Speciality Attraction
Dumfries and Galloway Tourist Board

Explore the Gretna Green story exhibition and discover the romance and intrigue surrounding this romantic Scottish village.

★ Re-enactments & live performances

★ Outdoor play area for children

★ Video presentations

LOCATION
Off the M74, on the England/Scotland Border

OPENING
1 Apr–30 Jun Mon–Sun 9am–6pm; 1 Jul–31 Aug Mon–Sun 9am–8pm; 1 Oct–31 Mar Mon–Sun 9am–5.30pm

ADMISSION PRICES
Adult £1.50 Under-12s Free

CONTACT
The World Famous Old Blacksmiths Shop Centre
Headless Cross
Gretna Green
Gretna
Dumfriesshire DG16 5EA
Tel 01461 338441
Fax 01461 338442
Email info@gretnagreen.com
Web www.gretnagreen.com

340

4 hrs

All year

Bedlam Paintball Edinburgh

The ultimate adrenalin rush can be found at Bedlam Paintball. Be prepared to utilise tactics, teamwork and quick-thinking as you experience any one of the five game scenarios available here.

★ Other venues at Glasgow & Edzell

LOCATION
If travelling from Edinburgh, Fife, Falkirk, Stirling, Livingston & the surrounding areas, Bedlam is off the A8000

OPENING
Open daily 9am–12pm & 1pm–4pm

ADMISSION PRICES
£30 per person

CONTACT
Bedlam Edinburgh
Milton Wood
Dundas Estate
South Queensferry
Edinburgh
Tel 07000 233526
Email info@bedlam.co.uk
Web www.bedlam.co.uk

The Britannia Experience

1–2 hrs

All year

LOCATION
Leith, north Edinburgh. Follow signs to Leith & Ocean Terminal

OPENING
Apr–Sep open 9.30am–4.30pm; Jan–Mar & Oct–Dec open 10am–3.30pm; Closed 25 Dec & 1 Jan

ADMISSION PRICES
Adult £8 Child £4 Family £20 Senior £6

CONTACT
The Britannia Experience
Ocean Terminal
Leith
Edinburgh EH6 6JJ
Tel 0131 5555566
Email enquiries@tryb.co.uk
Web www.royalyachtbritannia.co.uk

The Britannia Experience starts in the visitor centre where you can discover her fascinating story. Then step aboard her for a self-led audio tour, giving a unique insight into what life was like on board.

★ Children's audio handset available

---

3 Star Wildlife Attraction
Edinburgh and Lothians Tourist Board

Edinburgh Butterfly & Insect World

3 hours

All year

LOCATION
3 miles south of Edinburgh city centre on the A702. Just off the Edinburgh city bypass, the A720 at the Gilmerton exit

OPENING
In summer open daily 9.30am–5.30pm; In winter 10am–5pm; Closed 25, 26 Dec & 1 Jan

ADMISSION PRICES
Under-3s Free
Please phone for details of other prices

CONTACT
Edinburgh Butterfly & Insect World
Dobbies Garden World
Lasswade
Edinburgh EH18 1AZ
Tel 0131 6634932
Email info@edinburgh-butterfly-world.co.uk

Walk through an indoor tropical rain forest inhabited by thousands of the world's most beautiful butterflies.

★ Bugs & Beasties section

★ Reptile rooms

★ Meet the Beasties handling sessions

★ Indoor tropical rain forest

★ Minibeast exhibition

Edinburgh Castle

5 Star Historic Attraction
Edinburgh and Lothians Tourist Board

2 hrs

All year

Known throughout the world, this magnificent castle is Edinburgh's top tourist attraction.

★ Scottish Crown Jewels exhibition

★ The Stone of Destiny

★ Mons Meg cannon

LOCATION
Edinburgh city centre

OPENING
Apr–Sep open daily 9.30am–6pm; Oct–Mar daily 9.30am–5pm; Closed 25, 25 Dec

ADMISSION PRICES
Adult £7 Child £2
Under-5s Free

CONTACT
Travel Trade Team
Historic Scotland, Longmore House, Salisbury Place
Edinburgh EH9 1SH
Tel 0131 2259846
Email
hs.explorer@scotland.gsi.gov.uk

Edinburgh Classic Tour

Varies

All year

Join the buses on regular tours of this historic capital city with commentary provided. See the sights of this beautiful city from open-top buses.

3 Star Historic Attraction
Edinburgh and Lothians Tourist Board

LOCATION
Edinburgh city centre

OPENING
Please phone for timetable details

ADMISSION PRICES
Under-2s Free; Please phone for details of other prices

CONTACT
Edinburgh Classic Tour
LRT Coach Hire
27 Hanover Street
Edinburgh EH2 2DL
Tel 0131 5544494
Fax 0131 2257857

---

3 hrs

All year

Edinburgh Dungeon

4 Star Speciality Attraction
Edinburgh and Lothians Tourist Board

An indoor attraction depicting the darkest chapters of Scottish history. The Dungeon blends horror and humour to represent Scotland's bloody past.

★ Actors bring history to life   ★ Scary tableaux

★ Horror rides

LOCATION
Edinburgh city centre

OPENING
Open daily 10am–6pm; Closed 25 Dec

ADMISSION PRICES
Under-4s Free; Please phone for details of other prices

CONTACT
Edinburgh Dungeon
31 Market Street
Edinburgh
Tel 0131 2401000
Fax 0131 5566700/2401002
Email marketing@merlin-entertainments.com

Edinburgh Zoo

5 hrs+

All year

Enjoy a wild day out at this large wildlife attraction. It has over 1,000 wonderful animals – furry, feathery and scaly – from all over the world, including many endangered species.

★ Penguin Parade daily   ★ Hilltop Safari

LOCATION
10 minutes west of Edinburgh city centre, on the A8 towards Glasgow

OPENING
Apr–Sep open 9am–6pm; Oct–Mar open 9am–5pm; Nov & Feb open 9am–4.30pm

ADMISSION PRICES
Adult £7.50 Child £4.50
Family £22

CONTACT
Edinburgh Zoo
Corstorphine Road
Edinburgh EH12 6TS
Tel 0131 3349171
Web www.edinburghzoo.org.uk

Elgin Cathedral

2 hrs

All year

EDINBURGH

4 Star Historic Site Attraction
Edinburgh and Lothians Tourist Board

LOCATION
Elgin, on the A96

OPENING
Apr–Sep open daily 9.30am–6.30pm;
Oct–Mar open Mon–Sat 9.30am–4.30pm &
Sun 2pm–4.30pm; Closed Thurs pm & Fri
in winter & 25, 26 Dec

ADMISSION PRICES
Adult £2.50 Child £1

CONTACT
Elgin Cathedral
Longmore House
Salisbury Place
Edinburgh EH9 1SH
Tel 0131 6688800
Fax 0131 6688888
Email hs.explorer@scotland.gov.uk

The superb remains of a majestic and beautiful thirteenth-century cathedral which was almost destroyed in 1390 by Alexander Stewart, the infamous Wolf of Badenoch. You can also visit the bishop's home at Spynie Palace, two miles north of the town.

★ Re-enactments & live performances
★ Explore the magnificent West Towers

343

---

2 hrs

All year

The Granton Centre

In this major store for the National Museums of Scotland, you will discover thousands of weird and wonderful objects under one roof.

★ Classic motorbikes   ★ Ancient pottery
★ Massive turbines   ★ Moby the Whale bones

LOCATION
Off the A8 & the A902

OPENING
Tours every Tue at 10am &
2.30pm

ADMISSION PRICES
Under-12s Free. Visits must be
booked in advance. Booking fee
£1 per visitor

CONTACT
The Granton Centre
242 West Granton Road
Edinburgh EH5 1JA
Tel 0131 2474470
Fax 0131 5514106

Museum of Childhood

2 hrs

All year

This museum holds memories of everything you can imagine to do with childhood. The collection includes teddy bears and dolls, clothes and even castor oil.

LOCATION
City Art Centre, Edinburgh city
centre

OPENING
Please phone for details

ADMISSION PRICES
Please phone for details

CONTACT
Museum of Childhood
City Art Centre
High Street
Edinburgh
Tel 0131 5297903
Email daviecharles@hotmail.com

All day
All year

National War Museum of Scotland

The museum explores the Scottish experience of war and military service over the last 400 years.

★ Uniforms, insignia & equipment
★ Orders, decorations & medals
★ Fine decorative art
★ Documents & photographs
★ Weapons

LOCATION
Edinburgh Castle, Edinburgh city centre

OPENING
Apr–Oct open daily 9.45am– 5.30pm;
Nov–Mar open daily 9.45am–4.45pm

ADMISSION PRICES
Adult £7.50 Child £2

Senior £5.50

CONTACT
National War Museum of Scotland
Edinburgh Castle
Edinburgh EH1 2NG
Tel 0131 2257534
Email info@nms.ac.uk

3 hrs+

All year

Our Dynamic Earth

5 Star Speciality Attraction
Edinburgh and Lothians Tourist Board

A fantastic journey of discovery using dramatic special effects and state-of-the-art interactives that takes you from the beginning of time to the future.

LOCATION
At the foot of the Royal Mile, close to the Palace of Holyrood in Edinburgh city centre

OPENING
31 Mar–Nov open daily 10am–6pm; Nov–Mar open 10am–5pm (last admission 3.50pm); Phone for details of Christmas opening

ADMISSION PRICES
Adult £7.95 Child £4.50
Senior £4.50

CONTACT
Our Dynamic Earth
Holyrood Road
Edinburgh EH8 8AS
Tel 0131 5507800
Email enquiries@dynamicearth.co.uk
Web www.dynamicearth.co.uk

The People's Story

2 Star Museum Attraction
Edinburgh and Lothians Tourist Board

1–2 hrs
All year

This museum tells the story of the lives, work and leisure of the ordinary people of Edinburgh from the late eighteenth century to the present day.

★ Video presentation
★ Located in a sixteenth-century tolbooth

LOCATION
In the Canongate Tolbooth, towards the foot of the Royal Mile

OPENING
All year open Mon–Sun 10am–5pm & Sun 2pm–5pm during the Edinburgh Festival

ADMISSION PRICES
Free

CONTACT
The People's Story
163 Canongate
Edinburgh EH8 8BN
Tel 0131 5294057
Fax 0131 5563439

Royal Botanic Garden Edinburgh

2 hrs

All year

LOCATION
Off the A902, 1 mile north of the city, with entrances off Inverleith Row (Eastgate) & Arboretum Place (West Gate)

OPENING
Apr–Sep open daily 10am–7pm; Nov–Feb open daily 10am–4pm; Mar & Oct open daily 10am–6pm; Closed 25 Dec & 1 Jan

ADMISSION PRICES
Free

CONTACT
Royal Botanic Garden Edinburgh
20a Inverleith Row
Edinburgh EH3 5HR
Tel 0131 5527171
Email info@rbge.org.uk
Web www.rbge.org.uk

A **family favourite in the heart** of the capital of Scotland. 'The Botanics', with its beautifully landscaped grounds, provides a safe haven to discover and explore plant wonders from around the globe.

★ Storytelling
★ Workshops
★ Circus in summer
★ Exhibitions
★ Venue for the Edinburgh International Science Festival
★ Schools programme available

345

The Royal Observatory Visitor Centre

1–2 hrs

All year

LOCATION
3 miles south of the city centre. Leave the city bypass at Straiton Junction. Continue along the A701 & follow signs for the Royal Observatory

OPENING
Please phone for details

ADMISSION PRICES
Adult £2.60 Child £1.85
Family £6

CONTACT
Royal Observatory Visitor Centre
Blackford Hill
Edinburgh EH9 3HJ
Tel 0131 6688404
Web www.roe.ac.uk

Marvel at the interactive exhibits showing comets, the solar system and the seasons.

★ Special events throughout the year
★ Science festival
★ Storytelling festival

Witchery Tours

1–2 hrs

May–Aug

Witchery Tours take a light-hearted look at tales of witchcraft, plague and torture. Explore the eerie alleyways and creepy courtyards of the Old Town with your ghostly guide, who will blend history with humour and fact with fable.

★ 'Jump-ooters' make ghastly appearances
★ Walking tours run every evening by appointment
★ Re-enactments & live performances
★ Witchery Murder & Mystery tour
★ Witchery Ghosts & Gore tour every evening in summer – child rates on this tour

LOCATION
Meeting point outside the Witchery restaurant near Edinburgh castle in Central Edinburgh

OPENING
Open May–Aug; Tours start at 7pm, 8pm, 9pm,10pm (times may vary)

ADMISSION PRICES
Under-5s Free; Price depends on tour
Please phone for details

CONTACT
Cadies & Witchery Tours
537 Castlehill
Jollie's Close
Royal Mile
Edinburgh EH1 2ND
Tel 0131 2256745
Email lyal@witcherytours.demon.co.uk
Web www.witcherytours.com

The Writers Museum

2 hrs

All year

3 Star Museum
Edinburgh and Lothians Tourist Board

At this museum you can learn about the lives and work of Scotland's great literary figures, in particular Robert Burns (1759–96), Sir Walter Scott (1771–1832) and Robert Louis Stevenson (1850–94).

LOCATION
In the courtyard at the end of Lady Stair's Close, which runs off the Royal Mile, just a short distance from Edinburgh Castle

OPENING
Advance booking required

ADMISSION PRICES
Please phone for details

CONTACT
The Writers Museum
Lady Stair's Close, Lawnmarket
Edinburgh EH1 2PA
Tel 0131 5294901
Email enquiries@writers museum.demon.co.uk

Deep Sea World

1–2 hrs

All year

Scotland's National Aquarium has the world's longest underwater safari tunnel and one of Europe's largest collections of sand tiger sharks. Go on a voyage of adventure through coastal rockpools and into the shark-inhabited depths of the ocean.

LOCATION
12 miles outside Edinburgh in North Queensferry. From Edinburgh follow signs to Forth Road Bridge (1st exit after bridge)

OPENING
All year open daily 10am–6pm (last entrance 5pm); Closed 25 Dec

ADMISSION PRICES
Adult £6.95 Child £4.95
Family £21+

CONTACT
Deep Sea World
North Queensferry
Fife KY11 1JR
Tel 0906 9410077
Web www.deepseaworld.com

Inverkeithing Museum

1 hr+

WC

All year

LOCATION
Located in Inverkeithing. Take the 1st exit over the Forth Road Bridge from Edinburgh, Junction 1 on the M90

OPENING
All year open open Wed–Sun 11am–5pm
Closed public holidays

ADMISSION PRICES
Please phone for details

CONTACT
Fife Council Museums West
Dunfermline Museum
Viewfield
Dunfermline KY12 7HY
Tel 01383 313838
Fax 01383 313837
Email Lesley.Botten@fife.gov.uk

This is a small local history museum housed in the hospitium of the old Friary. It tells the story of Inverkeithing and nearby Rosyth and contains information about and artefacts belonging to Admiral Sir Samuel Greig, a son of Inverkeithing and the father of the modern Russian Navy.

★ Guided tours for individuals
★ Please note there is a very steep external staircase

347

---

3 Star Wildlife Attraction
Kingdom of Fife Tourist Board

Scottish Deer Centre

2 hrs+

All year

LOCATION
On the outskirts of Cupar, 12 miles from St Andrews on the A91

OPENING
Please phone for details

ADMISSION PRICES
Under-3s Free
Please phone for details of other prices

CONTACT
Scottish Deer Centre
Rankeilour Park
Bow-of-Fife
Cupar
Fife KY15 4NQ
Tel 01337 810391
Email simplythebest@ewm.co.uk

Enjoy a visit to this beautiful countryside centre, where a large herd of deer roam free. Under the guidance of expert rangers you are able to meet these majestic animals or even enjoy a nose-to-nose encounter with a stag.

★ Adventure play parks
★ Courtyard shopping
★ Trailer rides
★ Falconry displays

2 hrs

Easter–Oct

Scottish Vintage Bus Museum

Possibly Britain's largest collection of historic buses dating from the 1920s to 1980s. There are beautifully restored buses to see in the main exhibition hall, as well as buses under restoration in the large workshops.

★ Regular bus rallies

★ Reconstructed parcel office

★ Fire engines

LOCATION
In an ex Royal Navy stores depot at Lathalmond, near Dunfermline, Fife

OPENING
Easter–late Sep/early Oct open Sun 12.30pm–5pm

ADMISSION PRICES
Adult £3 Concession £1.50

CONTACT
Scottish Vintage Bus Museum
41 Oxford Street
Dundee
Tayside DD2 1TF
Tel 01383 623380
Fax 01383 623375

1 hr+

Easter–Oct

St Andrews Aquarium

3 Star Marine Centre
Kingdom of Fife Tourist Board

Enjoy a sense of discovery and enjoyment at the newly refurbished St Andrews Aquarium, which welcomes you to the wonderful world of the sea and its inhabitants – from shrimps to sharks, octopuses to eels, rays to seals.

★ Over 30 exhibition tanks

★ Touch some of the rays & fish

★ Look at sharks & piranhas

★ Harbour Habitat exhibition

LOCATION
At the Bruce Embankment near the Royal & Ancient Golf Club, St Andrews

OPENING
Easter–end Oct open daily 10am–6pm
Please call for winter opening details

ADMISSION PRICES
Adult £4.85 Child (4–14 years) £3.75
Senior £4 Concession £3.75 Price includes full use of all facilities all day

CONTACT
St Andrews Aquarium
The Scores
St Andrews
Fife KY16 9AS
Tel 01334 474786
Email info@standrewsaquarium.co.uk
Web www.standrewsaquarium.co.uk

Clydebuilt Scottish Maritime Museum

5 Star Museum Attraction
Greater Glasgow and Clyde Valley Tourist Board

3 hrs

All year

LOCATION
At junctions 25 & 26 on Glasgow's M8

OPENING
All year open Mon–Sat 10am–6pm & Sun 11am–5pm

ADMISSION PRICES
Adult £3.50 Child £1.75 Under-4s Free
Concession £1.75

CONTACT
Clydebuilt Scottish Maritime Museum
Braehead Shopping Centre
Kings Inch Road
Glasgow G51 4BN
Tel 0141 8861013
Fax 0141 8861015
Email clydebuilt@tinyworld.co.uk
Web www.scottishmaritimemuseum.org

Clydebuilt charts the development of Glasgow and the Clyde from 1700 to the present day. It tells the story of Glasgow's rivers, its ships and its people, through award-winning audio-visuals, computer interpretation, hands-on displays and video, and temporary exhibitions.

★ Steer your own ship in the virtual world of the river pilot

★ Learn to make a fortune as an ocean trader

★ Take control of a real steam engine

★ Go aboard the oldest Clydebuilt vessel still afloat

349

Glasgow Ski & Snowboarding Centre

Varies

All year

An artificial ski and snowboarding centre with three slopes that caters for children of all levels and offers lessons in group or private sessions.

★ Race training junior snow coaches

★ After school clubs

★ Freeride clubs

LOCATION
In Bellahouston Park

OPENING
In summer open Mon–Fri 9.30am–9pm & Sat & Sun 9.30am–6pm; In winter open Mon–Thurs 9.30am–11pm & Fri–Sun 9.30am–9pm; Closed 25 Dec & 1 Jan

ADMISSION PRICES
Please phone for details

CONTACT
Bellahouston Park
16 Dumbreck Road
Glasgow G41 5BW
Tel 0141 4274991
Email info@ski-glasgow.co.uk
Web www.ski-glasgow.co.uk

Glasgow Zoopark

1 Star Wildlife & Nature Attraction
Greater Glasgow and Clyde Valley Tourist Board

4 hrs

All year

Glasgow Zoopark is set in wooded parkland and has lions, tigers, bears, reindeer, snakes and monkeys.

★ Animal displays

★ Creepy crawlies

★ Flying macaws

★ Snakes

★ Birds of prey

★ Barbecues available on request

LOCATION
Near the A8 & A73 in Uddington outside the city centre

OPENING
In summer open daily 10am–6pm; In winter open 10am–5pm

ADMISSION PRICES
Adult £3 Child £3
Under-2s Free Concession £3

CONTACT
Glasgow Zoopark
Calderpark
Uddingston
Glasgow G71 7RZ
Tel 0141 7711185
Email zoo@glasgowzoopark.fsnet.co.uk
Web www.glasgowzoo.
topcities.com

3 hrs

All year

Museum of Transport

3 Star Museum Attraction
Greater Glasgow and Clyde Valley Tourist Board

This museum highlights the history of transport on land and sea. Vehicles range from horse-drawn carriages to motorcycles, fire engines, railway engines and motor cars.

★ Re-creation of a 1938 Glasgow street
★ Reconstructed underground station
★ Ship models

LOCATION
In Glasgow city centre

OPENING
All year open Mon–Thurs & Sat 10am–5pm;
Fri & Sun open 11am–5pm

ADMISSION PRICES
Free

CONTACT
Museum of Transport
1 Bunhouse Road
Glasgow G3 8DP
Tel 0141 287 2720
Fax 0141 287 2692
Web www.glasgow.gov.uk/cls

4 hrs

All year

People's Palace Museum

This collection displays the story of Glasgow, its people, and its impact on the world from 1175 to the present day.

★ Photographs
★ Film sequences
★ Many important collections

LOCATION
In the centre of Glasgow
off the A8

OPENING
All year open Mon, Tue, Wed,
Thu & Sat 10am–5pm, Fri & Sun
open 11am–5pm

ADMISSION PRICES
Free

CONTACT
People's Palace Museum
Glasgow Green
Glasgow
Scotland G40 1AT
Tel 0141 5540223
Fax 0141 5500892
Web www.glasgow.gov.uk/cls

The Piping Centre

4 Star Museum Attraction
Greater Glasgow and Clyde Valley Tourist Board

2 hrs

All year

The Piping Centre houses the National Museum of Scotland's fine collection of bagpipes, making it the most authoritative display of its kind. The priceless collection is presented in a lively, audio-visual format that is as entertaining as it is enlightening.

LOCATION
In Glasgow, off junction 16 of
the M8 & along the A804
towards the east

OPENING
Please phone for details

ADMISSION PRICES
Adult £3 Child £2
Concession £2

CONTACT
The Piping Centre
30–34 McPhater Street
Glasgow G4 0HW
Tel 0141 3530220
Email reception@thepipingcen-
tre.co.uk
Web www.thepipingcentre.co.uk

Scotkart

1 hr

All year

LOCATION
From Glasgow city centre follow Clydebank signs along the expressway then the Dunbarton road. At Yoker look for the brown tourist signs

OPENING
All year open daily 12pm–10pm; Please phone to check availability

ADMISSION PRICES
Under-16s £10 for 1 session, £18 for 2 sessions

CONTACT
Scotkart
John Knox Street
Clydebank
Glasgow G81 1NA
Tel 0141 6410222
Email sales@scotkart.co.uk
Web www.scotkart.co.uk

Experience the thrill, the speed and the buzz of Scotland's largest and fastest indoor karting centre. This indoor circuit features 200cc race karts. All the equipment, instruction and computer timings are included in the price.

★ 45mph race karts
★ Race commentary
★ Computer lap timing
★ Heated spectator area

351

---

3 Star Museum
Greater Glasgow and Clyde Valley Tourist Board

Scotland Street School Museum

3 hrs

All year

LOCATION
In the centre of Glasgow

OPENING
All year open Mon–Thur & Sat 10am–5pm, Fri & Sun open 11am–5pm

ADMISSION PRICES
Free

CONTACT
Scotland Street School Museum
225 Scotland Street
Glasgow G5 8QB
Tel 0141 2870500
Fax 0141 2870515
Web www.glasgow.gov.uk/cls

A fascinating museum that features restored period classrooms and a cookery room, a permanent display on the history of Scottish education and a programme of temporary exhibitions and activities.

★ Conservatory with plants from around the world
★ Ranger service always on hand
★ Ornamental garden
★ 8 miles of nature trails

★ Calderglen Classic Auto Rally
★ Scramble nets, chutes & climbing frames
★ Monthly Animal Magic sessions
★ Goats, guinea pigs, snakes & owls
★ Hidden Worlds wildlife experience

Arnol Blackhouse

2 hrs

All year

SCOTLAND

Visit a traditional Isle of Lewis thatched house museum and visitor centre, fully furnished, complete with attached barn, byre and stackyard. A peat fire burns in the open hearth with the smoke filtering out through the roof.

★ Guided tours all day
★ Video presentations

LOCATION
In Arnol village, Isle of Lewis

OPENING
Apr–Sep open Mon–Sat 9.30am–6.30pm;
Oct–Mar open Mon–Sat 9.30am–4.30pm

ADMISSION PRICES
Under-5s Free; Please phone for details of other prices

CONTACT
The Steward
Blackhouse
Arnol
Isle of Lewis
Western Isles HS2 9DB
Tel 01851 710395
Email hs.explorer@scotland.gsi.gov.uk
Web www.historic-scotland.gov.uk

352

Ballindalloch Castle

2 hrs

Varies

A magnificent sixteenth-century castle set in romantic gardens amongst the hills of Speyside.

★ Ballindalloch herd of Aberdeen Angus cattle
★ Superb rock garden
★ Herb garden
★ Walled garden

LOCATION
14 miles north-east of Grantown on Spey on the A95

OPENING
Please phone for details

ADMISSION PRICES
Under-5s Free; Please phone for other price details

CONTACT
Ballindalloch Castle
Ballindalloch AB37 9AX
Tel 01807 500206
Fax 01807 500210
Email enquiries@ballindallochcastle.co.uk
Web www.ballindallochcastle.co.uk

Bella Jane Boat Trips

Varies

Mar–Oct

Most Enjoyable Visitor Attraction
in Skye and Lochalsh
Talisker Quality Award

LOCATION
Take the B8083 from Broadford for 15
miles (45 mins by car)

OPENING
Mar–Oct open daily

ADMISSION PRICES
£10–20; Please book to avoid
disappointment

CONTACT
Bella Jane Boat Trips
Elgol
Isle of Skye IV49 9BJ
Tel 0800 7313089 (7.30am–10am)
Email bella@bellajane.co.uk
Web www.bellajane.co.uk

Bella Jane Boat Trips take you to the world famous Loch Coruisk and the
seal colony at the heart of the Cuillin on the Isle of Skye. During the
journey you will see a wealth of sealife and enjoy the breathtaking
scenery.

★ Excursions to Canna & Rum
★ Out of season charters available

The Bright Water Visitor Centre

3 hrs

Apr–Oct

3 Star Speciality Attraction
The Highlands Of Scotland Tourist Board

LOCATION
Take the Kyleakin exit at the Skye roundabout (at the end of the Skye Bridge)

OPENING
Apr–Oct open Mon–Sat 9.30am–5.30pm

ADMISSION PRICES
Free

CONTACT
The Bright Water Visitor Centre
The Pier
Kyleakin
Isle of Skye IV41 8PL
Tel & Fax 01599 530040
Email enquiries@eileanban.com
Web www.eileanban.com

A unique experience that unfolds the area's dramatic history and
celebrates the wealth of local wildlife.

★ Daily trips operated to the island of
Eilean Ban
★ Visit the Stevenson Lighthouse
★ Gavin Maxwell Museum (author of
Ring of Bright Water)
★ Award-winning wildlife hide
★ Tourist information
★ Visitor centre
★ Guided tours

Doune Broch Centre

1 hr

Varies

WC

A **walk-through chamber** with an exhibition depicting how people lived in the Broch. The surrounding area has many walks and cycle paths.

LOCATION
By the Doune Broch Monument

OPENING
Please phone for details

ADMISSION PRICES
Please phone for details

CONTACT
Doune Broch Centre
Carloway
Isle of Lewis HS2 9DY
Tel 01851 643338

Falls of Shin Visitor Centre

2 hrs+

All year

WC

Watch the salmon leap on a magnificent waterfall and enjoy the many other facilities at this rural visitor centre.

★ Walks

★ Children's playground

LOCATION
Between Lairg & Bonar Bridge on the B837

OPENING
Mar–Oct open daily; Nov–Feb weekends only; Please phone for opening hours

ADMISSION PRICES
Please phone for details

CONTACT
Falls of Shin Visitor Centre
Achany Glen
Lairg
Sutherland IV27 4EE
Tel 01549 402231
Fax 01863 766500

Family's Pride II

1 hr

Mar–Oct

Cruise in the spectacular Bay of Islands in a glass-bottomed boat. See seals, bird and porpoises above deck, then step below and see the amazing sights of the underwater world.

LOCATION
In Broadford, Isle of Skye, 8 miles from the Skye Bridge. There is a free minibus collection at the Information Centre if required

OPENING
Mar–Oct open daily
10.30am–4.45pm

ADMISSION PRICES
Adult £8.50
Under-12s £4.25

CONTACT
Glassbottom Boats
5 Scullamus, Breakish
Isle of Skye IV42 8QB
Tel 0800 7832175
Web www.glassbottomboat.co.uk

The Fun House

3 Star Visitor Attraction
The Highlands Of Scotland Tourist Board

1 day

All year

WC

The Fun House is a first choice for family entertainment with mini golf, a tree house, ten pin bowling, air hockey and soft play areas. There is also a creche for toddlers.

LOCATION
In a wooded riverside estate of 65 acres, on the ski road

OPENING
All year open daily from 10am

ADMISSION PRICES
Please phone for details

CONTACT
The Fun House
Hilton Coylumbridge Hotel
Aviemore
Inverness-shire PH22 1QN
Tel 01479 813081
Email enquiries@aviemorefun-house.co.uk
Web
www.aviemorefunhouse.co.uk

Highland Wildlife Park

3 Star Award
Highlands of Scotland Tourist Board

3 hrs+

All year

Kisimul Castle

1 hr+

Varies

Enjoy a wild day out in the heart of the Highlands, driving through a scenic main reserve and exploring the rest of the park on foot. You may see wolves and otters among the wildlife.

★ Outdoor play area   ★ Educational tours

The historic restored seat of the Macneils of Barra, chiefs of the Clan Macneil. Located on an island, it is reached by a small boat from the village of Castlebay.

LOCATION
15 minutes south of Aviemore, 2½ hours north of Edinburgh

OPENING
Open all year daily 10am–4pm (last entry 2pm)

ADMISSION PRICES
Under-3s Free; Please phone for details of other prices

CONTACT
Highland Wildlife Park
Kincraig, Kingussie
Inverness-shire PH21 1NL
Tel 01540 651270
Email info@highland-wildlifepark.org
Web
www.highlandwildlifepark.org

LOCATION
On a island in Castlebay, Isle of Barra

OPENING
Please phone for details

ADMISSION PRICES
Please phone for details

CONTACT
Kisimul Castle
Castlebay
Isle of Barra
Western Isles HS9 5XD
Tel 01871 810313
Email
hs.explorer@scotland.gsi.gov.uk
Web www.historic-scotland.gov.uk

355

4 Star Speciality Attraction
The Highlands Of Scotland Tourist Board

Landmark Forest Heritage Park

1 day

All year

LOCATION
7 miles north of Aviemore, 23 miles south of Inverness just off the A9 at Carrbridge

OPENING
Nov–Mar open 10am–5pm; April–mid July open 10am–6pm; Mid Jul–late Aug open 10am–6pm; Sep–Oct open 10am–5pm

ADMISSION PRICES
Under-4s Free; Please phone for details of other prices

CONTACT
Landmark Forest Heritage Park
Main Street
Carrbridge
Inverness-shire PH23 3AJ
Tel 01479 841613
Email landmarkcentre@compuserve.com
Web www.landmark-centre.co.uk

A highly popular visitor attraction, Landmark has a wide range of fun, discovery and adventure activities for all ages in all weather.

★ Wild Water Coaster
★ Red squirrel nature trail
★ Tree-top trail
★ Steam-powered sawmill
★ Microworld exhibition
★ Wildforest maze
★ Journey into Inner Space
★ Antcity
★ Log hauling by Clydesdale horse

Lewis Karting Centre

Varies

All year

Arrive and drive at this outdoor karting centre. There are karts for hire for children aged eight upwards and a Kiddie Kart section for the younger driver. The inflatable circuit makes it safe.

LOCATION
4 miles south of Stornoway on the A859

OPENING
All year open Tue–Sat; Please phone for details of timings

ADMISSION PRICES
From £4 for Juniors to £8 for Seniors

CONTACT
Lewis Karting Centre
Creed Enterprise Park
Lochs Road
Nr Stornoway
Isle of Lewis
Western Isles HS2 9JN
Tel 01851 700222
Web www.lewiscarclub.co.uk

Loch Ness 2000

4 Star Speciality Attraction
The Highlands Of Scotland Tourist Board

4 hrs

All year

Loch Ness 2000 is the Highlands, most popular visitor attraction, offering a fully automated seven-room walk-through story of Loch Ness.

★ Nessie shop
★ Boat trips on Loch Ness in summer

LOCATION
14 miles south of Inverness on the A82 road & 20 miles north of Fort Augustus on the A82

OPENING
Please phone for details

ADMISSION PRICES
Under-7s Free; Please phone for details of other prices

CONTACT
Loch Ness 2000
Drumnadrochit
Inverness-shire IV63 6TU
Tel 01456 450573
Email info@loch-ness-scotland.com
Web www.loch-ness-scotland.com

356

Lybster Harbour Heritage Centre

3 hrs

All year

Discover the amazing history of the picturesque port of Lybster with interactive displays, realistic sculptures and dynamic graphics.

★ Video presentations
★ Watch birds nesting by CCTV
★ Waterlines – the story of Lybster
★ Boat-building viewing gallery

4 Star Speciality Attraction
The Highlands Of Scotland Tourist Board

LOCATION
On the waterfront at Lybster

OPENING
All year open daily 11am–5pm

ADMISSION PRICES
Please phone for details

CONTACT
Lybster Harbour Heritage Centre
Lybster
Caithness KW3 6AH
Tel 01593 721520
Fax 01593 721325

Mallaig Marine World

3 hrs

WC

All year

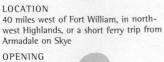

LOCATION
40 miles west of Fort William, in north-west Highlands, or a short ferry trip from Armadale on Skye

OPENING
Please phone for details

ADMISSION PRICES
Under-5s Free; Please phone for details of other prices

CONTACT
Mallaig Marine World,
The Harbour
Mallaig
Inverness-shire PH41 4PX
Tel 01687 462292
Web www.road-to-the-isles.org.uk/marine-world

A **highly original** marine aquarium and exhibition featuring the sea life of the west coast of Scotland. Models, photographs and a unique video (filmed locally) bring the story of Mallaig's fishing fleet to life.

★ Guided tours
★ Video presentations

357

1½ hr

Mar–Oct

Moray Firth Cruises

Enjoy a 1½ **hour cruise** on the Serenity out on the Moray Firth, where you will see the most northerly resident colony of dolphins in the world, common and grey seals, porpoise and Minke whales.

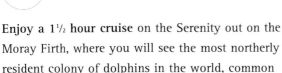

LOCATION
Pick the boat up in Inverness harbour

OPENING
Open Mar–end Oct; First cruise at 10.30am

ADMISSION PRICES
Adult £10 Child £7.50 Senior & Concession £8

CONTACT
Moray Firth Cruises
Shore Street Quay
Shore Street
Inverness IV1 1NF
Tel 01463 717900

Moray Firth Wildlife Centre

3 hrs

Mar–Dec

A **wildlife centre** with exhibitions about dolphins, ospreys, otters and wildfowl. Local boat trips are also available.

★ Full events programme
★ Nature reserve adjacent
★ Wildlife activity holidays

LOCATION
On the A96 at the mouth of the Spey, 5 miles north of Fochabers

OPENING
Mar–Dec open 11am–4pm; Jul–Aug open 10.30am–7pm

ADMISSION PRICES
Please phone for details

CONTACT
Moray Firth Wildlife Centre
Fochabers
Moray IV32 7PJ
Tel 01343 820339 Email
enquiries@mfwc.co.uk
Web www.mfwc.co.uk

3 hrs

All year

WC

Newtonmore Highland Folk Museum

A **fascinating glimpse into 300 years** of Highland life with a reconstructed eighteenth-century township, early twentieth-century school, clockmakers workshop and working croft.

★ Vintage buses on site

★ Children's play area

★ Reconstructed eighteenth-century farming township

★ Early twentieth-century school & mission church

★ Video presentations

★ Multilingual tapes available

LOCATION
½ mile north of Newtonmore & 2½ miles south of Kingussie

OPENING
Please phone for details

ADMISSION PRICES
Please phone for details

CONTACT
Newtonmore Highland Folk Museum
Duke Street
Kingussie
Inverness-shire PH21 1JG
Tel 01540 661307
Web www.highlandfolk.com

1 day

Apr–Oct

WC

Raasay Outdoor Centre

Seaprobe Atlantis

4 Star Visitor Attraction
Scottish Tourist Board

WC

1 hr

Easter–Oct

Raasay Outdoor Centre is situated in the historic mansion of Raasay House. Try your hand at sailing around the seas of Skye, kayaking around Raasay's sheltered bays or rock climbing and abseiling in some of the island's most beautiful locations.

In this fabulous semi-submersible glass-bottomed boat you can enjoy amazing underwater views of kelp beds, jellyfish, sea urchins and starfish. Visit the seals and, if you're lucky, you may catch sight of an otter.

★ Explore kelp forests   ★ Discover shipwrecks

LOCATION
Isle of Raasay is a 15 min ferry journey from the Isle of Skye. There is a direct bus route from Inverness & Glasgow

OPENING
Apr–Oct open daily 8am–11pm or fully residential

ADMISSION PRICES
Activities range from £22.50

CONTACT
Raasay House
Isle of Raasay, by Kyle
IV408 8PB
Tel 01478 660266
Web
www.raasayoutdoorcentre.co.uk

LOCATION
Kyle of Lochalsh, Ross-shire. Boat departs from below the Lochalsh Hotel. Follow road signs once on Skye

OPENING
Easter–Oct open daily 10.30am–evening

ADMISSION PRICES
For 1 hr trip: Adult £10
Child (5–12) £5 (1–4) £2.50

CONTACT
Seaprobe Atlantis
Old Ferry Slipway, Kyle of Lochalsh, Ross-shire
Tel 0800 9804846
Web www.seaprobeatlantis.com

Skyejet Wildlife Trips

1–2 hrs

Mar–Oct

The jet boat trip of a lifetime. Cruising in some of the most spectacular scenery in the world, you'll see seals, seabirds, whales and dolphins. A fascinating, fun experience for all.

LOCATION
Departing from the pontoons in Kyleakin, there is also a pick-up in Kyle of Lochalsh. Cross the Skye Bridge & follow the signs

OPENING
Mar–Oct open daily including Sun. All year charter available. In summer open am–late

ADMISSION PRICES
For 1 hr: Adult £12.50 Child £8.50 Family ticket from £30 Under-5s Free

CONTACT
Skyejet, 5 Scullarus, Breakish Isle of Skye IV42 8QB
Tel 0800 7832175
Web www.skyejet.co.uk

Small World

2 Star Fun and Games Attraction
Aberdeen and Grampian Tourist Board

1–2 hrs

All year

Small World is the ideal venue for kids on a wet day. It has a large softplay centre with slides, ropes, bouncy castle and ball pools. There is also an outdoor play area.

LOCATION
2 miles west of Forres on the main A96 Inverness–Aberdeen road. From Forres turn right at Brodie Castle crossroads towards Darnaway. The centre is 250 yards up the road, well signposted

OPENING
Please phone for details

ADMISSION PRICES
Please phone for details

CONTACT
Tearie Visitor Centre
Darnaway, Nr Forres
Moray
Scotland IV36 2ST
Tel 01309 641677
Email: small.world@tesco.net

359

Strathspey Steam Railway

2 Star Visitor Attraction
The Highlands Of Scotland Tourist Board

2 hrs

All year

This steam railway runs between Aviemore and Boat of Garten and on to Broomhill, near Nethybridge. Enjoy your journey through unspoilt countryside with mountainous views.

LOCATION
Boat-of-Garten village is off the A95 between Aviemore & Grantown-on-Spey, or off the B970 between Nethy Bridge & Inverdruie (near Coylumbridge)

OPENING
Please phone for details

ADMISSION PRICES
Please phone for details

CONTACT
Strathspey Steam Railway
Aviemore Station, Dalfaber Road Aviemore
Inverness-shire PH22 1PY
Tel 01479 810725
Web www.strathspeyrailway.co.uk

Treasures of the Earth

2 Star Tourist Attraction
The Highlands Of Scotland Tourist Board

2 hrs+

All year

One of Europe's finest collections of gemstones, crystals and fossils set in simulated caves, caverns and mining scenes.

LOCATION
In Corpach by Fort William

OPENING
In summer open 9.30am–7pm;
In winter 10am–5pm; Closed Jan

ADMISSION PRICES
Under-5s Free
Please phone for details of other prices

CONTACT
Treasures of the Earth
Corpach
Fort William
Inverness-shire PH33 7JL
Tel 01397 772283
Fax 01397 772133

2 hrs

Varies

Uist Animal Visitors Centre

WC

Working Sheepdogs

2 Star Wildlife and Nature Attraction
The Highlands Of Scotland Tourist Board

WC

2 hrs

All year

Come and see the Scottish Wildcats at this breeding centre. Enjoy watching birds of prey and other native Scottish creatures.

★ Cycling

★ Pony-trekking

★ Horse-riding

★ Children's play area

LOCATION
On the west side of North Uist, one of the Western Isles

OPENING
Please phone for details

ADMISSION PRICES
Under-2s Free; Please phone for details of other prices

CONTACT
Uist Animal Visitors Centre
Kyles Road, Bayhead
Isle of North Uist
Western Isles HS6 5DX
Tel & Fax 01876 510223
Email
castawaywad1fr@supanet.com

Participate in the working day of a Highland shepherd and his dogs. Help to shear a sheep and bottle-feed orphan lambs. Meet the friendly pups.

★ Re-enactments & live performances

★ Saturday demonstrations must be booked by phone in advance

LOCATION
5 miles north of Aviemore & 5 miles south of Kingussie on the B9152, on a working farm

OPENING
Demonstrations daily at 12pm & 4pm; Private bookings available

ADMISSION PRICES
Please phone for details

CONTACT
Working Sheepdogs
Leault Farm
Kincraig
Inverness-shire PH21 1LZ
Tel 01540 651310

2 hrs

All year

Almond Valley Heritage Centre

WC

3 Star Museum Attraction
Edinburgh and Lothians Tourist Board

An innovative museum exploring the history and environment of West Lothian with award-winning children's activities and interactive displays.

★ Farmsteading exhibition

★ Demonstrations & seasonal activities

★ Countryside walks

★ Tractor rides

★ Children's play areas

★ Narrow-gauge railway

★ Interactive displays

★ The story of Scotland's shale oil industry

LOCATION
2 miles from junction 3 of the M8 close to Livingston village

OPENING
Al year open Mon–Sat 10am–5pm

ADMISSION PRICES
Under-3s Free; Please phone for details of other prices

CONTACT
Almond Valley Heritage Centre
Millfield
Livingston
West Lothian EH54 7AR
Tel 01506 414957
Fax 01506 497771
Email info@almondvalley.co.uk
Web www.almondvalley.co.uk

Museum of Flight

3 hrs

All year

HIGHLANDS/LOTHIANS

A **superb aviation collection** with aircraft, engines, rockets, photographs, a reference library, archives, models, flying clothing, instruments and propellers.

- ★ Spitfires
- ★ 1914–18 exhibitions
- ★ Post-war military aircraft
- ★ Helicopters & rotorcraft
- ★ Motor gliders & microlights
- ★ Sailplanes
- ★ Hang-gliders
- ★ Rockets & missiles
- ★ Fuselage & cockpit sections
- ★ Pioneer aircraft
- ★ 1939–45 exhibition

LOCATION
Close to the A1 near Haddington; well signposted from the A1 in both directions

OPENING
All year open daily 10.30am–5pm; Closed 25 Dec & 1, 2 Jan; Late opening Jul & Aug until 6pm

ADMISSION PRICES
Adult £3 Child Free Concession £1.50

CONTACT
Museum of Flight
East Fortune Airfield
East Lothian EH39 5LF
Tel 01620 880308
Fax 01620 880355
Email museum_of_flight@sol.co.uk

361

Polkemmet Country Park

Varies

All year

Polkemmet country park is a very attractive area of mixed mature woodlands and grassy open spaces along the upper reaches of the River Almond.

- ★ Fantasy Forest
- ★ Large play area & picnic area
- ★ 9-hole golf course
- ★ 15-bay golf driving range

LOCATION
Between junctions 4 & 5 of the M8, midway between Edinburgh & Glasgow. Entry is from the B7066, on the outskirts of Whitburn

OPENING
Open all year but unattended 25, 26 Dec & 1, 2 Jan

ADMISSION PRICES
Free

CONTACT
Polkemmet Country Park
Whitburn
West Lothian EH47 0AD
Tel 01501 743905
Email mail@beecraigs.com

Scottish Railway Exhibition

1 hr+

Apr–Oct

The Scottish Railway Exhibition tells the story of the railways in Scotland. Carriages, wagons and locomotives are on display, including Glen Douglas, a Royal Saloon coach. The Bo'ness and Kinneil railway offers a seven-mile round trip by steam train.

LOCATION
Access by footbridge from Bo'ness Station, West Lothian, 8 miles west of the Forth bridges. Access via junction 3 or 5 of the M9

OPENING
Apr–Oct open weekends 11.30am–5pm; Jul & Aug open daily 11.30am–5pm except Mon

ADMISSION PRICES
Adult £1 Child 50p Concession 70p

CONTACT
Bo'ness Station
Union St, Bo'ness
West Lothian EH51 9AQ
Tel 01506 822298
Web www.srps.org.uk

Scottish Seabird Centre

4 Star Wildlife & Nature Attraction

Varies

All year

Set on a dramatic promontory at North Berwick, the centre allows visitors to explore the fascinating world of seabirds, including puffins, via remote cameras on the nearby islands of Fidra and Bass Rock.

LOCATION
At the harbour in North Berwick (30 minutes by train east of Edinburgh)

OPENING
Please phone for details

ADMISSION PRICES
Adult £4.95 Child £3.50
Family £13.50

Concession & Senior £3.50

CONTACT
Scottish Seabird Centre
The Harbour, North Berwick
East Lothian EH39 4SS
Tel 01620 890202
Fax 01620 890222
Web www.seabird.org

Balfour Castle

2 hrs

May–Sep

A Victorian castle surrounded by landscaped grounds and a plantation of trees.

★ Fishing

★ Walking

★ Victorian walled gardens

★ Ferry trip included

LOCATION
2 minutes from Shapinsay Harbour, reached by car ferry from Kirkwall on Orkney mainland, a 25-minute journey

OPENING
May–Sep open for guided tours every Sun & Wed

ADMISSION PRICES
Please phone for details

CONTACT
Balfour Castle
Balfour Shapinsay
Orkney KW17 2DY
Tel 01856 711282
Web www.balfourcastle.co.uk

Ferrycroft Countryside Centre

2 hrs

Varies

A hands-on family-oriented visitor centre displaying the natural and archaeological history of an area rich in beauty and wildlife.

★ Tourist information centre

★ Countryside ranger

★ Video presentations

★ Indoor & outdoor play area

LOCATION
Central Sutherland, on the shore of Loch Shin

OPENING
Please phone for details

ADMISSION PRICES
Please phone for details

CONTACT
Ferrycroft Countryside Centre
Lairg
Sutherland IV27 4TP
Tel & Fax 01549 402160
Fax 01549 402160

Historylinks Museum

3 hrs

May–Sep

This museum tells the story of Dornoch, from pre-history to the present time.

★ Video presentations

LOCATION
In Dornoch town centre

OPENING
May–Sep open Mon–Sat
10am–4pm

ADMISSION PRICES
Adult £2 Children Free

CONTACT
Historylinks Museum
The Meadows
Dornoch
Sutherland IV25 3SF
Tel 01862 811275
Email grahampark@supanet.com
Web www.dornoch.org.uk/historylinks

Kirbister Museum

1–2 hrs

Varies

The custodian at this folk museum describes the traditional farming life. The museum has the last traditional peat-burning central hearth and stone neuk bed.

LOCATION
In Kirbister, Birsay

OPENING
Please phone for details

ADMISSION PRICES
Please phone for details

CONTACT
Kirbister Museum
Kirbister
Birsay
Orkney KW17 2LR
Tel 01856 771268

The Orkney Museum

3 hrs

All year

Learn about the pre-history and social history of Orkney here.

★ Sixteenth-century Scottish vernacular architecture
★ Archaeological and social history collections

LOCATION
Kirkwall, Orkney, opposite St Magnus Cathedral

OPENING
Please phone for details

ADMISSION PRICES
Please phone for details

CONTACT
The Orkney Museum
Tankerness House
Broad Street
Kirkwall
Orkney KW15 1DH
Tel 01856 873191

Orkney Wireless Museum

2 hrs

Apr–Sep

An **extraordinary range** of wirelesses is displayed here, including wartime radios, domestic radios, valves, Italian prisoner-of-war craft, gimmick transistor radios and gramophones.

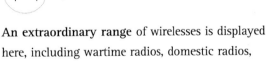

LOCATION
In central Kirkwall on the Orkney mainland, near Kirkwall Harbour

OPENING
Apr–Sep Mon–Sat 1pm–4.30pm & Sun 2pm–4.30pm

ADMISSION PRICES
Please phone for details

CONTACT
Orkney Wireless Museum
Kiln Corner
Junction Road
Kirkwall
Orkney KW15 1LB
Tel 01856 871400

Scapa Flow Visitor Centre & Museum

2 hrs

All year

A **British Navy base** in World Wars I and II, Scapa Flow is now a museum with many interesting relics from the war days. Advance booking is required.

LOCATION
Near Lyness Pier, on the island of Hoy

OPENING
Please phone for details

ADMISSION PRICES
Under-5s Free; Please phone for details of other prices

CONTACT
Scapa Flow Visitor Centre & Museum
Orkney Islands Council School Place
Kirkwal
Orkney KW15 1DH
Tel 01856 873535

3 hrs

All year

WC

Tomb Of The Eagles

A **visit to the Tomb of the Eagles** gives a valuable insight into the life of our neolithic ancestors. Visitors are given the opportunity to handle some of the original artefacts. Advance booking is required.

★ Guided tour of Bronze Age house
★ Children's indoor play area

LOCATION
South Ronaldsay, Orkney. Overlooking the Pentland Firth, mainland Orkney

OPENING
Apr–Oct open daily 10am–8pm; Nov–Mar open 10am–12pm (or by arrangement)

ADMISSION PRICES
Under-5s Free
Please phone for details of other prices

CONTACT
Tomb of the Eagles
Liddle
South Ronaldsay
Orkney KW17 2RW
Tel 01856 831339
Email info@tomboftheeagles.co.uk
Web www.tomboftheeagles.co.uk

2 hrs+

Varies

WC

Westray Heritage Centre

A **uniquely artistic,** permanent natural history display. There are annual historic exhibitions, hands-on children's models, family history displays and crafts.

★ Children's indoor play area

LOCATION
On the Island of Westray in Orkney. Located on the island of Westray

OPENING
Please phone for details

ADMISSION PRICES
Under-5s Free; Please phone for details of other prices

CONTACT
Westray Heritage Centre
9 Gill Pier
Westray
Orkney KW17 2DL
Tel 01857 677231

Atholl Country Life Museum

1–2 hrs

May–Sep

WC

This **lively museum** explores the reality of country life and the social history of the Atholl people. It uses detailed facts, historical photographs and stories set in a wide range of imaginative displays.

LOCATION
North of Pitlochry, on the A9

OPENING
May–Sep open daily 1.30pm–5pm; Jul & Aug from 10am on weekdays, or by arrangement

ADMISSION PRICES
Please phone for details

CONTACT
Atholl Country Life Museum
Blair Atholl
Pitlochry
Perthshire PH18 5SP
Tel 01796 481232

All day

Easter–Oct

Atholl Mountain Bike Hire

A full range of adult and child bikes is available here, as are bikes with child seats or stabilisers. The routes are safe and off-road.

★ Guided nature walks available

★ Children's events organised throughout summer

i

LOCATION
On the banks of the River Tilt, opposite Blair Castle Caravan Park

OPENING
Easter–mid-Oct open Tue–Sun 9am–6pm

ADMISSION PRICES
Adult: from £10 per day
Child: from £3 per day

CONTACT
Atholl Mountain Bike Hire
Allt na Fearn
Killiecrankie
Pitlochry
Perthshire PH16 5LN
Tel 01796 473553
Web
www.blairatholl.org.uk/activities

Auchingarrigh Wildlife Centre

4–5 hrs

All year

Set in 100 acres of beautiful Perthshire countryside with superb views, the centre has many animals and birds from all over the world.

★ Falconry display

★ Indoor play

★ Education packs for children

i

LOCATION
2 miles south of Comrie on the B827, 25 miles west of Perth & 20 miles north of Stirling. Follow the signs for Crieff

OPENING
Open daily 10am–dusk

ADMISSION PRICES
Adult £4.75 Child & Senior £3.75 Group £1 reduction

CONTACT
Auchingarrigh Wildlife Centre
Comrie
Perthshire PH6 2JS
Tel 01764 679469/670486

365

---

4 Star Visitor Attraction
Scottish Tourist Board

i

LOCATION
Between Aberdeen & Dundee, off the A90. On the A935 to Brechin turn off. It is well signposted from there

OPENING
In summer open Mon–Sat 9am–6pm, Sun 10am–6pm; In winter open Mon–Fri 9am–5pm, Sat 9am–6pm & Sun 10am–6pm

ADMISSION PRICES
Please phone for details

CONTACT
Brechin Castle Centre
Haughmuir, by Brechin
Angus
Tel 01356 626813
Email enquiries@brechincastlecentre.co.uk
Web www.brechincastlecentre.co.uk

Brechin Castle Centre

2 hrs+
All year

Brechin Castle is a country park with a working model farm and a children's activity area.

★ Guided tours of model farm

★ Miniature railway open Sat & Sun in Jun–Aug

★ Santa at Christmas

Children's Amusement Park

There is something for everyone, young and old, at this park, including bumper cars, bikes and boats, remote-controlled cars, boats and trucks, water lasers, children's rides and an amusement arcade.

3 Star Fun & Games Attraction

Perthshire Tourist Board

LOCATION
26 miles north of Perth on the A9

OPENING
Please phone for details

ADMISSION PRICES
Please phone for details; Not suitable for under-3s

CONTACT
Children's Amusement Park
Armoury Road
Pitlochry, Perthshire
Scotland PH16 5AP
Tel 01796 472876
Fax 01796 473320
Email info@matchett.co.uk

Dewar's Centre

Come and brush up on your skating skills, or take the plunge and learn to skate for the first time. Everyone is catered for, including the little ones, with 'Tiny Tots on Ice'.

LOCATION
Situated in the centre of Perth

OPENING
Open daily, but please check before coming as times vary; Closed 25, 26 Dec & 1, 2 Jan

ADMISSION PRICES
Skate & adult £5.50 Skate & junior child £4.50

CONTACT
Dewar's Centre
Glover St
Perth PH2 0TH
Tel 01738 624188
Email info@curlingscotland.com
Web www.curlingscotlan.co.uk

Jungle Kids

Britain's largest fully-themed children's play centre for under-12s. There is a separate toddlers' area, four themed party rooms and a quiet viewing lounge in which to relax.

★ 4 levels of play entertainment

★ Separate toddlers' area

★ Children's character parties available

★ Internet access

LOCATION
Follow the tourist signposts from Coupar Angus Road roundabout on the A90 to Dundee

OPENING
In summer open daily 10am–6.30pm; In winter open daily 11am–6pm

ADMISSION PRICES
Mon–Fri £2
Weekends & school holidays £3.25/£4.25

CONTACT
Jungle Kids
Dronley Road
Birkhill
Dundee DD2 5QD
Tel 01382 580540
Email fun@junglekids.sol.co.uk
Web www.junglekids.co.uk

Loch Rannoch Watersports

½–1 day

Apr–Oct

Try your hand at a variety of water-based activities, from canoeing and windsurfing to sailing, motor boating and kayaking.

★ Easter, summer & October holiday courses

★ Reindeer safaris during Christmas period

LOCATION
Signposted for Kinloch Rannoch off the A9 north of Pitlochry on Lochside, 1 mile past Kinloch Rannoch

OPENING
Apr–Oct open daily; In summer open 9.30am–7pm; In winter open 10.30am–5pm

ADMISSION PRICES
Activities priced individually

CONTACT
Loch Rannoch Watersports
Kinloch Rannoc
Perthshire
Tel 01882 632242
Web www.goforth.co.uk

Noah's Ark

4 Star Visitor Attraction
Scottish Tourist Board

2 hrs
All year

Noah's Ark is a specially equipped children's soft play barn for under-12s. There are three separate areas to ensure the safety of all the children. Indoor karting is available seasonally.

★ Italian Stell Karts   ★ Birthday parties

LOCATION
On the Perth western by-pass

OPENING
All year open daily
10.30am–6.30pm

ADMISSION PRICES
Adult Free Under-5s £3.25
Over-5s £3.75

CONTACT
Noah's Ark
Old Gallows Road
Western Edge
Perth PH1 1QE
Tel 01738 445568
Email info@noahs-ark.co.uk
Web www.noahs-ark.co.uk

Peel Farm

1–2 hrs

Mar–Dec

LOCATION
20 miles north of Dundee, off the B951 from Kirriemuir or the B594 from Alyth

OPENING
Mar–Dec open 9am–5pm; Open weekends from mid Oct 9am–5pm; Closed Jan & Feb

ADMISSION PRICES
Free

CONTACT
Peel Farm
Lintrathen, By Kirriemuir
Angus
Tel 01575 560205
Email Frances@peelfarm.com
Web www.peelfarm.com

There are many animals and birds at Peel Farm, as well as a walk along a varied and interesting farm trail that includes a gorge and waterfall.

★ Otters, mink, owls & woodpeckers

★ Deer park

★ Play area

★ Mill pond with ducks & geese

1–2 hrs

All year

R.R.S. Discovery

5 Star Visitor Attraction
Scottish Tourist Board

Enjoy the experience of looking around Captain Scott's famous Antarctic ship.

★ World War 1 exhibition

★ Learn about the Russian Revolution

★ Spectacular lighting

★ Special graphics & effects

LOCATION
In Dundee follow the signs for Historic Ships

OPENING
Apr–Oct open daily 10am–5pm; Nov–Mar open 10am–4pm

ADMISSION PRICES
Adult £5.95 Child £3.85 Senior £4.45 Concession £4.45

CONTACT
R. R. S. Discovery
Discovery Point
Discovery Quay
Dundee DD1 4XA
Tel 01382 201245
Email
info@dundeeheritage.sol.co.uk

Sensation Dundee

2–3 hrs

All year

If you thought science was boring, this museum may help you rethink. The hands-on experiments and investigations bring science to life.

★ Gyroscope

★ Reaction Attack

★ Ball Cannon

★ Soft play area

LOCATION
In Dundee city centre, 5 min walk from Dundee Station. Follow the brown tourist signs

OPENING
All year open daily; In summer open 9am–6pm; In winter open 9am–5pm

ADMISSION PRICES
Adult £5.50 Child £3.99
Concession £3.99

CONTACT
Sensation Dundee
Greenmarket, Dundee DD1 4QB
Tel 01382 228800
Web www.sensation.org.uk

1½ hrs

Mar–Nov

The Scottish Crannog Centre

Visit Scotland's only authentic recreation of an Iron Age loch-dwelling. Guided tours, exhibits, video and ancient crafts bring the past to life.

★ Regular 'hands-on' activities

★ Themed special events and re-enactments

★ Guided tours

LOCATION
6 miles west of Aberfeldy. Easy to access from Edinburgh & Glasgow

OPENING
Mid Mar–Oct open daily 10am–5.30pm (last admission 4.30pm); Nov open daily 10am–4pm (last admission 3pm)

ADMISSION PRICES
Adult £4.25 Child £3 Family £13+
Senior £3.85

CONTACT
The Scottish Crannog Centre
Kenmore
Lock Tay
Perthshire PH15 2HY
Tel 01887 830583
Email info@crannog.co.uk
Web www.crannog.co.uk

Blair Drummond Safari & Adventure Park

1 day

Apr–Oct

LOCATION
In Blair Drummond by Stirling junction 10 of M9, 4 miles along the A84 towards Callander

OPENING
Apr–Oct open daily 10am–5.30pm (last admission 4.30pm)

ADMISSION PRICES
Adult £8.50 Child £4.50 Under-3s Free
Senior £4.50

CONTACT
Blair Drummond Safari and Adventure Park
Blair Drummond
Stirling
Stirlingshire FK9 4UR
Tel 01786 841456
Email enquiries@safari-park.co.uk
Web www.safari-park.co.uk

Blair Drummond has a fascinating collection of animals from all over the world, including elephants, giraffes, lions, tigers, and rhinos. You can take a safari to Chimpanzee Island, watch the performing sea lion show or visit Pet Farm.

★ Adventure playground
★ Giant Astraglide
★ Pedal boats
★ Face painting
★ Flying Fox cable slide

369

Forest Hills Watersports

½–1 day

Mar–Dec

LOCATION
Off junction 10 of the M9 & junction 16 of the M8. Follow the signposts for Aberfoyle, & from Aberfoyle the centre is signposted to Forest Hills Watersports, 4 miles along the B829

OPENING
Mar–Dec open daily; In summer open 9.30am–8pm; In winter open 10.30am–5pm

ADMISSION PRICES
Activities priced individually

CONTACT
Forest Hills Watersports
Kinlochard
Aberfoyle
Stirlingshire FK8 3TL
Tel 01877 387775
Email info@gdforth.co.uk
Web www.gdforth.co.uk

The centre offers a range of 'wet' and 'dry' activities which can be combined or enjoyed individually. Watersports of all descriptions are available in addition to quad biking, mountain biking and 4x4 drives.

★ Cliff jumps
★ River scrambles
★ Raft building
★ Mountain biking
★ Kayaking
★ Canadian canoeing

Megazone

Varies

All year

Megazone laser adventure is a futuristic wasteland filled with smoke, sounds, flashing lights – and enemies. Stalk your opponents with the latest technology. Use stealth and cunning, strategy and skill to score points.

LOCATION
5 minutes walk from Grahamston Railway Station & Central Retail Park

OPENING
All year open Mon 4pm–10pm, Tue–Fri 12pm–10pm, Sat & Sun 10am–10pm; Closed 25 Dec & 1 Jan

ADMISSION PRICES
1st game £3.50 per person
Further games £2 per person

CONTACT
Megazone Falkirk
104 Grahams Road
Falkirk FK2 7BZ
Tel 01324 634828

Stirling Castle

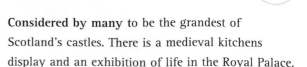

5 Star Historic Attraction

Argyll, The Isles, Loch Lomond, Stirling & Trossachs Tourist Board

3 hrs

All year

Considered by many to be the grandest of Scotland's castles. There is a medieval kitchens display and an exhibition of life in the Royal Palace.

★ Re-enactments & live performances

★ Outstanding architecture

LOCATION
At the head of Stirling's historic Old Town, off the M9

OPENING
Apr–Sep open daily 9.30am–6.30pm; Oct–Mar 9.30am–5pm

ADMISSION PRICES
Under-5s Free; Please phone for

details of other prices

CONTACT
Stirling Castle
Castle Wynd
Stirling
Stirlingshire FK8 1EJ
Tel 01786 450000
Fax 01786 464678

Aluminium Story Visitor Centre

2 hrs

Apr–Sep

Discover how a community and an industry harnessed hydro-electric power to produce aluminium for over 80 years.

★ Audio-visual display about the aluminium industry in the Highlands

LOCATION
At the head of Loch Leven, 7 miles from Glencoe

OPENING
Apr–end Sept open Mon–Fri 10am–6pm

ADMISSION PRICES
Free

CONTACT
Aluminium Story Visitor Centre
Linnhe Road
Kinlochleven PA40 5SJ
Tel & Fax 01855 831663
Email cultural.leisure@highland.gov.uk

Balmichael Visitor Centre

4 Star Speciality Attraction

Ayrshire and Arran Tourist Board

4 hrs

All year

This centre occupies a restored farm. It has quad bike tracks, an adventure playground, a putting green and a heritage area.

★ Indoor & outdoor play areas   ★ Restored mill wheel

LOCATION
7 miles from Brodick over the hill via the String Road, 3 miles from Blackwaterfoot

OPENING
All year open Wed–Sat 10am–6pm & Sun 12pm–5pm

ADMISSION PRICES
Please phone for details

CONTACT
Balmichael Visitor Centre
Shiskine
Isle Of Arran KA27 8DT
Tel 01770 860430
Web
www.thebalmichaelcentre.co.uk

The Big Idea

4 Star Speciality Attraction

Ayrshire and Arran Tourist Board

2 hrs+

All year

A **mind-blowing adventure** through the world of inventions, creations and innovations, where visitors interact with the exhibits using their own electronic key. It is not suitable for children under five.

LOCATION	CONTACT
The Harbourside, Irvine, on the A78	**The Big Idea**
	The Harbourside
OPENING	Irvine
Please phone for details	Ayrshire KA12 8XX
	Tel 08708 403100
ADMISSION PRICES	Fax 08708 403130
Adult £7.95 Child £5.95	Email caroline@bigidea.org.uk
Family £18 Senior £5.95	Web www.bigidea.org.uk

Calderglen Country Park

2–4 hrs

All year

This is a **large country park** with a visitor centre, children's zoo, conservatory, adventure playground and miles of fascinating trails to follow.

4 Star Award

Scottish Tourist Board

LOCATION	Zoo: Opening times vary
In Calderglen Country Park in East Kilbride on the Strathaven road, just out of town	ADMISSION PRICES
	Free
OPENING	CONTACT
Park: Open all year	**Visitor Services Officer**
Visitor Centre: In summer open 10.30am–5.30pm; In winter open 10.30am–4pm	Calderglen Country Park
	East Kilbride G75 0QZ
	Tel 01355 236644

371

Callendar House Museum

3 hrs

All year

Callendar House is an imposing mansion with a 600-year history, where you can go back in time to experience life in the 1820s.

★ Costumed interpreters   ★ Woodland walks

★ Boating

LOCATION	ADMISSION PRICES
From Callander Road (A803) enter Estate Avenue. Located ½ mile east of the town centre	Adult £3 Child £1.50 Under-6s Free Family £7 Senior £1.50
	CONTACT
OPENING	**Callendar House Museum**
All year open Mon–Sat 10am–5pm; Apr–Sep also open Sun 2pm–5pm	Callendar Park FK1 1YR
	Tel 01324 503770
	Email mmcfeat@falkirkmuseums.demon.co.uk

Chatelherault Country Park

4 hrs

All year

Chatelherault has a Georgian hunting lodge, a visitor centre, gallery, gardens and river and woodland walks.

★ White Cadzow cattle   ★ Ranger service

★ Adventure playground

LOCATION	CONTACT
2 miles from Hamilton town centre & 16 miles from Glasgow Airport	**Chatelherault**
	Carlisle Road
	Ferniegair
OPENING	Hamilton
All year open Mon–Sat 10am–5pm & Sun 12pm–5pm	South Lanarkshire ML3 7UE
	Tel 01698 426213
ADMISSION PRICES	Web
Free	www.southlanarkshire.gov.uk

The Ayrshire Country Life & Costume Museum

2 hrs+

All year

2 Star Museum Attraction

Ayrshire and Arran Tourist Board

A **country-life museum** and costume collection housed in a sixteenth-century building.

★ Horse-riding

★ Pony-trekking

LOCATION
On the A737 between Kilwinning & Dalry

OPENING
Please phone for details

ADMISSION PRICES
Under-5s Free
Please phone for details of other prices

CONTACT
The Ayrshire Country Life & Costume Museum
Dalgarven Mill
Dalgarven Dalry Road
Kllwinning
Ayrshire KA13 6PN
Tel 01294 552448
Fax 0141 5523987

---

2 hrs

All year

Dundonald Aviation Centre

The **Dundonald Aviation Centre** is a small museum dedicated to the promotion of interest in all aspects of aviation from World War I to the present day.

LOCATION
On the A759 midway between Kilmarnock & Troon in Ayrshire on the outskirts of Dundonald village

OPENING
All year open daily 10am–5pm

ADMISSION PRICES
Adults £1 Child 50p

CONTACT
Dundonald Aviation Centre
6 Ploughlands, Dundonald
Kilmarnock
Ayrshire KA2 9BT
Tel 01563 850215

Dundonald Castle

4 Star Historic Attraction

Ayrshire and Arran Tourist Board

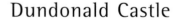

1 hr+

All year

The **castle's association with the Stewarts** gives Dundonald its special importance. It was built by Robert Stewart in 1371 to mark his succession to the throne of Scotland.

LOCATION
In the village of Dundonald on the A759, 6 miles from Ayr & 3 miles from Kilmarnock

OPENING
Please phone for details

ADMISSION PRICES
Under-5s Free; Please phone for details of other prices

CONTACT
Travel Trade Team
Longmore House
Salisbury Place
Edinburgh EH9 1SH
Tel 0131 668 8800
Email
hs.historic@scotland.gov.uk

2–4 hrs

All year

Finlaystone

Come and discover the woodland walks with waterfalls, extensive children's play areas and much more. Formal gardens overlook the River Clyde.

i

LOCATION
On the A8 west of Langbank, 10 minutes west of Glasgow Airport

OPENING
All year open daily
10.30am–5pm (tearoom closed Oct–Mar)

ADMISSION PRICES
Adult £3 Child £2
Concession £2

CONTACT
Finlaystone
Langbank
Renfrewshire PA14 6TS
Tel 01475 540505
Web www.finlaystone.co.uk

Varies
All year

Galleon Centre

This leisure facility has a swimming pool and ice rink, as well as a games hall which is suitable for badminton, football and table tennis.

★ Soft play area
★ Trampolining clubs
★ Swimming lessons
★ Fun swim sessions

i

LOCATION
Follow the signs for the town centre

OPENING
In summer open Sun–Fri
7am–11pm & Sat 9am–6pm; In winter Sun–Fri 7am–11pm & Sat 9am–6pm; Closed 25, 26 Dec & 1, 2 Jan

ADMISSION PRICES
Adult 90p Child 70p
Various activities priced separately

CONTACT
Galleon Centre
99 Titchfield Street
Kilmarnock KA1 1QY
Tel 01563 524014

373

---

3 hrs+

All year

Heads of Ayr Park & Off-Road Centre

An open farm hosting a collection of rare and exotic animals, birds and pets.

★ Quad bikes
★ Pony rides
★ Play parks

i

LOCATION
4 miles south of Ayr on the A719, just past Haven Craig Tara Holiday Park

OPENING
All year open daily 10am–5pm; Closed 25 Dec & 1 Jan

ADMISSION PRICES
Please phone for details

CONTACT
Heads of Ayr Park & Off-Road Centre
Dunure Road, Ayr
Ayrshire KA7 4LD
Tel 01292 441210
Web www.headsofayrpark.co.uk

2 hrs
Apr–Sep

Hunter House

4 Star Museum Attraction
Greater Glasgow and Clyde Valley
Tourist Board

Hunter House is the farmhouse where the medical pioneers John and William Hunter grew up.

★ Interactives
★ Computer games
★ Video presentations

i

LOCATION
On the A726, travelling east from East Kilbride

OPENING
Apr–Sep open Mon–Fri
12pm–4pm & weekends
12pm–5pm

ADMISSION PRICES
Free

CONTACT
Hunter House
Maxwellton Road, Calderwood
East Kilbride
South Lanarkshire G74 3LW
Tel 01355 261261

Inveraray Jail

4 Star Museum
Argyll, The Isles, Loch Lomond, Stirling and Trossachs Tourist Board

2 hrs

All year

Sit and listen to trials in the 1820 courtroom. Talk to guides dressed as warders, prisoners and the matron. Visit the two prisons and experience the sounds and smells as they would have been.

★ Not suitable for under-4s

★ Advance booking required

★ Stroll in the Airing Yards

★ Try the Crank Machine, Whipping Table & Hammocks

★ In Prison Today exhibition

LOCATION
Mid Argyll at the head of Loch Fyne

OPENING
Nov–Mar open daily 10am–5pm (last admission 4pm); Apr–Oct open 9.30pm–6pm (last admission 5pm)

ADMISSION PRICES
Please phone for details

CONTACT
Inveraray Jail
Church Square
Inveraray
Argyll PA32 8TX
Tel 01499 302381
Fax 01499 302195
Email inverarayjail@btclick.com

Kelburn Country Centre

4 hrs+

Easter–Oct

Kelburn is a historic country park with a castle, gardens, waterfalls and exhibitions to visit, as well as outdoor pursuits such as horse-riding.

★ Falconry centre

★ Secret Forest

★ Ranger events

★ Play areas

LOCATION
On the A78 between Largs & Fairlie

OPENING
Easter–Oct open daily; In summer open 10am–6pm; In winter 11am–5pm

ADMISSION PRICES
Adult £4.50 Child £3 Family (2+3) £13

CONTACT
Kelburn Country Centre
Fairlie
KA29 0BE
Tel 01475 568685
Email admin@kelburncountrycentre.com

L. A. Bowl Ltd

Fun for all the family with 16 fully computerised bowling lanes, amusements and pool tables.

★ Large-screen TV & satellite

LOCATION
In Ayr just off the A77 or A70.
South of Prestwick

OPENING
All year open daily 10am–late

ADMISSION PRICES
Please phone for details

CONTACT
L. A. Bowl Ltd
17 Miller Road
Ayr
Ayrshire KA7 2AX
Tel 01292 611511
Email labowl@ukgateway.net

Lamont City Farm

Come and meet all sorts of small animals including sheep, goats, ponies, pigs, hens, ducks and geese.

LOCATION
On the M8 travel to St James roundabout & take the Erskine cut-off. At the 3rd roundabout, turn left then 1st right into Barhill Road

OPENING
Open daily 10.30am–4.30pm;
Closed 25 Dec & 1 Jan

ADMISSION PRICES
Families free; Groups please phone for details

CONTACT
Lamont City Farm
Barhill Road
Erskine, Renfrewshire
Tel 0141 8125335
Web www.lamontcityfarm.co.uk

STRATHCLYDE

375

Lanark Visitor Centre

LOCATION
New Lanark is signposted from all major routes (A72/M74/A70) and is about 1 hrs drive from Glasgow, Edinburgh & Stirling

OPENING
All year open daily 11am–5pm except 25 Dec & 1 Jan

ADMISSION PRICES
Adult £4.95 Concession £3.95

CONTACT
Lanark Visitor Centre
New Lanark Conservation Trust
New Lanark Mills
Lanarkshire ML11 9DB
Tel 01555 661345
Email visit@newlanark.org
Web www.newlanark.org

This beautifully restored conservation village was once Britain's largest cotton manufacturing centre and now houses many exhibitions and activities to suit people of all ages.

★ Award-winning visitor centre

★ Amazing New Millennium Experience

★ Annie McLeod story

★ Restored Petrie steam-engine

★ Victorian engine house

★ Robert Owen's School for Children

★ Millworkers' house

★ Village store exhibition

★ The New Lanark Power Trail

★ Guided tours

Lochfyne Miniature Railway

2 hrs+

Varies

Loudoun Castle Theme Park

4 hrs+

Apr–Aug

This miniature 10½-inch gauge steam railway runs the length of Ardrishaig front green from Greenend Station to the John Smith memorial garden.

A combination of rides, rare species, animal and indigenous animals and plants in a historic setting.

★ Guided tours
★ Animal farm tour
★ Tour of woodlands
★ Video presentations
★ Outdoor play area for children

LOCATION
On the front green in Ardrishaig, Argyll, 2 miles south of Lochgilphead on the A83 Campbeltown Road, 40 miles south of Oban

OPENING
Please phone for details

ADMISSION PRICES
Please phone for details

CONTACT
Lochfyne Miniature Railway
19 McIntyre Terrace
Lochgilphead
Argyll PA31 8TF
Tel 01546 602918

LOCATION
On the A719 on the edge of Galston

OPENING
Apr–Aug open daily & specific days in Sep & Oct; Please phone for details & timings

ADMISSION PRICES
Under-3s Free; Please phone for details of other prices

CONTACT
Loudoun Castle Theme Park
Galston, Ayrshire KA4 8PE
Tel 01563 822296
Email loudouncastle@btinter-net.com

2–4 hrs

All year

Low Parks Museum

4 Star Museum Attraction

Greater Glasgow and Clyde Valley

Tourist Board

Motoring Heritage Centre

2 Star Museum

Argyll, The Isles, Loch Lomond, Stirling and Trossachs

Tourist Board

2 hrs

All year

Low Parks Museum combines displays on local history and industry with the collection of the Cameronians (Scottish Rifles) Regiment as well as a programme of changing exhibitions and activities.

The display tells the story of Scotland's motoring history with fine cars and unique archive film.

★ Horse-riding
★ Pony-trekking
★ Guided tours

LOCATION
In Hamilton just off the M74, west of Motherwell

OPENING
All year open Mon–Sat 10am–5pm & Sun 12pm–5pm

ADMISSION PRICES
Free

CONTACT
Low Parks Museum
129 Muir Street, Hamilton South Lanarkshire ML3 6BJ
Tel 01698 328232
Fax 01698 328412
Web
www.southlanarkshire.gov.uk

LOCATION
In Alexandria within walking distance of Balloch by Loch Lomond. Follow the A82 to Balloch.

OPENING
All year open daily 9.30am–5.30pm; Closed 25 Dec & 1 Jan

ADMISSION PRICES
Under-5s Free; Please phone for details of other prices

CONTACT
Motoring Heritage Centre
Loch Lomond Outlets
Main Street, Alexandria
West Dunbartonshire G83 0UG
Tel 01389 607862

Museum of Scottish Country Life

The museum was built on a farm and gives an insight into the working lives of the people of Scotland.

★ Events held throughout the year

★ Exhibitions on the environment, rural technologies & people

★ Demonstrations of farm techniques

LOCATION Just off the A749 or A726 south of Glasgow & west of East Kilbride	**ADMISSION PRICES** Admission £3 Concession £1.50 Under-18s Free
OPENING All year open Mon–Sun 10am–5pm; Closed 25, 26, 31 Dec & 1 Jan	**CONTACT** Museum of Scottish Country Life, West Kittochside East Kilbride G76 9HR Tel 01355 224181 Fax 01355 571290

Newmilns Ski Slope

Set among pine trees in the beautiful Ayrshire Countryside, Newmilns Dry Ski Slope offers all the fun of the world's most exciting sport, without the cost or the cold.

LOCATION Off the A77 on the A735	**CONTACT** Newmilns Ski Slope London Road Kilmarnock Ayrshire Tel 01563 554935
OPENING Please phone for details	
ADMISSION PRICES Please phone for details	

377

North Ayrshire Museum

Visit the North Ayrshire Museum and discover the history of this region from prehistoric times to the present day.

★ Temporary exhibitions all year   ★ Industrial history

★ Rich variety of artefacts   ★ Social history

LOCATION Just off the A81, north-east of Paisley	**CONTACT** North Ayrshire Museum Manse Street Saltcoats Ayrshire KA21 5AA Tel & Fax 01294 464174 Email namuseum@globalnet.co.uk
OPENING All year open Mon–Sat (not Wed) 10am–1pm & 2pm–5pm	
ADMISSION PRICES Free	

Oban Zoological World

A family-run zoo specialising in small mammals and reptiles.

★ Outdoor play area for children

★ Guided tours

LOCATION South of Oban	**CONTACT** Oban Zoological World Ariogan Cottage Upper Soroba Oban Argyll PA34 4SD Tel & Fax 01631 562481
OPENING Apr–Sep open 10am–6pm; Oct–Mar 11am–5pm	
ADMISSION PRICES Under-3s Free; Please phone for details of other prices	

Rowallan Activity Centre

Whether you want to play football, learn to ride or discover the thrill of paintballing, this multi-functional indoor and outdoor centre has something for everyone.

★ Wacky Warehouse
★ Soft play area
★ Parties catered for
★ Fishing

LOCATION
From the A77 Glasgow–Kilmarnock (Nr Fenwick) turn right (heading from Glasgow) at the Fenwick Hotel onto the B751 Kilmaurs. The centre is 1 mile on the left

OPENING
All year open 8am–1am; Closed 25 Dec & 1 Jan

ADMISSION PRICES
Free; Prices vary according to activity

CONTACT
Rowallan Activity Centre
Melklemosside
Fenwick
Ayrshire KA3 6AY
Tel 01560 600769

Scottish Sealife & Marine Sanctuary

Scotland's leading marine animal rescue centre cares for abandoned seal pups and also has resident common seals and displays of native marine life.

3 Star Marine Attraction
Argyll, The Isles, Loch Lomond, Stirling and Trossachs Tourist Board

LOCATION
10 miles north of Oban on A828

OPENING
Please phone for details

ADMISSION PRICES
Under-4s Free; Please phone for details of other prices

CONTACT
Scottish Sealife & Marine Sanctuary
Barcaldine
By Oban
Argyll PA37 1SE
Tel 01631 720386
Email oban@sealife.fsbusiness.co.uk
Web www.sealsanctuary.co.uk

South Bank Farm Park

A working farm with rare and minority breeds of farm animals and poultry.

LOCATION
In East Bennan on the Isle of Arran

OPENING
Please phone for details

ADMISSION PRICES
Please phone for details

CONTACT
South Bank Farm Park
East Bennan
Isle of Arran KA27 8
Tel 01770 820221

Summerlee Heritage Park

4 Star Historic Attraction
Greater Glasgow and Clyde Valley Tourist Board

Take a trip on Scotland's only electric tramway and visit a huge undercover exhibition hall with working machinery and period room settings.

★ Re-created mine & miners' cottages

★ Compton cinema organ

LOCATION	CONTACT
Off the M8 in Coatbridge on the way into Glasgow	**Summerlee Heritage Centre**
	Heritage Way
OPENING	Coatbridge
All year open daily 10am–5pm, except Nov–Mar 10am–4pm; Closed 25, 26 Dec & 1, 2 Jan	Lanarkshire ML5 1QD
	Tel 01236 431261
	Fax 01236 440429
ADMISSION PRICES	
Free	

Tam O'Shanter Experience

3 Star Speciality Attraction
Ayrshire and Arran Tourist Board

Visit the Tam O'Shanter Experience, explaining the infamous tale of Tam O'Shanter.

★ Visit the Burns Monument   ★ Kirk Alloway

★ Brig O'Doon

LOCATION	CONTACT
In the village of Alloway 5 miles South of Ayr town centre	**Burns National Heritage Park**
	Murdochs Lone Alloway, Ayr
OPENING	Ayrshire KA7 4PQ
Apr–Sep open 9am–5.30pm; Oct–Mar open 9am–5pm	Tel 01292 443700
	Email
	info@burnsheritagepark.com
ADMISSION PRICES	
Adult £1.40 Child 70p	
Under-5s Free	

Vikingar!

4 Star Speciality Attraction
Ayrshire and Arran Tourist Board

A multi-media experience taking you from the first Viking raids to their defeat at the Battle of Largs.

★ Swimming pool   ★ Cinema

★ Theatre   ★ Soft play centre

LOCATION	CONTACT
Opposite the RNLI lifeboat station on the A78, ½ mile into Largs	**Vikingar!**
	Greenock Road
	Largs
OPENING	Ayrshire KA30 8QL
Feb–Nov open daily; Please phone for details	Tel 01475 689777
	Email
	anyone@vikingar.prestel.co.uk
ADMISSION PRICES	
Adult £3.80 Child £2.90	

West Dumbarton Activity Centre

A community leisure facility where workshops are organised and children can play badminton, tennis, football, archery and judo. Taster classes offer children various activities at a subsidised cost.

LOCATION	ADMISSION PRICES
Off the A82, 2 minutes from Dumbarton town centre. Follow the blue post signs	From 50p–£1 depending on the activity
	CONTACT
OPENING	**West Dumbarton Activity**
Mon–Fri open 9am–9pm, Sat & Sun 10am–5pm; Holiday programmes for children Mon–Fri 10am–4pm	**Centre,** 73 Ardoch Crescent Brucehill, Dumbarton
	Tel 01389 607298

Index of Place Names

382

Acknowledgements
& picture credits

Picture Researcher: Lynda Marshall

The Publishers would like to acknowledge the contribution of the British Tourist Authority to this publication, made through allowing access to the information on their website: www.visitbritain.com

The Publishers would also like to thank all contributors who provided information, and particularly all those who kindly supplied photographs for use in this book.

The Publishers would like to thank the following for permission to reproduce copyright material:

Corbis Ltd: pp.35T, 40T, 44T, 60T, 67T, 117T, 120T, 122T, 142B, 147T, 151B, 155B, 158B, 165B, 173T, 181T, 255B, 255T, 262T, 273T, 283T, 288B, 301T, 306T, 325T, 348T, 358T, 365B.

The Image Bank: pp.14T, 14B, 17B, 24B, 34B, 35B, 52B, 63B, 86B, 87B, 88T, 110T, 110B, 115B, 123B, 125B, 131T, 138T, 140T, 142T, 154B, 159B, 167T, 179T, 187T, 191B, 267B, 268B, 271T, 273T, 280B, 290T, 291T, 299T, 326T, 335T, 340T, 348B, 351T, 356B, 372T.

TAXI: pp.29T, 32T, 36B, 90B, 95B, 118T, 119B, 123T, 126T, 127T, 138B, 139B, 143T, 147B, 161T, 164B, 168B, 174T, 175B, 240T, 271B, 304T, 309B, 331T, 347B, 369B, 378T.

Stone: pp.2, 67T, 126B, 167B, 182T, 284B, 297B, 298T, 311T, 314B, 350T.

Sean Conboy: 141T

Anglian Water: 176B

RSPB Images: 317T